D0200610

# The Global Factory

# The Global Factory

*Foreign Assembly*
*in International Trade*

JOSEPH GRUNWALD *and* KENNETH FLAMM

THE BROOKINGS INSTITUTION
*Washington, D.C.*

THE BROOKINGS INSTITUTION
*1775 Massachusetts Avenue, N.W., Washington, D.C. 20036*

*Library of Congress Cataloging in Publication data:*

Main entry under title:
The Global factory.
1. International business enterprises. 2. International division of labor.
3. Comparative advantage (Commerce) I. Flamm, Kenneth S., 1951– .
II. Grunwald, Joseph, 1920– .
HD2755.5.G58 1985 338′.06 84-23122
ISBN 0-8157-3304-6
ISBN 0-8157-3303-8 (pbk.)

9 8 7 6 5 4 3 2 1

THE BROOKINGS INSTITUTION is an independent organization devoted to nonpartisan research, education, and publication in economics, government, foreign policy, and the social sciences generally. Its principal purposes are to aid in the development of sound public policies and to promote public understanding of issues of national importance.

The Institution was founded on December 8, 1927, to merge the activities of the Institute for Government Research, founded in 1916, the Institute of Economics, founded in 1922, and the Robert Brookings Graduate School of Economics and Government, founded in 1924.

The Board of Trustees is responsible for the general administration of the Institution, while the immediate direction of the policies, program, and staff is vested in the President, assisted by an advisory committee of the officers and staff. The by-laws of the Institution state: "It is the function of the Trustees to make possible the conduct of scientific research, and publication, under the most favorable conditions, and to safeguard the independence of the research staff in the pursuit of their studies and in the publication of the results of such studies. It is not a part of their function to determine, control, or influence the conduct of particular investigations or the conclusions reached."

The President bears final responsibility for the decision to publish a manuscript as a Brookings book. In reaching his judgment on the competence, accuracy, and objectivity of each study, the President is advised by the director of the appropriate research program and weighs the views of a panel of expert outside readers who report to him in confidence on the quality of the work. Publication of a work signifies that it is deemed a competent treatment worthy of public consideration but does not imply endorsement of conclusions or recommendations.

The Institution maintains its position of neutrality on issues of public policy in order to safeguard the intellectual freedom of the staff. Hence interpretations or conclusions in Brookings publications should be understood to be solely those of the authors and should not be attributed to the Institution, to its trustees, officers, or other staff members, or to the organizations that support its research.

# Foreword

STRUCTURAL shifts in the international distribution of industrial production have become a major concern. This is particularly true of the decline of traditional industries in the older, economically advanced countries and their rise in the emerging countries of the third world. In some instances, parts of industries have been displaced: labor-intensive operations have been transferred from high-wage to low-wage areas, while the capital-intensive and knowledge-intensive portions of production have remained in place. Such shifts are part of an adjustment process whereby firms in industrial countries adapt to the increasing pressures of international competition and changing comparative advantage. To the extent the adjustment is successful, economic dislocations and the pressures for protectionism are reduced.

In this volume the authors examine industrial collaboration between developed and developing countries, focusing on the transfer of assembly operations abroad. In particular, they analyze those activities that involve the United States and three of its near neighbors: Mexico, Haiti, and Colombia. They also consider in detail the worldwide internationalization of production in the semiconductor industry.

Joseph Grunwald conceived the idea for this project in 1978, when he reviewed the modes of collaboration between U.S. firms and those of developing countries. In 1979, after the United Nations Development Programme (UNDP) had decided to provide major financial support and Kenneth S. Flamm had joined the project, the basic research got under way. In 1979 and 1980 the United Nations Conference on Trade and Development (UNCTAD) sponsored two international seminars, coordinated by Brookings, in Mexico City under the auspices of El Colegio de México. Attended by professionals from Latin America, North America, Europe, and Asia, the seminars laid the groundwork for the study, examining papers on related research, obtaining information about work in progress, and collecting comments on the authors' draft overview of the project. In addition, representatives of the World Bank, the United Nations, and institutions in developing countries presented background papers.

Joseph Grunwald, a senior fellow in the Brookings Foreign Policy Studies program when this book was written, is now president of the Institute of Americas at the University of California–San Diego; Kenneth S. Flamm is a research associate in the Brookings Foreign Policy Studies program. Leslie Delatour and Karl Voltaire, two Haitian economists now with the World Bank, are coauthors with Grunwald of the Haiti chapter; Delatour also provided Grunwald and Flamm with access to many assembly plants in Haiti. Juan José Echavarría of the Fundación para la Educación Superior y el Desarrollo of Bogotá collaborated with Grunwald on the Colombian case study. El Colegio de México prepared some materials for the Mexican case study. Professors C. Berthomieu and A. Hanaut of the University of Nice wrote a report on subcontracting relations of the European Community, cited in chapter 2.

The authors submitted an earlier version of this study to UNCTAD in Geneva in October 1981. Several outside readers, including Werner Baer, Richard Eckaus, and Albert Fishlow, made helpful comments on that report. Others commented on sections of the report: Robert Noyce of the Intel Corporation and Lenny Siegel of the *Global Electronics Information Newsletter* on the semiconductor chapter; and Victor Urquidi, president of El Colegio de México, and members of his staff, particularly M. Martínez del Campo, and Sidney Weintraub on the Mexican chapter. The authors then reorganized, shortened, and updated the report for the present book.

The authors wish to thank many others who assisted them in the project. Andy Rylyk and the staff of the U.S. International Trade Commission, as well as staff members of the U.S. Department of Commerce and the U.S. Customs Service in Washington and on the Mexican border, generously provided unpublished statistics and other information. Special tabulations on magnetic tapes prepared by the International Trade Commission were particularly helpful. S. Abbas and S. Laird of UNCTAD provided administrative and substantive support. John D. Steinbruner, director of the Brookings Foreign Policy Studies program, suggested important improvements in the manuscript; Hugh Schwartz of the Inter-American Development Bank (IADB) commented on several early drafts. The authors benefited from conversations with Richard Bolin of the Flagstaff Institute and Shinzo Kobori of the C. Itoh Trading Company. Reactions from participants at various seminars given by the authors, including those at the IADB and the World Bank, were also useful in making revisions. William Mitchell and Richard Campbell of the Bermudez and Nogales industrial parks helped with access to assembly firms and accompanied the authors on many visits to plants.

Jeff Marzilli, Karen Licker, and Jacquelyn A. Mitchell provided research assistance; David Barkin and Jacqueline M. Honoré helped to prepare the tables; and Julia Sternberg, Antoinette K. Buena, and Susan E. Nichols gave secretarial support at various stages of the project. David Howell Jones edited the manuscript, Bruce J. Dickson checked it for accuracy, and Twin Oaks Indexing Collective prepared the index.

The authors owe a special debt to Gabriel Valdés, who was assistant administrator of the UNDP, and the late Cecilio Morales, who was manager of social and economic development at the IADB, for recognizing the relevance of the subject matter and making this study possible.

The project received early and generous financial support from the Tinker Foundation as well as from the United Nations Development Programme and the United Nations Conference on Trade and Development. The Inter-American Development Bank provided funding primarily for the collaboration of Latin American institutions and economists. The U.S. Department of State and the U.S. Agency for International Development provided additional funding.

The views expressed in this book are those of the authors and should not be ascribed to the persons or organizations whose assistance is acknowledged, or to the trustees, officers, or other staff members of the Brookings Institution.

BRUCE K. MAC LAURY
*President*

*January 1985*
*Washington, D.C.*

# Contents

## Tables

## Figures

# The Global Factory

CHAPTER ONE

# The Setting

THE slowdown in the world economy during the 1970s increased economic strains between the rich countries and the poor countries. The conventional wisdom of "what is good for industrial countries is good for developing countries" began to be challenged, and demands for a "new international economic order" appeared in forums of the United Nations.

The source of many of these tensions is the emergence in many developing countries of export-led industrialization programs that have threatened some labor-intensive industries in developed countries. Because huge international disparities in wages have persisted while costs of transport and communications have dropped, underdeveloped regions have become increasingly competitive in the production of labor-intensive goods.

The choices available to the industrial economies are relatively few and generally untried. One response is the "high tech" option, the aim of which is to generate increases in productivity in order to maintain high wages for workers and large returns for investors through the development of new technology. Such an effort requires continued large investment in areas in which returns are not easily identified or calculated.

Outright protectionism is another choice. Even before the oil-price explosion, the first symptoms of a new protectionism appeared in industrial countries in the form of the long-term trade arrangements for textiles. "Orderly marketing arrangements," actions against real and imagined export subsidies or dumping by developing countries, and other protectionist measures have multiplied.

A third choice is to adapt to the changing pattern of international comparative advantage, integrating production operations across national boundaries. Such an internationalization of industry is based on the complementarities between factors of production in developing and developed countries, with unskilled assembly being performed in low-wage areas in which there is an abundance of untrained labor and more highly skilled operations being performed in the developed countries that have an abundance of skilled labor and technological and scientific resources. Sharing in the manufacture of products might provide a partial reconciliation between the promotion of nontraditional exports from developing countries and the rising pressures to protect economic activities in the industrial countries.

Transferring some production processes abroad, with one side primarily furnishing labor services, the other primarily components, is a substitute neither for the traditional exchange of primary goods for manufactured products nor for the "nontraditional" export of products emerging from the newly industrializing countries and their imports of capital goods and technology. This complementary intraindustry trade is a relatively new addition to the changing international division of labor.[1]

Foreign assembly in world trade, which involves the internationalization of industrial operations performed within a single industry, is the subject of this book. There are benefits and costs on both sides of the coproduction relationship.[2] Without attempting to undertake formal benefit-cost analyses, the authors have tried to evaluate the positive and negative aspects of assembly operations abroad. The aim is to examine the nature of these activities and to arrive at some conclusions about ways in which they might evolve and affect the future of North-South economic relations.

## The International Reorganization of Production

In present-day discussions of the changing international division of labor, manufacturing industries are often divided into those using stable, widely understood technology to make relatively simple products—traditional industries—and those using rapidly developing technology to make

1. Even this form is not new. Already in the eighteenth century the German term *Veredelungsverkehr* (upgrading trade) implied that each country undertakes those stages of a production process that give it the greatest value added. See Peter F. Drucker, "Production Sharing, Concepts and Definitions," *Journal of the Flagstaff Institute,* vol. 3 (January 1979), pp. 2–9.

2. Peter Drucker coined the term "production sharing" for this relationship. See his article, "The Rise of Production Sharing," in *Wall Street Journal,* March 15, 1977. For a description of the various modes of coproduction between developing and developed countries, see Joseph Grunwald, "North-South Intra-Industry Trade: Sharing Industrial Production between Developing and Developed Countries," in *Las organizaciones regionales en el nuevo orden internacional* (Madrid: Instituto de Cooperación Intercontinental, 1978), pp. 81–97.

a continuous stream of quickly obsolete new products—high-tech industries.[3] The traditional industries have generally been associated with fairly labor-intensive technologies and, because of the persistence of low wage rates in the third world and the relatively low development cost of establishing a production capability in these older products, these industries have been the leading edge of the burgeoning exports of manufactures produced in developing countries.

The high-tech industries, on the other hand, depend for their success on access to the specialized resources required for research and development and highly complex production processes. These industries have therefore been located in the industrial countries. As products mature, technology diffuses, high-tech products eventually become traditional products, and production moves to more competitive locations abroad. This is roughly the product-cycle description of international trade first advanced by Raymond Vernon in 1966.[4]

While production overseas to serve local markets—stimulated by protection and transport costs and, in some instances, lower production costs—has long been a feature of direct foreign investment by U.S. producers of manufactures, volume manufacture in foreign locations for reexport to the home market or other export markets is a qualitatively new feature of foreign manufacturing operations that emerged in the late 1960s.[5] In developing Asia, more than a quarter of sales of U.S. affiliates went to the United States in 1977, up from less than 10 percent in 1966. In electrical machinery, in particular, some 70 percent of output was shipped back to the United States in 1977 (see tables 1-1 and 1-2).

A similar phenomenon appears to have taken place in Japanese multinationals. Japanese data for 1975, presented in table 1-3, show a significant

3. See, for example, Jagdish N. Bhagwati, "Shifting Comparative Advantage, Protectionist Demands and Policy Response," and Ronald P. Dore, "Adjustment in Process: A Lancashire Town," in Bhagwati, ed., *Import Competition and Response* (University of Chicago Press for National Bureau of Economic Research, 1982); and Ira C. Magaziner and Robert B. Reich, *Minding America's Business: The Decline and Rise of the American Economy* (Harcourt Brace Jovanovich, 1982).

4. Raymond Vernon, "International Investment and International Trade in the Product Cycle," *Quarterly Journal of Economics,* vol. 80 (May 1966), pp. 190–207.

5. See Mira Wilkins, *The Maturing of Multinational Enterprise: American Business Abroad from 1914 to 1970* (Harvard University Press, 1974), for the history of U.S. direct foreign investment; and Lawrence G. Franko, *The European Multinationals* (Harper & Row, 1976), for European investment. Significant volumes of Japanese direct foreign manufacturing investment in the postwar period did not begin until the late 1960s. See Sueo Sekiguchi, *Japanese Direct Foreign Investment* (Tokyo: Japan Economic Research Center, 1977).

Table 1-1. *Exports of U.S. Foreign Manufacturing Affiliates to the United States as Percent of Total Sales, 1966 and 1977*

| | Location of affiliates[a] | | | | | | | | | |
|---|---|---|---|---|---|---|---|---|---|---|
| | Europe | | Japan | | Latin America | | Asia and the Pacific | | All countries | |
| Industry | 1966 | 1977 | 1966 | 1977 | 1966 | 1977 | 1966 | 1977 | 1966 | 1977 |
| All manufacturing | 2 | 2 | 3 | 4 | 2 | 4 | 10 | 27 | 6 | 8 |
| Food | n.a. | 2 | n.a. | 0 | n.a. | 4 | n.a. | 18 | 3 | 2 |
| Chemicals | 1 | 1 | | 0 | n.a. | 1 | n.a. | 2 | 2 | 2 |
| Metals | 1 | 1 | n.a. | 1 | n.a. | 7 | n.a. | n.a. | 1 | 6 |
| All machinery | 4 | 3 | 3 | n.a. | * | 10 | n.a. | 63 | 4 | 7 |
| Nonelectrical | n.a. | 3 | n.a. | 5 | n.a. | 2 | n.a. | 24 | n.a. | 4 |
| Electrical | n.a. | 2 | n.a. | n.a. | n.a. | 18 | n.a. | 70 | n.a. | 12 |
| Transportation equipment | n.a. | 2 | n.a. | n.a. | n.a. | 4 | n.a. | n.a. | n.a. | 17 |
| Other | n.a. | 2 | n.a. | 2 | n.a. | 3 | n.a. | 12 | n.a. | 7 |

Sources: U.S. Department of Commerce, Bureau of Economic Analysis, *U.S. Direct Investment Abroad, 1977* (Government Printing Office, 1981), pp. 138, 158, and *U.S. Direct Investment Abroad, 1966* (GPO, n.d.), pp. 199, 201.
n.a. Not available.
*0.3 percent.
a. Figures for 1966 refer to majority-owned affiliates, figures for 1977 to all affiliates.

Table 1-2. *Distribution, by Industry, of Exports of U.S. Foreign Manufacturing Affiliates to the United States, 1977*

Percent

| | Location of affiliates | |
|---|---|---|
| Industry | Latin America | Asia and the Pacific[a] |
| All manufacturing | 100 | 100 |
| Food | 12 | 6 |
| Chemicals | 7 | 2 |
| Metals | 14 | n.a. |
| Nonelectrical machinery | 3 | 5 |
| Electrical machinery | 35 | 79 |
| Transportation equipment | 17 | n.a. |
| Other | 13 | 7 |
| *Addendum* | | |
| Value of all exports by manufacturing affiliates (millions of U.S. dollars) | 1,409 | 2,165 |

Sources: Same as table 1-1. Figures are rounded.
n.a. Not available.
a. Not including Japan

share of sales as exports to Japan from Asian affiliates, though at a smaller proportion than exports to the United States from U.S. affiliates. When not investing abroad in order to secure material resources, Japanese firms

Table 1-3. *Distribution of Sales of Japanese Foreign Subsidiaries, 1975*
Percent

| | *Location of investment* | | | |
|---|---|---|---|---|
| | *Latin America* | | *Asia* | |
| *Industry* | *Exports to Japan* | *Other exports* | *Exports to Japan* | *Other exports* |
| All manufacturing | 7 | 10 | 26 | 21 |
| Textiles | 6 | 21 | 28 | 27 |
| Wood, paper, and pulp | 43 | 0 | 48 | 23 |
| Iron and steel | 0 | 3 | 10 | 12 |
| Electrical machinery | 0 | 8 | 29 | 25 |
| Transportation equipment | * | 2 | 13 | 13 |
| Other | 0 | 11 | 30 | 24 |

Source: Japanese Ministry of International Trade and Industry (MITI), as reported in Sueo Sekiguchi, *Japanese Direct Foreign Investment* (Tokyo: Japan Economic Research Center, 1977), p. 117.
* 0.3 percent.

seemed more inclined than U.S. firms to use their foreign affiliates as low-cost platforms for exports into markets other than Japan.[6]

European firms, by way of contrast, showed relatively little propensity to serve their home markets through exports from affiliates located in low-wage areas.[7] There were a number of possible explanations for their reluctance to move abroad: high European Community (EC) tariffs and other barriers to trade had considerable effect in inhibiting foreign production;[8] a strong, well-organized trade-union movement possibly also exercised considerable influence in restraining firms from relocating; and the important fact of significant state participation in ownership of many European multinationals, particularly in the electronics industry, may have placed further political constraints on exports to the home market from foreign locations. Nevertheless, large outflows of European direct investment continued throughout the 1960s and 1970s into the establishment of numerous foreign subsidiaries for the purpose of penetrating protected foreign markets.

The growing participation of foreign affiliates of national firms in exports of manufactures from developing countries to markets in industrial countries probably also served to reduce political resistance to these imports. As table 1-4 makes clear, imports of manufactures into the industrial markets increased in relation to total consumption of manufactures.

6. See also Kunio Yoshihara, *Japanese Investment in Southeast Asia* (University Press of Hawaii, 1978), pp. 37–38.
7. See Franko, *The European Multinationals,* pp. 126–32.
8. See the discussion of European trade policy in chapter 3 for a clear example.

Table 1-4. *The Importance of Manufactured Exports of Developing Countries to the Principal Industrial Markets, 1968–77*

| *Country or countries and period* | *Apparent consumption of manufactures (U.S. dollars)* | *Imports as percent of consumption* | *Imports from developing countries as percent of all imports* |
|---|---|---|---|
| *United States and Canada* | | | |
| 1968 | 64.8 | 3.1 | 24 |
| 1970–71 | 705.6 | 3.9 | 24 |
| 1974–75 | 1,143.9 | 5.2 | 33 |
| 1976–77 | 1,391.9 | 5.2 | 34 |
| *Japan* | | | |
| 1968 | 127.4 | 3.9 | 22 |
| 1970–71 | 188.3 | 4.0 | 23 |
| 1974–75 | 409.8 | 4.7 | 31 |
| 1976–77 | 494.9 | 4.4 | 36 |
| *European Community* | | | |
| 1968 | 344.0 | 5.6 | 20 |
| 1970–71 | 456.4 | 7.7 | 19 |
| 1974–75 | 902.2 | 8.4 | 20 |
| 1976–77 | 1,067.5 | 8.9 | 20 |

Source: United Nations Conference on Trade and Development (UNCTAD), *Handbook of International Trade and Development Statistics, 1980* (New York: UNCTAD, 1980), table 7.1. Data are for eleven industrial product groups, in current prices.

The movement abroad was not restricted exclusively to large U.S. multinationals. There are many smaller firms involved in these trade links from the United States and other countries. The small firms, in fact, tend to stick closer to home—U.S. firms to Mexico and the Caribbean, Japanese firms to Taiwan and Korea, and Western European firms to Eastern Europe and the Mediterranean. In familiar nearby areas with which communication links are good, and where a considerable overhead investment in learning the local ways is not necessary, even small firms can afford to move out of the country—and they may be forced to do so by their competition.

Thus, those observers who claim that the 1960s and 1970s marked a new stage in the evolution of the world capitalist system appear to be correct, insofar as the operations of U.S. multinational firms seem to have switched, on a fairly large scale for the first time, to overseas production of manufactured exports for the home market.[9] Asia and Latin America be-

9. Among those who have made such a claim are Folker Fröbel, Jürgen Heinrichs, and Otto Kreye in *The New International Division of Labour,* trans. Pete Burgess (London: Cambridge University Press, 1980).

came the primary locations for these operations and electrical machinery the principal product.

One way to regard the phenomenon of production abroad is as a system of production geared to retaining competitiveness for firms in developed countries after a product has entered the down side of the product cycle. That is, the firms that developed the product continue to produce economically by eventually relocating or subcontracting assembly production facilities in low-wage developing countries. They must generally have some other competitive cost advantage, such as access to capital, marketing, administration, or technology, for this strategy to work, since an indigenous firm producing a standard product in its native business environment presumably could do so at no greater—and possibly at lower—cost. Also, production processes must permit such a division of labor, and transportation costs should not be excessive.

Production of more traditional products such as textiles and apparel, radio and television receivers and, to a certain extent, automobiles has been integrated vertically across national boundaries in response to foreign competition for some time. But production abroad is even more important in certain high-tech electronics industries, where the products are anything but traditional. Semiconductors alone account for about 40 percent of the value of U.S. components reimported into this country after overseas assembly, and more than 80 percent of U.S. semiconductor production is probably assembled abroad.

The technical characteristics of the product that determine transport cost, the separability of labor-intensive operations from other steps in production, and the capital intensity of assembly operations are critical to the decision whether to produce abroad. High value-to-weight ratios of apparel and electronics reduce transport costs as a barrier to trade, and production operations are easily separated into distinct steps—manufacture of components, assembly, testing, and packaging—that do not require physical contiguity. All these products require relatively small inputs of capital and large inputs of unskilled labor in the assembly stage, when labor-intensive methods are used.

While assembly abroad is important in the U.S. economy—in 1981 perhaps 15 percent of U.S. imports of manufactures, 22 percent of those from developing countries, and very much higher percentages of imports of certain items of apparel and electronics were assembled abroad—the amount of controversy generated by such production arrangements gives them a disproportionate prominence. To critics in the third world they symbolize not only a development strategy concentrated on export promotion, "industrialization by invitation," and the continued deepening of external links to a fluctuating world economy, but also, since they are often under the control of foreign investors, a strategy guaranteed to extend the power of multinational corporations as a political and economic pressure group within the host state. Considerable debate often surrounds the questions how much employment these activities generate, what its quality is, what their net contribution to the balance of payments of the host country is, what kinds of technology are transferred, whether industrialization is fostered, how much economic instability is caused by dependence on export markets, and what the social effects of this type of development are. Proponents of production sharing as part of an industrialization policy generally claim that the net balance is positive.

Production sharing also generates considerable friction within the industrial countries. Labor groups view with alarm a presumed "export" of jobs, although assembly abroad can increase the use of domestically produced components and stave off competition from low-cost foreign imports, thereby avoiding the departure of the entire industry. The workers displaced in industries in which assembly production is moved out of the country, it is argued, are especially vulnerable to adjustment problems. Some fear the loss of U.S. competitiveness through the leakage of technology used in foreign plants or the deterioration of the balance of payments in important industries.

Two factors seem to guarantee that overseas production arrangements will remain for some time a significant issue in foreign economic policy discussions in the industrial countries. First, in many of the industries in which import penetration has been most pronounced and trade policy most highly charged with political pressures—sectors such as apparel, electronics, and automobiles—firms have reorganized their operations to use assembly abroad as an integral part of their strategy for survival. Second, in apparel as in electronics, the constant cycle of change and obsolescence has been an obstacle to automation. Automation, because it generally requires large fixed investments, is normally economical only when large production runs are guaranteed. In electronics, rapid innovation and continuous technological change have posed a barrier to automation, while in apparel, the principal barrier has been the frequent and unpredictable changes in fashions and styles.

Transferring assembly abroad has been the cutting edge of continued growth in the foreign investments of transnational industrial enterprises.

U.S.-owned assets in foreign manufacturing subsidiaries, for example, increased faster in overseas assembly areas than in other regions of the world between 1966 and 1977.[10]

## Basic Questions

Three broad sets of questions must be answered in interpreting these recent trends in the internationalization of industry. This book is organized as an analysis of these basic issues.

First, just how important in the aggregate are overseas production arrangements? What are their characteristics? Is coproduction a universal phenomenon, or is it confined to a limited array of regions, countries, or products?

Second, what have the causes of growth in overseas production been, and how have they been reflected in the evolution of these arrangements? To what extent has growth abroad been tied to developments in industrialized and industrializing economies? Can particular characteristics of products and policies that have determined the nature of these relationships be identified? The importance of technological and economic factors, national policy measures, and historical and political circumstances in explaining the rise of production sharing ought to be evaluated.

Third, what have the effects of overseas production on home and host economies been? Can the arguments made by proponents and critics of these arrangements be evaluated reasonably?

Because overseas investment is dominated by a relatively small set of products and countries, it is difficult to answer these questions without a detailed and specific analysis of the circumstances of its development. Accordingly, the heart of this book is a set of case studies in which the authors attempt to come to grips with the causes and effects of production abroad.

The first set of concerns will be addressed in the next chapter through presentation of a statistical picture and analysis of production-sharing arrangements. The overall significance of overseas production activity in the United States, Japan, and Europe will be examined, and the reasons for important differences will be analyzed.

Chapter 3 is a case study of the semiconductor industry. Other than

10. Based on data given in Ned G. Howenstine, "Growth of U.S. Multinational Companies, 1966–77," *Survey of Current Business,* April 1982, pp. 34–46.

some items of apparel, it was the first industry to go abroad and remains the most important single U.S. industry dominated by foreign sourcing arrangements. The author will attempt to illuminate the second and third sets of questions, where the dynamics of the movement abroad are detailed. The nature of production abroad will be analyzed as a response to foreign competition and its effects on the domestic industry.

In chapters 4 through 6 these same two sets of questions will be examined, but through the lenses of the developing countries' experiences with export platforms. The effects on national development objectives in Mexico, Haiti, and Colombia have been examined in some detail. The selection of Mexico is obvious: it is the country with the largest volume of U.S. production activities. It is also among the most highly industrialized countries in the third world. At the other extreme on the economic scale in this hemisphere is Haiti, where substantial assembly operations are also handled for U.S. firms. Colombia, the subject of the third case study, has a checkered history of coproduction with the United States. The question there is why assembly activities did not take off as consistently as elsewhere in the region. The diversity of the three cases affords the opportunity to review the issues, problems, and aspects of coproduction that are basic to the relationship and those that are country-specific.

In chapter 7 the evidence assembled in the aggregate overview and case studies on the nature, extent, causes, and effects of offshore assembly and investment will be reviewed. In chapter 8 the prospects for future growth of these arrangements and their usefulness in reconciling the divergent objectives of developed and developing countries will be evaluated. Policy implications will be discussed from the perspectives of the United States and the developing countries. The conclusions will include consideration of the possible effects of automation.

CHAPTER TWO

# A Survey

ASSEMBLY abroad has grown dramatically during the last few decades. Before wage differentials became an important factor in this trade, coproduction, linked to technology and skill specialization, was primarily a phenomenon of the industrial countries. Production sharing among industrial countries has therefore involved fairly sophisticated goods with technologically advanced production processes.[1]

Coproduction between industrial and developing countries, which has been stimulated by the improvement in transport and communications, is a comparatively recent phenomenon. Since the mid 1960s, when relevant data were first tabulated, trade derived from production abroad has grown faster than total international trade. The emergence of overseas assembly activities followed naturally from the growing worldwide competition in manufactures in the period following World War II, as Western Europe recovered and Japan quickly became an important industrial power. The United States faced the new competition first because its wages were so high in relation to those of the rest of the world. As domestic labor-intensive production became less and less economical, U.S. firms began to look to other countries, breaking production into stages and carrying out the labor-intensive processes in countries where wages were low. In response to essentially the same situation, industrially advanced countries of Europe imported low-cost labor, and Japan turned to automation when wages rose to high levels.

Part of the analysis presented in this chapter is based on detailed product and country tables on U.S. 806/807 imports, including partial comparisons with total U.S. imports, calculated from tabulations made from magnetic tapes provided by the U.S. International Trade Commission.

1. Environmental and safety standards have also been influential, as when, for example, foreign automobiles can be imported only with special antipollution and safety equipment made in the importing country. The value of these domestically produced components has generally constituted a very small proportion of the value of such imports.

While firms in all industrial countries have engaged in foreign assembly, U.S. firms have done by far the most. Because of higher degrees of protection, the production activities abroad of European countries have remained at a comparatively low level. In Japan, such activities have been used primarily as a means of penetrating foreign markets, although it appears that more recently Japanese companies have reimported a growing volume of products assembled for them abroad. On the other side of the coproduction relationship, the principal participants are developing countries in the Far East and in and around the Caribbean basin, as shown in table 2-1.

## Assembly Abroad and the United States

The items assembled abroad for U.S. firms have become an important part of the supply of certain manufactured products, although they are still only a small part of total national output and trade. More than half of U.S. sales of certain products in textiles and electronics are assembled abroad. The imports of products assembled abroad have reached a level of almost a sixth of total U.S. imports of manufactures and about a quarter of imports of manufactures from developing countries.

### *U.S. Tariff Items 806.30 and 807.00*

The chief source of information on products assembled abroad that reach the U.S. market is a set of statistics maintained by the U.S. International Trade Commission (ITC) of imports entering the United States under tariff items 806.30 and 807.00 (henceforth 806/807), which permit the duty-free entry of U.S. components sent abroad for processing or assembly. The countries of the European Community (EC) have similar tariff provisions—on "outward processing" trade—and some statistics on their coproduction trade are therefore available separately.[2]

2. Japan also has special tariff arrangements that permit duty-free reentry of Japanese-made components assembled abroad, but their use appears to be much more restricted than is the case in the United States and the EC. U.S. Tariff Commission, *Economic Factors Affecting the Use of Items 807.00 and 806.30 of the Tariff Schedules of the United States,* Publication 339 (USTC, September 1970), p. 32; and United Nations Conference on Trade and Development (UNCTAD), *International Subcontracting Arrangements in Electronics Between Developed Market-Economy Countries and Developing Countries* (New York: United Nations, 1975), pp. 21–22.

Table 2-1. *U.S. 806/807 Imports from Fifteen Countries, 1969 and 1983*
Millions of dollars

| | *1969* | | *1983* | |
|---|---|---|---|---|
| *Country of assembly* | *Total 806/807 imports* | *Value of duty-free U.S. components* | *Total 806/807 imports* | *Value of duty-free U.S. components* |
| *Industrial countries* | | | | |
| West Germany | 627.4 | 11.6 | 2,736.7 | 58.9 |
| Japan | 137.9 | 25.4 | 6,489.6 | 175.5 |
| Canada | 340.1 | 118.7 | 1,425.9 | 467.0 |
| *Developing countries* | | | | |
| Mexico | 150.0 | 97.9 | 3,716.9 | 1,908.7 |
| Malaysia | 0.4 | 0.1 | 1,203.2 | 695.7 |
| Singapore | 11.6 | 3.8 | 983.3 | 275.9 |
| Philippines | 5.2 | 3.5 | 725.9 | 455.6 |
| Korea | 23.8 | 15.9 | 575.6 | 340.4 |
| Taiwan | 68.7 | 23.8 | 568.5 | 100.7 |
| Hong Kong | 91.4 | 51.3 | 448.1 | 72.2 |
| Haiti | 4.0 | 2.4 | 197.4 | 139.4 |
| Brazil | 4.1 | 2.5 | 193.1 | 27.4 |
| Dominican Republic | 0.1 | 0.1 | 161.0 | 111.6 |
| El Salvador | 0.2 | 0.1 | 79.6 | 45.3 |
| Colombia | 0.4 | 0.2 | 29.8 | 20.0 |
| Fifteen countries | 1,465.3 | 357.3 | 19,534.6 | 4,894.3 |
| All countries | 1,841.8 | 442.6 | 21,845.7 | 5,447.1 |

Source: U.S. Tariff Commission, *Economic Factors Affecting the Use of Items 807.00 and 806.30 of the Tariff Schedules of the United States,* Publication 339 (Washington, D.C.: USTC, September 1970), pp. A-57, A-87; and special tabulation from the U.S. International Trade Commission, 1983.

Essentially, 806 permits the reimport of "fabricated" but in effect unfinished metal products into the United States for further processing; 807 permits only the "assembly" of finished goods for reexport to the United States for final consumption (see the appendix to this chapter). Through the years, the definition of *assembly* has been expanded through a series of decisions in the U.S. customs courts.[3] Imports under 807 are by far the more important of the two items; they amounted to more than $21 billion in 1983, whereas imports under 806 amounted to less than a half-billion dollars.

Only the value of the U.S. components of those items that are reimported in products fabricated or assembled abroad is exempt from duty.

3. See Alan G. Lebowitz, "Item 807.00," Mandel and Grunfeld Seminar (New York: Mandel and Grunfeld, 1979).

U.S. trade statistics record the total value of such imports, including the duty-free U.S. components and the dutiable value added abroad. The product classification is fairly detailed but, except for the larger aggregates, the groupings are occasionally not comparable from year to year. By definition these tariff items deal with U.S. parts and components that come back to the United States, often for further processing and for sale domestically or abroad. The statistics, therefore, do not show complementary intraindustry trade in products that do not return to the United States. Such production-sharing activities may be of significant extent. There are other omissions, such as production-sharing trade either covered under the Generalized System of Preferences (GSP), which provides for full tariff exemption, or excluded from 806/807 because the provisions of the legislation are not met.

As a special sort of trade liberalization, U.S. tariff items 806/807 will tend to lower the prices of U.S.-made components in relation to the prices of inputs from the foreign country in which assembly operations are located. This will encourage the use of U.S. components if the tariff on the assembled product is significant. In unprotected industries, 806 and 807 have no economic effects. In protected industries, however, barring large transport costs, a foreign component must actually be cheaper than a U.S. component for its use to be economical in production for the U.S. market.

The 806/807 U.S. tariff sections, then, facilitate imports into the U.S. market, but in a way that clearly serves to foster greater U.S. export of components and parts for assembly at the same time. This effect, however welcome, was probably not intended by explicit design. Labor unions certainly do not consider the export effect to be of great significance.[4] The 806/807 tariff items can be expected to be used for the import to the United States of goods produced abroad whenever foreign-produced components are either unavailable or are available only at a cost that exceeds the U.S. component price less the savings realized after tariff-sparing and transport costs have been taken into account.[5]

4. The AFL-CIO became concerned about 806/807 in 1966, when U.S. firms began to make increasing use of it under the Mexican Border Industrialization Program. U.S. organized labor has sought its repeal since then on numerous occasions. See *Special Duty Treatment or Repeal of Articles Assembled or Fabricated Abroad,* Hearing before the Subcommittee on Trade of the Committee on Ways and Means, 94 Cong. 2 sess. (Government Printing Office, 1976), statement by Nathaniel Goldfinger, pp. 96–101.

5. There may also be some small cost to the firm for the administration and maintenance of forms, statistics, and records required by the special customs procedures for entry of 806/807 imports.

*The Principal Products*

Since 1966, U.S. 806/807 imports have grown faster than a rapidly growing U.S. import bill, rising from less than 4 percent to almost 10 percent of total U.S. imports of merchandise in 1983. The growth has been much more rapid in relation to imports of selected groups of manufactures.[6] Table 2-2 pinpoints a limited number of industrial products imports of which showed significant growth in their shares of the U.S. market during the period 1966–76. Those products include some relatively unsophisticated manufactures, such as apparel, footwear, pottery, and simple metal products, and a number of more technologically advanced items, such as textile machinery, radio and television receivers, semiconductors, automobiles and motorcycles, and watches and clocks. Overseas production has been a particularly important factor in the fast-rising imports of this group.

Although most of the eleven product lines detailed in table 2-3 have dominated U.S. 806/807 imports since these data became available, their importance has increased significantly. They accounted for less than two-thirds of U.S. 806/807 imports in 1969, the first year for which such detailed information was collected, but reached well over 80 percent of the total in 1982. Thus it can be seen that U.S. 806/807 imports are largely confined to motor vehicles and parts, apparel, and various types of electrical equipment.[7] Almost all the motor vehicle imports come from industrial countries, almost all the other 806/807 imports from developing countries.

*Semiconductors.* Large-scale assembly of U.S. products in other countries originated in the U.S. semiconductor industry. It began in Asia as a response of U.S. semiconductor manufacturers to low-cost transistors imported from Japan. The other significant alternative—automation of

6. The importance of production sharing is greater than 806/807 figures indicate. First, U.S. components processed and assembled abroad and sold in any market outside the United States are not identified in U.S. statistics. Then there are the exclusions from 806/807 data noted in the appendix to this chapter. Furthermore, because 806/807 trade is largely in semifinished goods, it is sometimes difficult to determine the market value of such shipments. This is true not only of intrafirm deliveries, which make up a good part of 806/807 trade and suffer from the usual problems of transfer pricing, but also of independent arm's-length transactions. Independent contracting relationships often require that inputs be furnished in kind, and if they are dutiable there will be the temptation to undervalue such transfers. Thus, 806/807 statistics are probably understatements of the true importance of such imports in relation to other imports.

7. The most dramatic increase can be observed in game machines, 807 imports of which rose roughly 300-fold, almost exclusively because of the emergence of video games.

Table 2-2. *U.S. Manufacturing Industries Whose Markets Were Significantly Penetrated by Imports, 1966 and 1976*[a]

Percent of new supply imported

| *Industry* | *1966* | *1976* |
|---|---|---|
| Sugar | 20 | 29 |
| Wine and brandy | 18 | 26 |
| Bottled liquors | 25 | 27 |
| Canned and cured seafoods | 18 | 23 |
| Miscellaneous textile goods | 53 | 64 |
| Knit outerwear sport shirts | * | 23 |
| Other men's and boys' sport shirts | * | 20 |
| Raincoats | * | 47 |
| Leather clothing | * | 50 |
| Shingles and cooperage stock | * | 29 |
| Pulp-mill products | 33 | 33 |
| Medicinal and botanical products | 16 | 26 |
| Women's footwear | * | 27 |
| All other footwear | * | 57 |
| Luggage | * | 22 |
| Women's handbags and purses | 12 | 32 |
| Earthenware food utensils | 33 | 61 |
| Other pottery products | 21 | 39 |
| Electrometallurgical products | * | 37 |
| Steel nails | 19 | 34 |
| Refined copper | 11 | 20 |
| Zinc-refining products | 16 | 44 |
| Nonferrous refining products | 44 | 40 |
| Textile machinery | 14 | 30 |
| Sewing machines | 40 | 47 |
| Radio and television receivers | 10 | 43 |
| Semiconductors | * | 20 |
| Passenger cars | * | 20 |
| Motorcycles, bicycles, and parts | 46 | 51 |
| Watches and clocks | 17 | 32 |
| Dolls and stuffed animals | 13 | 25 |

Sources: U.S. Department of Commerce, Bureau of the Census, *U.S. Commodity Exports and Imports as Related to Output,* 1975 and 1976, 1966 and 1967.

* Less than 10 percent of the new supply was imported.

a. Four-digit SIC products imports of which were equal to 20 percent of new supply—domestic output and imports together—and were valued at more than $100 million in 1976.

labor-intensive operations—was impractical because of the rapid rate of technological innovation and product obsolescence in the industry. The share of semiconductors, already the most important single product assembled abroad that flowed into the U.S. market in 1969, in 806/807 imports has tripled since then. The industry, which will be examined in detail in chapter 3, illustrates many of the complexities and issues related to the use of foreign production and provides an important example of

Table 2-3. *Importance of Significant Groups of Products Imported under Tariff Items 806.30 and 807.00, 1969 and 1982*

Millions of dollars; percentage composition in parentheses

| Product group | 1969 Total value | 1969 Duty-free value of U.S. components | 1982 Total value | 1982 Duty-free value of U.S. components |
|---|---|---|---|---|
| Motor vehicles and parts | 771.3 | 18.9 | 8,360.8 | 176.1 |
| | (42) | (4) | (46) | (4) |
| Semiconductors and parts | 106.2 | 62.4 | 3,131.5 | 1,987.1 |
| | (6) | (14) | (17) | (42) |
| Television receivers and parts | 87.1 | 37.4 | 943.3 | 226.2 |
| | (5) | (8) | (5) | (5) |
| Office machines and parts | 96.9 | 38.7 | 764.0 | 208.8 |
| | (5) | (9) | (4) | (4) |
| Radio apparatus and parts | 51.1 | 8.5 | 299.7 | 77.7 |
| | (3) | (2) | (2) | (2) |
| Textile products | 34.8 | 23.1 | 649.7 | 398.3 |
| | (2) | (5) | (4) | (8) |
| Equipment for making, breaking, and connecting electrical circuits | 6.5 | 3.3 | 263.9 | 145.1 |
| | (*) | (0.7) | (1) | (3) |
| Electrical conductors | 4.2 | 2.8 | 244.4 | 147.6 |
| | (*) | (0.6) | (1) | (3) |
| Motors and generators | 7.7 | 2.4 | 220.2 | 111.6 |
| | (*) | (0.5) | (1) | (2) |
| Internal combustion engines and parts | 16.1 | 5.3 | 212.5 | 79.7 |
| | (0.9) | (1) | (1) | (2) |
| Game machines and parts | 0.7 | 0.4 | 211.3 | 29.1 |
| | (*) | (*) | (1) | (0.6) |
| Total, eleven product groups | 1,182.6 | 203.2 | 15,301.3 | 3,587.3 |
| | (64) | (46) | (84) | (76) |
| Total, all 806/807 imports | 1,838.8 | 442.1 | 18,275.5 | 4,703.3 |
| | (100) | (100) | (100) | (100) |

Sources: U.S. Tariff Commission, *Economic Factors Affecting the Use;* printouts from magnetic tapes specially prepared by the ITC; and ITC, *Imports under Items 806.30 and 807.00 of the Tariff Schedules of the United States, 1979-82,* Publication 1467 (ITC, January 1984).

* Less than 0.5 percent.

coproduction as an adjustment strategy for a U.S. industry that is threatened by foreign imports.

*Textiles.* Although the apparel industry was in fifth place in U.S. 807 imports in 1982, it constituted the second most important use of U.S.

components for reimport in assembled products.[8] Imports from Latin American countries, especially Mexico, predominate among these products. The technology used in the manufacture of apparel is one of the most labor-intensive, and 807 imports have grown rapidly as a share of both total imports and domestic production. Although "voluntary" quotas, which impose national ceilings on exports, obscure the economic meaning of trends in the location and level of exports, the most rapid growth in 807 imports of apparel has been from Haiti, the Dominican Republic, El Salvador, Nicaragua, and Barbados, countries in which wage rates are among the lowest in Latin America.

Interestingly, while most 807 imports of apparel come from Latin America, they represent only a small share of total U.S. imports of apparel, most of which come from Southeast Asia. A principal reason for this dichotomy is that Latin American manufacturers of fabrics, producing for relatively small markets and protected by trade policies aimed at promoting import substitution, are high-cost sources of inputs. In Southeast Asia, domestic fabrics of high quality are available to exporters at internationally competitive prices. Thus, Latin America can be internationally competitive in exports of apparel largely through the duty-free entry and reexport of imported fabrics for the U.S. market. This explains the predominance of U.S. 807 imports in the garment trade with Latin America.

*Television sets and components.* After semiconductors, the second largest group of 806/807 imports from developing countries is television apparatus and parts. In many ways, the experiences of U.S. producers of television sets with production sharing represent the extremes of the international realignment of an industry. As was true of the manufacturers of most of the other electronic products, the U.S. television industry was heavily influenced by Japanese competition. U.S. firms, struggling to survive, moved many of their television assembly operations to Mexico, to Taiwan, and, later, to Singapore. By the end of the 1960s, roughly half of U.S. imports came in under tariff item 807, most of them from the factories of U.S. firms in Mexico and Taiwan.

As U.S. firms went abroad and wages in Japan continued to rise, Japanese producers also went abroad, and by the early 1970s Japanese firms in Taiwan and Korea were exporting a substantial number of black-and-white television sets. In addition, since the technology of producing television sets, especially the less complex black-and-white models, was by then

8. There are no 806 imports of apparel.

well known, indigenous producers in Taiwan and Korea entered the export market. Exports from Japan of black-and-white sets declined and were gradually replaced in the U.S. market by imports from Taiwan and Korea.[9]

These changes greatly affected the U.S. television industry. Although some 20 percent of monochrome receivers sold in the United States in 1976 were still nominally produced there, substantial imports of subassemblies and parts from locations in Mexico and Taiwan were incorporated into these sets. In 1960 there were twenty-seven U.S. firms assembling television sets; by 1976 there were only twelve. Of these twelve, however, two had been acquired by Japanese firms, one was owned by a Dutch multinational, and one was a new Japanese subsidiary.

During the early 1970s this history repeated itself with color television. The Japanese again promoted small solid-state television sets aggressively. American producers responded by transferring some of their production of complete sets abroad and, in addition, set up operations abroad to produce parts, subassemblies, and incomplete sets in large volume to be used in color television sets assembled and finished in the United States. Between 1971 and 1976 the proportion of the value of color television subassemblies and parts produced in overseas operations by U.S. firms for their own use went from 23 percent to more than 90 percent; these do not include purchased parts and subassemblies, some of which were also produced abroad.

When, during the mid 1970s, the United States exacted "voluntary" orderly marketing agreements (OMAs) from Far Eastern countries that limited their exports of television sets to the United States, Japanese producers reacted by setting up assembly operations in the United States. Because subassemblies and parts were not covered by OMAs, Japanese subsidiaries in the United States imported them from Japan and low-wage developing countries.[10] By 1979, all the principal Japanese producers and

9. U.S. Department of Commerce, *The U.S. Consumer Electronics Industry* (GPO, 1975); U.S. International Trade Commission (ITC), *Television Receivers, Color and Monochrome, Assembled or Not Assembled, Finished or Not Finished, and Subassemblies Thereof,* Publication 808 (ITC, March 1977); ITC, *Television Receiving Sets from Japan,* Publication 1153 (ITC, June 1981); and ITC, *Color Television Receivers and Subassemblies Thereof,* Publication 1068 (ITC, May 1980).

10. Because a chassis with the picture tube installed was classified as an incomplete receiver and was therefore not subject to OMA limitations, the assembly of color sets in the United States often involves nothing more than the addition of a cabinet, knobs, and perhaps a few other minor components. See ITC, *Color Television Receivers,* p. A-3. A subassembly is less nearly finished than an incomplete receiver.

some Taiwanese producers had established assembly plants in the United States, turning conventional expectations about trade patterns upside down.

The result was that imports of complete receivers dropped sharply as imports of incomplete receivers and subassemblies rose.[11] The bulk of the imports of complete receivers came from Japan, Taiwan, and Korea, with little reliance on item 807. The bulk of incomplete receivers and subassembly imports came from Mexico, nearly all of it under U.S. tariff item 807, trailed by imports from Japan, Taiwan, and Singapore. While in 1980 almost three quarters of imports from Taiwan and Singapore came in under 807, less than 1 percent of those from Japan were in that category.

Thus, by an ironic twist, while U.S. producers were going abroad to stay competitive in color television sets, Japanese—and Taiwanese—producers were moved by U.S. trade restrictions to set up shop in the United States. During the early 1980s U.S. consumers were purchasing "Japanese" television sets assembled in the United States, while U.S. producers were relocating larger and larger shares of "American" output to factories abroad, especially those in Mexico. Furthermore, Japanese producers may soon be put in the odd position of performing in the United States more of the work that goes into the assembly of their sets than is done for the so-called American set produced by U.S.-owned producers abroad.[12] With the implicit threat of renewed import restrictions hanging over their heads, Japanese producers are likely to continue to automate their U.S. plants, using more capital-intensive technologies to reduce labor costs, while most U.S. producers compete on the basis of the more labor-intensive assembly technologies that are most economical abroad.

*Motor vehicles.* Although motor vehicles and parts are the single most important product group in 807 imports, constituting almost half of the total and almost three quarters of such imports from developed countries, they do not fit into the general pattern of shared production. They are typical of 806/807 imports from the industrial countries in that U.S.-made components, often used to meet product safety standards or the tastes of local consumers, account for a minor share of the value of a basically

11. Ibid., tables 2–4.

12. U.S. firms have shifted from imports of subassemblies to more nearly finished but incomplete receivers from Mexico. Because in addition to the foreign parts, these have some U.S. components, they are imported under 807.

foreign-made product. The products imported from industrial countries embody considerably more than 90 percent foreign value added, and in motor vehicles it is close to 98 percent.[13] On the other hand, the total value of products imported from developing countries under 807 is on the average about equally divided between value added abroad and U.S. components.[14]

While still a tiny part of U.S. production, automotive imports from developing countries have been expanding rapidly under U.S. tariff provision 807. They were stimulated primarily by a Mexican decree that tied the production of automobiles by U.S.-owned firms in the lucrative Mexican market to the volume of their exports.[15] While the decree may have given the initial impetus to the growth of imports of automobile parts from Mexico to the United States, various studies project that the "outsourcing" of components used in U.S. production of automobiles will become increasingly common.[16] U.S. labor unions have responded to this trend and to rising imports of automobiles by lobbying for legislation to impose national-content requirements on cars sold in the United States.

## Intrafirm Trade

Much 806/807 trade is internal to the multinational operations of U.S. firms. In 1969, the U.S. Tariff Commission, the predecessor of the ITC, found that more than half the value of U.S. duty-free components reimported under 806/807 came from U.S.-owned investments. The remainder came from U.S. firms dealing with independent contractors and jobbers

13. The exception is Canada, which uses a larger share of U.S. components because of the U.S.-Canadian automotive agreement.

14. The principal exception is Brazil, which contributed about 86 percent of the value of its 807 exports to the United States in 1983 (see table 2-1).

15. Essentially, the decree obliged U.S. automobile producers to balance their imports with an equivalent value of exports. See Douglas Bennett and Kenneth E. Sharpe, "Transnational Corporations and the Political Economy of Export Promotion: The Case of the Mexican Automobile Industry," *International Organization,* vol. 33 (Spring 1979), pp. 177–201.

16. A recent survey showed U.S. auto companies forecasting a 40 percent imported component content in 1990, up from 2 percent in 1978. See "Detroit's Jobs That Will Never Come Back," *Business Week,* May 23, 1983, pp. 168–70. See also a University of Michigan study reported in the *New York Times,* July 6, 1981; and studies by both Arthur Anderson and Company and the U.S. Department of Transportation reported in *Business Week,* August 31, 1981, p. 60.

Table 2-4. *The Relation of U.S. 806/807 Imports and Related-Party Imports of Selected Product Groups from Fifteen Countries to Total U.S. Imports, 1978*[a]

Percent of total imports

| | *Television receivers and parts* | | *Motor vehicles* | | *Motor vehicle parts* | | *Semiconductor parts* | | *Parts for office machines* | |
|---|---|---|---|---|---|---|---|---|---|---|
| *Country of assembly* | *806/807 imports* | *Related-party imports* | *806/807 imports* | *Related-party imports* | *806/807 imports* | *Related-party imports* | *806/807 imports* | *Related-party imports* | *806/807 imports* | *Related-party imports* |
| Mexico | 99.7 | 99.8 | * | 51.5 | 62.5 | 49.1 | 94.5 | 99.3 | 82.5 | 97.2 |
| Malaysia | * | 69.0 | * | * | * | * | 96.6 | 99.0 | 9.7 | 98.7 |
| Singapore | 21.7 | 94.3 | * | * | * | 57.6 | 96.1 | 99.5 | 8.5 | 44.9 |
| Taiwan | 61.9 | 87.4 | * | 99.9 | * | 23.4 | 86.5 | 84.3 | 14.5 | 18.6 |
| Hong Kong | 65.8 | 74.6 | * | 100.0 | * | 35.0 | 94.1 | 86.4 | 70.1 | 78.0 |
| Korea | * | 45.8 | 32.8 | 100.0 | 37.5 | 77.0 | 95.8 | 95.6 | 44.8 | 91.5 |
| Philippines | * | * | * | * | * | 34.4 | 96.6 | 42.8 | 37.4 | 35.8 |
| Brazil | * | 100.0 | * | * | 36.8 | 68.9 | 97.9 | 99.1 | 70.5 | 91.9 |
| Haiti | 61.4 | 34.5 | * | * | * | * | 70.8 | * | 97.6 | 83.0 |
| El Salvador | * | * | * | * | * | * | 99.6 | 99.9 | 68.9 | 98.6 |
| Dominican Republic | * | * | * | * | * | * | * | * | 50.0 | 100.0 |
| Colombia | * | * | * | * | * | * | 100.0 | 100.0 | * | 44.4 |
| West Germany | 0.5 | 37.8 | 70.9 | 97.2 | 0.3 | 63.7 | 1.0 | 90.7 | 0.3 | 75.5 |
| Canada | 78.9 | 82.3 | 12.8 | 82.3 | 1.1 | 33.3 | 8.2 | 49.9 | 69.7 | 92.9 |
| Japan | 1.1 | 74.5 | 16.4 | 95.7 | 12.4 | 82.6 | 0.9 | 80.0 | 1.8 | 54.3 |
| Fifteen countries | 41.4 | 82.0 | 33.4 | 95.6 | 9.2 | 59.9 | 85.4 | 90.6 | 23.6 | 66.0 |
| All countries | 41.1 | 81.4 | 32.7 | 95.6 | 9.6 | 60.1 | 84.5 | 90.8 | 20.5 | 68.6 |

Source: Calculated from data on magnetic tapes prepared specially by the ITC and the Bureau of the Census.
* Less than 0.1 percent.

abroad and from foreign firms securing U.S. components for their exports to the United States.[17]

In 1977, almost $3 billion of U.S. imports, excluding food, chemicals, and primary metals, came from U.S. manufacturing affiliates in developing countries, while $3.3 billion of the imports under 806/807 came from developing countries.[18] While no direct conclusions can be drawn from this juxtaposition, it is known that "a large part of the [807] trade is by U.S. firms and their foreign affliliates."[19]

This conclusion is supported by an examination of U.S. "related party"

17. U.S. Tariff Commission, *Economic Factors Affecting the Use,* pp. 6–7, 147–49.

18. U.S. Department of Commerce, Bureau of Economic Analysis, *U.S. Direct Investment Abroad, 1977* (GPO, April 1981), p. 159.

19. ITC, *Import Trends in TSUS Items 806.30 and 807.00,* Publication 1029 (ITC, January 1980), p. 11.

Table 2-4 (*continued*)

| *Textile products* | | *Equipment for electrical circuits* | | *Watches and clocks* | | *Eight product groups* | | *All products* | |
|---|---|---|---|---|---|---|---|---|---|
| *806/807 imports* | *Related-party imports* | *806/807 imports* | *Related-party imports* | *806/807 imports* | *Related-party imports* | *806/807 imports* | *Related-party imports* | *806/807 imports* | *Related-party imports* |
| 86.5 | 62.6 | 97.9 | 96.1 | 82.0 | 84.3 | 89.6 | 83.9 | 65.3 | 71.3 |
| * | * | 17.8 | 82.9 | 88.6 | 96.5 | 91.3 | 94.3 | 85.5 | 91.4 |
| * | 0.3 | 4.7 | 94.3 | 83.4 | 96.5 | 60.3 | 76.5 | 46.6 | 74.1 |
| 0.1 | 1.3 | 3.0 | 39.7 | 76.8 | 75.7 | 28.5 | 37.2 | 12.3 | 20.8 |
| 0.1 | 2.7 | 21.6 | 35.3 | 32.0 | 28.0 | 14.1 | 15.9 | 10.1 | 17.2 |
| 0.9 | 7.6 | 32.7 | 16.0 | 49.4 | 25.3 | 23.7 | 34.4 | 10.2 | 24.3 |
| 13.3 | 37.4 | 99.4 | 2.4 | 92.2 | 93.8 | 56.6 | 44.7 | 36.3 | 37.6 |
| * | 12.8 | 80.0 | 89.3 | 50.9 | 20.3 | 44.2 | 63.0 | 19.0 | 43.0 |
| 91.1 | 19.1 | 98.2 | 10.6 | * | * | 91.1 | 24.8 | 78.5 | 29.2 |
| 83.9 | 54.0 | 98.8 | 99.9 | 96.3 | 99.9 | 89.5 | 84.3 | 80.3 | 74.9 |
| | | | | | | | | | |
| 97.9 | 70.8 | 48.1 | 97.2 | * | * | 94.6 | 72.6 | 69.1 | 64.1 |
| 64.7 | 25.5 | * | 100.0 | * | * | 64.6 | 25.6 | 17.9 | 23.3 |
| 0.1 | 24.2 | * | 67.1 | 0.4 | 12.7 | 57.3 | 90.1 | 27.7 | 68.6 |
| 4.5 | 46.5 | 11.4 | 45.3 | 10.0 | 51.9 | 12.3 | 48.5 | 9.1 | 45.1 |
| 1.0 | 18.7 | * | 66.5 | 1.0 | 73.0 | 12.2 | 84.9 | 7.2 | 73.2 |
| | | | | | | | | | |
| 8.7 | 11.5 | 26.1 | 69.0 | 33.6 | 57.6 | 28.6 | 70.7 | 16.2 | 56.7 |
| 8.8 | 11.9 | 21.1 | 66.4 | 25.0 | 55.0 | 27.1 | 69.4 | 13.7 | 52.2 |

a. Total imports of products in each group include all items in the Tariff Schedule of the United States (TSUS) in that group that contain 807 imports.

imports in areas where 806/807 is important.[20] In table 2-4 related-party imports are compared with 806/807 imports in 1978. Although the data do not permit determination of the share of 806/807 that is between related parties, it is clear that somewhere between half and all the imported television sets under 806/807 and between 90 and 100 percent of the semiconductors and motor vehicles are related-party transactions. When these statistics are disaggregated at the level of the individual country, the relationship is even more striking (see table 2-4). While a related-party transaction does not necessarily indicate an internal production flow, because it can also describe flows between purchasing and sales affiliates as well as between production affiliates, when considered alongside the other available evidence these data seem to indicate clearly that 806/807 imports are dominated by the trade of multinational firms, especially those based in the United States.

20. "Related party" statistics were available from the U.S. Bureau of the Census for certain years after 1975. They covered trade between parties in which an ownership relation of 5 percent or more exists between importer and exporter. No data are available showing which 806/807 imports are related-party transactions. The Census Bureau no longer provides data on related-party transactions.

The principal exception is the apparel industry. In 1969, according to the U.S. Tariff Commission, about two fifths of the imports of wearing apparel under 807 were by contractors or jobbers dealing with foreign subcontractors in which they had no financial interest.[21] In 1978, less than 12 percent of all imports of textiles and apparel were among related parties. On the other hand, in 1978 more than 90 percent of the imports of semiconductors and more than 80 percent of the imports of television receivers and parts were among related parties, not to mention motor vehicles, 96 percent of the imports of which were related-party imports from other industrial countries. While not all these are intrafirm transactions, it is likely that the figures do reflect the significance of transnational firms in 806/807 imports.

## Foreign Assembly in Europe and Japan

Foreign production arrangements by European and Japanese firms are significantly different from those made by U.S. firms. European firms do relatively little production abroad for the home market, except in the apparel industry, for which assembly is done principally in Eastern Europe. The barriers to imports into the European market of those products generally produced abroad—textiles and electronics—are probably the most significant factor in the explanation of this pattern.

Foreign production by Japanese firms is also concentrated in electronics and apparel, but it is considerably larger in relation to imports and domestic production than is that of European firms. Japanese employment in electronics in Southeast Asia, for example, is of roughly the same order of magnitude as that of U.S. electronics affiliates. It differs from U.S. production abroad, however, in that its output is primarily for export markets rather than the home market and in that many of the electronic products shipped by Japanese firms seem less complex than the electronic products typically shipped by U.S. firms.

Import quotas in developed countries have also influenced production patterns in obvious ways. It seems likely that Japanese production by Asian affiliates is affected by various sorts of trade preference extended by developed countries to producers in developing countries. Japan, though heavily committed to foreign production in certain product lines, generally ships relatively little back to the home market; more than 70 percent of the

21. U.S. Tariff Commission, *Economic Factors Affecting the Use,* pp. 43–44.

output of its Asian manufacturing affiliates generally goes to local or other export markets.[22]

### *The European Community*

As does the United States, the countries of the EC permit the return of goods temporarily exported abroad for fabrication with the payment of duty on the value added. The concept of outward-processing trade in the EC is roughly comparable to the concept of 806/807 imports in the United States. Assessment by customs officials in the EC of the value added differs from U.S. procedures, but in principle the outward-processing provisions of the EC are very similar to the provisions of items 806 and 807 of the U.S. Tariff Schedule. The countries of the EC, however, are subject to more complicated procedures for allowing partial relief of duty on the reimport of assembled or processed goods.[23]

22. This is true for all products except wood, paper, and pulp; see table 1-3. Asian manufacturing affiliates of U.S. firms shipped roughly the same percent of Asian output to local or other export markets, except in electrical machinery, where 70 percent of output went back to the United States.

23. Until 1975 most members of the EC offered some form of duty relief for goods reimported after treatment abroad. Application of these provisions, however, varied from country to country within the Community. In 1975 the Council of the European Community issued a directive regarding the "harmonizing of outward-processing regulations." "Inward arrangements" allowing for the exemption of any export duty on goods processed within the Community have been in effect since 1969.

The directive makes duty relief consistent and uniform throughout the Community. In essence, the directive states that the duty upon reimportation of a good after treatment is to be reduced by the amount of duty that would have been charged upon import of the originally exported components had they been imported alone at the time of reentry of the product.

For statistical purposes each of the countries of the EC has adopted a name for the type of outward-processing transaction discussed here. The names are as follows:

*Belgium*—Régime du perfectionnement passif, Regeling Passive Veredeling
*Denmark*—Passiv Foraedling
*France*—Exportation temporaire industrielle
*Germany*—Passiver Veredelungsverkehr
*Ireland*—Outward processing
*Italy*—Temporanea esportazione per perfezionamento passivo
*Luxembourg*—Régime du perfectionnement passif
*Netherlands*—Voorwaardelijke vrijstelling voor goederen welke worden wederingevoerd na te zijn bewerkt, verwerkt of hersteid (passive veredeling)

West Germany and the Netherlands have published statistical information on the so-called outward-processing trade for some time, and in 1978 the European Community released the first such complete records for the entire EC.

Karen Licker assisted in preparing this footnote.

The tariff charge is equal to the difference between the tariff rate on the imported article into which it is incorporated and the rate to which it would be subject if it were imported alone. Instead of deducting the value of European components from dutiable value before assessing the tariff charges, as would be done in the case of the U.S. 807 item, the tariff is levied and then the value of the tariff charges on the exported component if it were imported *alone* is credited toward that tariff charge.

Thus, components exported by members of the EC are in effect subject to duty upon reimport. In semiconductors, for example, it may be uneconomical to import integrated circuits into Europe after assembly in Asia because of the wide gap between the 17 percent tariff applicable to assembled integrated circuits upon reimportation and the 9 percent tariff on unfinished silicon chips that is credited. Since finished goods generally face greater tariff barriers than unassembled materials and components, this can be a formidable barrier to import of products assembled abroad. The European system diverges from U.S. practice in two other significant ways: all transactions must have the prior approval of the national customs authority, and only residents of member countries are allowed to have the processing carried out abroad.

Imports of products assembled in developing countries by the European Community as a whole, as well by individual countries, are minimal (see table 2-5). In 1978, for example, reimports of products processed abroad amounted to about $261 million, while U.S. 806/807 imports from developing countries amounted to about $4.133 billion, approximately sixteen times as great. The bulk of these imports was in textiles, primarily garments, and in electronics. In fact, only in these two categories of product do reimports of products processed abroad account for a significant portion of imports (see tables 2-6 and 2-7). Most garments reimported into European countries are assembled in Eastern Europe.[24]

France and Germany account for 78 percent of such imports from developing countries (see table 2-8). Reimports generally come from Southeast Asia, except in France, which takes almost two-thirds of its reimports from its former colonies in North Africa.

The small scale of European operations abroad is evident in a recent survey of foreign employment by German-owned affiliates.[25] It was found

24. This is documented by Folker Fröbel, Jürgen Heinrichs, and Otto Kreye in *The New International Division of Labour,* trans. Pete Burgess (London: Cambridge University Press, 1980).

25. Ibid.

Table 2-5. *Geographic Origin of Outward-processing Reimports by the Netherlands and West Germany, 1978*

Percent

| *Group of countries* | *Netherlands* | *West Germany* |
|---|---|---|
| European Community | 80 | * |
| Rest of Western Europe | 6 | 14 |
| Eastern Europe | 5 | 69 |
| Asia | 1 | 13 |
| Other | 9 | 4 |
| All | 100 | 100 |

Sources: The Netherlands, Central Bureau voor de Statistiek, *Maandstatistiek van de buitenlandsie handel,* January 1979, table 8; West Germany, Statistisches Bundesamt Wiesbaden, *Zusammenfassende Übersichten für den Aussenhandel,* vol. 1 (Stuttgart and Mainz: W. Kohlhammer, 1979), table 2.4.2, pp. 112–13. Figures are rounded.
* 0.2 percent.

Table 2-6. *Outward-processing Reimports from Developing Countries by Members of the European Community, 1978*

Millions of units of European account (UEA);[a] percentages of total imports of items in parentheses

| *Product* | *EC* | *West Germany* | *France* | *Italy* | *Netherlands* | *United Kingdom* |
|---|---|---|---|---|---|---|
| Leather, shoes | 13.2 | 8.8 | 4.4 | * | * | * |
| | (0.22) | (0.42) | (0.45) | (*) | (*) | (*) |
| Textiles, garments | 60.2 | 27.4 | 24.4 | 0.05 | 2.4 | 1.0 |
| | (0.89) | (1.07) | (3.29) | (0.02) | (0.20) | (0.10) |
| Machinery | 10.4 | 1.3 | 0.7 | 0.3 | 7.8 | 0.3 |
| | (0.03) | (0.02) | (0.01) | (0.01) | (0.24) | (0.01) |
| Electrical, electronics | 109.6 | 66.4 | 19.6 | 16.6 | 0.01 | 5.9 |
| | (0.65) | (1.5) | (0.68) | (0.83) | (*) | (0.24) |
| Clocks, watches, optical and photographic equipment | 6.7 | 2.7 | 2.4 | 0.2 | 0.03 | 1.2 |
| | (0.08) | (0.12) | (0.10) | (0.03) | (*) | (0.08) |
| Games, toys, sporting goods | 3.2 | 0.6 | 1.7 | * | * | 0.9 |
| | (0.20) | (0.14) | (0.51) | (*) | (*) | (0.33) |
| Other | 14.4 | 7.5 | 1.7 | 2.9 | 1.5 | 0.04 |
| | (0.06) | (0.12) | (0.09) | (0.05) | (0.03) | (0.02) |
| All | 217.7 | 114.8 | 54.9 | 20.2 | 11.6 | 9.3 |

Sources: Imports, official Eurostat figures for 1978; outward-processing reimports from developing countries, C. Berthomieu and A. Hanaut, "Recent Studies and Data from Western Europe on Production Sharing and the International Division of Labour," revised, paper submitted to the Brookings Institution (March 1980).
* Zero or negligible.
a. 1 UAE = U.S. $1.20.

that a total of 23,000 employees in assembly operations for German electrical engineering firms were in South and Southeast Asia in 1975; in 1977 U.S. firms in Asia employed 200,000 workers in the electrical industry. German electrical engineering affiliates employed only 96,000 in the developing countries throughout the world. Since little German production for

Table 2-7. *Outward-processing Reimports by Countries of the European Community from Their Developing-Country Trading Partners, 1978*

Thousands of units of European account (UEA)[a] and percent

| Region and developing country | West Germany | | France | | Italy | | Netherlands | | United Kingdom | | Total EC | |
|---|---|---|---|---|---|---|---|---|---|---|---|---|
| | *Amount* | *Percent* | *Amount* | *Percent* | *Amount* | *Percent* | *Amount* | *Percent* | *Amount* | *Percent* | *Amount* | *Percent* |
| *Mediterranean Africa* | | | | | | | | | | | | |
| Morocco | 517 | 0.5 | 12,574 | 24.7 | 47 | 2.0 | 40 | 0.6 | 2 | 0.0 | 13,178 | 6.5 |
| Tunisia | 2,438 | 2.2 | 18,934 | 37.2 | 2,372 | 12.2 | 1,074 | 15.0 | 0 | 0.0 | 25,362 | 12.5 |
| Algeria | 0 | 0.0 | 10 | * | 56 | 0.3 | 0 | 0.0 | 0 | 0.0 | 71 | * |
| Egypt | 0 | 0.0 | 0 | 0.0 | 123 | 0.6 | 0 | 0.0 | 0 | 0.0 | 128 | * |
| Libya | 0 | 0.0 | 0 | 0.0 | 56 | 0.3 | 0 | 0.0 | 0 | 0.0 | 56 | * |
| Subtotal | 2,955 | 2.6 | 31,518 | 62.0 | 2,654 | 13.6 | 1,114 | 15.6 | 2 | * | 38,795 | 19.0 |
| *Latin America* | | | | | | | | | | | | |
| Brazil | 4,783 | 4.3 | 12 | * | 59 | 0.3 | 142 | 2.0 | 0 | * | 5,014 | 2.3 |
| *Southeast Asia* | | | | | | | | | | | | |
| Malaysia | 26,597 | 23.9 | 3,033 | 6.0 | 15 | * | 8 | * | 1,746 | 21.4 | 32,311 | 16.0 |
| Singapore | 20,135 | 18.0 | 1,619 | 3.2 | 16,441 | 84.5 | 0 | 0.0 | 656 | 8.0 | 40,694 | 20.0 |
| Philippines | 14,274 | 12.8 | 529 | 1.0 | 0 | 0.0 | 0 | 0.0 | 1,064 | 13.1 | 15,867 | 7.8 |
| South Korea | 5,755 | 5.2 | 11,330 | 22.3 | 0 | 0.0 | 0 | 0.0 | 643 | 7.9 | 17,773 | 8.8 |
| Taiwan | 21,143 | 19.0 | 1,918 | 3.8 | 8 | 0.0 | 46 | 0.6 | 1,757 | 21.6 | 25,951 | 12.8 |
| Hong Kong | 15,756 | 14.0 | 919 | 9.8 | 284 | 1.4 | 5,811 | 81.6 | 2,275 | 27.9 | 26,270 | 13.0 |
| Subtotal | 103,660 | 93.0 | 19,348 | 38.0 | 16,748 | 86.0 | 5,865 | 82.4 | 8,141 | 100.0 | 158,856 | 78.4 |
| Total | 111,438 | 100.0 | 50,872 | 100.0 | 19,461 | 100.0 | 7,121 | 100.0 | 8,143 | 100.0 | 202,665 | 100.0 |

Sources: Berthomieu and Hanaut, "Recent Studies and Data from Western Europe," table I3. Figures are rounded.
* Less than 0.1 percent.
a. 1 UEA = U.S.$1.20.

Table 2-8. *Outward-processing Reimports by Countries of the European Community from Their Developing-Country Trading Partners, by Commodity Group, 1978*

Thousands of units of European account (UEA)[a]

| *Region and developing country* | *Leather and shoes* | *Textiles and garments* | *Machinery* | *Electrical and electronic products* | *Clock and watchmaking, optical and photographic equipment* | *Games, toys, and sporting goods* | *Other* | *Total* |
|---|---|---|---|---|---|---|---|---|
| *Mediterranean Africa* | | | | | | | | |
| Morocco | 800 | 7,462 | 637 | 3,779 | 0 | 0 | 500 | 13,178 |
| Tunisia | 3,517 | 17,755 | 0 | 893 | 70 | 540 | 2,587 | 25,362 |
| Algeria | 0 | 0 | 44 | 7 | 1 | 0 | 19 | 71 |
| Egypt | 0 | 0 | 36 | 0 | 92 | 0 | 0 | 128 |
| Libya | 0 | 0 | 4 | 3 | 0 | 0 | 49 | 56 |
| Subtotal | 4,317 | 25,217 | 721 | 4,682 | 163 | 540 | 3,155 | 38,795 |
| *Latin America* | | | | | | | | |
| Brazil | 309 | 0 | 0 | 3,668 | 98 | 0 | 939 | 5,014 |
| *Southeast Asia* | | | | | | | | |
| Malaysia | 416 | 917 | 0 | 24,736 | 1,262 | 0 | 4,980 | 32,311 |
| Singapore | 0 | 4,363 | 0 | 35,433 | 227 | 0 | 671 | 40,694 |
| Philippines | 0 | 1,785 | 1,136 | 12,888 | 0 | 0 | 58 | 15,867 |
| South Korea | 0 | 8,239 | 0 | 9,208 | 0 | 3 | 323 | 17,773 |
| Taiwan | 4,224 | 3,348 | 86 | 15,803 | 2,128 | 64 | 298 | 25,951 |
| Hong Kong | 3,576 | 13,038 | 4,567 | 2,691 | 1,170 | 37 | 1,191 | 26,270 |
| Subtotal | 8,216 | 31,690 | 5,789 | 100,759 | 4,787 | 104 | 7,521 | 158,866 |
| Total | 12,842 | 56,907 | 6,510 | 109,109 | 5,048 | 644 | 11,615 | 202,675 |

Source: Berthomieu and Hanaut, "Recent Studies and Data from Western Europe," table I2.
a. 1 UEA = U.S.$1.20.

export markets is found outside Southeast Asia, except in the Mediterranean and North African countries, it can be concluded that exports are not a strong motivation for German investments in foreign electronics industry affiliates.

Many of the German firms involved in foreign production of apparel are smaller companies.[26] As is true of U.S. firms, much of the apparel trade involves subcontracts with independent foreign subcontractors.

This relatively minor use of production-sharing arrangements by the European countries is largely the result of two factors: the preference shown in the past by large industrial countries in Europe to import work-

26. In the German apparel industry some 70 percent of all firms maintain some form of production abroad. Ibid., p. 107.

ers rather than export components abroad to them for processing and the substantial protection given to the European market. Imports of electronic products and apparel, the goods usually associated with foreign assembly, are subject to high tariff rates in the EC. Furthermore, there are quotas on imports of apparel. National content requirements, such as those limiting intra-EC duty-free trade to electronic products containing less than 3 percent imported semiconductor components, also pose a formidable nontariff barrier to production abroad.

### *Japan*

Prodded by the rising costs of Japanese labor, increasing problems with congestion and pollution at home in the traditional manufacturing industries, lower levels of protection for the Japanese home market, and exchange-rate revaluations, the Japanese began making direct investments in coproduction during the late 1960s.[27] Excluding several large investment projects in chemicals and natural resources, these investments in developing countries were largely in textiles and electrical equipment.[28] Japanese garment makers and manufacturers of textile fibers stepped up their foreign investments, particularly in Hong Kong, in order to circumvent OMAs imposed on Japanese exports of apparel to the United States and Western Europe. Tariffs imposed on textile imports by developing countries have also stimulated Japanese production abroad. In general, the large East Asian markets have become quite important to Japanese textile producers, who supply these markets through their local affiliates and subcontractors.[29]

The Japanese electronics industry in East Asia is even more dependent on exports. A 1979 survey by the Japan Electrical Machinery Industry Association makes strikingly clear what large volumes of investment and employment are involved. Of 193,000 workers said to be employed by Japanese electrical equipment affiliates throughout the world, some 134,000 were in these East Asian affiliates.[30] Of these, in turn, some 89,000

27. See Kunio Yoshihara, *Japanese Investment in Southeast Asia* (Honolulu: University Press of Hawaii, 1978), chapter 1.

28. Sueo Sekiguchi, *Japanese Direct Foreign Investment* (Tokyo: Japan Economic Research Center, 1977), p. 73 and note 5.

29. Yoshihara, *Japanese Investment,* p. 23, and chapter 4.

30. Japanese Electrical Machinery Industry Association (JEMIA), *Internationalization and Its Impact on the Electronics Industry of Japan* (Tokyo, June 1980), in Japanese, p. 2.

worked in the manufacture of components; the balance, 45,000, were employed in consumer and industrial electrical products.[31]

The distribution of employment in Japanese electrical affiliates in various countries in 1979 in relation to total employment in electronics and to employment in U.S. electrical affiliates in 1977 is summarized in table 2-9. Together, in recent years, U.S. and Japanese electrical equipment affiliates have employed a third to a half or more of those employed in electronics industries in all the principal East Asian countries other than Hong Kong.[32]

Exports of electrical goods by Japanese producers in Korea had much to do with the rise of Korea in the international electronics market. Yoshihara claims that Japanese affiliates accounted for almost all the exports of electronic equipment from Korea in 1973.[33] Another study shows that some 89 percent of Korean exports of electric and electronic equipment were shipped by foreign firms—U.S., Japanese, and others—in 1974. Japanese investment in electronics in Korea ($35 million) also exceeded U.S. investment (about $13 million) by a margin greater than two to one.[34] In contrast to Japanese investment, most of which was in production intended for export, U.S. investment was geared primarily toward the domestic Korean market.

In the other important Asian location of Japanese investment in electronics, Taiwan, Japanese influence does not predominate. Taiwanese fig-

31. Ibid. These 1979 Japanese Asian electrical affiliate employment figures contrast with the 1977 employment of about 158,000 for U.S. electrical and electronics affiliates in developing Asia and the Pacific, of which some 101,000 were in components. See U.S. Department of Commerce, *U.S. Direct Investment Abroad, 1977,* p. 149, table II.G.4. Thus, Japanese and U.S. electronics employment in production-sharing arrangements in Asia were of roughly the same magnitude in the late 1970s, with employment in the manufacture of components outnumbering workers in other product lines about two to one.

32. The figures in table 2-6 confirm that Japanese firms through some degree of foreign ownership accounted for about 46 percent of Korean electronics employment in 1979. See JEMIA, *Internationalization and Its Impact,* p. 180. In Taiwan, on the other hand, U.S. and Japanese employment in the electronics industry were of roughly the same size—and together must have constituted nearly half of total industrial employment there. In Singapore and Malaysia, U.S. employment in electronics outnumbered Japanese employment more than two to one, assuming continued growth of employment in U.S. affiliates after 1977, and together must have accounted for about two-thirds of the total work force in the electronics industry. Only in Hong Kong are U.S. and Japanese firms of merely marginal importance, accounting probably for at most a quarter of employment in the industry.

33. Yoshihara, *Japanese Investment,* p. 175 and table 5.13.

34. See Chung H. Lee, "United States and Japanese Direct Investment in Korea: A Comparative Study," *Hitotsubashi Journal of Economics,* vol. 20 (February 1980), pp. 28, 29, 39.

Table 2-9. *Employment of Foreign Affiliates in the Asian Electronics Industry*

| | *Distribution of output, circa 1978 (percent)* | | | | | |
|---|---|---|---|---|---|---|
| *Country* | *Consumer goods* | *Industrial products* | *Components* | *Total number of workers, circa 1978 (thousands)* | *Number of employees in Japanese affiliates, 1979 (thousands)* | *Number of employees in U.S. affiliates, 1977 (thousands)* |
| Korea | 41 | 9 | 50 | 180 | 38 | 8 |
| Taiwan | 46 | 4 | 50 | 230 | 54 | 48 |
| Hong Kong | 78 | 5 | 17 | 94 | 2 | 19 |
| Singapore | 48 | 2 | 50 | 60 | 14 | 25 |
| Malaysia | 10 | ... | 90 | 55 | 11 | 24 |

Source: Japan Electrical Machinery Industry Association, *Internationalization and Its Impact on the Electronics Industry of Japan* (Tokyo: JEMIA, June 1980), in Japanese, pp. 33, 180; and U.S. Department of Commerce, Bureau of Economic Analysis, *U.S. Direct Investment Abroad, 1977* (Government Printing Office, April 1981), table II.G.3.

ures show that roughly 61 percent of the dollar value of foreign commitments in electronics and electrical equipment between 1952 and 1974 came from the United States and 17 percent came from Japan.[35]

Japanese investments for export in the textile and electronics sectors in Southeast Asia also seem to be undertaken by smaller firms than is generally true of U.S. investments in the region. Roughly half the number of investments in electronics, or 30 percent of the value, and a third of the investments in textiles have been undertaken by firms not listed on the Tokyo stock exchange.[36] Even among the listed firms, the tendency is for relatively small firms to predominate. These small Japanese affiliates tend to stay close to home, a tendency reflected in the high degree of concentration of such investments in Taiwan and Korea. Only in more distant Singapore do large Japanese firms predominate.[37]

Statistics also seem to show an accelerating trend toward overseas production; table 2-10 indicates that there was a substantial shift toward foreign production of several Japanese consumer electronic products between 1978 and 1979. Much of the increased foreign investment in the production of color television sets has gone to the U.S. market because of trade restrictions. The vast bulk of other products produced abroad, however, is to be found in the nearby Asian countries.

While Japan has special tariff-sparing arrangements similar to the provisions of U.S. 806/807, they do not seem to be in wide use. The secretar-

35. See Gustav Ranis, "Industrial Development," in Walter Galenson, ed., *Economic Growth and Structural Change in Taiwan* (Cornell University Press, 1979), p. 249.

36. Yoshihara, *Japanese Investment*, pp. 163–65.

37. Ibid., pp. 28, 31.

Table 2-10. *Japanese-made Units Produced in Foreign Countries, by Product, 1978–79*

Percent

| Product | Percent produced abroad | | Distribution of foreign production, 1979 | | | |
|---|---|---|---|---|---|---|
| | 1978 | 1979 | Western Europe | North America | Asia | Other |
| Videotape recorders | 0 | 0 | ... | ... | ... | ... |
| Color television sets | 27 | 30 | 8 | 50 | 29 | 10 |
| Black-and-white television sets | 41 | 49 | 3–6 | | 85 | 9–12 |
| Radios | 59 | 69 | * | | 93 | 7 |
| Tape recorders | 27 | 34 | * | | 96 | 4 |
| Automobile radios | 6 | 3 | 2–4 | | 86 | 10–12 |
| Automobile stereos | 2 | 4 | | | | |
| Stereos | 21 | 32 | 6–10 | | 72 | 18–22 |
| High-fidelity amplifiers | 5 | 8 | 1–3 | | 95 | 2–4 |
| Record players | * | 3 | | | | |
| Tape decks | 5 | 6 | | | | |
| FM tuners | 9 | 9 | | | | |
| Speaker systems | 10 | 12 | 80 | | 20 | * |

Source: JEMIA, *Internationalization and Its Impact*, pp. 3–4.
* Negligible.

iat of the United Nations Conference on Trade and Development (UNCTAD) once suggested that reexport to the Japanese market was discouraged by government authorities, who have discretionary authority over the duty-free reimport of exported Japanese components, which U.S. customs authorities do not have over U.S. imports under 806/807.[38] At any rate, the output of Japanese overseas production of electronics articles is directed toward non-Japanese markets.

Japanese investors in other Asian countries have been acutely aware of the political nature of barriers to trade and have shown considerable resourcefulness in adapting to changes in the rules of the game. It is clear, for example, that they have been influenced in their choice of sites for production of goods for international export markets by the existence of trade preferences in important markets that accept output manufactured in suitable host developing countries.[39] The political intervention that has repeat-

38. See UNCTAD, *International Subcontracting Arrangements*, pp. 21–22.

39. For evidence that Japanese firms have the Generalized System of Preferences (GSP) and quotas in mind when they choose production locations abroad, see the case studies of international subcontracting presented by Sang-Seol Lee, "International Subcontracting in ESCAP [Economic and Social Commission for Asia and the Pacific] Countries," paper presented at the UNDP/UNCTAD–Brookings Seminar on North-South Complementary Intra-Industry Trade, Mexico City, July 16–20, 1979.

edly occurred in their export of color television sets, automobiles, and—more recently—integrated circuits has taught the Japanese that their share of the market for advanced products in the United States and Europe must often be purchased with the transfer of some part of production into the target market. Alternatively, the political protection offered by a joint venture with a national who possesses some claim to part of the GSP limit or export quota of a developing country can be used.[40]

A recent industry report suggested that Japanese producers will carefully coordinate the shift of items with lower value added to their overseas production bases while keeping items with higher value added in Japan, in order to maintain employment.[41] In electronic components, in particular, overseas production by Japanese industry has the purpose of expanding the Japanese share of the global export market.[42] As can be seen from table 2-7, large volumes of television, radio, tape recorder, and stereo equipment are simultaneously produced at home and abroad by Japanese firms, suggesting that Japanese producers will retain much of their domestic production of these products in Japan, while supplying expanding export markets from overseas plants whenever they can.

## Appendix: Explanation of Items 806.30 and 807.00

The United States International Trade Commission (ITC) gives the following summary of the U.S. customs treatment of 806/807:

> Items 806.30 and 807.00 are included in schedule 8, part 1, subpart B, of the [Tariff Schedule of the United States]. Pursuant to the provisions of item 806.30, articles of metal (except precious metal) that have been manufactured, or subjected to a process of manufacture, in the United States, exported for processing, and then returned to the United States for further processing are subject to duty only on the value of the foreign processing. Under item 807.00, imported

40. Note, incidentally, that Japanese foreign investment is much more likely to be found in a joint venture than is U.S. investment. See Yoshihara, *Japanese Investment,* pp. 39–46.

41. JEMIA, *Internationalization and Its Impact,* pp. 257–61. Perhaps the situation is best described by these comments from a Japanese commercial attaché in Singapore, when asked if recent wage hikes would bring more sophisticated operations into foreign-owned plants: " 'There is little prospect of more sophisticated ventures being established in Singapore,' Mr. Nayashima said. 'Japanese firms keep their businesses in Japan until they lose their competitiveness. Then, they move out to take advantage of lower wages or to establish export markets abroad.' " *Asian Wall Street Journal Weekly,* March 23, 1981, p. 20.

42. JEMIA, *Internationalization and Its Impact,* pp. 257–61.

> articles assembled in foreign countries with fabricated components that have been manufactured in the United States are subject to duty upon the full value of the imported product less the value of the U.S.-fabricated components contained therein. No further processing in the United States is required for articles imported under item 807.00.[43]

The 807.00 provision covers

> articles assembled abroad in whole or in part of fabricated components, the product of the United States, which (a) were exported in condition ready for assembly without further fabrication, (b) have not lost their physical identity in such articles by change in form, shape, or otherwise, and (c) have not been advanced in value or improved in condition abroad except by being assembled and except by operations incidental to the assembly process such as cleaning, lubricating, and painting.[44]

The bureaucratic requirements for 806.30 are more onerous than those for 807.00:

> Before the exportation of an article for processing abroad under item 806.30, the owner or exporter must file . . . a certificate of registration describing the article(s) exported. The owner or exporter must state the name of the U.S. manufacturer . . . and . . . must further provide the name of the person who will further process the articles upon their return to the United States. . . . The article must be examined by a customs officer and laded for export under customs supervision.[45]

Section 807 of the Tariff Schedule of the United States (TSUS) came into being in 1963 as a technical change suggested by the Tariff Classification Study of the U.S. Tariff Commission, which codified into law prevailing practices that had arisen as a result of decisions of the customs court in the 1950s. The only substantive change introduced by this legislation was to eliminate the "constructive segregation" requirement, whereby assembled components had to be able to be removed without injury from the item of which they were part. Slight changes in this section were legislated in 1965 and 1966.[46]

The 806 and 807 statistics, maintained by the ITC, go back in rudimentary form to 1966. Detailed statistics for 807 are available only from 1969, those for 806 from 1972. (Broad 806 classifications are also available from

43. ITC, *Imports under Items 806.30 and 807.00 of the Tariff Schedules of the United States, 1979–1982,* Publication 1170 (ITC, 1984), pp. 1-2. "The admission of an article under either of these tariff items does not relieve it from quantitative limitations imposed under other provisions of law, such as certain textile articles covered by the Arrangement Regarding International Trade in Textiles" (ibid., p. 4, n. 2).

44. Ibid., p. 4.

45. ITC, *Import Trends in TSUS Items,* p. 10.

46. U.S. Tariff Commission, *Economic Factors Affecting the Use,* pp. 15–20.

1969 and are used in table 2-2.) The ITC maintains these data in disaggregated form—by country and by product—on magnetic tape, in addition to those published in its less detailed reports.

There are several problems in the valuation of 806/807 imports. Since a large share of 806/807 transactions represents the transfer between related firms of semifinished products which therefore have no observable market value, products assembled abroad are given a constructed value as they pass through U.S. customs. Essentially, customs value is defined as variable production costs plus a markup particular to the country and product.

This problem is not confined to trade within a single firm. Even when independent contractors are involved, the contracting firm often supplies inputs gratis, in which case problems arise in valuing an input with an arbitrary price. Independent subcontractors, for example, are frequently lent machinery by their U.S. principals, given technical and administrative assistance, and so forth, the value of which could be omitted from all sales contracts and invoices without financial prejudice to either side.

Except for the costs of certain special tools and dies unique to a specific product, depreciation and other capital costs ought properly to be considered general expenses. The legal status of research, development, and design costs is ambiguous. When directly allocable to a U.S.-made component, they are not considered a cost of fabrication. When numerous production stages take place inside and outside the United States before a finished product emerges, it is not clear what allocation of basic technical, administrative, and research overhead should have been made to the various stages of production. Does the silicon chip from which an integrated circuit is assembled overseas and then shipped back to the United States for testing and packaging embody the research cost that went into it as a chip before it was exported, as an assembled integrated circuit, or as a packaged integrated circuit after it has passed electrical tests and is actually ready for sale?

As might be imagined, the U.S. Customs Service has had great difficulty in interpreting this statute. Informal interviews undertaken by the authors early in 1980 with customs officials at various ports of entry along the U.S.-Mexican border, where a great deal of 806/807 trade enters the United States, disclosed a great deal of variation in customs practice. Some import specialists ask for actual fabrication costs, general expenses, and profit; others make elaborate calculations, comparing various cost ratios among the operations for which they are responsible, in an effort to monitor "usual" expenses and profit; many simply accept with minimal scrutiny whatever declaration is made. Often a wide variety of practices is followed within a single port of entry. The result of valuation procedure is in effect to price the article at its declared cost of manufacture overseas plus, possibly, a markup for general expenses and profit. No imputation of U.S.-based research and development expenditure, administrative overhead, or marketing costs is generally made.

In addition, the values on official documents that are reported to the U.S. Census Bureau, which is the official custodian of U.S. trade statistics, are substantially revised as more accurate and timely cost information is received by customs import specialists. These revisions are often not attributed to the individual transactions to which they apply and are frequently resolved after the deadline for sending revised data to the Census Bureau has passed. A report came from one customs post that the official transaction values for imports of electronic components sent to the Census Bureau were generally 8–12 percent lower than revised appraisals made later, in many cases too late for the revisions to be picked up by the Census Bureau.

CHAPTER THREE

# Internationalization in the Semiconductor Industry

KENNETH FLAMM

THE U.S. semiconductor industry illustrates one way in which production of a technologically complex, sophisticated, nontraditional product can be internationalized, with little possibility of real competition from producers based in developing countries. The dynamics of this internationalization were not vastly different from those of production of more traditional products abroad—low-wage foreign competition, in the form of imported Japanese transistors, led to the establishment of operations in other countries in the early 1960s. The semiconductor industry was the first U.S. industry to go abroad on a large scale. Because of this early start and the highly competitive nature of the U.S. semiconductor industry, even products in the manufacture of which the United States had clearly maintained a technological lead soon began to be assembled abroad.

The evolution of the U.S. semiconductor industry represents one path by which industry has come to terms with the changes that have made the postwar decades a distinctive stage in the evolution of the modern world economy: a dramatic decline in all sorts of trade barriers, including an enormous reduction in the cost of international transport and communication; the quickening of the pace at which technology is diffused across national boundaries; continuing international disparities in wages and standards of living; and the great leap in the importance of the multinational firms that accompanied these changes.

But it is not the only model. The Western European and Japanese semiconductor industries have taken different paths on critical policy issues, and each illustrates potential strengths and weaknesses of those alternatives.

All the diverse national policies have produced an essentially global semiconductor industry, with product, capital, or technology flowing across national boundaries while, for the most part, internalized within the limits of a single multinational firm. In a certain sense, since the trade associated with overseas production consists largely of the internal transfers of multinational corporations, the rise of a global semiconductor industry reflects a shift in the functions of the multinational firm. Until the early 1960s, most of the output of multinational electronics subsidiaries was produced for foreign markets. Tariff and tax barriers determined whether a company would export through a foreign sales affiliate or would produce behind foreign tariff walls. Superior management, marketing skills, technical knowledge, or preferential access to capital markets made multinationals competitive with foreign entrepreneurs overseas. Foreign operations were basically versions of big national companies in the home market.

Technological advances in transport and communication, the development of a basic industrial infrastructure in many developing countries, and the creation of free-trade and export-processing zones in unfinished manufactures in the developing world have made new forms of organization possible. Multinational producers of electronic products can now transfer to distant regions where costs are lower the production departments that supply their output to their primary markets. Foreign affiliates, rather than being sales offices or scaled-down versions of home operations, can now specialize in the production or assembly tasks of the organization, while home offices can specialize in the skill- and technology-intensive operations in which their costs are lower.

## Semiconductors and Their Importance

The development of semiconductor technology can be traced back to World War II, when the unreliability of silicon diodes used in radar prompted the U.S. government to sponsor a huge research program in the fundamental properties of germanium and silicon, which involved thirty to forty U.S. research laboratories.[1] Nevertheless, the transistor, the most important early semiconductor device, was actually invented at the civilian

1. A complete and entertaining history of semiconductors can be found in Ernest Braun and Stuart Macdonald, *Revolution in Miniature,* 2d ed. (Cambridge University Press, 1982); see pp. 26–30 for this point.

Bell Laboratories, which did not receive a research and development grant from the military for semiconductors until after its invention.[2]

The transistor gradually replaced many types of vacuum tube amplifiers, because it was more reliable, was smaller, consumed less power, and cost less to manufacture. It soon became clear that devices constructed with semiconductor materials could perform most other electronic functions, including those of various types of diodes, resistors, and capacitors.[3]

At the outset it was recognized that the transistor was of great strategic value. Military users financed a large share of the research and development that went into semiconductors during the 1950s, directly through grants and indirectly through purchase of new devices at premium prices. In addition, roughly $36 million was spent between 1952 and 1959 on grants to provide funds to individual firms to build semiconductor production capacity far in excess of what was then required.[4] In 1959, the first integrated circuit was developed; it consisted of several different electronic devices constructed on the surface of a single piece of semiconductor material.[5]

The decision to use integrated circuits in the Minuteman intercontinental ballistic missile (ICBM) of the Air Force and in the Apollo space program of the National Aeronautics and Space Administration (NASA) gave the industry another big push in the 1960s. Industry sources estimate the government to have paid for roughly half of all research and development in the industry during the years in which the integrated circuit was being developed and brought to the mass market.[6]

2. A semiconductor device (SCD) was so named because its principle of operation involved the application of electric currents to normally nonconductive crystalline materials which had been treated with small amounts of impurities to permit the flow of electric current. The transistor is a semiconductor amplifier, in which the application of an input regulates the flow of electric current through the semiconductor medium.

3. Inductors are the most important electronic component that cannot be replicated in a semiconductor device. See James D. Meindl, "Microelectronic Circuit Elements," *Scientific American,* vol. 237 (September 1977), p. 70.

4. John G. Linvill and C. Lester Hogan, "Intellectual and Economic Fuel for the Electronics Revolution," *Science,* vol. 195 (March 18, 1977), p. 1109. See also John E. Tilton, *International Diffusion of Technology: The Case of Semiconductors* (Brookings Institution, 1971), pp. 92–93. Braun and Macdonald, in *Revolution in Miniature,* p. 71, report that the industry in 1955 had the capacity to produce 15 million transistors a year, whereas the actual output was 3.6 million.

5. It was developed, independently, by Jack Kilby and Robert Noyce.

6. From 1958 through the early 1970s. See U.S. Department of Commerce, Industry and Trade Administration, Office of Producer Goods, *A Report on the U.S. Semiconductor Indus-*

The importance of semiconductors quickly spread beyond purely military applications. As the price dropped and production increased, they became an important input into the young computer industry. Cheap semiconductors lowered the cost of moving and storing data, lowered the costs of the computers into which they were built, and thereby did much to stimulate demand for computers.

The decline in the price with improvements in technology was quite remarkable. Figure 3-1 depicts semiconductor price indexes between 1967 and 1981 in real terms. Furthermore, as more and more circuit elements were crammed onto a single semiconductor chip, integrated circuits went from fewer than sixty-four components per circuit in the early 1960s (small-scale integration), to more than a thousand in the early 1970s (large-scale integration), and finally to more than sixteen thousand in the late 1970s (very large scale integration or VLSI). The price per electronic function has thus declined some 100 to 1,000 times the decline shown in the figure. One calculation shows the price of an electronic function in a computer memory declining from $50 in the mid 1960s to less than $0.005 in 1979.[7]

Table 3-1 shows that in the early 1960s military consumption in the United States peaked at almost half the total U.S. demand for semiconductors, and all the demand for integrated circuits. In 1965, producers of the Minuteman missile were the largest users of integrated circuits, accounting for 20 percent of all sales by the U.S. semiconductor industry.[8] But commercial use increased much more rapidly until, by 1981, military sales accounted for only 10 percent of the semiconductors sold in the United States.

The fact that they are a critical input in the computer and telecommuni-

---

*try* (Government Printing Office, 1979), p. 8; Linvill and Hogan, "Intellectual and Economic Fuel," p. 1108. Even at civilian Bell System Laboratories, the military services paid for a quarter of Bell's semiconductor research during the period 1949–58. The first practical application of the transistor in laboratory equipment was undertaken by Bell for the navy in 1949. The early development of the power transistor was financed at Bell by the air force, as was the first transistorized computer. See C. Warren, B. McMillan, and B. Holbrook, "Military Systems Engineering and Research," in *A History of Engineering and Science in the Bell System,* vol. 2, *National Service in War and Peace* (Bell Telephone Laboratories, 1978), pp. 617–48.

7. United States International Trade Commission (ITC), *Competitive Factors Influencing World Trade in Integrated Circuits,* Publication 1013 (Washington, D.C.: ITC, 1979), p. 21.

8. Norman J. Asher and Leland D. Strom, *The Role of the Department of Defense in the Development of Integrated Circuits* (Arlington, Va.: Institute for Defense Analyses, May 1977), pp. 21–22.

Figure 3-1. *Declines in Semiconductor Prices, 1967–82*

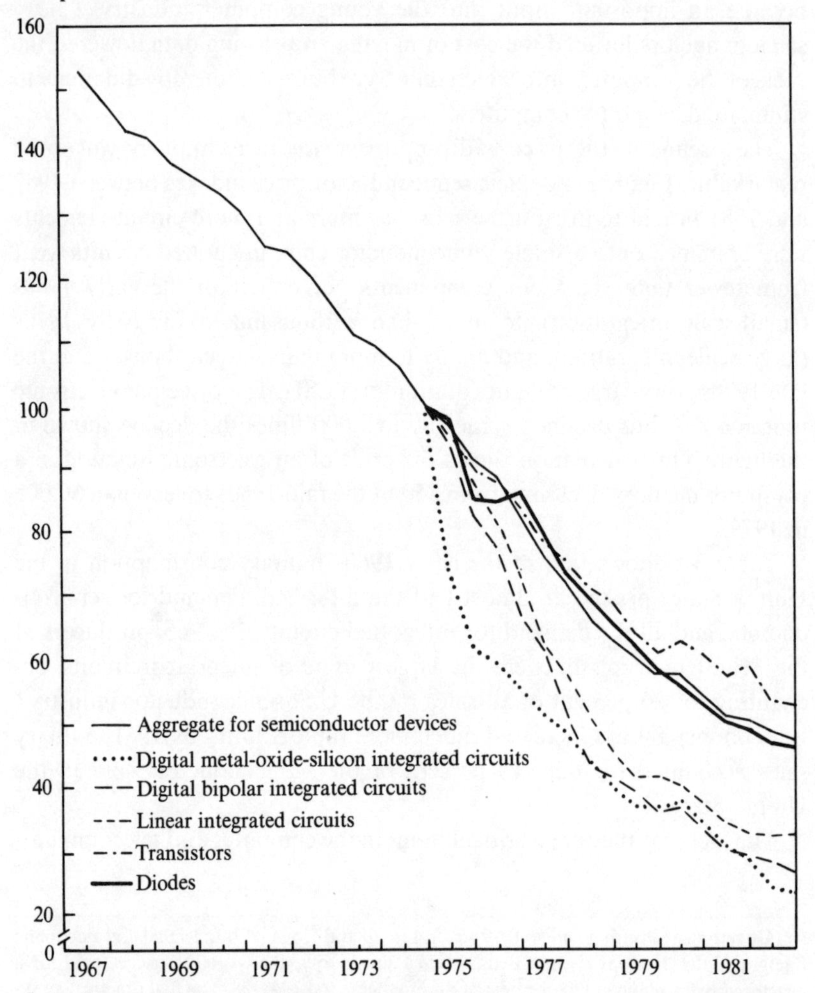


Source: Prices are real indexes, divided by producer price index for finished goods; producer prices from unpublished series furnished by the U.S. Bureau of Labor Statistics.

cations industries is as much responsible for the economic and strategic importance of semiconductors as any purely military use. As table 3-2 makes clear, the greatest consumption of semiconductors, at least since the early 1960s, has been in those two sectors. After correction for changes in the prices of semiconductor devices and outputs, the figures show that the number of semiconductors in computers tripled between 1963 and 1972 and increased five to seven times in various types of telecommunications

Table 3-1. *Military Sales as Percentage of All Sales in the U.S. Semiconductor Market, Selected Years, 1958–81*

| *Year* | *All semiconductors* | *Integrated circuits* |
|---|---|---|
| 1958 | 39 | n.a. |
| 1960 | 48 | n.a. |
| 1962 | 39 | 100 |
| 1964 | 28 | 85 |
| 1966 | 27 | 53 |
| 1968 | 25 | 37 |
| 1972 | 24 | n.a. |
| 1979 | 14 | n.a. |
| 1981 | 10 | n.a. |

Sources: 1958–68, John Tilton, *International Diffusion of Technology: The Case of Semiconductors* (Brookings Institution, 1971), pp. 90–91; 1972, William Finan, "The International Transfer of Semiconductor Technology Through U.S.-Based Firms," Working Paper 118 (National Bureau of Economic Research, 1975), p. 96; 1979, U.S. Department of Commerce, Industry and Trade Administration, *A Report on the U.S. Semiconductor Industry* (Government Printing Office, September 1979), p. 77; 1981, Larry Waller, "Cadence Slow for Military Sales," *Electronics*, August 25, 1982, p. 75.
n.a. Not available.

Table 3-2. *Semiconductor Use, by Sector, 1963, 1967, and 1972*

| | *As percent of value of output of user industry* | | | *As percent of value of total semiconductor production* | | |
|---|---|---|---|---|---|---|
| *Sector*[a] | *1963* | *1967* | *1972* | *1963* | *1967* | *1972* |
| Computers and calculators | 5.0 | 2.8 | 5.5 | 21.0 | 11.0 | 16.0 |
| Electrical measurement instruments | 1.6 | 1.9 | 2.9 | 2.1 | 2.1 | 1.8 |
| Radio and television receivers | 1.3 | 1.8 | 2.1 | 5.0 | 6.0 | 3.3 |
| Telephone and telegraph equipment | 3.6 | 3.1 | 5.3 | 9.0 | 6.3 | 9.4 |
| Radio and television communications equipment | 2.2 | 2.9 | 4.7 | 24.0 | 21.0 | 18.0 |
| Semiconductors | 0.51 | 1.1 | 1.8 | 0.51 | 1.1 | 1.8 |
| Other electronic components | 1.6 | 3.0 | 2.9 | 6.5 | 12.1 | 6.2 |
| Aircraft and parts | 0.17 | n.a. | 1.1 | 3.8 | n.a. | 7.7 |
| Photographic equipment | 0.03 | 0.04 | 1.8 | 0.1 | 0.11 | 4.1 |
| Communications other than radio and television | n.a. | 0.08 | 0.13 | n.a. | 1.1 | 1.7 |
| Personal and repair services | 0.32 | 0.72 | 0.91 | 4.0 | 6.2 | 6.8 |
| Business services | n.a. | 0.04 | 0.46 | n.a. | 0.70 | 7.3 |
| *Deliveries to final demand* | | | | | | |
| Net exports | ... | ... | ... | 4.8 | 11.2 | 4.2 |
| Federal defense use | ... | ... | ... | 5.6 | 5.4 | 3.7 |
| Federal use other than for defense | ... | ... | ... | 0.61 | 0.86 | 0.95 |

Source: U.S. Department of Commerce, Input-Output Tables, 1963, 1967, and 1972.
n.a. Not available.
a. Sectors included are those that used more than 1 percent of the semiconductor devices produced in 1972.

equipment.[9] The growth in their use in certain other types of equipment was even more spectacular.

Computers have become the most important commercial use for semiconductors. From 1964 to 1966, total industry sales of integrated circuits were about 77 million units, whereas internal production by IBM alone was 130 million units.[10] In 1977, the single most important product line was computer memory chips, which accounted for at least 17 percent of all shipments of semiconductor devices in the United States, or about 28 percent of the production of integrated circuits; microprocessors, which contain the processing units of computers, accounted for another 4 percent or so of semiconductor devices produced.[11] Of the 60 percent of the U.S. semiconductor output that consisted of integrated circuits, in fact, approximately 86 percent were some form of digital logic circuit.

Since the production of semiconductors is one of the most technologically dynamic sectors of the U.S. economy, it is not surprising to find both the semiconductor industry and its principal customers in the ranks of the most rapidly growing U.S. industries. Between 1972 and 1978 semiconductor sales, in constant dollars, grew at an annual compound growth rate of almost 20 percent, the highest of any American manufacturing industry;

9. An index (1972 = 100) of real use of SCDs per unit of output is (n.a. means not available):

| *User sector* | *1963* | *1967* |
|---|---|---|
| Computers and calculators | 33 | 44 |
| Radio and television receivers | 23 | 76 |
| Telephone and telegraph equipment | 21 | 43 |
| Radio and television communication equipment | 15 | 45 |
| Semiconductors | 28 | 61 |
| Aircraft and parts | 4.5 | n.a. |
| Photographic equipment | 0.61 | 1.9 |
| Communications other than radio and television | n.a. | 45 |
| Personal repair services | 10 | 58 |
| Business services | n.a. | 6.1 |

Method: Percent of value of output of user industry in table 3-2 deflated to 1972 dollars using SCD and output price indexes. Output price indexes based on four-digit SIC output price indexes (cross-weights used) published in the U.S. Census of Manufactures data corresponding to year; except the indexes for computers, aircraft and parts, communications, and services, which are taken from U.S. Department of Labor, Bureau of Labor Statistics, *Time Series Data for Input-Output Industries* (GPO, 1979).

10. See William Harding, "Semiconductor Manufacturing in IBM, 1957 to the Present: A Perspective," *IBM Journal of Research and Development,* vol. 25 (September 1981), p. 652.

11. U.S. Department of Commerce, Bureau of the Census, *1977 Census of Manufactures,* vol. 2, pt. 3, p. 36E-24 (GPO, 1980).

the average in all U.S. manufacturing was 3.2 percent a year.[12] Table 3-3 was constructed by selecting from 161 U.S. industries, as defined by the U.S. Department of Labor in its input-output studies, those sectors whose real annual growth rates exceeded 7 percent in either period, 1958–76 or 1959–73; the latter period excludes the distorting effects of the 1973 oil price rises and the recession of 1975–76. This criterion was met by twenty-two industries, of which seventeen were in manufacturing, two in transportation and communication, and three in services.

Of the seventeen high-growth manufacturing industries, three—plastic products, plastics and synthetic rubber, and synthetic fiber products—were based on cheap petrochemicals and two—floor coverings and bicycles—were based on new products associated with postwar affluence. Of the remaining twelve manufacturing sectors, five were principal users of semiconductor devices, and three—service industry machinery, medical and dental instruments, and optical and ophthalmic equipment—were significant users of electronic equipment containing semiconductors. Communications and business services, also on the high-growth list, are large purchasers of semiconductor devices. This indicates that the manufacture of semiconductor devices is not only a highly important growth industry, but is also one with important linkages to other growth industries.

Casual observation would suggest that many of these are forward linkages to other growth industries, with innovative products that are cheaper generating new demands in new markets. Industry analysts claim that the average value of semiconductor content in electronic equipment went from less than 1 percent to almost 5 percent of value between 1970 and 1979.[13] In computer applications, that percentage has risen from about 1.5 percent to about 6 percent of the value of equipment; in consumer and automotive applications, from almost zero to 6 percent; in industrial applications, from zero to nearly 2 percent; and in government and military applications, from 1.5 percent to about 2.5 percent. Since the prices of semiconductor devices were dropping rapidly in relation to the general level of producer prices and in relation to the prices of almost all specific industrial products as well, the real semiconductor content of all these products was rising even faster than these percentages seem to indicate.

It is this critical link to the computer and telecommunications indus-

12. U.S. Department of Commerce, *1982 U.S. Industrial Outlook* (GPO, 1982), pp. xvi–xvii.

13. "Can Semiconductors Survive Big Business?" *Business Week,* December 3, 1979, p. 68.

Table 3-3. *Growth of Output and Jobs in High-Growth U.S. Industries, 1958–76 and 1959–73*[a]

| *Sector (standard industrial classification)* | *Product* | *Growth rate of output*[b] *(percent)* | | *Growth rate of jobs*[b] *(percent)* | | *Output, 1976 (millions of dollars)* | *Employment, 1976 (thousands of jobs)* |
|---|---|---|---|---|---|---|---|
| | | *1958–76* | *1959–73* | *1958–76* | *1959–73* | | |
| *Manufacturing* | | | | | | | |
| 307 | Plastic products | 11.5 | 12.4 | 7.4 | 8.5 | 20,480 | 351 |
| 2821–22 | Plastics and synthetic rubber | 9.7 | 9.7 | 1.6 | 2.0 | 20,240 | 100 |
| 283 | Drugs | 8.2 | 8.3 | 3.0 | 3.1 | 14,746 | 168 |
| 367 | Electronic components | 7.9 | 8.8 | 3.8 | 4.3 | 11,349 | 372 |
| 358 | Service industry machinery | 7.6 | 9.3 | 3.8 | 4.4 | 10,235 | 163 |
| 351 | Engines, turbines, and generators | 6.2 | 7.3 | 2.1 | 2.8 | 10,058 | 113 |
| 3573–74 | Computers and peripherals | 9.5 | 9.5 | 5.2 | 5.8 | 9,825 | 248 |
| 3861 | Photographic equipment and supplies | 10.2 | 11.0 | 4.3 | 4.8 | 9,192 | 130 |
| 225 | Hosiery and knit goods | 7.3 | 8.6 | 1.4 | 1.8 | 8,870 | 259 |
| 365 | Radio and television sets | 8.4 | 9.3 | 1.6 | 2.6 | 7,275 | 129 |
| 2823–34 | Synthetic fibers | 9.3 | 9.6 | 3.2 | 4.2 | 6,497 | 105 |
| 3661 | Telephone and telegraph apparatus | 6.8 | 8.7 | 2.7 | 3.6 | 5,832 | 133 |

| | | | | | | | |
|---|---|---|---|---|---|---|---|
| 384 | Medical and dental instruments | 8.7 | 8.9 | 5.6 | 5.8 | 5,554 | 109 |
| 379 | Other transport equipment | 12.3 | 16.0 | 11.8 | 14.7 | 5,437 | 123 |
| 227 | Floor coverings | 9.8 | 11.8 | 3.9 | 4.6 | 3,657 | 60 |
| 383, 385 | Optical and ophthalmic equipment | 8.9 | 9.0 | 3.1 | 3.0 | 2,151 | 64 |
| 375 | Cycles, bicycles, and parts | 11.4 | 12.5 | 3.1 | 3.4 | 1,054 | 24 |
| *Transportation* | | | | | | | |
| 45 | Air transportation | 9.1 | 10.2 | 5.1 | 5.9 | 20,798 | 370 |
| *Communication* | | | | | | | |
| 48 | Communications, except radio and television (SIC 438) | 7.6 | 7.7 | 2.2 | 2.6 | 48,069 | 1,028 |
| *Services* | | | | | | | |
| 73, 7692, 7694[c] | Miscellaneous business services | 7.9 | 8.6 | 6.7 | 7.1 | 63,279 | 2,173 |
| 806 | Hospitals | 7.7 | 7.8 | 5.2 | 5.4 | 43,480 | 2,490 |
| 722, 807, 809[d] | Other medical services | 8.1 | 8.5 | 10.6 | 10.8 | 17,610 | 1,139 |

Source: U.S. Department of Labor, Bureau of Labor Statistics, *Time Series Data for Input-Output Industries,* Bulletin 2018 (GPO, 1979).

a. High-growth industries are those whose annual growth rates are greater than 7 percent.

b. Constant-dollar annual growth rates, estimated by the BLS using the regression method.

c. Includes part of SIC 7699; excludes 731 and 7396.

d. Excludes SIC 8099.

tries, rather than military uses, that has led to the keen international competition that now grips the industry. The widely perceived promise of rapid technological advance explains the depth of worldwide interest in the promotion of national semiconductor industries. Before examining the variety of national policies and their effects on the structure of production in various countries, it may be worth while to look at the economics of semiconductors and their manufacture.

## Semiconductor Economics

Certain physical features of semiconductors, and the production processes used in their manufacture, are important determinants of the pattern of international trade and production in the industry. The most important physical feature of semiconductors is that their manufacture involves a number of physically discrete steps. In the beginning, of course, a firm must invest in the research and development of the design for a new device. For integrated circuits the production process itself can be broken into three distinct steps: chip fabrication, chip assembly, and testing of the finished device.[14]

A second distinctive feature of semiconductors, one that allows the stages of production to be separated geographically, is their great value in relation to their weight. Transport costs are a much smaller fraction of value than of almost any other important good that is traded internationally.[15] Transport costs generally amount to between 1 percent and 2.5

14. In the manufacture of an integrated circuit, ultrapure silicon crystals are sliced into wafers, polished, and processed with photochemical, electrochemical, or ion-beam techniques to implant precisely controlled amounts of impurities in each wafer. A grid of devices is created on each wafer, and faulty devices are tested and marked. The grid is scribed and broken into "dice." The individual chips are then bonded to the final package and are connected to external wire leads. The final assembly is encapsulated in a metal, ceramic, or plastic case, tested, rated according to its electrical characteristics, packaged, and shipped to the final consumer. The sequence of steps is generally similar, though considerably less complex technologically, in the production of discrete SCDs such as transistors and diodes.

15. In a sample of 155 four-digit industries taken from the 1963 U.S. Census of Manufactures, SCDs had the highest value-to-weight ratio of any industry. F. M. Scherer and others, *The Economics of Multi-Plant Operation* (Harvard University Press, 1975), pp. 437–39. SCDs were worth, on an average, $30.40 a pound. The runners-up were radio and communications equipment ($12.36), radio and telegraph apparatus ($12.05), computing machines ($7.68), and scientific instruments ($6.30). Richard Moxon's calculations of value-to-weight ratios for electronic products show SCDs, again, with the highest such ratios, based on 1967 U.S.

percent of the value of a shipment.[16] Because transport costs tend to be related to weight, more highly integrated devices—which are more valuable per ounce of silicon—are cheaper to fly around. Thus, the more complex state-of-the-art circuits are cheaper in relation to their value to route to foreign assembly sites than simpler components.

Very low transport costs make a widely dispersed geographic pattern of specialization in production economical. As will be seen in the next sections, the response of the industry has been to develop an extensive two-way trade in semiconductors, with components being shipped from developed countries to developing countries in which wages are low and returning as assembled devices to be marketed in the large industrial countries.

Semiconductors are also a research-intensive product. The electronic components industry spent 7 percent of sales on research and development in 1977.[17] This was far above the average of 3.1 percent of sales spent by all U.S. manufacturing firms in 1977. Estimates of research and development costs as a percentage of sales of semiconductor devices and integrated circuits in 1977 are about 8.5 percent and 16.4 percent, respectively, placing the industry among the most research-intensive in the United States.[18]

The design of a new semiconductor device, like more basic types of research, makes intensive use of highly skilled scientific manpower. Before the use of computer-aided design systems, which became widespread in the early 1980s, the development of an advanced microprocessor chip required roughly one or two years each of the time of six design engineers. In 1978, there were only a few more than two thousand engineers in the entire

---

Census data. Richard Moxon, *Offshore Production in the Less Developed Countries—A Case Study of Multinationality in the Electronics Industry,* Bulletin No. 98-99 (New York University, July 1974), pp. 86–87. In a Japanese study integrated circuits were found to have the highest price per kilogram of any major Japanese export—twice that of computers, and more than sixty times that of color television sets. Cited in Kunio Yoshihara, *Japanese Investment in Southeast Asia* (University Press of Hawaii, 1978), p. 134. Price per kilogram (in yen) was 100 for steel, 500 for automobiles, 1,000 for bearings, 3,000 for color television sets, 10,000 for cameras, 100,000 for computers, and 200,000 for integrated circuits.

16. These figures for 1978 are based on calculations from data furnished on magnetic tape by the U.S. International Trade Commission. Discrete devices are generally more costly and integrated circuits (ICs) less costly to transport.

17. These calculations are based on National Science Board, National Science Foundation, *Science Indicators 1978* (GPO, 1979).

18. For SCDs in general, see J. Rada, *The Impact of Microelectronics* (Geneva: International Labour Office, 1980), p. 23; for ICs, the figure is calculated from tables A-21 and A-36, ITC, *Competitive Factors.*

United States who had the requisite skills.[19] The design facilities of the principal producers of semiconductors are generally located in areas in which trained electrical engineers are concentrated or near universities at which these skills are produced: "Silicon Valley," near Stanford University, and the cluster of design and research facilities in the northeastern Washington–Boston urban belt are prime examples of this phenomenon.

The availability of highly skilled manpower, then, is the prime determinant of the location of facilities for the design of semiconductor devices. Many companies locate research facilities far from their primary area of operations.[20] Naturally, small-scale pilot production facilities are often sited alongside research and design centers, and considerable support employment clusters around them.

Of the various stages of actual production, the fabrication of chips for sophisticated products is probably the most costly and capital-intensive. Extraordinarily expensive machinery is required for the creation of the etched silicon chip that contains an integrated circuit; a typical production line that in 1965 required about $1 million in equipment required an expenditure of $50 million or more in 1980. In 1982 a single state-of-the-art electron-beam etching machine cost more than a million dollars.[21] Highly automated chip-fabrication lines run by computers have recently been put into production.[22]

The assembly of the silicon chip—bonding it to its leads and packaging it—is where the greatest technological diversity exists and where the effect of overseas production is most often felt. Since the mid 1970s, many of the larger semiconductor firms have experimented with machines that automate the bonding process.[23] The alternative is manual assembly, which

19. See Arthur Robinson, "Are VLSI Microcircuits Too Hard to Design?" *Science,* July 11, 1980, p. 258; I. R. Saddler, "Can VLSI Growth Continue?" *Military Electronics/Countermeasures,* February 1980, p. 98.

20. A young British firm, Inmos, with headquarters in England and production facilities in Wales, located its main design center in Colorado Springs, Colorado. See Colin Norman, "Inmos Enters the 64K RAM Race," *Science,* May 8, 1981, pp. 642–44. The principal U.S. semiconductor firms have design facilities in Israel and Japan, thousands of miles from their main production locations; the attraction is the large concentration of research engineers. See *Business Week,* April 20, 1981, pp. 44–48; "U.S. Semiconductor Makers Set Up Centers for Research in Japan," *Asian Wall Street Journal Weekly,* June 2, 1980.

21. *Business Week,* July 21, 1980, p. 189: National Materials Advisory Board, National Research Council, *An Assessment of the Impact of the Department of Defense Very-High-Speed Integrated Circuit Program* (National Academy Press, 1982), p. 136.

22. "Automated Semiconductor Line Speeds Custom Chip Production," *Electronics,* January 27, 1981, pp. 121–27.

23. Douglas W. Webbink, *The Semiconductor Industry: A Survey of Structure, Conduct and Performance,* Federal Trade Commission (GPO, 1977), p. 57.

means workers bonding and encapsulating chips by hand under a microscope.

The predominantly manual nature of the technology used until recently by most U.S. firms in the assembly and packaging of semiconductors is apparent when the statistics are compared to aggregate statistics for other industries. In 1976, semiconductor devices were estimated to have required roughly fifty-four man-years of direct labor input per million dollars of output. Of all the manufacturing industries found in the 367-sector U.S. input-output tables, only lace goods, combing plants, and cooking utensils and pottery—all much less important industries—required greater input of labor.[24] Motor vehicles and computers, in contrast, required about nine man-years and twenty-three man-years of direct labor, respectively. The manufacture of apparel using purchased material required about thirty-five man-years per million dollars of output in 1976.

Two features of manual and automated assembly processes are important determinants of their economic usefulness. First, since automated assembly involves substantial fixed expenditures on equipment and its setup, the primary factor in the profitability of automated assembly is the volume of production to be undertaken. For long production runs it makes sense to undertake a large fixed investment in an automated line. The fixed costs of manual assembly methods, with much higher variable costs per unit assembled, are much smaller and shorter production runs therefore make much more sense.

Since average product life, historically, has tended to be rather short in the semiconductor industry, because of the unflagging rhythm of technological advance in the design of semiconductor devices, automated assembly facilities have not been in widespread use during most of the history of the industry.[25] More than half the transistors introduced during the late 1950s, for example, were obsolete within two years; semiconductors used in computer systems during the mid 1970s are said to have had about the

24. Testimony of Howard D. Samuel, U.S. Department of Labor, "Multilateral Trade Negotiations," Hearings before the Subcommittee on International Finance of the Senate Committee on Banking, Housing, and Urban Affairs, 96 Cong. 1 sess., April 4, 1979.

25. An important recent exception is that of some computer-oriented chips, whose very large market size makes automated assembly economically feasible. Andy McCue, "U.S. Firm's Plan to Assemble Semiconductors on West Coast Could Threaten Asian Producers," *Asian Wall Street Journal Weekly,* June 23, 1980, p. 16. High-volume chip designs are being assembled on automated U.S. lines with growing frequency. See, for example, Pieter Burggraaf, "Motorola's Goal: Full Assembly Automation," *Semiconductor International,* March 1984, pp. 120–22.

same life span.[26] At IBM memory products have historically had about a one-year life.[27] This rapid rate of obsolescence in products means relatively short lives for production equipment as well; the average life of equipment in the industry is probably some three to five years.[28]

Length of production run, of course, is not the only determinant of optimal assembly technique. As capital becomes cheaper in relation to the cost of labor, automation becomes more and more attractive economically. Because large firms may have both large production volumes and access to cheaper capital, they might be expected to be more highly automated—as they seem to be in the U.S. semiconductor industry.[29]

The other important factors in the choice between manual and automated assembly are quality—the number of defective assemblies produced—and reliability—the frequency of failure in use. Because they occur less randomly, defects are much easier (and therefore cheaper) to detect with an automated process. While extremely low defect rates can be obtained with an automated assembly line, automated production may be more costly. How much the ultimate consumer is willing to pay for higher quality is one of the determinants of whether or not to automate.[30]

26. See Tilton, *International Diffusion of Technology,* p. 83; Webbink, *The Semiconductor Industry,* p. 131.

27. Harding, "Semiconductor Manufacturing in IBM," p. 653.

28. Because of the structure of the investment tax credit in the late 1970s, manufacturers actually depreciated their equipment over a period of four to eight years. See U.S. Department of Commerce, Industry and Trade Administration, Office of Producer Goods, *U.S. Semiconductor Industry* (GPO, September 1979), p. 54.

29. See Webbink, *The Semiconductor Industry,* p. 57. In addition to IBM, AT&T is also reported to have automated all stages of its operation. The dangers of investing in highly automated production equipment were graphically illustrated to the U.S. industry by the experience of Philco, a major producer, in the late 1950s. Philco developed a highly automated production line for transistors, with a considerable reduction in costs, only to find its products, and its stock of technology and equipment, obsolete after only a few years and so ended up withdrawing from the transistor business. See Tilton, *International Diffusion of Technology,* p. 83; Webbink, *The Semiconductor Industry,* p. 57. IBM completed the automation of its transistor assembly line in 1959, only to find it running just as its last germanium transistor was introduced. In IBM's case, however, a huge internal demand may have made the company economically viable, and IBM appears to have been convinced that better process control—and quality—justified a continuing commitment to automation. See Harding, "Semiconductor Manufacturing in IBM," pp. 648–49. Nonetheless, the relatively short lives of new SCDs have historically been a healthy deterrent to automation for most U.S.-produced semiconductors.

30. This point is often overlooked in the continuing debate over the quality of U.S. and Japanese microchips. See, for example, "Japan Makes Them Better," *The Economist,* April 26, 1980, pp. 55–56; "U.S. Reject Rate Still Trails Japanese," *Electronics,* November 6, 1980, p. 46; "U.S. Makes Raising Processor Quality," *Electronics,* December 18, 1980, p. 41; and "Perception Lag Nags U.S. Chip Makers," *Electronics,* April 21, 1982, p. 42.

The last stage of semiconductor production is the testing of the finished product. Testing a complex integrated circuit requires the use of expensive computerized test equipment and therefore tends to be a capital-intensive process.

These four basic steps—design, chip fabrication, assembly, and testing—are characterized by important learning effects; that is, important reductions in unit cost are obtained as production experience is accumulated. The so-called learning curve or experience curve is estimated to reduce the unit cost of producing a semiconductor device 20–30 percent every time cumulated production doubles.[31] These economies are thought to be primarily the product of improvements in yields from basic production processes, rather than of experience on the part of production workers. Most of the learning economies occur in the more capital-intensive stages of manufacture.

This means that assembly costs tend to be a more important component of the cost of producing a mature product than a new one. Since process yields improve much more quickly than any other factor in production cost, chip fabrication costs decline in relation to assembly costs as a technology matures.[32] In the design of new products, reduction in the cost of fabrication means that more complex products are increasingly economical to produce.[33]

The costs of detecting and replacing a defective chip in the manufacture of electronic equipment generally increase with the complexity and cost of the equipment. The market for chips is therefore differentiated by quality and density, for use in different sorts of application.

The large fixed overhead in these fabrication processes also creates certain economies of scale; similar economies of scale may exist in the final testing of complex devices, which requires costly testing equipment.[34] Manual bonding, assembly, and encapsulation operations, on the other hand, are labor-intensive and offer few significant economies of scale or

31. Tilton, *International Diffusion of Technology,* p. 85. These ideas about learning curves were developed in the late 1960s by the Boston Consulting Group (BCG), a private management-consulting firm. For a more recent derivation of this figure, see Harding, "Semiconductor Manufacturing in IBM," p. 652.

32. See William F. Finan, "The International Transfer of Semiconductor Technology Through U.S.-Based Firms," Working Paper No. 118 (New York: National Bureau of Economic Research, December 1975), p. 21.

33. See Robert N. Noyce, "Large-Scale Integration: What Is Yet to Come?" *Science,* vol. 195 (March 18, 1977), pp. 1102–06.

34. See Finan, "The International Transfer," chapter 3, for a more complete discussion of mid-1970s technology and its various economies.

learning to U.S. producers.[35] Expenditures for research and development are another important source of economies of scale.

There are noticeable international differences in the types of assembly technique used in the manufacture of semiconductors.[36] To explain these differences—and even more significant variations in the characteristics of different national semiconductor industries—the main industrial policies affecting the semiconductor industry that have been pursued in Western Europe, Japan, and the United States will be outlined briefly.

## The Effects of National Industrial Policy

National policies have had important effects on the international patterns of specialization in the production of semiconductors. Certain characteristics of the industry—especially the significance of economies of learning and scale for reduction of costs and of extensive research-and-development programs—have led to various proposals for rationalization of the industry, protection from international competition, public investment, and other kinds of national industrial policy.

The implication of significant economies of learning and scale for competitiveness is that the best strategy for reducing production cost is to concentrate experience and output in as small a number of firms as possible; this may, however, have negative effects on innovation if, as Tilton found, small firms are leaders in the development and diffusion of new and untried technologies.[37] Market share will be a critical determinant of the speed with which production experience can be accumulated. A variant of the infant-industry argument for protection can therefore be offered for

35. Though producers who have automated more of the bonding operations may enjoy economies of scale in these operations.

36. See, for example, "Tape Automated Bonding Meets the Challenge of VLSI," *Electronics,* December 18, 1980, pp. 100–05.

37. See Tilton, *International Diffusion of Technology,* p. 59. This point seems to have been of particular concern to U.S. policymakers studying the effects of Japanese competition on the U.S. semiconductor industry. A recent CIA intelligence estimate concluded that

> without competing directly against major U.S. semiconductor firms now in existence, the Japanese may be able, in the long term, to become industry leaders simply because their strategy will preclude the emergence and growth of small, innovative U.S. firms.

See U.S. Central Intelligence Agency, *Japanese Microelectronics: A Thrust for Leadership* (Washington, D.C.: CIA, May 1979), p. 13. Released under the Freedom of Information Act, January 30, 1980.

the erection of trade barriers around national markets in order to allow national firms to acquire the volume of cumulative output that will make them competitive with established foreign producers.[38]

Finally, the sunken costs of research and development present a public-goods problem to producers, since new technologies diffuse rapidly to competitors. The temporal "window" in which a producer can charge a premium over the cost of manufacture for a new device or technology to pay back the generally large costs of research and development incurred in its creation may be brief. Government financial support of research programs, tied perhaps to centralized coordination and sharing of research among competing national firms, is a rational policy response when new technology and its benefits cannot be appropriated in full by the firm that undertakes the research. The historical record indicates that firms cannot generally prevent competitors from swiftly acquiring new techniques and that patent and licensing barriers are an ineffective means of protecting proprietary information in this industry.[39]

It may be argued, in fact, that the failure of the market to guarantee innovators a period of rents on their new technology long enough to stimulate the socially correct amount of risky investment is an important justification for state intervention.[40] The existence of significant economies of learning and of scale may create a tendency toward concentration, again offering justification for intervention.

Also, because the abilities of individual firms to bear risk may be limited by the imperfections of financial institutions, government intervention may be desirable merely because of the great riskiness of research investment that is nevertheless socially worth while. It is possible to conclude that a rationale for government intervention in research and development is readily available, since, to quote Kenneth Arrow, "we expect a free enterprise economy to underinvest in invention and research (as compared

38. It is offered in Jan S. Hogendorn and Wilson B. Brown, *The New International Economics* (Addison-Wesley Publishing Co., 1979), pp. 240–43.

39. See Finan, "The International Transfer," chapter 4; Webbink, *The Semiconductor Industry,* pp. 96–101; CIA, *Japanese Microelectronics,* pp. 6–8; and Marie Therese Flaherty, "Field Research on the Link between Technological Innovation and Growth: Evidence from the International Semiconductor Industry," *American Economic Review,* vol. 74 (May 1984), pp. 67–72.

40. See Kenneth Arrow, "Economic Welfare and the Allocation of Resources for Invention," in Richard Nelson, ed., *The Rate and Direction of Inventive Activity* (Princeton University Press for the National Bureau of Economic Research, 1962), pp. 609–25.

with an ideal) because it is risky, because the product can be appropriated only to a limited extent, and because of increasing returns in use."[41]

Learning and scale effects, as well as the importance of sizable investment in research and development, may explain a principal feature of growth in the semiconductor industry. On the one hand, as Tilton first noted, small firms account for a disproportionately large number of innovations.[42] On the other hand, an industry shakeout generally occurs later, leaving several large firms producing the vast bulk of a specific product line; small firms are often taken over by larger, established firms or end up becoming large firms, as such economies of scale and learning come into play.

A wave of mergers and acquisitions in the late 1970s suggests that such a shakeout was then taking place.[43] The picture is complicated, however, by a growing tendency toward vertical integration, with large users of semiconductors guaranteeing the security of their technology and the stability of their supply by buying out their suppliers, and by the acquisition of technology or access to the U.S. market by foreign firms through the purchase of smaller U.S. firms.

The disproportionate number of innovations found in small firms may be related to the position of these firms in the market. An established monopoly may have less to gain from developing an innovation than will an outside inventor, because the outside inventor realizes an additional profit by seizing the monopoly position. This argument can be used to explain another empirical characteristic of innovations in the U.S. semiconductor industry: engineers and scientists often leave a large firm that is unwilling to pioneer a new process or idea and start their own small firm to do so, grow to become a major force in the industry, then find in turn their own staff leaving to work on ideas they are slow to finance. While the sociology of the large firm certainly has some influence in this process, a new idea will always be more attractive economically if it propels a firm to a dominant position in an industry, instead of improving on an established position of market power.

41. "Economic Welfare," p. 619. These arguments for private return falling short of social return on invention may be offset by pecuniary transfers that arise as innovating firms expand at the expense of existing firms in the industry. See Morton I. Kamien and Nancy L. Schwartz, *Market Structure and Innovation* (Cambridge: Cambridge University Press, 1982), chapter 2, for a summary of this literature.

42. Finan, in "The International Transfer," chapters 3 and 4, also offers a useful discussion of this point, as does Webbink, in *The Semiconductor Industry,* pp. 104–12.

43. See "Can Semiconductors Survive Big Business?" *Business Week,* December 3, 1979, p. 68.

In discussions of the effects of government policies, it should be remembered that only in the United States does the semiconductor industry contain a large number of independent producing firms. The European industry is dominated by large, integrated producers of electronic products, and Japanese production takes place in even larger, integrated industrial conglomerates.[44]

### *Western Europe*

The common external tariff of the European Community on semiconductors—17 percent—is high enough to offer significant protection to producers within the boundaries of the Common Market. There have been, moreover, a number of additional policies in various member countries that have further restricted imports:[45] France and Britain are reported to have had a system of informal administrative quotas; both the British and French have used their military procurement activities to favor domestically produced output selectively on the grounds of national security; much of the procurement by EC governments, including the purchase of state telecommunications enterprises, offers similar incentives to national producers; and EC "Rules of Origin," limiting intra-EC duty-free trade to electronic products containing less than 5 percent imported integrated circuits limit the demand for foreign components.

There are also some carefully controlled ways of evading these high EC tariffs. First, the tariff on silicon wafers not yet cut into chips and on other parts of semiconductor devices is only 9 percent, encouraging the establishment of assembly operations to cut, bond, test, and package chips for the European market within the EC tariff walls. In fact, of thirty-four U.S.-owned European producers of semiconductor devices inventoried in the spring of 1974, eighteen were assembly operations.[46] Fifteen U.S. operations were complete manufacturing plants and one was an assembly operation serving third-country markets.

44. For more on the industrial organization of the industry at home and abroad, see Webbink, *The Semiconductor Industry;* CIA, *Japanese Microelectronics;* U.S. Department of Commerce, *U.S. Semiconductor Industry;* and Michael Borrus, James Millstein, and John Zysman, *International Competition in Advanced Industrial Sectors: Trade and Development in the Semiconductor Industry,* prepared for the Joint Economic Committee, 97 Cong. 2 sess. (GPO, 1982).

45. See Finan, "International Transfer," pp. 71–75; U.S. Department of Commerce, *U.S. Semiconductor Industry,* pp. 95–98; and ITC, *Competitive Factors,* pp. 54–67.

46. Finan, "International Transfer," p. 58.

Semiconductors were also eligible for duty-free import into the EC from designated developing countries under the Community's generalized scheme of preferences (GSP). In addition to per country preferential trade ceilings—20 percent of total EC imports as of 1978—semiconductor devices have been subject to special quotas and a 40 percent maximum on the value of imported inputs processed into the final product.[47] In 1978, the entire EC quota of semiconductors under the GSP was set at about $9 million—7.6 million EC units of account—or a little more than 0.35 percent of the estimated European consumption of semiconductors.[48] As has been true of earlier GSP quotas, the primary effect of the quota system has probably been to favor selected national firms with tariff-created rents.[49]

Yet another method of penetrating the tariff barriers of the EC is to use the so-called outward-processing regulations of the EC, which were reviewed briefly in chapter 2. As indicated there, the duty relief, which is set equal to the tariff that would have been levied on the untransformed component export, is not very attractive when the component exported is subject to duty at a rate much lower than the rate on the final product, as is true of the duty on semiconductors. Therefore, as will be seen, foreign assembly is not a significant factor in imports of semiconductors into the EC.

Finally, in addition to protecting their national manufacturers of semiconductor devices, most countries of the EC have extended significant subsidies to their industries, especially in the financing of research and development.[50] State funds appropriated in West Germany for microcir-

47. See Richard Cooper, "The European Community's System of Generalized Tariff Preferences: A Critique," *Journal of Development Studies,* vol. 8 (July 1972), p. 379; R. E. Baldwin and T. Murray, "MFN Tariff Reductions and Developing Country Trade Benefits under the GSP," *Economic Journal,* vol. 87 (March 1977), pp. 30–46; Commission of the European Community, *Practical Guide to the Use of the European Communities' Scheme of Generalized Tariff Preferences* (Brussels: European Economic Community [EEC], May 1979), p. 233; the 40 percent maximum was set by Regulation no. 148/79, issued in 1979 by the Commission of the European Community; see the *Official Journal of the European Communities,* L 25/33 (January 31, 1979).

48. The European consumption estimate is from "Japan/Europe Markets Forecast 1980," *Electronics,* January 3, 1980, p. 147.

49. Cooper, "The European Community's System," pp. 383–84.

50. This discussion is based on the U.S. Department of Commerce, Industry and Trade Administration, *Global Market Survey—Electronic Components* (Washington, D.C.: DOC, June 1978); "Europe Joins Microchip Race," *New York Times,* January 29, 1980; ITC, *Competitive Factors,* pp. 75–77; "U.S. Losing Ground in the Lab," *Electronics,* March 13, 1980, pp. 81–86; "SGS Plans a Global Attack," ibid., July 14, 1982, pp. 115–16; and "Britain's Troubled Chip Maker," *Business Week,* August 2, 1982, p. 52.

cuit research and development programs by national firms during the late 1970s are said to have amounted to $300 million for a two-year period; the figure for France is about the same; and the United Kingdom appropriated $300 million for a three-to-five-year period. In 1977, research grants made by the French government are said to have represented a third of the amount spent for research and development by electronics firms. In 1982, the Mitterrand government was considering a sizable expansion—$20 billion for the following five years—of its investment in electronics research.[51] The Netherlands and Italy are also reported to have provided important government financial support for research and development of semiconductor technology. The EC had proposed a Community-wide program that would have cost $100 million a year for the five years ended in 1982, and current proposals for a ten-year program of joint research in information technologies, including microelectronics, call for up to $1 billion.[52] These funds will supplement national research programs.

Members of the EC, perhaps mindful of the possible competitive advantage to be had from concentrating production experience and subsequent learning economies in a small number of firms, have also attempted to "rationalize" their industries by encouraging mergers or concentrating their aid on a single national "champion" firm. In France, Sescosem, a subsidiary of the French industrial giant Thomson-CSF, has received a disproportionate share of government aid in the past. In Germany, Siemens receives the most support, while in the Netherlands, Philips is the only national producer. SGS-ATES, in Italy, is a government-controlled enterprise responsible for 60 percent of employment in the Italian semiconductor industry. The British government has been financing the development of a young firm, Inmos, in an effort to recapture its own market.

### *Japan*

The tariff applied to most discrete semiconductor devices was—before the Tokyo Round cuts—6 percent in Japan, while integrated circuits, light-emitting diodes, and certain other products were levied 12 percent. These rates, while not as steep as those prevailing in the European Community, offered significant protection to national producers.

Import quotas were also used to protect the Japanese market. In 1972,

51. "France Urged to Reorganize Electronics," *Electronics,* June 2, 1982, pp. 105–06.
52. *Electronics,* August 25, 1982, p. 8; and "French Want National as Partner," ibid., September 8, 1982, pp. 104–06.

at the end of the Kennedy Round tariff cuts, the very high tariffs that protected Japanese markets during the 1960s were lowered and were superseded by quotas on particularly sensitive items. These quotas included integrated circuits and computer parts, but were discontinued in the mid 1970s.[53] As in the EC, U.S. businessmen claim that government procurement policies favor domestic suppliers.[54]

In fact, some spokesmen for U.S. industry have asserted that Japanese government procurement of advanced computers has subsidized the production of advanced semiconductor components in much the same way that military demand supported the U.S. industry during the late 1950s and early 1960s.[55] The Japanese government, by subsidizing the lease of computers, has acted to increase the use of recent models in the private sector as well.[56]

Japan also has a GSP, which is much like that of the EC. As in the EC, besides the per country limits, the use of these preferences for specific products is limited by the setting of overall quotas. By 1978, the overall quota had risen to about $62 million—equal to about 24 percent of 1978 imports of integrated circuits—and actual imports from developing countries under the GSP came to $44 million.[57]

53. In 1974 for ICs; 1975 for computer parts. See Yoshihara, *Japanese Investment,* p. 146; and U.S. General Accounting Office, *United States–Japan Trade: Issues and Problems* (Washington, D.C.: GAO, September 1979), pp. 27–28.

54. See U.S. Department of Commerce, Industry and Trade Administration, "Country Market Survey, Electronic Components, Japan," in *Global Market Survey—Electronic Components* (DOC, August 1978), p. 10.

55. In recent years, however, the typical computer used by the U.S. federal government has been six years behind the state of the art (according to Erich Bloch of IBM, as quoted in *Electronic Engineering Times,* May 25, 1981, p. 91).

56. See GAO, *United States–Japan Trade,* p. 28.

57. Ippei Yamazawa, "Manufactured Exports from Thailand and the Japanese Market," *Hitotsubashi Journal of Economics,* vol. 20 (February 1980), p. 7. Figures on all imports of ICs are based on official Ministry of Finance statistics for imports of finished ICs. In fact, all Japanese imports of ICs from developing countries came to only $44 million, all from Asia, implying that virtually all imports of ICs from Asia entered under GSP. See ITC, *Competitive Factors,* table A-56. U.S. affiliates in developing countries apparently used these provisions to make duty-free exports to Japan during the 1970s, but this is of marginal importance in U.S.-controlled exports to Japan. See Finan, "The International Transfer," p. 75; and U.S. Department of Commerce, *U.S. Semiconductor Industry,* p. 92.

It is interesting to speculate that the establishment of plants for production of silicon wafers by Monsanto and Dow in Malaysia and by General Instrument in Taiwan (the latter also diffuses the wafers in the same plant) represented a trend toward increasing national content in order to qualify for the Japanese and European GSP systems, or perhaps even for

The Japanese also have a tariff provision much like the European outward-processing regulations. The Japanese components of certain designated manufactured imports, with the prior authorization of customs authorities, can be granted duty relief. Various types of semiconductor device and computer parts are on the list of eligible products.[58] American manufacturers have asserted that Japanese-produced semiconductors enter Japan from abroad under these provisions.[59] As a result of the multilateral trade negotiations, tariffs are now a much less important influence on production for the Japanese market.[60]

Most important, state industrial policy and government promotion have indisputably been influential in shaping the growth of the electronics industry, as of other favored industries.[61] In 1957, the Japanese government enacted a Temporary Measure for the Promotion of the Electronics Industry, with the main objective of inducing the private sector to focus "preferentially upon the electronics industry, by encouraging national consensus that the electronics industry was the perfect industry for Japan's socio-economic state, and therefore, was the industry that should form the core [of] industrial Japan."[62] The mandate was renewed by the 1978 Spe-

---

the U.S. system. The inclusion of SCDs in the list of items eligible for the U.S. GSP has been under study, and discrete semiconductors—but not ICs—were placed on the list in 1981. See Malaysia, Federal Industrial Development Authority (FIDA), *Malaysia—Your Profit Centre in Asia* (Kuala Lumpur, 1978), p. 27; and *Free China Review,* February 1980, pp. 40–41, on wafer production; ITC, *Summary of Trade and Tariff Information—Semiconductors,* Publication 841 (ITC, July 1982), p. 6.

58. Conversation with Japanese embassy officials, May 1980. See also U.S. Tariff Commission, *Economic Factors Affecting the Use of Items 807.00 and 806.30 of the Tariff Schedules of the United States,* Publication 339 (Washington, D.C.: USTC, September 1970), p. 32.

59. See, for example, the statement of W. J. Sanders III before the Subcommittee on Trade of the House Committee on Ways and Means, 94 Cong. 2 sess., March 24, 1976, pp. 42, 50.

60. See *New York Times,* May 12, 1981. The agreement was largely the result of pressure by the U.S. industry. In the Tokyo Rounds, both the United States and Japan agreed to reduce their levies on semiconductor imports to 4.2 percent, and an agreement was reached in 1981 to accelerate the reduction so that it took effect by mid 1982.

61. For three recent interpretations of Japanese industrial policy in the semiconductor industry, see Borrus and others, *International Competition in Advanced Industrial Sectors;* U.S. Office of Technology Assessment, *U.S. Industrial Competitiveness—A Comparison of Steel, Electronics, and Automobiles* (Washington, D.C.: OTA, July 1981); and Semiconductor Industry Association, *The Effect of Government Targetting on World Semiconductor Competition* (Washington, D.C.: Verner, Liipfert, Bernhard, and McPherson, 1983).

62. To quote a quasi-official Japanese source, *Look Japan,* May 10, 1981, p. 24. The "socio-economic state" alluded to is a scarcity of raw materials, energy, and land, and an abundance of skilled labor.

cial Measure Law Concerning the Promotion of Specialized Machine and Information Industry. The largest Japanese semiconductor companies seem to specialize in different product lines, and this rationalization of the industry is sometimes credited to government sponsorship as well.[63]

This government-established consensus was given teeth by the extensive powers of the Ministry of Finance and the Ministry of International Trade and Industry (MITI) to channel capital into favored industries. Because a large amount of personal interest income is in effect untaxed in Japan and interest payments are deductible from corporate taxes, there is a substantial incentive to finance corporate investment by the issuance of debt.[64] Since the Ministry of Finance often exercised direct administrative controls over bank portfolios, it had considerable discretion to channel bank lending in directions that were consistent with its priorities. Banks, in turn, were in effect guaranteed the solvency of these "guided" loans, and favored firms' risk of bankruptcy was substantially reduced by the tacit promise of government intervention.[65]

63. See Borrus and others, *International Competition in Advanced Industrial Sectors,* pp. 65–70; and "Semiconductors Face Worldwide Challenge," *Electronics,* May 19, 1982, p. 137.

64. See Joseph A. Pechman and Keimei Kaizuka, "Taxation," in Hugh Patrick and Henry Rosovsky, eds., *Asia's New Giant: How the Japanese Economy Works* (Brookings Institution, 1975), on the Japanese tax system.

The Miller-Modigliani theorem, stating that firms are theoretically indifferent between debt and equity finance, assumes the absence of taxes and costly bankruptcy. With the most common sorts of tax structure—that is, interest on debt deductible from taxable corporate income, and roughly comparable personal tax rates on interest, dividends, and capital gains—firms ought to prefer debt. With uncertainty and the possibility of costly bankruptcy (but no taxes), firms ought to prefer equity, which requires no fixed service and therefore reduces the probability of bankruptcy. With both, there will be an optimal financial structure using both debt and equity. See Roger Gordon and Burton Malkiel, "Corporation Finance," in Henry J. Aaron and Joseph A. Pechman, eds., *How Taxes Affect Economic Behavior* (Brookings Institution, 1981), pp. 131–98.

65. This is roughly the same account of the way the government guided capital investment as can be found in GAO, *United States–Japan Trade,* p. 185. Many of the same points are made in Gardner Ackley and Hiromitsu Ishi, "Fiscal, Monetary, and Related Policies," in Patrick and Rosovsky, *Asia's New Giant,* especially pp. 203–05. On the functioning of "window guidance" by the Bank of Japan, see Yoshio Suzuki, *Money and Banking in Contemporary Japan* (Yale University Press, 1980), pp. 166–81. See also Eisuke Sakakibara, Robert Feldman, and Yuzo Haroda, *The Japanese Financial System in Comparative Perspective,* U.S. Congress, Joint Economic Committee, 97 Cong. 2 sess. (GPO, 1982), for a slightly different interpretation.

The interpretation of great amounts of debt used in Japanese corporate finance as the product of the tax structure and implicit government guarantees of priority investments is also made by James Abegglen and William Rapp, "The Competitive Impact of Japanese

In addition, subsidies to capital investment in the electronics industry have included special depreciation allowances, special funding for technological development, and government underwriting of the operations of three laboratory groups developing very large scale integration (VLSI) technology.[66] Other more general tax policies grant special tax write-offs for investment in export promotion.[67] A new generation of programs to fund research and development in the electronics industry was being initiated by MITI in 1981, with the focus on developing advanced computers.[68] It is estimated that support through 1990 will amount to roughly $1 billion. Officially coordinated loans by the Japan Development Bank to the electronics industry, said to have signaled virtual guarantees of the loans of Japanese private banks to the industry, have recently increased in importance.[69]

---

Growth," in Jerome Cohen, ed., *Pacific Partnership: United States–Japan Trade* (Lexington, Mass.: Lexington Books, 1972), p. 35.

Leaders in the semiconductor industry have focused on the high Japanese debt-to-assets (or debt-to-equity) ratio as symptomatic of the competitive disadvantages of the American industry in its access to capital markets. See "Trade and Technology" (pt. 3), testimony of Robert Noyce and John Welty before the Subcommittee on International Finance of the Senate Committee on Banking, Housing, and Urban Affairs, 96 Cong. 2 sess., January 15, 1980. Noyce, for example, cites figures that imply equity to be 22 percent and 86 percent of the assets of Japanese and U.S. semiconductor companies, respectively. The Japanese figure is roughly the same as in all Japanese industry in the aggregate, while the U.S. SCD industry uses substantially more equity than U.S. industry in general. Henry C. Wallich and Mabel I. Wallich, "Banking and Finance," in Patrick and Rosovsky, *Asia's New Giant,* p. 267, cite figures of roughly 18 percent and 51 percent for industry in general in Japan and the United States in 1972; Abegglen and Rapp, "The Competitive Impact," p. 34, cite figures of 21 percent and 56 percent equity in Japan and the United States in 1968.

66. See GAO, *United States–Japan Trade,* pp. 178–84; U.S. Department of Commerce, "Country Market Survey, Electronic Components, Japan," in *Global Market Survey,* p. 8; CIA, *Japanese Microelectronics,* p. 11. The program was funded at about $240 million in 1976 U.S. dollars. See also ITC, *Competitive Factors,* p. 77.

67. GAO, *United States–Japan Trade,* pp. 179–84.

68. See "Japan Polishes Creativity Image," *Electronics,* August 11, 1982, pp. 96–97. The Japan Research Development Corporation is funding still another semiconductor research program. The new cycle of MITI semiconductor research was just getting under way in 1981. MITI then asked the parliament to approve a logic-circuit research program in the $100 million range. *Electronic News,* March 30, 1981.

69. See Abegglen and Rapp, "The Competitive Impact," p. 35; and Nobuyoshi Namiki, "Japanese Subsidy Policies," in Steven Warnecke, ed., *International Trade and Industrial Policies* (Holmes and Meier, 1978), p. 128. The influence of these loans is regarded by some as overrated or no longer of great importance. See Philip H. Trezise and Yukio Suzuki, "Politics, Government, and Economic Growth in Japan," in Patrick and Rosovsky, *Asia's New Giant,*

Before 1968, the purchase of foreign technology was strictly controlled by the government. Though most controls were lifted in 1968, the government retained the authority to apply them.[70] By denying access to the technology of foreign consumer goods to Japanese producers, the controls may well have stimulated investment in basic industrial electronics technology. Most recently, a common route to the acquisition of U.S. technology by Japanese firms has been acquisition of or investment in U.S. firms, a movement undoubtedly facilitated by the removal of all official controls on direct foreign investment in 1971.[71]

Although the control of direct foreign investment in Japan was substantially liberalized in the mid 1970s, U.S. firms still complain about obstacles to entering the Japanese market with a subsidiary.[72] In the past, certainly, Japanese policy has been protective of the market shares of Japanese firms. Texas Instruments—apart from the more recent entry of Motorola, the only successful U.S. producer of semiconductor devices with a history of manufacturing in Japan—was allowed to invest only after agreeing to make its patents on integrated circuits available to Japanese firms and to limit its output so that Japanese firms were guaranteed 90 percent or more of the national market.[73]

*United States*

As a result of the Kennedy Round tariff negotiations, tariff rates on semiconductors were cut by more than half from the pre-1968 rate of 12.5 percent to the 6 percent rate effective in 1972. This left the United States, in the 1970s, with probably the lowest tariffs on semiconductor devices in the industrial West. By mid 1982, the rate had dropped to 4.2 percent, as had the Japanese tariff. Even more important, U.S. tariff items 806.30 and

---

pp. 795–97 and table 11-4; Namiki, "Japanese Subsidy Policies," pp. 126–29; and Japan Development Bank (JDB), Annual Report (Tokyo, 1979). While historically, during the period 1951–72 JDB loans for the "development of technology" (two of the three categories are in the electronics and computer industries) accounted for only about 6.5 percent of loans made, such loans accounted for between 10.5 percent and 13 percent of new lending by the JDB between 1975 and 1979; about $1.8 billion in loans was outstanding in 1979.

70. Merton Peck and Shuji Tamura, "Technology," in Patrick and Rosovsky, *Asia's New Giant,* p. 546.

71. CIA, *Japanese Microelectronics,* pp. 6–8.

72. ITC, *Competitive Factors,* pp. 59–60.

73. Tilton, *International Diffusion of Technology,* p. 147; and Pack and Tamura, "Technology," p. 552.

807.00 were introduced in the early 1960s.[74] This arrangement is more liberal than the European outward-processing procedures.

By the late 1970s, the 806/807 tariff provisions were in widespread use throughout the U.S. semiconductor industry. Fully 83 percent of U.S. imports of semiconductors were brought in under these provisions. The percentage was even higher—90 percent—for the integrated circuits that made up the overwhelming bulk—79 percent—of U.S. imports of semiconductor devices.[75] In 1978, imports of semiconductor devices under 806/807 alone accounted for some 15 percent of the total value of all U.S. 806/807 imports and 34 percent of the value of the duty-free U.S. components of all such imports (see table 3-6). The U.S. Generalized System of Preferences, on the other hand, is not widely used by the industry because integrated circuits are not eligible. About 11 percent of U.S. imports of transistors and diodes, however, made use of the GSP in 1981. It would be used more if integrated circuits were eligible.[76] In late 1984 proposals to eliminate all tariffs on most semiconductors, as well as on other high-technology items, were being discussed by makers of U.S. trade policy.

The United States has not protected its domestic market against foreign entry through restrictions on direct investment. Large foreign investments in U.S. producers of semiconductor devices were a prominent feature of the evolution of the U.S. industry during the late 1970s.[77] Such purchases served not only to allow foreign firms to sell directly in the U.S. market but also as an important conduit for the acquisition of U.S. technology by Western European and Japanese producers.

While the United States has no explicit government-sanctioned restrictive procurement practices, the situation is not strictly comparable to that in Western Europe and Japan. Telecommunications are under the control of state-affiliated concerns in most foreign countries, while the U.S. Bell System was until the end of 1983 a publicly regulated monopoly. The equipment-manufacturing subsidiary, Western Electric (now part of

74. Actually, a provision similar to 806.30 existed before 1963. See U.S. Tariff Commission, *Economic Factors Affecting the Use,* pp. 14–26. It was, however, more restrictive than item 807.00.

75. Data refer to customs value and are based on information furnished by the ITC.

76. International Trade Commission, *Summary of Tariff and Trade Information—Semiconductors,* Publication 841 (ITC, July 1982), p. 6. In 1976, the first year of the GSP, U.S. importers rapidly switched from the use of 806/807 to the use of GSP for eligible items. ITC, *Study of the Effects of the Generalized System of Preferences on U.S. Trade in the Program's First Year of Operation, 1976,* Staff Research Study No. 12 (ITC, March 1978), pp. 38–39.

77. ITC, *Competitive Factors,* p. 106; and CIA, *Japanese Microelectronics,* pp. 6–9.

AT&T Technologies), along with IBM, is among the largest producers of semiconductor devices in the world; all of its output was used internally.[78]

Furthermore, because defense applications account for a significant volume of U.S. demand, procurement restrictions that affect the manufacture of classified items limit foreign sales in this market. Industrial security regulations of the U.S. Department of Defense also prohibit the manufacture of classified products in foreign facilities.[79]

The importance of the defense market in the United States also obscures the question whether the U.S. industry receives public subsidies. Since military users are generally willing to pay premium prices for new standards of reliability and performance—and the research-and-development costs of new devices with military applications as well—it was argued earlier that the U.S. government has, in effect, financed a significant portion of the development costs of U.S. technology. Also, the development of the modern computer, which is the largest single customer of the semiconductor industry, came about through projects undertaken for the military.[80] Thus, indirectly as well as directly, the U.S. military has been an outstanding patron of the national semiconductor industry.[81] In Japan, by way of contrast, military expenditure for the procurement of semiconductor devices was virtually nil, while European military sales accounted for 14 percent of consumption in 1972.[82]

Opinion concerning the commercial potential of the research, however, diverges widely, although participants in the Very High Speed Integrated Circuit (VHSIC) program of the U.S. Department of Defense are already

78. IBM was number three and Western Electric number four in 1972. See U.S. Department of Commerce, *The U.S. Semiconductor Industry,* p. 89; Webbink, *The Semiconductor Industry,* pp. 21–22; and "Europe Joins Microchip Race," *New York Times,* January 29, 1980. In 1981, all U.S. shipments of integrated circuits amounted to about $7.8 billion. IBM alone accounted for roughly $1.9 billion of IC production, Western Electric $350 million. See ITC, *Summary of Trade and Tariff Information—Semiconductors,* p. 27; and "Semiconductors Face Worldwide Challenge," *Electronics,* May 19, 1982, p. 135.

79. U.S. Department of Commerce, *The U.S. Semiconductor Industry,* p. 77.

80. See, for example, Kenneth Flamm, "Technology Policy in International Perspective," in Subcommittee on Economic Goals and Intergovernmental Policy of the Joint Economic Committee, *Policies for Industrial Growth in a Competitive World,* 98 Cong. 2 sess. (GPO, 1984), pp. 23–51.

81. Most recently, the U.S. Department of Defense has been involved in another major research effort of a magnitude comparable to current Japanese and European efforts. "VHSIC Funding Raised to Nearly $80 Million," *Electronics,* April 21, 1982, p. 57; and ITC, *Competitive Factors,* p. 75.

82. Finan, "The International Transfer," p. 96.

spinning off commercial variants.[83] Clearly, civilian research undertaken for commercial application is likely to yield a greater return, dollar for dollar, than research specifically tailored to military applications. This, in fact, has been a continuing source of criticism within the U.S. semiconductor industry.[84]

The absence of publicly financed and disseminated research on new semiconductor technologies has led to proposals within the industry for the formation of joint research ventures, to avoid the duplication of costly basic research. Research programs financed by some of the larger firms have already been set up with the sponsorship of leading American universities.[85]

### *Summary*

A variety of government policies has affected the structure of the semiconductor industries in the United States, Western Europe, and Japan. Public subsidies to research and development, whether through explicit grants to industry or through military procurement and loan guarantees,

83. See ITC, *Competitive Factors,* pp. 75–76; and Jerry Streb, "Technology Transfer from the VHSIC Program," *Military Electronics/Countermeasures,* February 1980, pp. 100–05. Honeywell is using packaging similar to that developed for its VHSIC circuits in its new DPS 88 high-speed mainframe computer and other high-speed logic circuits developed for the program, and Texas Instruments was using its military technology in the 256 K memory chips it had planned to introduce in 1983. See "CML and Flip TAB Join Forces in the DPS 88's Micro Packages," *Electronics,* November 3, 1982, pp. 93–99; "3000-Gate Array Has 600-ps Delays," ibid., February 10, 1983, pp. 175–76; and "VHSIC Proposals Take Six Fast Tracks," ibid., September 22, 1981, p. 95. The VHSIC program is considered by the military services to be the single most important program now being undertaken that will affect the capabilities of future U.S. weapons. The military was stimulated to consider similar research projects in the areas of software, machine intelligence, and advanced semiconductor materials. See "Pentagon Moves to Expand VHSIC," *Electronics,* May 5, 1982, pp. 96–98.

84. To quote Robert Noyce, "There are very few research directors anywhere in the world who are really adequate to the job . . . and they are not often career officers in the Army." Quoted in Braun and Macdonald, *Revolution in Miniature,* p. 143.

85. The Semiconductor Industry Association has created a research cooperative to finance university research; twelve U.S. companies were also involved in establishing a for-profit joint research venture; see *Business Week,* April 20, 1981, p. 39; "Semiconductors Face Worldwide Challenge," *Electronics,* May 19, 1982, p. 140; "Joint U.S. R&D Consortium Is Incorporated," ibid., September 8, 1982, p. 56; and "R&D Co-op Gets Set to Open Up Shop," ibid., March 24, 1983, pp. 89–90. In late 1982 negotiations were under way between the United States and Japan to allow each other's firms to participate in all nonmilitary government-funded research consortia. "U.S., Japan Pact Would Bolster Joint Research," *Wall Street Journal,* November 1, 1982. Such programs appear to have stalled, however.

have affected all three markets significantly. Government grants for research and development may have had some effect on the pattern of international specialization.

Government financing of research and subsidization and promotion of capital expenditure in explicitly commercial applications have been particularly important in Japan. As mentioned earlier, the long-run goal of Japanese planners is to create a strong national computer industry. The low rates of return implicit in a highly subsidized investment are presumably balanced by the technological externalities that an advanced electronics industry transmits to other sectors of the economy.

Barriers to trade have also been an important determinant of global product flows. The U.S. market has certainly been the least protected, as might have been predicted, given its past dominance of world markets. The European market is the most protected at the moment, Japan being somewhat more open to imports. All the large world markets grant various sorts of preference to imports from developing countries. Items imported into the United States under tariff items 806 and 807 probably account for most import preferences extended to developing countries.

Barriers to direct investment together with trade restrictions determine whether a foreign firm chooses to export, or to invest behind a tariff wall. Again, the United States has the fewest barriers to such investment. The policies of most countries of the EC have probably favored direct investment in a manufacturing subsidiary, undoubtedly with the explicit intention of acquiring foreign technology. Japanese policy toward direct foreign investment—formal and informal—has probably been the most restrictive. Historically, U.S. investment was permitted only in exchange for a closely held technology and after some limits to penetration of the national market had been established.

## The Internationalization of Semiconductor Production: The United States

The political and economic constraints on semiconductor firms, outlined in the preceding section, have varied considerably from country to country. Not surprisingly, the result has been strikingly different systems for the organization of production; firms that operate from different national bases take radically different approaches to the location of production facilities. A brief history of the internationalization of production by U.S., Japanese, and Western European producers will explain much of this pattern.

Assembly of semiconductors abroad by U.S. manufacturers can be traced from 1961, when Fairchild, later to become one of the largest U.S. producers, set up a manufacturing affiliate in Hong Kong, exporting to the U.S. market.[86] Other companies quickly imitated Fairchild.

In many ways the circumstances of Fairchild's move overseas were a preview of events that were to repeat themselves in the late 1970s. Fairchild began its foreign operations with the assembly of transistors, a product whose technology had become well known by the late 1950s, sparking considerable competition, and pressure on prices, from Japanese producers.

Table 3-4 shows how quickly Japanese producers mounted a formidable threat to U.S. companies. Japanese production of transistors, two-thirds of which was slated for eventual use in the ubiquitous transistor radio, almost quintupled between 1957 and 1958.[87] The Japanese were able to mount this successful offensive because wages in the Japanese industry at that time were considerably lower than those in the United States. The basic technology for transistor production was then widely propagated by AT&T's Bell Laboratories, whose liberal licensing policy embodied no significant discrimination between American and foreign firms.[88] The year of the big push in production, 1957, coincided with the Japanese decision embodied in the Special Measures Law described earlier to promote the electronics industries.

Confronted with low-cost foreign competition, American producers followed one or the other of two paths. One was to invest heavily in capital equipment and automate the production of transistors. This was the path taken by Philco, a path that led to disaster because of the rapid pace at which existing types of transistor became obsolete with continuing technological advances. The other path, pioneered by Fairchild, was to beat the

86. See Y. S. Chang, *The Transfer of Technology: Economics of Offshore Assembly, The Case of the Semiconductor Industry,* UNITAR Research Report, no. 11 (New York: United Nations Institute for Training and Research, 1971), pp. 40–44.

87. Apocryphal stories are still told within the U.S. semiconductor industry describing how some Japanese producers even stuck extra transistors onto their circuit boards, often with no actual electrical connection to the radio circuit, since the number of transistors in the radio was often used by consumers as a measure of quality.

88. Tilton, *International Diffusion of Technology,* pp. 75–76, 119.

Table 3-4. *U.S. and Japanese Transistor Output during the Transition to Overseas Production, 1957–68*

Output in millions of units

| Year | Output | | Percent of Japanese transistors used in radios | Percent of transistor radios exported |
|---|---|---|---|---|
| | United States | Japan | | |
| 1957 | 29 | 6 | 67 | n.a. |
| 1958 | 47 | 27 | 67 | n.a. |
| 1959 | 82 | 87 | 55 | 77 |
| 1960 | 128 | 140 | 48 | 70 |
| 1961 | 191 | 180 | 41 | 67 |
| 1962 | 240 | 232 | 34 | 76 |
| 1963 | 300 | 268 | 35 | 81 |
| 1964 | 407 | 416 | 33 | 69 |
| 1965 | 608 | 454 | 30 | 75 |
| 1966 | 856 | 617 | 26 | 86 |
| 1967 | 760 | 766 | 23 | 83 |
| 1968 | 883 | 939 | 20 | 90 |

Sources: For the United States, Electronic Industries Association, *Electronic Market Data Book, 1977* (Washington, D.C.: EIA, 1977), table 77, p. 115; for Japan, Tilton, *International Diffusion of Technology*, pp. 156–57.

Japanese by taking the labor-intensive stages of production to Far Eastern locations where wages were even lower than in Japan. This was a successful strategy, quickly copied by other U.S. producers.

Still, the Japanese, having acquired large volumes of sales concentrated in a relatively small number of firms, were able to ride down the learning curve and maintain fierce competition in established product lines. The lesson learned was that a competitive advantage, once lost, is exceedingly difficult to regain. The importance of maintaining a position at the cutting edge of technology and responding quickly to potential competitive threats became clear. Thenceforth U.S. producers were to move production to low-cost locations as soon as the manufacturing technology for a newly developed product became sufficiently stable to make the establishment of overseas assembly lines feasible.

The general pattern of investment in overseas factories for assembly of semiconductor devices that developed in the next twenty years or so can be seen as a series of waves of activity. As information about the costs and risks of setting up assembly operations in a particular region was accumulated, the entire industry tended to follow the successful pioneers who had experimented with operations in a specific country.[89]

89. Fairchild, in particular, set up first in Korea and Singapore, as well as in Hong Kong. See Chang, *The Transfer of Technology*.

The rush by semiconductor firms into production abroad quickly spread beyond Hong Kong. In 1964 and 1965, significant investments were made in Korea and Taiwan. After 1967, producers moved into Mexico; from 1968 on, important plants were also located in Singapore. In 1972 Malaysia became an important area for export production, while Indonesia, Thailand, and the Philippines became popular locations in the mid to late 1970s.[90]

In table 3-5 U.S. imports of semiconductor devices are disaggregated by country of origin, from 1964, when they were first given a separate statistical classification, until 1969. While somewhat imprecise—detail by country of small export volumes went unreported in published statistics—the figures suggest the importance of certain economic and political factors. In 1966 both Mexico and Taiwan established export-processing zones, permitting the duty-free import of materials used in manufacture for export—the Mexican Border Industrialization Program and the Kaohsiung Export Processing Zone. Sizable exports of semiconductor devices to the United States followed in 1967. Korea liberalized its trade policy in 1965–66, permitting the drawback of duties paid on imported inputs used in exports, setting up in-bond processing arrangements, and establishing additional export incentives; again, significant export of semiconductor devices began in 1967. Hong Kong, it should be remembered, the original low-wage source of U.S. imports of assembled semiconductors, is a free port.

Coincident with this sudden increase in imports from new low-wage suppliers—and sharp drops in the growth rate of exports from the industrial countries—was the 1966–67 U.S. economic slowdown, which greatly reduced the growth in demand for imports of semiconductor devices. It was a premonition of the sharp reactions to the recessions of the 1970s that were later to trouble the industry. The almost static behavior of imports in 1967 suggests that a shakeout had taken place in the industry, with supplies from low-wage developing countries displacing higher-cost European exports.

The almost unchanged level of exports from Hong Kong in 1967 and

90. The sequential nature of investment abroad in the semiconductor industry can be seen, to some extent, by looking at the years in which subsidiaries were established abroad. Studies by Chang (*The Transfer of Technology,* 1971) and Finan ("The International Transfer of Semiconductor Technology," 1975), which report the date of establishment of U.S. overseas operations present in different samples of U.S. SCD firms in 1971 and 1974, respectively, support the general chronology outlined above. Note that the 1971 and 1974 samples differ in composition and definition. Also, only *current* assembly operations are considered.

Table 3-5. *U.S. Imports of Semiconductors from Fifteen Countries as Percentage of Total Imports, 1964–69*

| *Region and country* | *1964* | *1965* | *1966* | *1967* | *1968* | *1969* |
|---|---|---|---|---|---|---|
| *Western Hemisphere* | | | | | | |
| Canada | 3 | 1 | 1 | 1 | 1 | 1 |
| Mexico | n.a. | n.a. | n.a. | 6 | 21 | 18 |
| Netherlands Antilles | n.a. | n.a. | n.a. | n.a. | 2 | 2 |
| *Europe* | | | | | | |
| United Kingdom | 1 | 1 | 1 | 1 | 1 | * |
| France | 8 | 12 | 4 | 2 | 1 | * |
| West Germany | 1 | * | * | 2 | 2 | 2 |
| Ireland | * | 9 | 19 | 18 | 15 | 12 |
| Netherlands | 24 | 12 | 8 | 2 | 3 | 2 |
| Portugal | n.a. | n.a. | n.a. | n.a. | * | 2 |
| Italy | 2 | 4 | 3 | 1 | 1 | 1 |
| *Asia* | | | | | | |
| Singapore | n.a. | n.a. | n.a. | n.a. | n.a. | 7 |
| Korea | n.a. | n.a. | n.a. | 2 | 3 | 5 |
| Hong Kong | 22 | 37 | 43 | 42 | 28 | 30 |
| Taiwan | n.a. | n.a. | * | 7 | 11 | 9 |
| Japan | 36 | 23 | 17 | 14 | 10 | 8 |
| Fifteen countries | 97 | 98 | 96 | 98 | 99 | 100 |
| *Addenda* | | | | | | |
| Total value of SCD imports (millions of dollars) | 8.4 | 24 | 42 | 43 | 72 | 104 |
| Nominal growth rate of SCD imports (percent) | n.a. | 186 | 75 | 2 | 67 | 44 |

Source: Calculated from U.S. Department of Commerce, Bureau of the Census, *FT 246, U.S. Imports,* various years.
n.a. Not available.
* Less than 1 percent.

the precipitous drop in its share of the import market in 1968 are probably linked to the riots and political disturbances that shook that British colony in 1967, as well as to the tightening of local labor markets as investment boomed. Growing concern about diversification of the country-specific political risk inherent in overseas assembly operations and about lower wages are likely to have influenced the establishment of subsidiaries in Singapore in 1969.

Imports assembled abroad are unfortunately not distinguished from wholly foreign imports in these data. Information on U.S. imports under the 806/807 tariff classifications, in which overseas production returning to the United States is presumably captured reasonably well, is first available for the year 1966.[91] Table 3-6 details the total value of U.S. imports of semiconductor devices from 1966 through 1983 and the values for imports that entered under tariff items 806.30 and 807.00 as well. Estimates of 806.30 imports of semiconductor devices from developing countries are not available until 1969 but these imports cannot have amounted to more than about $200,000 before 1968.[92] By 1966, it is clear, foreign assembly already dominated U.S. imports; 62 percent of U.S. imports entered under 807 alone. By 1969, it is estimated, U.S. imports under 806/807 accounted for more than 90 percent of the semiconductor devices entering the country.[93]

When current-dollar imports are adjusted for inflation with a producer price index, as is done in table 3-6, the particular sensitivity of the semiconductor industry to the effect of general economic recession stands revealed. The growth of constant-dollar assembly imports—and of other imports as well—slowed considerably in 1971 and dropped 12 percent in 1975, whereas growth rates during the fatter years of the 1970s had been 30 to 60 percent. A similar slowdown began after the onset of the 1979 recession.

91. The data might have a positive bias if foreign producers using a small proportion of U.S. content chose to export with 806/807, a negative bias if U.S. producers chose not to go to the bureaucratic trouble and costly paperwork of using 806/807 or if foreign firms' assembly exports to the United States had no components manufactured here. Both problems are probably small.

92. According to U.S. Tariff Commission estimates, *all* 806 imports from the developing countries that exported to the United States amounted to about $800,000 in 1967. In 1968, the possible maximum rises to $5.8 million. In 1969, in the aggregate, only 10 percent of all 806 imports were SCDs. See U.S. Tariff Commission, *Economic Factors Affecting the Use,* pp. A-87 to A-88.

93. The figures for 806/807 imports, as well as total imports, reflect revisions in published statistics. Compare them, for example, to ITC, "Background Materials on Articles Assembled and Fabricated Abroad, Item 806.30 and 807.00 of the Tariff Schedules of the United States" (Washington, D.C., unpublished report, 1976), appendix tables; and U.S. Department of Commerce, *The U.S. Semiconductor Industry,* pp. 60–62. As a further example of such discrepancies, the U.S. Tariff Commission, in *Economic Factors Affecting the Use,* published an estimate of 1969 806/807 imports of SCDs equal to $127 million. The official figure published for *all* SCD imports was $104 million for that same year (see *The U.S. Semiconductor Industry,* table 4.1). The last figure was revised upward to $111 million by Commerce in 1979, still well below the ITC figure of $134 million (*Economic Factors Affecting the Use,* p. A-46). See U.S. Department of Commerce, Bureau of the Census, *U.S. Commodity Exports and Imports as Related to Output 1976 and 1975* (Washington, D.C., November 1979), table 3b. The net effect of accepting the unrevised Commerce Department statistics would be to increase the proportion of imports entering under 806/807 prior to 1970.

Table 3-6. *U.S. Imports of Semiconductors, 1966–83*[a]

| Year | *807 imports (millions of dollars)* | *806/807 imports (millions of dollars)* | *Total U.S. imports (millions of dollars)* | *806/807 imports as percent of total*[b] | *806/807 imports (millions of 1967 dollars)*[c] | *Percent increase in 806/807 imports in 1967 dollars* | *Price index of SCDs* |
|---|---|---|---|---|---|---|---|
| 1966 | 31 | n.a. | 50 | 62 | n.a. | n.a. | n.a. |
| 1967 | 36 | n.a. | 50 | 72 | n.a. | n.a. | 100.0 |
| 1968 | 67 | n.a. | 86 | 78 | n.a. | n.a. | 96.5 |
| 1969 | 106 | 127 | 134 | 95 | 130 | n.a. | 96.6 |
| 1970 | 127 | 160 | 168 | 95 | 167 | 28 | 95.7 |
| 1971 | 130 | 178 | 187 | 95 | 190 | 14 | 93.6 |
| 1972 | 162 | 254 | 329 | 77 | 277 | 46 | 91.8 |
| 1973 | 223 | 413 | 611 | 68 | 447 | 61 | 92.4 |
| 1974 | 346 | 684 | 953 | 72 | 688 | 54 | 99.4 |
| 1975 | 312 | 617 | 802 | 77 | 605 | −12 | 102.0 |
| 1976 | 556 | 879 | 1,098 | 80 | 909 | 50 | 96.7 |
| 1977 | 864 | 1,120 | 1,358 | 82 | 1,231 | 35 | 91.0 |
| 1978 | 1,329 | 1,478 | 1,775 | 83 | 1,733 | 41 | 85.3 |
| 1979 | 1,852 | 1,916 | 2,427 | 79 | 2,267 | 31 | 84.8 |
| 1980 | 2,451 | 2,506 | 3,326 | 75 | 2,763 | 22 | 90.7 |
| 1981 | 2,798 | 2,825 | 3,553 | 80 | 3,111 | 13 | 90.8 |
| 1982 | 3,106 | 3,131 | 4,128 | 76 | 3,510 | 13 | 89.2 |
| 1983 | 3,368 | 3,383 | 4,881 | 69 | 3,726 | 6 | 90.8 |

Sources: Trade data, 1966–69, U.S. Tariff Commission, *Economic Factors Affecting the Use of Items 807.00 and 806.30 of the Tariff Schedules of the United States,* Publication 339 (GPO, September 1970), appendix tables; 1970–76, 806/807 data are ITC estimates; see ITC, "Background Materials on Articles Assembled and Fabricated Abroad, Items 806.30 and 807.00 of the Tariff Schedules of the United States," unpublished report (Washington, D.C., 1976), appendixes B and C; total imports, U.S. Department of Commerce, Bureau of the Census, *U.S. Commodity Exports and Imports as Related to Output, 1976 and 1975* (GPO, November 1979), table 3B; 1977–80, 806/807 data, ITC, *Imports under Items 806.30 and 807.00 of the Tariff Schedules of the United States, 1977–80,* Publication 1170 (ITC, July 1981), appendix B; total imports, ITC, *Summary of Trade and Tariff Information,* Publication 841 (ITC, July 1982), p. 26, table 1; 1981–83, 806/807 data from ITC, *Imports under Items 806.30 and 807.00 of the Tariff Schedules of the United States, 1979–82,* Publication 1467 (ITC, January 1984) and unpublished computer printouts from the U.S. Department of Commerce; total imports, unpublished printouts from the Department of Commerce; price index of SCDs, U.S. Department of Labor, Bureau of Labor Statistics, producer price index for "Semiconductors and Related Devices," unpublished.

n.a. Not available.

a. The figures reflect revisions in the trade statistics originally published.

b. 807 only for 1966–68.

c. Calculation of 1967 dollars made by using price index for SCDs.

The serious effect of general economic conditions on the industry, as well as the more recent changes in location of production that were made as the U.S. industry grew through the 1970s, are clearly defined when the countries of origin of 806/807 imports are considered, as in table 3-7. Note that data for years earlier than 1972 do not include 806.30 imports; some discontinuity in the distribution of imports across countries occurs in 1972 because of the definitional changes in the statistics.

Dramatic changes in the geographic origin of foreign-assembled imports into the United States also took place in the 1970s. Before 1976, some 20–30 percent of U.S. 806/807 imports came from sources in the

Western Hemisphere, mainly from Mexico. From 1976 on, that figure dropped precipitously into the range of 10 to 15 percent.

That smaller level of imports from within the Western Hemisphere masks even more pronounced shifts within the hemisphere. Before 1976, the share of imports of semiconductor devices that came from Mexico hovered around 20 percent and accounted for almost all Western Hemisphere imports. After 1976, Mexico dropped to only 5 percent, while El Salvador and Barbados rose to 2 percent or more each, and Haiti and Brazil peaked at 1 percent of the market. There has been some resurgence in semiconductor assembly in Mexico, concentrated in the heavier, discrete devices, since the late 1970s.

Geographical diversification also had much to do with the evolution of Asian exports of semiconductor devices to the United States. The Asian share of U.S. 806/807 imports zoomed from 50–60 percent in the early 1970s to an 80–90 percent share by the late 1970s. While 10 to 12 percentage points of that 30 percent increase was at the expense of exporters in the Western Hemisphere, another 15 percent was accounted for by the virtual disappearance of Western European exports.

Within Asia, diversification of supply was also important. Exports from Hong Kong continued to decline precipitously, while Singapore and Malaysia seem to have benefited from the drop in Hong Kong's importance. During the mid to late 1970s, Thailand, Indonesia, and the Philippines were principal beneficiaries of the increased location of production in Asia. Malaysia is now the preeminent Asian location for assembly of U.S. semiconductors, followed by the Philippines, Korea, and Taiwan.

The details of table 3-7 point to the possible importance of political and institutional changes in the location decisions of producers. Political difficulties and instability gripped Mexico in 1975–76, the years preceding the drop in Mexico's relative importance. It is difficult to infer causality, however, because of labor difficulties—strikes, work stoppages—and a devaluation of the peso in 1975–76, while sizable wage increases had been decreed in 1975.

In Haiti, exports of semiconductor devices to the United States began in 1972, the year after the death of dictator François Duvalier, an event which coincided with what has been delicately described as a shift in "the Government's general disposition toward industrial expansion."[94] In the

94. See Inter-American Development Bank, "Opportunities for Industrial Investment in Haiti," unpublished report, May 1979, pp. 37–38.

Table 3-7. *Market Shares of the Principal Exporters of Semiconductor Devices Brought into the United States under Tariff Items 806.30 and 807.00, 1969–83*[a]

Percent

| *Region and country* | *1969* | *1970* | *1971* | *1972* | *1973* | *1974* | *1975* | *1976* | *1977* | *1978* | *1979* | *1980* | *1981* | *1982* | *1983* |
|---|---|---|---|---|---|---|---|---|---|---|---|---|---|---|---|
| Western Hemisphere | 25 | 26 | 30 | 22 | 20 | 24 | 20 | 15 | 11 | 10 | 10 | 11 | 11 | 11 | 14 |
| Canada | 2 | 1 | 2 | * | 1 | * | * | * | * | * | 3 | 4 | 4 | 2 | 4 |
| Mexico | 22 | 26 | 28 | 21 | 19 | 20 | 18 | 11 | 6 | 5 | 5 | 5 | 5 | 5 | 5 |
| El Salvador | 0 | 0 | 0 | 0 | 0 | * | 1 | 3 | 3 | 3 | 2 | 2 | 2 | 2 | 2 |
| Haiti | 0 | 0 | 0 | * | * | 1 | * | * | 1 | 1 | * | * | * | * | * |
| Barbados | * | 0 | * | 0 | * | * | * | * | * | * | * | * | * | 2 | 3 |
| Netherlands Antilles | 1 | * | * | 1 | * | 1 | * | * | 0 | 0 | 0 | 0 | 0 | 0 | * |
| Brazil | 0 | * | * | 0 | 0 | * | 1 | 1 | 1 | 1 | * | * | * | * | * |
| Western Europe | 14 | 15 | 15 | 11 | 7 | 4 | 2 | 2 | 1 | * | 1 | * | * | * | * |
| United Kingdom | * | * | 6 | 2 | 0 | 0 | 0 | 0 | * | 0 | 0 | * | * | * | * |
| Ireland | 12 | 11 | 4 | 7 | 4 | 3 | 2 | 2 | 1 | * | 1 | * | * | * | * |
| Portugal | 2 | 4 | 5 | 4 | 3 | 1 | * | * | * | * | 0 | 0 | 0 | 0 | 0 |
| Asia | 61 | 56 | 55 | 67 | 72 | 70 | 76 | 82 | 87 | 88 | 87 | 88 | 87 | 89 | 85 |
| Hong Kong | 30 | 25 | 18 | 17 | 15 | 12 | 9 | 9 | 7 | 6 | 4 | 4 | 3 | 3 | 1 |
| Korea | 14 | 13 | 17 | 18 | 17 | 16 | 13 | 17 | 19 | 15 | 12 | 9 | 8 | 10 | 14 |
| Taiwan | 9 | 5 | 7 | 7 | 9 | 9 | 6 | 6 | 8 | 5 | 4 | 4 | 4 | 4 | 4 |
| Singapore | 6 | 10 | 13 | 25 | 24 | 16 | 20 | 23 | 21 | 20 | 20 | 22 | 20 | 17 | 11 |
| Malaysia | * | * | * | * | 6 | 15 | 23 | 21 | 24 | 30 | 29 | 30 | 30 | 32 | 31 |
| Japan | 2 | 3 | * | * | * | * | 1 | * | * | * | 4 | * | * | * | * |
| Thailand | 0 | 0 | 0 | 0 | 0 | * | 0 | * | 1 | 3 | 2 | 3 | 4 | 3 | 4 |
| Indonesia | 0 | * | * | 0 | 0 | * | * | * | 1 | 1 | 2 | 2 | 2 | 2 | 2 |
| Philippines | 0 | 0 | 0 | 0 | 1 | 2 | 4 | 6 | 6 | 8 | 10 | 14 | 16 | 18 | 18 |

Sources: 1969–78, calculated from data furnished on magnetic tape by the ITC; 1979–82, U.S. Department of Commerce, Bureau of the Census, *FT 246, U.S. Imports;* 1983, unpublished data from the Department of Commerce. Figures are rounded.

* Less than 1 percent.

a. 807 only, 1969–71; 806/807 combined, 1972–83.

Netherlands Antilles there was an outbreak of rioting in 1969, followed by large drops in exports in 1970 and 1971; labor problems continued in the early 1970s, as did large fluctuations in the export share of this territory. In Portugal, the military coup of April 1974 was accompanied by a sharp drop in 806/807 exports, which continued until 1977.

Malaysian exports of semiconductor devices, which had begun in 1969, did not reach significant levels until 1973, two years after the rioting that had troubled that country in 1969–70. In Taiwan, exports dropped in 1978, the year during which it became clear that the United States would normalize its relations with China and break its ties to Taiwan (actually announced in December). In Thailand, a military junta was installed in 1976, ending a period of turbulent but democratic rule; significant levels of 806/807 production of semiconductor devices began the following year. In the Philippines, the declaration of martial law by strongman Ferdinand Marcos in 1972 was followed by rapid growth in exports of semiconductor devices to the United States. The political turbulence in Korea that followed the assassination of President Park was followed by a drop in Korea's share of the export market during the early 1980s.

The last few cases also emphasize the inherent futility of this sort of casual empiricism. Not only major political changes, but also major institutional shifts in economic policies occurred just before large volumes of 806/807 exports from the Philippines, Malaysia, and Thailand were made. Malaysia opened the doors of its first export-processing zone in 1972. Thailand simplified procedures to rebate duties and taxes on inputs used in the export production of promoted investments as of 1977, while the Philippines' Bataan export-processing zone began operation in 1973.[95] Similarly, substantial 806/807 exports from El Salvador began after an export-processing zone opened its doors in 1975. Table 3-8, which shows the spread of export-processing zone arrangements among the principal producers of semiconductor devices emphasizes the coincidence of these policies with increasing exports in tables 3-5 and 3-7.

It is, in fact, impossible to attribute rises and declines in exports to specific political events and changes in economic policy without controlling for the effects of other economic variables, of which the most impor-

95. See World Bank, "Thailand's Industrial Sector: The Changing Role of Policies" (Washington, D.C., November 1978), pp. 23–24. Note that while the Bataan export-processing zone opened its doors in 1973, most foreign assemblers of electronics established operations outside the zone, near the Manila airport. See "Electronics Fever Hits Philippine Zones," *Philippine Daily Express,* November 2, 1979.

Table 3-8. *Dates of Establishment and Beginning of Operations of Export-processing Zones*

| *Country* | *Date established* | *First year of operation* |
|---|---|---|
| Ireland | 1958 | n.a. |
| Mexico | n.a. | 1966 (Border Industrialization Program) |
| El Salvador | 1974 | 1975 |
| Haiti | 1974 | 1974 (industrial park) |
| Netherlands Antilles | ... | Free port |
| Brazil | 1968 | 1968 |
| Hong Kong | ... | Free port |
| Korea | ... | 1966[a] (export industrial estates) |
| Taiwan | 1966 | 1966 |
| Singapore | 1968[b] | Free port |
| Malaysia | 1972 | 1972 |
| Philippines | 1969 | 1973 |

Sources: Date established, Jean Currie, "Investment: The Growing Role of Export Processing Zones," Special Report no. 64 (London: The Economist Intelligence Unit, June 1979); and United Nations Conference on Trade and Development (UNCTAD), "The Use of Free Zones as a Means of Expanding and Diversifying Exports of Manufactures from the Developing Countries" (New York: United Nations, June 1973); first year of operation, Folker Fröbel, Jürgen Heinrichs, and Otto Kreye, *The New International Division of Labor,* tr. Pete Burgess (London: Cambridge University Press, 1980), table 3-18.

n.a. Not available.

a. Drawback system also begun in 1965–66.

b. Jurong Town Corporation established.

tant is the cost of labor. Important changes in the relative costs of assembly labor in various producing countries occurred during the period 1969–78.

For the moment, it is sufficient to observe that production shifted out of areas such as Mexico and Hong Kong, where relative wage levels were increasingly higher, and into countries such as El Salvador, Malaysia, Thailand, Indonesia, and the Philippines, where labor was cheaper. Singapore's much-publicized policy, put into effect durng the early 1980s, of increasing wages in order to change the mix of skills in its industrial employment was followed by a considerable decline in its share of U.S. assembly imports. Table 3-9 contains estimates of the relation of dollar-equivalent compensation to unskilled labor in the principal producing countries to that in the United States for the years 1969 through 1982.

In spite of the multiplicity of factors that may have contributed to growth in the geographically diversified spread of assembly of semiconductor devices for export to the United States, there is little doubt that political factors had much to do with it. Semiconductor manufacturers have explicitly acknowledged the influence of country-specific political risk in their sourcing decisions, in interviews with researchers, and in public testimony.[96]

Though it is clear that overseas production, in successive waves of investment, became a prominent feature of the operations of U.S. semiconductor firms, it is very difficult to establish the quantitative importance of these arrangements. To some extent, the lack of available information is symptomatic of the deficiencies of national statistical procedures, which are ill suited to the task of documenting production flows within an international firm.[97]

Another problem is that, since the vast majority of 806/807 transactions represent the transfer of semifinished products between related firms and thus have no observable market value, foreign production is given a constructed value as it passes through U.S. customs.[98] Essentially, customs value is defined as declared production costs, plus the normal profit particular to the country and product. The effect of this valuation procedure is a serious understatement of the market value of 806/807 imports.[99]

96. See Chang, *The Transfer of Technology,* pp. 34–38; Moxon, *Offshore Production in the Less Developed Countries,* pp. 45–47; and M. T. Flaherty, "Business History of C-MOS Integrated Circuits," Working Paper 86-07, Graduate School of Business Administration, Harvard University, 1981, p. 13. In testimony before the Subcommittee on Trade of the House Committee on Ways and Means, 94 Cong. 2 sess., March 24, 1976, David Packard (of Hewlett-Packard) remarked that he was "concerned about our long-term exposure in Malaysia and wondered whether [Hewlett-Packard] could solve the problem by automating the assembly process and transferring it to the United States. . . . We found that if we had to do this work in the United States, the increased costs would force us out of this particular business."

97. In the United States, for example, Census Bureau estimates of the value of shipments by U.S. establishments include devices assembled from U.S. components overseas and entered as 806/807 imports to be finished in the United States; these figures exclude devices assembled, tested, and finished overseas, even if they were made from U.S. components, entered under 806/807, and eventually shipped within the United States by a U.S. firm.

The conventional manner of calculating apparent consumption—taking the value of U.S. industry shipments, adding imports, and subtracting exports—would double count many U.S. imports and exports of SCDs. As noted earlier, the figures of the Bureau of the Census for U.S. shipments already include the final value of unfinished 806/807-type imports when the value of U.S. shipments is calculated. Similarly, parts of SCDs exported to be fabricated into 806/807 imports are actually consumed inside the United States when they return as 806/807 imports. Thus, the appropriate way to calculate U.S. apparent consumption is to take U.S. final shipments, add the value of imports *other than* unfinished 806/807 imports, and subtract the value of U.S. exports of SCDs *less* the U.S. content of unfinished 806/807 imports.

98. See ITC, *Import Trends in TSUS Items 806.30 and 807.00,* Publication 1029 (ITC, January 1980), p. 11.

99. No imputation of U.S.-based research and development expenditure, administrative

Table 3-9. *Dollar Indexes of Total Hourly Compensation in the International Electronics Industry, 1969 and 1974–82*[a]

United States = 100

| *Foreign producer of SCDs* | *1969*[b] | *1974*[c] | *1975*[d] | *1975*[e] | *1976*[d] | *1977*[d] | *1977*[e] | *1978*[d] | *1979*[d] | *1980*[d] | *1981*[d] | *1982*[d] |
|---|---|---|---|---|---|---|---|---|---|---|---|---|
| Canada | 78 | n.a. | 93 | n.a. | 99 | 94 | n.a. | 87 | 83 | 84 | 83 | 84 |
| Mexico | 21 | n.a. | 23 | 28 | 26 | 20 | 15 | 22 | 22 | 25 | 30 | n.a. |
| El Salvador | n.a. | 50 | n.a. | n.a. | n.a. | n.a. | n.a. | n.a. | n.a. | n.a. | n.a. | n.a. |
| Netherlands Antilles | 22 | n.a. | n.a. | n.a. | n.a. | n.a. | n.a. | n.a. | n.a. | n.a. | n.a. | n.a. |
| Brazil | n.a. | n.a. | n.a. | 11 | n.a. | n.a. | 10 | n.a. | n.a. | n.a. | n.a. | n.a. |
| United Kingdom | 44 | n.a. | 49 | 47 | 44 | 44 | 48 | 51 | 60 | 74 | 64 | 57 |
| Portugal | n.a. | n.a. | 36 | n.a. | 33 | 28 | n.a. | 25 | 24 | 27 | 24 | n.a. |
| Hong Kong | 10 | 12 | 11 | 12 | 12 | 13 | 17 | 14 | 14 | 15 | 14 | 14 |
| Korea | 10 | 8 | 6 | 7 | 7 | 8 | 9 | 10 | 12 | 11 | 11 | 11 |
| Taiwan | 8 | n.a. | 8 | 7 | 8 | 9 | 10 | 9 | 10 | 13 | 12 | 12 |
| Singapore | 9 | 11 | 12 | 12 | 11 | 11 | 10 | 12 | 13 | 14 | 15 | 15 |
| Malaysia | n.a. | 7 | n.a. | 9–10 | n.a. | n.a. | 9 | n.a. | n.a. | n.a. | n.a. | n.a. |
| Japan | 1 | n.a. | 47 | 49 | 46 | 51 | 59 | 66 | 59 | 54 | 53 | 46 |
| Thailand | n.a. | n.a. | n.a. | 5 | n.a. | n.a. | 8 | n.a. | n.a. | n.a. | n.a. | n.a. |
| Indonesia | n.a. | n.a. | n.a. | 5 | n.a. | n.a | 4 | n.a. | n.a. | n.a. | n.a. | n.a. |
| Philippines | n.a. | 4 | n.a. | 6 | n.a. | n.a. | 6 | n.a. | n.a. | n.a. | n.a. | n.a. |

n.a. Not available.

a. National currencies converted to dollars at prevailing exchange rates.

b. U.S. Tariff Commission, *Economic Factors Affecting the Use,* p. 170; firm-level ratios for office machinery, consumer electronics, and semiconductors have been averaged together.

c. From data on foreign compensation in UNCTAD, *International Subcontracting Arrangements in Electronics between Developed Market-Economy Countries and Developing Countries* (New York: UNCTAD, 1975), p. 20, table 10; U.S. compensation is based on hourly earnings in semiconductors from U.S. Department of Labor, Bureau of Labor Statistics (BLS), *Industry Wage Survey: Semiconductors, September 1977,* Bulletin 2021 (GPO, April 1979) and on unpublished BLS estimates of supplementary compensation (August hourly earnings in the United States, 1974 = $3.82 × 1.30 = $4.97).

d. From unpublished estimates of the BLS, Office of Productivity and Technology.

e. Based on estimates of total monthly compensation of unskilled labor made by Arthur D. Little, Inc., for use in comparisons of international manufacturing costs of electronic products.

Nevertheless, a rough index can be constructed using 806/807 import statistics to show the proportion of semiconductors that were assembled abroad (see appendix A). Such an index has been constructed in table 3-10. It shows that the proportion of the total value of U.S.-based shipments added abroad almost doubled between 1971 and the mid 1970s. The recessions of 1970–71 and 1974–75 were accompanied by particularly large increases in the share of foreign assembly facilities in total value added.[100] After peaking in 1976, this index declined somewhat during the late 1970s and has been stable since 1979.

To assess the magnitude of these flows some base-year estimate of the proportion of U.S. semiconductor output that was assembled abroad is needed. The 1970 survey by the U.S. Tariff Commission established that most firms operating in that year began their foreign assembly operations in 1967 or 1968—excluding, of course, the pioneers.[101] Furthermore, in 1969 all 806.30 semiconductors and "most" 807.00 assembly imports underwent further processing in the United States,[102] so figures on *quantities*

---

overhead, or marketing cost is generally made. Since marketing, research, and administrative overhead account for a large portion of the price of a finished SCD, the customs value of an 806/807 import significantly understates the market value of devices imported under tariff items 806/807. Cost data reported by Finan in 1975, for example, show corporate overhead—*excluding* direct manufacturing overhead—and profit equal to about 35 percent of sales price, or 54 percent of manufacturing cost. See Finan, "The International Transfer," table 3-3. Detailed statistics from the 1977 U.S. Census of Manufactures show that producers of SCDs marked up purchased devices by about two-thirds before reselling them. See U.S. Department of Commerce, *1977 Census of Manufactures,* table 3-A. In a recent study of manufacturing costs of ICs it was concluded that market prices ranged from 2 to 3.5 times production cost. See Howard Dicken, "How to Determine Fair Market Prices for Integrated Circuits," *Defense Electronics,* June 1980, pp. 79–83.

As might be imagined, the U.S. Customs Service had great difficulty in interpreting this statute. An informal survey in early 1980 of customs practices at various ports of entry along the U.S.-Mexican border, where a great deal of 806/807 trade enters the United States, disclosed a great deal of variation in actual practice. Some import specialists ask for actual fabrication cost, general expenses, and profit; others make elaborate calculations comparing various cost ratios among the operations for which they are responsible, in an effort to monitor "usual" expenses and profit; many simply accept with minimal scrutiny whatever declaration is made. Often, a wide variety of practices are followed within a single port of entry.

100. Note that this index probably *understates* the true increase in the fraction of U.S.-based shipments assembled abroad (see appendix A).

101. U.S. Tariff Commission, *Economic Factors Affecting the Use,* p. 98.

102. Ibid. This means that they are counted in the U.S. "shipments" figures.

Table 3-10. *Foreign Value Added in Relation to Total Value Added in Domestic and Export Shipments Passing through U.S. Facilities, Semiconductor Industry, 1969–81*[a]

Millions of U.S. dollars

| Year | *806/807 dutiable value (1)* | *Value added in U.S. establishments (2)* | *U.S. industry value added (1 + 2) (3)* | *Foreign value added ÷ industry value added (1 ÷ 3) (percent) (4)* | *Index of foreign value added ÷ industry value added (1971 = 100) (5)* |
|---|---|---|---|---|---|
| 1969 | 58 | 1,061 | 1,119 | 5.2 | 72 |
| 1970 | 69 | 972 | 1,041 | 6.6 | 92 |
| 1971 | 84 | 1,076 | 1,160 | 7.2 | 100 |
| 1972 | 125 | 1,735 | 1,860 | 6.7 | 93 |
| 1973 | 226 | 2,373 | 2,599 | 8.7 | 120 |
| 1974 | 373 | 2,738 | 3,111 | 12.0 | 166 |
| 1975 | 326 | 2,182 | 2,508 | 13.0 | 180 |
| 1976 | 477 | 2,859 | 3,336 | 14.3 | 198 |
| 1977 | 503 | 3,407 | 3,910 | 12.9 | 178 |
| 1978 | 592 | 4,203 | 4,795 | 12.3 | 170 |
| 1979 | 734 | 5,592 | 6,326 | 11.6 | 160 |
| 1980 | 926 | 7,055 | 7,981 | 11.6 | 160 |
| 1981 | 1,023 | 7,730 | 8,753 | 11.7 | 161 |

Sources: Column 1, official U.S. trade statistics as compiled by the ITC, various publications; column 2, 1969–77, U.S. Department of Commerce, Bureau of the Census, *Census of Manufactures;* 1978–81, *Annual Survey of Manufactures,* various years.

a. SCDs assembled from U.S.-made chips and shipped in the United States to domestic and foreign markets, also referred to in the text as U.S.-based shipments.

of 806/807 imports can be used to measure the fraction of U.S. shipments of semiconductor devices that were processed abroad. This is done in table 3-11 for the period 1969–71.

The results show an increase in the share of U.S. semiconductor shipments processed abroad, from about 40 percent in 1969 to about 46 percent in 1971, during the depths of the 1970–71 recession. If the share of foreign assembly in U.S.-based shipments increased 1.7 to 2 times between 1971 and 1978, in line with the discussion of table 3-10, the implication is that between 78 percent and 92 percent of U.S. semiconductors were assembled abroad in 1978.

Unfortunately, this procedure cannot reasonably be extended into the mid and late 1970s, because the Department of Commerce ceased estimat-

Table 3-11. *Production of Semiconductor Devices and Components Abroad in Relation to U.S. Shipments, 1969–71*

Millions of units and percent

| *Item* | *1969* | *1970* | *1971* |
|---|---|---|---|
| *All semiconductors* | | | |
| Number shipped in the United States (millions of units) | 3,387 | 3,126 | 2,773 |
| Number imported under 806/807 (millions) | 1,365 | 1,319 | 1,275 |
| Percentage imported under 806/807 | 40 | 42 | 46 |
| *Integrated circuits* | | | |
| Number shipped in the United States | 278 | 292 | 406 |
| Number imported under 806/807 | n.a. | 241 | 275 |
| Percentage imported under 806/807 | ... | 83 | 68 |
| *Transistors* | | | |
| Number shipped in the United States | 1,192 | 1,064 | 997 |
| Number imported under 806/807 | 646 | 548 | 482 |
| Percentage imported under 806/807 | 54 | 52 | 48 |

Source: Shipments are official U.S. Department of Commerce and ITC estimates; 806/807 imports are official trade statistics. Both are found in ITC, *Transistors and Diodes,* Publication 715 (ITC, 1975), tables 2, 4, 6, and 8.
n.a. Not available.

ing quantities of semiconductors shipped, and because during this period a growing number of U.S. manufacturers began to test and finish their semiconductors in overseas facilities.[103] In the latter case, the finished semiconductors imported under 806/807 are no longer counted in the value of U.S. semiconductor shipments, as defined by the U.S. Census Bureau.

It is possible, however, to estimate the proportion of U.S.-based integrated circuit shipments that were processed abroad during the mid to late 1970s. These estimates, which are based on the results of a 1979 ITC survey of most U.S. producers, are documented in table 3-12. They indicate that between 1974 and 1978 the percentage of U.S. shipments that involved processing abroad increased from about 79 percent to 82 percent.

103. This trend was noted in ITC, *Competitive Factors,* p. 6. The U.S. Department of Commerce, in *The U.S. Semiconductor Industry,* p. 64, expresses the opinion that the increasingly costly and capital-intensive nature of the testing process for ICs has led to a shift in testing facilities back to the United States, to take advantage of economies of scale in centralized facilities. The additional riskiness perceived in placing expensive equipment in foreign locations may also explain part of this shift. During the early 1970s, most testing of U.S. devices intended for the U.S. market was probably done in the United States. See Finan, "The International Transfer," pp. 18–19.

Table 3-12. *Importance of Foreign Assembly in U.S. Shipments of Integrated Circuits, 1974–78*

| *Item* | *1974* | *1975* | *1976* | *1977* | *1978* |
|---|---|---|---|---|---|
| | | | *Millions of units* | | |
| 1. Assembled in the United States | 250 | 176 | 245 | 314 | 372 |
| 2. Imported under 806/807 | 935 | 670 | 1,011 | 1,325 | 1,666 |
| 3. Total U.S. units (1 + 2) | 1,185 | 846 | 1,256 | 1,639 | 2,038 |
| 4. Finished in the United States | 648 | 441 | 611 | 773 | 944 |
| | | | *Percent of total* | | |
| 5. Assembled and finished in the United States (1 ÷ 3) | 21 | 21 | 20 | 19 | 18 |
| 6. Assembled abroad, finished in the United States [(4 − 1) ÷ 3] | 34 | 31 | 29 | 28 | 28 |
| 7. Assembled and finished abroad [(3 − 4) ÷ 3] | 45 | 48 | 51 | 53 | 54 |

Sources: Items 1 and 4, ITC, *Competitive Factors Influencing World Trade in Integrated Circuits,* Publication 1013 (ITC, November 1979), table A-2. Item 2 was calculated by dividing the value of 806/807 imports reported by U.S. firms by the average unit value of U.S. 806/807 imports of integrated circuits for 1974–78, under the assumption that the composition and value of 806/807 imports reported in the survey was identical to the number given in the official U.S. trade statistics for that year; see ITC, *Integrated Circuits and Their Use in Computers* (ITC, May 1979), table 8. Dollar unit values used were

| *1974* | *1975* | *1976* | *1977* | *1978* |
|---|---|---|---|---|
| 0.43 | 0.60 | 0.47 | 0.48 | 0.53 |

These are based on the tabulation given in ITC, *Integrated Circuits and Their Use,* table A-2. The two sets of figures, in millions of dollars, are as follows:

| | *1974* | *1975* | *1976* | *1977* | *1978* |
|---|---|---|---|---|---|
| Official U.S. trade statistics | 446 | 476 | 690 | 910 | 1,245 |
| ITC survey (November 1979) | 402 | 402 | 475 | 636 | 883 |

The discrepancies probably arise because not all U.S. producers of integrated circuits were covered by the survey; not all 806/807 imports are made by U.S. producers; and the fiscal years to which company figures refer may be different from the calendar years to which U.S. trade statistics refer.

The proportion of U.S.-shipped integrated circuits finished abroad increased from about 45 percent to 54 percent during that period.[104]

Foreign assembly of U.S. manufactured products, then, grew mightily during the late 1960s and 1970s and now dominates production shipped

104. Several final scraps of information suggest that more than 70–80 percent of all U.S.-based semiconductor shipments are assembled abroad. According to a 1979 market report by the consulting firm of Frost and Sullivan (whose methodology is unknown), 71 percent of the semiconductors consumed in the United States at that time were assembled abroad. See "Report Cites Growth in Semiconductor Market," *Northern California Electronic News,* January 7, 1980. A leading producer of equipment embodying SCDs estimated in 1982 that 85–95 percent of the devices shipped by merchant houses—that is, excluding captive producers, such as IBM and AT&T—were assembled abroad. See "Automation May Erase Offshore Edge," *Electronics,* April 21, 1982, p. 95. Since IBM and AT&T, which, according to ITC, *Summary of Trade and Tariff Information—Semiconductors,* p. 2, assemble their output in the United States, accounted for about 28 percent of U.S. shipments of ICs in 1981, these figures suggest that 70–80 percent of all output is assembled abroad; see ibid., table 3, and "Semiconductors Face Worldwide Challenge," *Electronics,* May 19, 1982, p. 135.

from the United States. This offers a marked contrast to production arrangements in Europe and Japan.

## Foreign Assembly of Semiconductors in Western Europe and Japan

While information on assembly abroad by European and Japanese firms is much more difficult to obtain, it is clear that it is a much less important part of their operations than it is of the operations of U.S. firms—a point made clearly in table 3-13. As an upper bound to imports of integrated circuits assembled abroad the fraction of production accounted for by imports from the Asian countries has been calculated. Less than 5 percent of Japanese production of integrated circuits and less than 20 percent of production by members of the EC could have been accounted for by foreign-assembled imports in the late 1970s.[105]

These bounds do not take into account as overseas production the output of Japanese affiliates in place behind the tariff walls of the United States and the Common Market. With the definition of foreign production broadened to include output that never reenters Japan, table 3-14 gives the available figures for 1977.

It was estimated that by 1980 some 10 percent of Japanese integrated circuits were made in overseas plants, and all indications are that this upward trend continued as Japanese producers accelerated their move into the European and U.S. markets with local production facilities.[106]

Relatively little of the Japanese foreign production is reexported into Japan. This can be seen by examining figures compiled by the ITC on the operations of the ten largest Japanese producers of integrated circuits, who in 1978 accounted for some 85 percent of the production of integrated circuits within Japan (see table 3-15). According to the ITC, these large Japanese producers had facilities located in Ireland, Korea, and Taiwan, all of which exported their output only to related parties; therefore, the

105. These figures ought to be considered upper bounds to possible imports by national firms of devices assembled abroad, since they may include exports from Asian affiliates of U.S. firms and even from indigenous Asian producers or assemblers. In 1978 it was estimated that about $33 million in imports of ICs from foreign subsidiaries of U.S. producers of SCDs entered Japan. See the Consulting Group, BA Asia Limited, *The Japanese Semiconductor Industry: An Overview* (Hong Kong: BA Asia Limited, 1979), p. 109.

106. See "Going for a Bigger Bite of the EC Chip Market," *Business Week,* October 6, 1980, p. 47.

Table 3-13. *Imports and Production in the Japanese and European Markets for Integrated Circuits, 1974–78*

Millions of U.S. dollars

| *Countries and year* | *Imports* | *Imports from assembly-oriented countries*[a] | *Shipments* | *Ratio of imports to shipments (percent)* | *Ratio of imports from assembly-oriented countries to shipments (percent)* |
|---|---|---|---|---|---|
| *Japan* | | | | | |
| 1974 | 179 | 27 | 253 | 71 | 11 |
| 1975 | 134 | 25 | 260 | 52 | 10 |
| 1976 | 199 | 45 | 435 | 38 | 10 |
| 1977 | 187 | 27 | 517 | 36 | 5 |
| 1978 | 255 | 44 | 909 | 28 | 5 |
| *European Community*[b] | | | | | |
| 1974 | 309 | 41 | 330 | 94 | 12 |
| 1975 | 266 | 30 | 313 | 85 | 10 |
| 1976 | 526 | 90 | 378 | 139 | 24 |
| 1977 | 555 | 74 | 465 | 119 | 16 |

Source: Calculated from data in ITC, *Competitive Factors,* tables A-56, A-59, A-67, and A-70.
a. All of Asia except Japan.
b. Less Luxembourg, Ireland, and Denmark.

Table 3-14. *Japanese Semiconductor Output, 1977*

| *Item* | *Number (thousands)* | *Value (millions of U.S. dollars)*[a] |
|---|---|---|
| Discrete production | 9,892 | 1,015 |
| Discrete production abroad | 1,186 | 47 |
| Percent of total production | 12 | 5 |
| Production of integrated circuits (ICs) | 828 | 774 |
| Production of ICs abroad | 67 | 22 |
| Percent of total production | 8 | 3 |

Source: The Consulting Group, BA Asia Limited, *The Japanese Semiconductor Industry: An Overview* (Hong Kong, 1979); calculated from data provided by the Japanese Ministry of International Trade and Industry (MITI) and the Japanese Ministry of Finance (MOF), reported on p. 37.
a. Converted from yen at 274 yen to the dollar.

related-party imports in table 3-15 place an upper bound on Japanese imports from overseas locations of the top ten producers. While the importance of such related-party imports of integrated circuits has grown rapidly, it is still minuscule in relation to Japanese domestic production.

The overseas integrated circuit plants of the top Japanese firms in Ko-

Table 3-15. *Shipments of Integrated Circuits by the Ten Largest Japanese Producers, 1974–78*[a]

| *Item* | *1974* | *1975* | *1976* | *1977* | *1978* |
|---|---|---|---|---|---|
| Total Japanese production of ten largest producers (millions of U.S. dollars) | 268 | 331 | 516 | 643 | 1,135 |
| Exports as percent of Japanese production of ten largest producers | 1.3 | 4.0 | 5.3 | 12.8 | 18.0 |
| Related-party imports as percent of Japanese production of ten largest producers | 0.6 | 1.1 | 1.8 | 3.7 | 1.8 |
| Production of ICs by the ten largest producers as percent of all Japanese production | 61 | 84 | 78 | 85 | 85 |

Sources: ITC, *Competitive Factors,* tables A-43, A-49, A-55, A-58; and U.S.-Japan Trade Council, Council Report, December 7, 1979, table 8.

a. Nippon Electric Company, Hitachi, Toshiba, Matsushita, Mitsubishi, Sharp, Sanyo, Sony, Fujitsu, and Oki.

rea and Ireland also sold some of their output in those countries; in Korea, some of those local sales were to other affiliates of the Japanese parent firms, which presumably used the purchases in equipment being assembled in Korea. The top ten firms also had much more extensive overseas operations in discrete semiconductor devices, with only a small portion of their employment in integrated circuits. Their total overseas semiconductor employment grew very rapidly from 1974 to 1978, but it was still small in relation to Japanese employment.[107]

At least in part because of increasing trade friction with U.S. and European producers, Japanese producers began to invest more heavily in production and assembly facilities in U.S. and European markets during the early 1980s.[108] It appears doubtful that much of their overseas production of sophisticated integrated circuits will be coming from the less developed Asian countries typically linked to such production. On the other hand, production elsewhere in Asia by Japanese firms of simpler integrated circuits and discrete semiconductors, while still constituting a fairly small part of global output, has been increasing rapidly.[109]

107. ITC, *Competitive Factors,* p. 44.

108. "Toshiba Plans to Start Production in the U.S.," *Asian Wall Street Journal Weekly,* March 14, 1981, p. 3; "Top Four Japanese IC Makers Expand U.S. Operations," ibid., July 13, 1981, p. 21; and "NEC Plans $100 Million U.S. Plant," *New York Times,* June 27, 1981.

109. "Four Semiconductor Firms Boost Output in Southeast Asia," *Asian Wall Street Journal Weekly,* July 27, 1981, p. 15; and "Japan's Electronic Firms Cut Reliance on Offshore Plants," ibid., August 17, 1981, p. 21.

The apparently meager use of foreign production facilities by Japanese semiconductor firms warrants further examination. Until the early 1970s, imports were discouraged by trade barriers, and foreign investment by Japanese firms was tightly controlled; it might therefore be argued that these historical restraints account for the small volume of overseas production by Japanese producers of semiconductor devices.

As long ago as 1963, Japanese investments in the production of passive electronic components—simple devices, such as resistors and capacitors—were permitted in Hong Kong.[110] The stimulus to this policy was undoubtedly international competition, since by then Japanese wages had started to move well above the levels prevailing in the less developed Asian countries, where U.S. producers were just beginning to assemble their most labor-intensive products.

Japanese foreign investments in active components, which include, along with semiconductors, various types of electronic tube, were not approved until 1969, in Korea and Taiwan. Korea and Taiwan provide to a Japanese investor many of the same advantages that Mexico offers to a U.S. investor. They are quite close—Korea is a one-hour ferryboat ride from western Japan—have much lower wages, and have a long history of political, cultural, linguistic, and ethnic ties to Japan. After the 1970–71 recession, a whole rash of approvals followed between 1972 and 1974, and a number of Japanese firms moved into Malaysia as well, to produce electrical tubes and semiconductors. Few of these investments involved the production of integrated circuits; most were directed toward simpler discrete devices.[111]

By 1979, Japanese producers of semiconductors had spread themselves all over Asia. Table 3-16 shows Japanese semiconductor firms in most of the same locations in which U.S. firms have established affiliates. It is also clear that these affiliates, in increasing numbers, were producing more sophisticated devices, including simpler types of integrated circuit. Nevertheless, as the foregoing discussion has made clear, Japanese production abroad at the end of the 1970s was a very much less significant—though growing—part of global production than was that of U.S. firms.

A more detailed examination of the circumstances of Japanese foreign investments in the production of semiconductors will shed further light on

110. See Yoshihara, *Japanese Investment,* p. 214.

111. Ibid., pp. 161, 213.

Table 3-16. *Foreign Investments by Japanese Firms in the Production of Semiconductor Devices, 1979*[a]

Number of instances of investment

| *Country* | *Discrete SCDs* | *Integrated circuits* |
|---|---|---|
| United States | 0 | 2 |
| Mexico | 1 | 0 |
| Argentina | 2 | 0 |
| Korea | 4 | 4 |
| Taiwan | 2 | 1 |
| Hong Kong | 0 | 2 |
| Thailand | 1 | 1 |
| Singapore | 3 | 2 |
| Malaysia | 3 | 4 |
| Other | 0 | 1 |
| All countries | 16 | 17 |

Source: Japan Electrical Machinery Industry Association, *Internationalization and Its Impact on the Electronics Industry of Japan* (Tokyo: JEMIA, June 1980, in Japanese), p. 51.

a. Investments listed here correspond to those made by firms that responded to a survey undertaken by JEMIA.

the motivation for and growth of such operations. Table 3-17 summarizes details of such investments by members of the Japan Electrical Machinery Industry Association (JEMIA).

It seems clear that penetration of foreign markets is the primary aim of such investment. Only three countries—Korea, Taiwan, and Malaysia—had Japanese-owned plants that reported exports to Japan. Also, the establishment of such operations accelerated during the late 1970s. Of the twenty-four such investments made by members of JEMIA, a fourth were made after 1978, and half were made after 1975.

Patterns are also visible in the establishment of subsidiaries by country. Cheap or stable supplies of labor were cited as a reason for investment in low-wage Asian countries such as Korea, Taiwan, the Philippines, and Malaysia. Access to domestic markets appears to have been more important in Hong Kong and Singapore, with nearness to equipment industries that use semiconductors especially important in Singapore. In seventeen of the twenty-four investments, there was some sort of financial incentive.

By the end of 1979, however, production by such overseas facilities in Asia must still have been relatively small. While no employment figures are available for some of the investments surveyed and thus no complete figure

Table 3-17. *Foreign Investments by Japanese Firms in the Production of Semiconductors, 1965–79*[a]

Number of instances of investment in the production of SCDs

| *Country* | *Total number* | *Period* | | | | *Principal reasons cited for investment* | | | | |
|---|---|---|---|---|---|---|---|---|---|---|
| | | *1965–70* | *1971–74* | *1975–77* | *1978–79* | *Reexport to Japan* | *Production for foreign markets*[b] | *Labor supply*[c] | *Financial incentives*[d] | *Other related producers in country* |
| United States | 2 | 0 | 0 | 0 | 2 | 0 | 2 | 0 | 0 | 0 |
| Mexico | 1 | 1 | 0 | 0 | 0 | 0 | 1 | 0 | 1 | 0 |
| Brazil | 2 | 2 | 0 | 0 | 0 | 0 | 2 | 0 | 1 | 0 |
| Korea | 5 | 2 | 2 | 1 | 0 | 1 | 2 | 5 | 4 | 0 |
| Taiwan | 4 | 1 | 1 | 1 | 1 | 2 | 0 | 3 | 2 | 0 |
| Hong Kong | 2 | 0 | 0 | 1 | 1 | 0 | 1 | 0 | 1 | 0 |
| Philippines | 2 | 0 | 0 | 1 | 1 | 0 | 0 | 2 | 1 | 0 |
| Singapore | 2 | 0 | 0 | 1 | 1 | 0 | 2 | 0 | 2 | 2 |
| Malaysia | 4 | 0 | 3 | 1 | 0 | 1 | 1 | 3 | 4 | 0 |
| Nine countries | 24 | 6 | 6 | 6 | 6 | 4 | 11 | 13 | 16 | 2 |

Source: JEMIA, *Internationalization and Its Impact.*
a. Only investments by members of JEMIA in facilities in which semiconductors are produced are included.
b. "To increase third-country markets," "to increase domestic markets," or "difficult to export from Japan."
c. "Stable labor supply," "good quality labor," or "cheap labor."
d. "Subsidy from host country," "easy access to domestic capital," or "cheap capital."

on employment can be given, the information can be used to calculate some general orders of magnitude. Of nineteen Asian operations, twelve reported employment. Of those twelve, the seven establishments producing only semiconductors employed about 9,300 workers; if establishments with a broader product mix are included, employment is about 13,700. It seems safe to suppose that Japanese semiconductor employment in Asia probably lay between 10,000 and 20,000 workers in 1979. Since the ten largest Japanese producers of integrated circuits, who accounted for the great bulk of Japanese output of semiconductor devices, employed roughly 33,000 workers in semiconductors in 1978, this is significant in relation to Japanese domestic employment.[112]

The U.S. industry, by way of contrast, employed fewer than 100,000 employees in assembly operations in Asia and Latin America in 1977, and about 64,000 production workers and roughly 50,000 nonproduction employees were employed domestically.[113]

The 1979 ITC study of competition in the international market for integrated circuits also showed all foreign employment by the principal U.S. producers of integrated circuits to be roughly equal to domestic employment in U.S. producers' semiconductor operations.[114] Thus, the Japanese industry had considerably fewer employees abroad in relation to its size than the U.S. industry.

But the salient feature of Japanese electronic production abroad is that it is used primarily to supply local and third-country export markets, in contradistinction to U.S.-based operations. This point is clear from the trade statistics of Korea, Singapore, and Hong Kong. Japanese producers are using electronic equipment assembly operations located in those countries as a vehicle for making significant exports of semiconductor devices

112. ITC, *Competitive Factors,* p. 116, table A60.

113. The only really solid figures on employment abroad by U.S. producers of semiconductors appear in the 1977 survey by the Department of Commerce of U.S. foreign direct investment. That survey contains data for "electronic component"-producing affiliates of U.S. firms in a number of regions. Exports to the United States from Asia and the Pacific, excluding Japan, Australia, and New Zealand, accounted for some 83 percent of sales. The data on U.S. imports of electronic components from the Far East, excluding Japan, indicate that some 75 percent of these were semiconductors. See U.S. Department of Commerce, unpublished compilation of official trade statistics; and Bureau of Economic Analysis, *U.S. Direct Investment Abroad, 1977* (GPO, April 1981). Thus, production of electronic components by U.S. affiliates in Asia in 1977 was overwhelmingly given over to the manufacture of semiconductors; these data on the Asian operations of U.S. affiliates will be used as a proxy for U.S. production of semiconductors abroad in 1977.

114. See ITC, *Competitive Factors,* pp. 100–01.

produced in Japan. In those three countries as a whole, the ratio of imports of parts for semiconductor devices to exports of semiconductor devices ranged from about 0.7 to 0.8 (see table 3-18). The ratio was much lower in the parts and product trade of most European countries and much higher for Japanese exports of parts to imports of product. Japan seems to have been a net exporter of parts to the European countries, through assembly operations in other Asian countries.[115]

Also, since, as noted earlier, all Asian imports of integrated circuits in 1978 entered under the Japanese GSP scheme, and most Japanese foreign affiliates are in Asia, it is almost certainly true that the foreign production of Japanese producers that enters Japan must have made significant use of Japan's generalized tariff preference scheme. Given the fairly high tariff barriers that were protecting the Japanese market during this period, the existence of these preferences may have been an important means of making some foreign production economical.

There is every sign that the general pattern of continued Japanese investment in overseas facilities for the purpose of penetrating third-country export markets will continue. Japanese production abroad, while expanding, continues to be concentrated on discrete devices and the simpler types of integrated circuit used in consumer applications. With the highly automated, large-scale facilities for assembly of integrated circuits used in Japan dramatically cutting costs by means of large production runs—as is true for the sophisticated memory chips in the production of which Japan is most competitive—the gains from using low-cost assembly labor may be minimal in products geared to the mass market. In some instances, products assembled abroad may even be more expensive than those made in Japan, which highlights the fact that the primary purpose of Japanese facilities abroad is to supply components for the electronic imports of non-Japanese markets.[116]

In the EC, by way of contrast, tough protective measures against im-

115. It is also interesting to note that large volumes of parts are being exported from Malaysia to Hong Kong and Singapore, confirming the impression of a growing trend to the establishment of more complex operations in Hong Kong and Singapore.

116. NEC, the largest Japanese producer of ICs, is reported to have found its production costs slightly higher in Malaysia than in Japan. See "Japan's Electronic Firms Cut Reliance on Offshore Plants," *Asian Wall Street Journal Weekly,* August 17, 1981, p. 2. The only Japanese producer in Malaysia to ship most of its output back to Japan was Hitachi. Further expansion abroad is likely to follow the same pattern. The responses of a sample of Japanese producers of semiconductors, queried about their plans for expansion of facilities abroad, supported this hypothesis. Of twelve manufacturing operations planned for 1980 in Asia,

Table 3-18. *Principal Exporters of Parts for Semiconductor Devices to Korea, Singapore, and Hong Kong, 1978*

| *Country from which parts are exported* | *Importing country* | | | | | |
|---|---|---|---|---|---|---|
| | *Value of parts imported (millions of U.S. dollars)* | | | *Ratio of imports of parts to exports of SCDs* | | |
| | *Korea* | *Singapore* | *Hong Kong* | *Korea* | *Singapore* | *Hong Kong* |
| France | 11.8 | 0.0 | 1.8 | 0.66 | 0.00 | 0.60 |
| West Germany | 0.2 | 14.4 | 2.1 | 0.20 | 0.26 | 0.12 |
| Italy | 0.0 | 12.2 | 0.0 | 0.00 | 0.56 | 0.00 |
| Japan | 47.1 | 39.6 | 39.6 | 1.10 | 2.00 | 5.60 |
| United Kingdom | 0.7 | 2.3 | 1.3 | 3.50 | 0.19 | 0.16 |
| United States | 165.7 | 325.2 | 68.8 | 0.86 | 0.84 | 0.72 |
| Netherlands | 4.3 | 0.00 | 5.4 | 0.52 | 0.00 | 0.42 |
| Korea | ... | 0.0 | 3.2 | ... | 0.00 | 0.64 |
| Singapore | 5.3 | ... | 10.2 | 0.48 | ... | 0.65 |
| Hong Kong | 7.6 | 3.6 | ... | 0.12 | 0.14 | ... |
| Malaysia | 0.6 | 22.2 | 3.1 | 3.00 | 1.50 | 0.80 |
| Taiwan | 0.0 | 0.00 | 8.7 | 0.00 | 0.00 | 0.67 |
| Philippines | 0.0 | 1.6 | 1.2 | 0.00 | 0.40 | 0.19 |
| Thailand | 0.2 | 0.8 | 6.4 | 0.40 | 0.62 | 0.00 |
| All countries | 245.2 | 424.3 | 155.3 | 0.69 | 0.75 | 0.79 |

Source: Official trade statistics of Korea, Singapore, and Hong Kong, 1978.

ports of semiconductor devices seem to have been effective, so even the much lower wages available in Asia have not sparked a mass movement abroad. Since available GSP quotas were quite limited, such tariff relief was available to only a small number of Asian imports produced by EC and foreign nationals.

While no disaggregated statistics on EC outward-processing trade are published, it can be established that the outward-processing provisions were used for at least some imports of semiconductor devices.[117] The EC

only one was to supply the more sophisticated metal oxide silicon (MOS) types of IC, which include less complex chips as well as highly integrated computer chips; four were slated to produce simpler linear ICs, and seven were scheduled to produce simple discrete devices, probably destined for use in consumer electronics. Japan Electrical Machinery Industry Association (JEMIA), *Internationalization and Its Impact on the Electronics Industry of Japan* (Tokyo: JEMIA, June 1980, in Japanese), p. 227.

117. According to official EC (Eurostat) statistics, semiconductors accounted for roughly 15.6 million European units of account out of a grand total of 18.6 million EC units of account imported from the Philippines in NIMEXE section 85—electronic goods—in 1978. According to Berthomieu and Hanaut, outward-processing imports from the Philippines in NIMEXE 85 amounted to 12.9 million units of account. See C. Berthomieu and A. Hanaut, "Recent Studies and Data from Western Europe on Production Sharing and the International Division of Labor—A Survey (1979, revised 1980; mimeographed), p. 56.

system is much less advantageous to producers, however, than the U.S. 806/807 system.

Thus, production abroad, through the mid 1970s, was a less important aspect of the global operations of European and Japanese firms than it was for U.S.-based firms. Japanese firms, however, have been rapidly increasing the number of their foreign affiliates in both industrial and developing areas and seem to be transferring a growing share of the manufacture of less complex semiconductor devices to their affiliates in developing countries. The Japanese operations seem to be geared primarily toward export to foreign markets, and the affiliates in low-wage Asian countries seem especially inclined to export to Europe.

## The Effects on the U.S. Economy

The shift of semiconductor assembly tasks to foreign plants has had significant effects on the structure of the industry in the industrial countries in which it is based. In an ideal world of frictionless competitive markets, the benefits to the home economy of movement abroad would be measured by the lower prices paid by producers for assembled semiconductors, reflected in lower prices to consumers for the finished goods using these assembled inputs.[118]

In a real world economy with rigidities, adjustment costs, and a host of structural and institutional imperfections, however, the question of the effects of this international transfer is not so easily resolved.[119] Changing the number and mix of workers in an industry may impose costs on various groups within the economy. If some workers are displaced, they will have to seek new employment, be retrained, or face involuntary unemployment.

The effects of foreign assembly on the domestic labor force will be examined briefly here. Because usable data are available in detail only for the United States and because the United States is the only national

118. This statement, of course, ignores considerations of distribution, which could also be eliminated by an ideal system of lump-sum transfers.

119. For a discussion of optimal policy in the presence of such costs, see Harvey E. Lapan, "International Trade, Factor Market Distortions, and the Optimal Dynamic Subsidy," *American Economic Review,* vol. 66 (June 1976), pp. 335–46; Lapan, "International Trade, Factor-Market Distortions, and the Optimal Dynamic Subsidy: Reply," ibid., vol. 68 (December 1978), pp. 956–59; Edward J. Ray, "Factor-Market Distortions and Dynamic Optimal Intervention: Comment," ibid., vol. 69 (September 1979), pp. 715–17; and Lapan, "Factor-Market Distortions and Dynamic Optimal Intervention: Reply," ibid., pp. 718–20.

semiconductor market in which production abroad is the dominant feature of supplies to that market, the discussion will be focused on the U.S. industry.

### *The Economic Benefits of Production Abroad*

The social cost, in dollar value, of "bringing home" semiconductor assembly, instead of producing other goods and trading them at fixed international prices for assembly services abroad, can be approximated.[120] The resources required to assemble a semiconductor domestically come at the expense of other output, with value exceeding the costs with foreign assembly. To measure this loss, estimates of *m,* additional U.S. assembly costs as a fraction of the total cost with overseas assembly, and $\eta_{Qp}$, the price elasticity of demand for semiconductors as an input, are needed. Estimates of these two parameters, based on historical relations, are derived in appendix B.

The social cost of bringing home foreign production is a welfare loss with value *V*. By taking a second-order approximation, that change can be expressed as a fraction of the original value of semiconductor output with overseas assembly ($P_oQ_o$):[121]

$$\frac{V}{P_oQ_o} = m\,(1 + \frac{m\eta_{Qp}}{2}). \quad (3\text{-}1)$$

Semiconductor demand seems rather elastic with respect to the effective price of an electronic function on a chip; to make a rough estimate, the effect of a 10 percent drop in price might be bracketed at between a 15 percent and a 30 percent increase in demand. The apparent sensitivity of demand for semiconductor devices to price fluctuations is entirely consistent with the highly volatile demand for electronic equipment throughout the business cycle, which would also seem to indicate a high income elasticity of demand by consumers for the electronics in which they are em-

120. I also assume that foreign exchange is available in perfectly elastic supply and that foreign imports are not permitted to substitute for U.S.-produced semiconductors as U.S. semiconductors become more costly. This means that protection isolates the domestic market from international competition. See appendix B.

121. See Zvi Griliches, "Research Costs and Social Returns: Hybrid Corn and Related Innovations," *Journal of Political Economy,* vol. 66 (October 1958), pp. 419–31. This is the formula for what Griliches calls Loss 1.

bodied. A reasonable figure for the cost savings from assembly abroad would be from 7 percent to 13 percent of average cost in the late 1970s.

Performing the welfare calculations of equation 3-1, using a variety of parameter values through the plausible range, gives the magnitudes shown in table 3-19. If a price elasticity estimate of −2.3 is the preferred choice, the calculations suggest that transferring foreign assembly to domestic plants would be roughly equivalent to a windfall loss of income to consumers of about 8 percent of the value of their consumption of semiconductor devices, give or take perhaps 3 percent. With U.S. semiconductor shipments in 1983 estimated at about $12 billion, the loss would have been roughly $960 million, plus or minus perhaps $360 million.[122] This is a respectable sum but it is not overwhelmingly large.

Since the implicit assumption is that protectionist policies will prevent imports from displacing U.S. products as U.S. prices rise, the calculations of welfare loss overestimate what the loss would be without protectionist policies. Average prices for semiconductor output would then be lower, and the welfare loss would be smaller.

These calculations, of course, ignore both the costs of retraining and relocating workers who were displaced by foreign production and the costs of any unemployment they may have suffered. While they may give a useful approximation of the costs of relocating foreign assembly to the United States, they must certainly underestimate the social costs of the original movement abroad. Although no real data on the number of workers actually displaced are available, it is clear that a significant number were affected. Between April 1975 and July 1982 roughly 8,500 workers in the semiconductor industry were certified as eligible for trade-adjustment assistance, while the petitions of almost 3,000 were denied.[123] This is a relatively large number, since the bulk of the movement abroad took place before 1975. While statistics for this earlier period are unavailable, a number of petitions for adjustment assistance made to the ITC, involving 806/807 imports, were approved then.[124]

122. See ITC, *Summary of Trade and Tariff Information—Semiconductors,* Publication 841 (ITC, August 1984), table 1.

123. Unpublished statistics of the U.S. Department of Labor, Employment and Training Administration. I thank Michael Podgursky for bringing them to my attention.

124. ITC investigations numbered TEA-W-196 and TEA-W-255 approved the petitions of workers at General Electric transistor and diode plants when production was moved abroad in 1973 and 1974. See ITC, *Transistors and Diodes,* Publication 715 (ITC, 1975). Investigations TEA-W-82 through TEA-W-88 involved workers at seven Sprague Electric Company plants in the United States.

Table 3-19. *Value of Welfare Loss as Percent of the Consumption of Semiconductor Devices with Transfer of Foreign Assembly to the United States, Late 1970s*

| *Parameter values* | | |
|---|---|---|
| *Estimated cost advantage of assembly abroad (m)* | *Elasticity of demand for semiconductor devices* ($\eta_{QP}$) | *Value of welfare loss as percent of consumption of semiconductor devices* |
| 0.13 | −1.5 | 12 |
| 0.13 | −2.3 | 11 |
| 0.13 | −3.0 | 10 |
| 0.07 | −1.5 | 7 |
| 0.07 | −2.3 | 6 |
| 0.07 | −3.0 | 6 |

Source: Equation 3-1; see text.

### *Effects of Foreign Assembly on the Structure of U.S. Employment*

The export of labor-intensive assembly operations has had vastly different effects on different groups within the U.S. semiconductor labor force. Table 3-20 displays basic information on employment in the U.S. industry. The first and most obvious feature of employment is that it has been growing quite slowly in relation to output. Between 1963 and 1980, it approximately tripled. The value of shipments during the same period increased almost sixteen times; since prices for semiconductors were declining, real growth was even greater. Certainly, some large part of the divergence in growth rates must have been caused by the use of foreign assembly arrangements.

Second, recession and economic slowdown have had drastic effects on employment in the U.S. industry. Employment growth rates fell sharply during the 1966–67 economic slowdown and dropped steeply during and after the 1970 recession. During the 1974–75 recession, employment in the U.S. industry fell more than 27 percent in 1975 alone. Declines were also registered during the 1981 economic slowdown. The semiconductor work force seems therefore to have been hit somewhat harder during economic slowdown than most of the manufacturing work force.

Third, workers in the U.S. semiconductor industry are concentrated in nonproduction employment. In 1977, the average for all U.S. manufacturing and for electrical equipment was in excess of 2.2 production workers

Table 3-20. *Structure of Employment in the U.S. Semiconductor Industry, 1958 and 1963–81*

| Year | Total employment (thousands) | Annual growth rate (percent) All employment | Annual growth rate (percent) Production workers | Number of production workers per non-production employee | Hourly wage per production worker (dollars) | Ratio of wages per production work hour, semiconductor devices to all manufacturing (percent) |
|---|---|---|---|---|---|---|
| 1958 | 23.4 | n.a. | n.a. | 3.0 | 1.90 | 87 |
| 1963 | 56.3 | 5.6[a] | 4.5[a] | 2.0 | 2.19 | 86 |
| 1964 | 55.3 | −1.8 | 1.3 | 2.2 | 2.27 | 87 |
| 1965 | 67.4 | 21.9 | 28.2 | 2.6 | 2.31 | 86 |
| 1966 | 82.2 | 22.0 | 21.4 | 2.6 | 2.32 | 83 |
| 1967 | 85.4 | 3.9 | −2.0 | 2.1 | 2.60 | 89 |
| 1968 | 87.4 | 2.3 | 4.5 | 2.2 | 2.80 | 90 |
| 1969 | 98.8 | 13.0 | 14.5 | 2.3 | 2.83 | 87 |
| 1970 | 88.5 | −10.4 | −13.0 | 2.1 | 3.07 | 89 |
| 1971 | 74.7 | −15.6 | −24.5 | 1.6 | 3.33 | 90 |
| 1972 | 97.6 | 30.7 | 28.4 | 1.5 | 3.61 | 91 |
| 1973 | 120.0 | 23.0 | 27.9 | 1.6 | 3.73 | 89 |
| 1974 | 133.1 | 10.9 | 9.2 | 1.6 | 3.93 | 86 |
| 1975 | 96.7 | −27.3 | −35.8 | 1.2 | 4.34 | 86 |
| 1976 | 102.5 | 6.0 | 10.5 | 1.3 | 4.46 | 82 |
| 1977 | 112.9 | 11.2 | 7.8 | 1.2 | 5.31 | 90 |
| 1978 | 130.8 | 14.7 | 15.9 | 1.3 | 5.57 | 90 |
| 1979 | 142.9 | 9.3 | 10.2 | 1.3 | 5.85 | 86 |
| 1980 | 160.7 | 12.5 | 7.6 | 1.2 | 6.90 | 93 |
| 1981 | 169.5 | 5.5 | −2.7 | 1.0 | 8.15 | 101 |

Source: Calculated from U.S. Department of Commerce, Bureau of the Census, *Census of Manufactures* and *Annual Survey of Manufactures,* various years; data refer to manufacturing establishments, excluding administrative office and auxiliary operations.

n.a. Not available.

a. Growth rate 1958–63/65.

per nonproduction employee; the corresponding figure for the semiconductor devices sector was 1.3, a little more than half this average.[125]

Furthermore, recession seems to have been a catalyst to the reorganization of employment in the U.S. industry. The ratio of production workers to nonproduction employees declined during the 1970–71 and 1974–75 recessions, and the new and lower ratios of production employment persisted after the recessions. During the most recent recession, in the early 1980s, worldwide semiconductor employment again dropped significantly,

125. Statistics are taken from U.S. Department of Commerce, *1977 Census of Manufactures.*

with U.S. employment taking the brunt of the cutbacks.[126] The industry was reorganized significantly during recessions; higher-cost U.S. assembly operations were shut down, and when demand again picked up they were replaced with assembly plants abroad.

Greater insight into the effects of assembly abroad on the structure of U.S. semiconductor employment can be had from an examination of the detailed information displayed in table 3-21. The data reveal little change in the structure of production employment until the period 1967–72. During that period, however, the number of assembly laborers per nonproduction employee was roughly halved, while the number of nonassembly production workers per nonproduction employee increased slightly. This radical shift supports the claim that the bulk of the movement toward foreign assembly took place between 1967 and 1972, though it is also explained in part by changes in manufacturing technique. The slight increase in other types of production employment may be the result of the increasing complexity of chip fabrication and the greater numbers of production workers required to handle materials and inspection and testing of output assembled abroad.

Between 1972 and 1977, the use of assembly workers again dropped, though to a much smaller degree than it had between 1967 and 1972. This is consistent with the continued, more gradual expansion of foreign assembly in production for the U.S. market. The number of nonassembly production employees per nonproduction employee remained essentially constant during this period.

What little direct information exists supports the view that the expansion of production employment abroad coincided with major recessions. Table 3-22 gives an analysis of U.S.-based and worldwide production employment in semiconductors by U.S. producers of integrated circuits during the period 1974–78. Since makers of integrated circuits accounted for the bulk of U.S. output and employment in semiconductor devices during this period, the table probably reflects the worldwide distribution of employment with fair accuracy. It shows a marked increase in the share of foreign employment in the manufacture of semiconductor devices follow-

126. Some manufacturers trimming their operations in early 1981 reported that the bulk of their shutdowns affected their U.S. employment and not their foreign operations. See "Semicon Firms Wriggle Work Schedules," *Electronic News,* March 30, 1981; "Layoff Set by Texas Instruments," *New York Times,* May 30, 1981; and "Asian Semiconductor Output and Sales Humming Along despite Slump in U.S.," *Asian Wall Street Journal Weekly,* September 14, 1981, p. 14.

Table 3-21. *Structure of Production Employment in the U.S. Semiconductor Industry, 1963, 1967, 1972, and 1977*

| Year | Number of production workers (thousands) | Estimated number of workers in assembly of product[a]: Number (thousands) | Estimated number of workers in assembly of product[a]: As percent of all production workers | Ratio of assembly workers to nonproduction employees | Ratio of nonassembly workers to nonproduction employees |
|---|---|---|---|---|---|
| 1963 | 37.5 | 28.4 | 76 | 1.51 | 0.48 |
| 1967 | 57.9 | 44.6 | 77 | 1.63 | 0.48 |
| 1972 | 58.4 | 30.6 | 52 | 0.78 | 0.71 |
| 1977 | 63.5 | 28.7 | 45 | 0.57 | 0.69 |

Source: U.S. Department of Commerce, Bureau of the Census, *Census of Manufactures, Selected Metalworking Operations* (Washington, D.C., various years).

a. The estimate of the number of workers in assembly of product was calculated under the assumption that the composition of employment in manufacturing establishments not covered by the special survey of metalworking operations, in which, depending on the year, 10–30 percent of all workers were employed, was identical to that of establishments that completed the special survey.

Table 3-22. *Worldwide Employment by U.S. Producers of Semiconductors, 1974–78*[a]

Thousands of workers

| Year | Number of production workers engaged in production of integrated circuits: Total | Foreign subsidiaries | Percent foreign | Total number of employees producing semiconductors: Total | Subsidiaries | Percent foreign |
|---|---|---|---|---|---|---|
| 1974 | 74 | 41 | 55 | 156 | 70 | 45 |
| 1975 | 63 | 35 | 56 | 127 | 59 | 46 |
| 1976 | 81 | 50 | 62 | 150 | 78 | 52 |
| 1977 | 88 | 52 | 59 | 161 | 81 | 50 |
| 1978 | 103 | 61 | 59 | 179 | 89 | 50 |

Source: ITC, *Competitive Factors,* tables A-33 and A-34. The data are for a sample that includes all the principal U.S. producers.

a. For U.S. producers of integrated circuits only.

ing the 1974–75 recession; it also confirms that growth in foreign employment during the mid to late 1970s was gradual compared to what must have been explosive growth during the late 1960s and early 1970s.

The significance of the transfer of production employment to plants abroad during and after major recessions is the implication that recessions may be considerably less harmful to foreign employment than to domestic production employment in the United States. Slackening demand may lead producers to close their least profitable operations, which are probably more often than not in the United States, where the cost of assembly labor is high.

Since significant variation in output and employment throughout the business cycle seems to be a primary characteristic of the semiconductor industry, it might be asked what effect the transfer of assembly operations out of the country has had on the stability of employment within the U.S. industry. In an attempt to answer this question, the deviations in production and nonproduction employment from their trend growth during the period 1963–80 were examined.[127] The results are plotted in figure 3-2.

Between 1963 and 1980 production employment grew at an annual rate of 3 percent, while nonproduction employment grew at 8 percent per year. As can be seen from figure 3-2, fluctuation of actual employment around the levels predicted by this average growth rate were substantially more severe in production employment. The movement toward more assembly abroad, however, seems to have had little or no discernible effect on the instability of U.S. production employment, suggesting that assembly employment is not affected by business cycle fluctuations or is affected only somewhat more than other types of production employment. Before 1968 or so, production employment may have deviated slightly less from its trend, but the difference seems to be of little significance. The same may be said of nonproduction employment.

That is not to say, of course, that production abroad has had no effect on the stability of U.S. employment. Since the use of foreign assembly seems to have been associated with a shift toward more U.S. nonproduction employment, which shows less variation from its trend, the changing composition of U.S. employment in the manufacture of semiconductor devices has served to stabilize total U.S. employment.[128]

Strikingly, the production labor force in semiconductors is overwhelmingly female. This has been true historically since at least the early 1960s

127. That is, regressions of the form $\ln X = a + bt$ were calculated for dependent variable $X$ corresponding to production and nonproduction employment in the U.S. industry and $t$ a time trend variable with value 0 in 1963, incremented by 1 in every subsequent year. Coefficient $b$ is an estimate of the trend growth rate. Between 1963 and 1980, $b$ was equal to 0.034 for production workers, 0.08 for nonproduction workers. Deviations from trend employment were then calculated by comparing actual employment to that predicted by the trend growth equation.

128. That is to say, for a given average volume of semiconductor employment, increasing the proportion of that employment which is nonproduction workers reduces the variations in total employment. This follows from the fact that variation of nonproduction employment around its predicted mean is less than the variance of production employment, and their covariance is positive—that is, the fluctuations tend to move together (see figure 3-2).

To put this more formally, suppose that total employment equals $(S_N\epsilon_N + S_P\epsilon_P)\,L$, with

Figure 3-2. *Variation of Production Employment and Nonproduction Employment around the Trend Growth Rate over the U.S. Business Cycle, 1963–80*

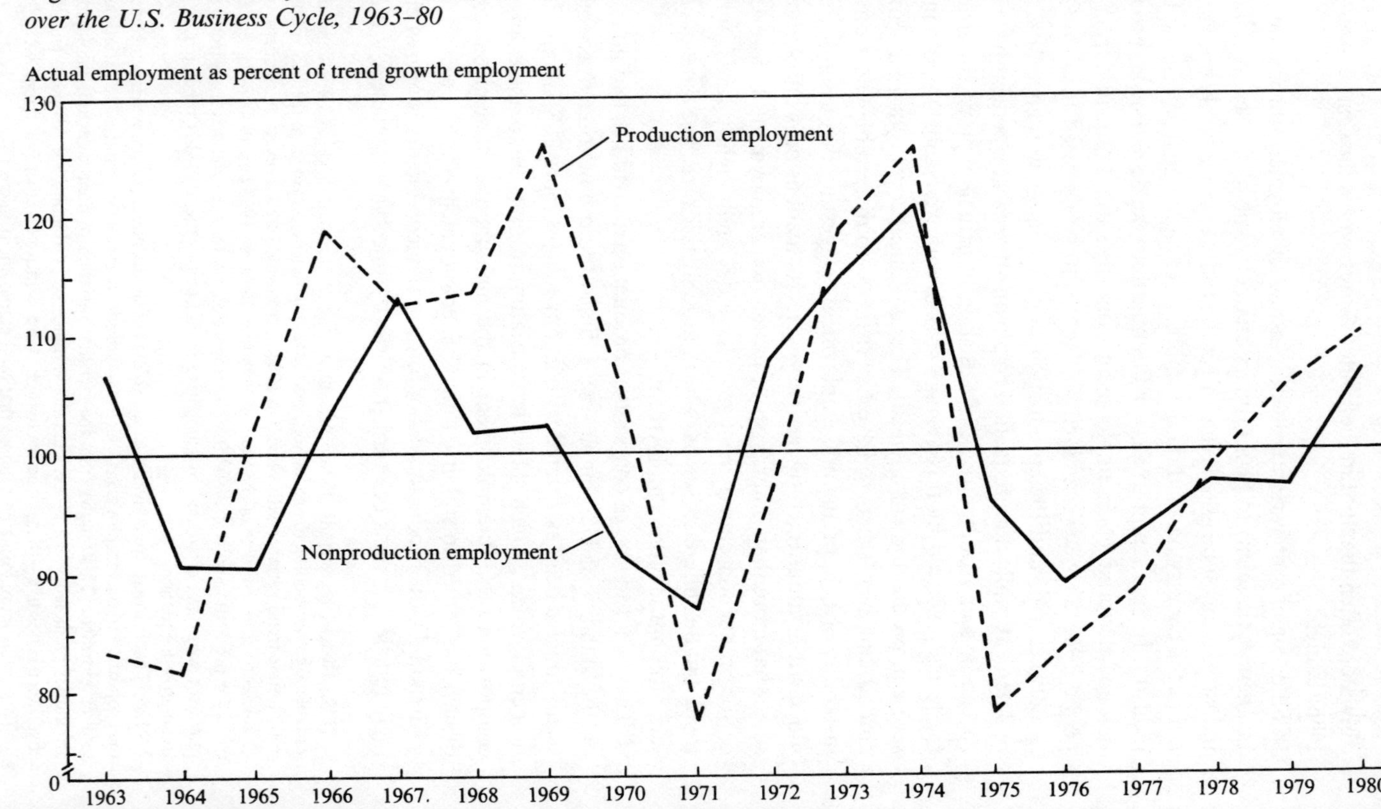

and shows little prospect of changing.[129] The occupation with the largest majority of female workers in fact, is assembly, in which more than 90 percent of the workers are women.

The preponderance of women in this work force is in part attributable

---

$S_N$ and $S_P$ the fractional shares of nonproduction and production employment, respectively, in total employment, $L$ ($S_N + S_P = 1$), and that $\varepsilon_N$ and $\varepsilon_P$ are (mean 1) random errors associated with fluctuations around expected employment at any moment in time. Let $\sigma_N^2$, $\sigma_P^2$, and $\sigma_{NP}$ be the variances and covariance of these random fluctuations.

The variance of total employment is then equal to

$$L^2 [S_N^2 \sigma_N^2 + (1 - S_N)^2 \sigma_P^2 + 2S_N (1 - S_N) \sigma_{NP}]$$

and its derivative with respect to $S_N$—that is, the effect on variance of an increase in the portion of employment made up of nonproduction workers—is

$$2L^2\sigma_P^2\left[S_N\left(\frac{\sigma_N^2}{\sigma_P^2} + 1 - 2\frac{\sigma_N}{\sigma_P}R_{NP}\right) + \left(R_{NP}\frac{\sigma_N}{\sigma_P} - 1\right)\right]$$

with $R_{NP}$ the correlation coefficient of $N$ and $P$.

Using the residuals of the estimated equations described in the preceding footnote, consistent estimates of $R_{NP}$, $\sigma_N^2$, and $\sigma_P^2$, taking on values of about .652, .00952, .0267, respectively, are calculated.

For an increase in $S_N$ to *reduce* variation in overall employment, it is necessary that

$$S_N < \frac{1 - \frac{\sigma_N}{\sigma_P} R_{NP}}{\frac{\sigma_N^2}{\sigma_P^2} + 1 - 2\frac{\sigma_N}{\sigma_P} R_{NP}},$$

which, using these estimates, requires that $S_N < 1.06$.

With the observed pattern of employment fluctuation, therefore, any increase in the employment share of nonproduction workers appears to reduce the instability of overall employment, since $S_N$ must always lie between 0 and 1.

129. The following statistics portray the situation in the U.S. semiconductor industry:

| | *Women as percentage of all workers* | |
|---|---|---|
| *Occupation* | *1962* | *1977* |
| Assembly | 90–100 | 92 |
| Inspecting and testing | 90–99 | 88 |
| Processing and fabrication | 65–90 | n.a. |
| Processing only | n.a. | 73 |
| Custodial and janitorial services | 5 | 14 |
| All production work | 70–72 | 71 |

U.S. Department of Labor, Bureau of Labor Statistics, *Industry Wage Survey: Semiconductors September 1977,* Bulletin 2021 (GPO, 1979), pp. 7–8; and *Employment Outlook and Changing Occupational Structure in Electronics Manufacturing,* Bulletin 1363 (GPO, October 1963), p. 38.

to the preference of employers for women workers in work that requires close tolerance—that is, in routine and monotonous tasks that require manual dexterity and for which great physical strength is not particularly useful. It may also be attributable in part to the generally lower wage rates paid to women and to a lesser propensity of women to organize in unions. Labor force analysts attribute the high labor-force participation rates of women in areas where there are electronic industries to this demand, which draws into the labor force women who had not previously been a formal part of it.[130]

Whatever the cause of the predominance of female workers, it carries with it the implication that the phenomenon of assembly abroad has imposed relatively greater costs on female workers as the U.S. assembly force has contracted. Since in many instances it appears that formal female participation in the labor force was stimulated by preference of employers, the transfer of assembly to foreign locations may have exacerbated unemployment among women workers and imposed upon the female labor pool a disproportionate share of the costs of adjusting to shifts in the location of production.

In a Labor Department survey conducted in September 1977 about a fifth of semiconductor production workers were found to be unionized;[131] almost all the unionized plants were in the Northeast, defined to include the mid-Atlantic states. This is probably accounted for largely by the production of the Bell system. About half the production workers in the Northeast were unionized.

### *Net Employment in the U.S. Semiconductor Industry*

The estimates of price elasticity constructed in appendix B can be used to assess the net effect of the trend toward foreign assembly on employment within the U.S. industry. The net effect will reflect a balance between two conflicting forces. On the one hand, foreign assembly leads to a decrease in the unit requirements for U.S. labor per semiconductor. On the

130. See Albert H. Rubenstein and Victor L. Andrews, *The Electronics Industry in New England to 1970* (Boston: Federal Reserve Bank of Boston, December 1959), p. 9. See also the discussion of the female labor force in chapter 4 of this book.

131. U.S. Department of Labor, Bureau of Labor Statistics, *Industry Wage Survey,* p. 2. The unionized workers held a 61 percent wage advantage over their counterparts in unorganized plants, throughout the country, though the advantage drops to 48 percent when only plants in the Northeast are examined and to 31 percent when only large plants in the Northeast are examined.

other hand, a decline in the price of semiconductors leads to increased demand and greater employment. Together, these effects determine the elasticity of the demand for labor with respect to the share of assembly done abroad.

If, as before, it is assumed that during the late 1970s perhaps 70 percent of U.S. semiconductors were assembled abroad, the roughly 29,000 workers shown in table 3-21 who in 1977 worked in assembly occupations in the U.S. industry would have been assembling perhaps 30 percent of U.S. output. If all that year's shipments had instead been assembled in the United States, perhaps another 68,000 assembly jobs would have been created in the U.S. semiconductor industry, more than doubling the 1977 production work force. Higher semiconductor prices would have reduced demand, however, and therefore employment, so further adjustments are required.

Assume, as before, that a reasonable range for the price elasticity of demand for semiconductors is from $-1.5$ to $-3.0$ and that the average semiconductor would be 7–13 percent more expensive without foreign assembly.[132] Column 1 of table 3-23 gives the net gain in U.S. assembly employment after the effects of higher prices on U.S. demand for semiconductors have been taken into account. If it is assumed that both production workers other than assemblers and nonproduction employees are used in fixed proportion to output, the loss of nonassembly employment on account of rising prices can also be calculated and is shown in column 2. Column 3 gives the net gains in employment when changes of both types are added together.

Thus, gains in U.S. assembly employment that might be produced by policies that would force assembly back onto U.S. soil might be offset to a large extent by losses in nonassembly employment. Furthermore, there is good reason to believe that these figures are underestimates of the true losses in nonassembly employment that would be caused by bringing assembly home. Employment in research and development may, to a certain degree, be an input from which increasing returns would be realized in use; a large research effort may be required to produce even a small market

132. Assuming constant returns to scale and given U.S. factor prices, the demand for labor per unit of output will be constant for all types of skill. As in appendix B, the average SCD price used as a base for the calculation of cost differential ($m$) is a weighted average of cost with U.S. and foreign assembly. Note that since a more labor-intensive technology is presumably used in foreign assembly, more assembly jobs would be lost abroad than would be gained in the United States per assembly line transferred back.

Table 3-23. *Direct Effect on Employment of Returning All Semiconductor Assembly to the United States*

Thousands of jobs

| *Demand elasticity* | *Cost differential (m)* | *Net gain, assembly jobs* | *Net loss, nonassembly jobs* | *Net gain, all jobs* |
|---|---|---|---|---|
| −1.5 | 0.07 | 57 | 9 | 48 |
| | 0.10 | 53 | 13 | 40 |
| | 0.13 | 48 | 17 | 32 |
| −2.3 | 0.07 | 52 | 14 | 38 |
| | 0.10 | 45 | 20 | 25 |
| | 0.13 | 38 | 26 | 13 |
| −3.0 | 0.07 | 47 | 18 | 29 |
| | 0.10 | 38 | 26 | 13 |
| | 0.13 | 30 | 33 | −4 |

Source: Author's calculations, described in text. It is assumed that 70 percent of assembly is done abroad and that labor, given U.S. factor prices, is used in fixed proportion to output. The cost differential, *m*, is the same as that used in table 3-19. Figures are rounded.

share. This feature of a high-tech business, along with any economies of scale and learning-curve effects, would push unit costs even higher than the differentials assumed in these calculations.

The estimates suggest a gain of 30,000–60,000 assembly jobs in 1977 if assembly in the United States were required, offset by a loss of 10,000–30,000 jobs in other semiconductor employment. The net effect on employment might be a gain of up to 50,000 jobs, but at a high price: a gain in unskilled employment, but a significant loss in skilled employment caused by reduced demand. The price elasticity of demand for semiconductors is the key parameter, with a more price-elastic demand leading to a contractionary effect on production because of increased costs.

These estimates assume that protectionist policies prevent foreign imports from displacing U.S. products as the U.S. prices of semiconductor devices rise. To take these displacement effects properly into account would require an estimate of the degree to which foreign imports would be substituted for U.S. output as prices rose—an estimate that would be very difficult to obtain. Since the relative importance of assembly costs in output price is fairly small, substitution of foreign imports would probably reduce these job-creation estimates by a small amount. Also, the effect of increases in the prices of semiconductors on other industries has not been considered. Cheaper semiconductors displace other types of components and the workers who produce them. Used as inputs in the electronic equipment industry, they may reduce the demand for labor in the user industries if elimination of the need to wire many discrete components into equipment in lieu of a single integrated circuit more than compensates for the increase in demand for the product attributable to the passing on to the consumer of lower costs. Cheaper semiconductors may also increase demand for workers in industries that supply inputs to the semiconductor sector. The net effects are difficult to predict but are probably not large.

### *The Balance of Payments*

Finally, the effect of assembly abroad on the balance of payments in the U.S. semiconductor industry can be considered. In table 3-24 exports and imports are decomposed into trade not related to foreign assembly and an item that gives the approximate net balance of trade related to foreign assembly. While the 806/807 dutiable value figure is an overstatement of the net drain on foreign exchange attributable to the production-sharing arrangements of U.S. producers—some of the dutiable content may be U.S. materials that are materially transformed abroad or are otherwise ineligible for duty-free reentry—it is clear that production arrangements abroad have absorbed a growing share of the surplus of trade in finished semiconductors. In 1982 foreign assembly for the first time pushed the balance of trade in semiconductors into the red.

This is not to say, of course, that those arrangements have caused the balance of payments to decline. It may well be that by reducing U.S. production costs they have led to an expansion of exports and prevented growth in foreign imports. Also, to some extent, products in which the United States has not yet faced significant international competition might be vulnerable to such competition in the face of price increases. While a quantitative analysis of this question is, in principle, possible, there is little or no information available on the price elasticity of U.S. semiconductor imports and exports in the presence of accelerating Japanese competition in international markets.

### *Summary*

In this section the effects of U.S. production abroad on the structure of the U.S. semiconductor industry have been traced. Assuming that protection prevented an influx of foreign imports, some simple calculations sug-

Table 3-24. *Adjusted Balance of Payments of the U.S. Semiconductor Industry, 1969–82*

Millions of U.S. dollars

| Year | *Nonassembly exports*[a] *(1)* | *Nonassembly imports*[b] *(2)* | *806/807 dutiable value (3)* | *Net balance (1 − 2 − 3) (4)* |
|---|---|---|---|---|
| 1969 | 278 | 8 | 58 | 212 |
| 1970 | 326 | 8 | 69 | 249 |
| 1971 | 276 | 9 | 84 | 183 |
| 1972 | 341 | 75 | 125 | 141 |
| 1973 | 662 | 198 | 226 | 238 |
| 1974 | 937 | 269 | 373 | 295 |
| 1975 | 745 | 185 | 326 | 234 |
| 1976 | 984 | 219 | 477 | 288 |
| 1977 | 886 | 232 | 503 | 151 |
| 1978 | 1,036 | 290 | 592 | 154 |
| 1979 | 1,421 | 511 | 734 | 176 |
| 1980 | 1,870 | 820 | 926 | 124 |
| 1981 | 1,768 | 728 | 1,023 | 17 |
| 1982 | 1,794 | 997 | 1,156 | −359 |

Sources: U.S. Department of Commerce, Bureau of the Census, printouts of total exports and imports of SCDs to 1978; data for 1979 and 1980, ITC, *Summary of Trade and Tariff Information—Semiconductors,* and ITC, *Imports under Items 806.30 and 807.00,* July 1981; data for 1981 and 1982, Bureau of the Census, *FT 246, Imports,* 1981, 1982, and ITC, *Imports under Items 806.30 and 807.00,* January 1984.

a. Total exports less U.S. content of 806/807 imports.

b. Total imports less 806/807 imports.

gest that the relocation of U.S. plants from other countries back to the United States would have been equivalent, roughly, to a welfare loss on the order of perhaps 10 percent of the value of U.S. consumption.

In making these calculations I have ignored the social costs of readjusting and retraining the workers displaced when the move abroad was first made. Such costs may have been substantial, and their effect may have fallen disproportionately on low-income, unskilled women in the U.S. labor force. To some extent participation of these women in the labor force may have been the direct result of the previous employment practices of U.S. electronic firms. On the other hand, there is some evidence that shifting these production jobs abroad may have stabilized employment in the U.S. semiconductor industry as a whole, since nonproduction employment is affected less by business-cycle fluctuations.

The magnitude of these employment losses has been substantial, with perhaps 30,000 to 60,000 jobs associated with the repatriation of U.S. semiconductor assembly back to the United States. But it is assumed that protectionist policies eliminate the danger that a rise in U.S. costs will lead to loss of market share to foreign imports. In the long run, very little in the way of employment might be gained without production abroad if the industry remained open to international competition.

Finally, a cursory examination of the balance of payments in the U.S. industry shows that the imported value added in products assembled abroad substantially reduced what otherwise would have been a very large positive balance of trade in finished goods. Again, however, the cost increases associated with a return of assembly to the United States might have substantially cut U.S. producers' share of the domestic market—in the absence of protection—and driven the balance of payments into the red.

In sum, foreign assembly arrangements have indirectly benefited the U.S. consumer. Significant numbers of workers, however, have been displaced by the movement abroad, and unskilled female workers, in particular, are likely to have suffered the costs of adjustment.

## Effects of Foreign Assembly on Developing Countries

In evaluating the effects of assembly abroad, a host government is likely to focus on five sets of socioeconomic effects. First, because most developing countries are faced with significant problems of open unemployment and underemployment, the effects of operations that absorb unskilled labor are bound to be of fundamental importance. Second, because foreign exchange is generally a scarce—often rationed—commodity in these host countries, the net effect on the balance of payments and the availability of foreign exchange are of great importance. Third, many developing countries have selected industrialization as an explicit development strategy, and the contribution of foreign assembly to this process is of interest. Similarly, the possible importance of this type of foreign investment in transferring more advanced technology to the developing areas must be considered. Finally, the possible long-term implications of orienting the industrial economy to foreign markets and to technical developments over which the host has little or no control raise the issue of the effects of this type of manufacture on the stability of the host economy and its dependence on foreign markets.

*Employment*

While reliable and detailed information is difficult to obtain, the data do permit some conclusions. The available information on employment in the electronics industries of the principal Asian assembly countries is summarized in table 3-25. It is clear that while employment in the electronics sector grew rapidly in all these countries during the 1970s, it absorbed a fraction of the labor force that ranged from about 1 percent in Malaysia to 7 percent in Singapore. If only industrial employment is considered, however, electronics becomes considerably more important.

In Singapore, where electronics is most important, the industry accounts for 7 percent of both GNP and the labor force, a fifth of manufacturing value added, and a quarter of the manufacturing work force.[133] About 60 percent of electronic output consists of components, mainly integrated circuits and other semiconductors.[134] About 95 percent of employment and of output are accounted for by multinational electronics firms.[135]

Foreign subsidiaries of firms located in industrial countries also dominate employment in many of the other Asian electronics industries. The available data on the foreign and domestic employment of U.S. and Japanese electronic component firms are summarized in table 3-26. Both countries' firms had about 100,000 workers each in Asia in the late 1970s.[136] Employment, along with output, seems to have taken off in the early 1970s, after slower growth through most of the 1960s.[137]

133. Wolfgang Hillebrand and others, "Industrial Restructuring in Singapore—Technological Decision-Making and International Cooperation in the Electronics Industry" (Berlin: German Development Institute, 1981; mimeographed), pp. 14–15.

134. Ibid., pp. 15, 19, 52. ICs alone constituted almost 40 percent of electronics exports in 1980, other semiconductors (and tubes) another 14 percent. Domestic sales of components amounted to less than 10 percent of exports.

135. Ibid., p. I.

136. Most of the U.S. firms manufacturing components, as noted earlier, are manufacturers of semiconductors, while only 10–20 percent of Japanese employment is on SCD lines.

137. Some fragmentary information indicates the way semiconductor employment abroad has grown. Employment by the principal semiconductor firms of all nationalities in 1971 and 1974 was surveyed in an UNCTAD study of production sharing in electronics. The firms in the sample accounted for about 51.4 percent of world semiconductor sales in 1972. This can be seen from the market shares of the firms in the sample as published in Webbink, *The Semiconductor Industry,* p. 22.

The results suggest that semiconductor producers of all nationalities in the developed countries employed about 20,000 workers in their foreign semiconductor operations in 1971 and perhaps three to four times as many in 1974. Roughly three quarters of the employment

Table 3-25. *Significance of Employment in Asian Electronics Industries, Selected Years, 1970–79*

| Country | Employees in Asian electronics industries (thousands) | | | | | | Population of working age, 1979[a] (millions) | Percent of labor force in industry, 1979 |
|---|---|---|---|---|---|---|---|---|
| | 1970 | 1971 | 1972 | 1973 | 1975 | 1979 | | |
| Korea | n.a. | n.a. | n.a. | 86 | n.a. | 180 | 23.1 | 30 |
| Taiwan | n.a. | n.a. | n.a. | 99 | n.a. | 230 | 10.6[b] | 27[b] |
| Hong Kong | 37 | 45 | 41 | n.a. | n.a. | 94 | 3.3 | 57 |
| Singapore | 11 | n.a. | 27 | 24 | 32 | 67 | 1.6 | 38 |
| Malaysia | 6 | 7 | n.a. | n.a. | n.a. | 55 | 7.2 | 16 |
| Philippines | n.a. | n.a. | n.a. | n.a. | 21 | 35 | 30.1 | 17 |

Sources: Population of working age and percent of labor force in industry, World Bank, *World Development Report, 1981* (New York: Oxford University Press, 1981), tables 1 and 19; employment in electronics industries, JEMIA, *Internationalization and Its Impact,* p.180; "Hong Kong Outlook: Sweet and Sour," *Electronics,* December 7, 1970, pp. 115–16; "New Offshore Explosion," ibid., December 4, 1972, pp. 69–72; S. C. Suh, "Development of a New Industry through Exports: The Electronics Industry in Korea," in Wontack Hong and Anne O. Krueger, eds., *Trade and Development in Korea* (Seoul: Korea Development Institute, 1975), p. 117; Wolfgang Hillebrand and others, "Industrial Restructuring in Singapore: Technological Decision-Making and International Cooperation in the Electronics Industry," mimeographed (Berlin: German Development Institute, 1981), p. 15; U.S. Department of Commerce, Global Market Survey, *Electronics Industry Production and Test Equipment* (GPO, April 1974); and "Philippines Plans to Stress Growth in 80's," *Asian Wall Street Journal Weekly,* June 9, 1980, p. 17.

n.a. Not available.

a. Between the ages of fifteen and sixty-four.

b. Figure for 1977.

Table 3-26. *Foreign Employment of Foreign Affiliates of U.S. Firms, 1977, and Japanese Firms, 1979*

Thousands of employees

| Country or region of employment | Producers of electronic components (SIC 367) | | |
|---|---|---|---|
| | U.S. firms, 1977 | | |
| | Majority-owned affiliates | All affiliates | Japanese firms, 1979, all affiliates |
| All foreign employment | 185 | 219 | 99 |
| Europe | 52 | 62 | 0.1 |
| Japan | 3 | n.a. | ... |
| Other countries of Asia and the Pacific | 95 | 101 | 89 |
| Latin America | 24 | 37 | 5 |
| North America | ... | ... | 1 |
| *Addendum* | | | |
| Home industry employment, electronic components | ... | 374 | 228[a] |

Sources: U.S. firms, U.S. Department of Commerce, Bureau of Economic Analysis, *U.S. Direct Investment Abroad, 1977,* pp. 149, 295; Japanese firms, JEMIA, *Internationalization and Its Impact,* p. 2; home industry employment, U.S. Department of Commerce, Bureau of the Census, *1977 Census of Manufactures* (GPO, 1980); and U.S. Department of Commerce, Industry and Trade Administration, "Country Market Survey, Electronic Components, Japan," in *Global Market Survey: Electronic Components* (GPO, June 1978).

n.a. Not available.

a. For 1978.

The great bulk of U.S. operations are located in Taiwan, Singapore, Malaysia, and Hong Kong. It seems likely that at least half of electronics employment in Singapore—most of which is probably in semiconductors—and Malaysia was associated with U.S. subsidiaries, and perhaps a quarter of electronics employment in Hong Kong and Taiwan was generated by U.S. subsidiaries.[138]

While these figures represent a respectable number of jobs, they are at best a marginal contribution to the reduction of unemployment in most Asian countries. It might be argued that there are multiplier effects, since foreign assembly operations might stimulate the growth of industries that could use the assembled components in exports of other electronic goods. Even in Singapore, however, where integration of the components industry into a local electrical equipment industry is most advanced, local sales constituted less than 13 percent of component production and about 17 percent of all electronics output in 1979.[139]

---

in 1971, and roughly 85 percent in 1974, was by U.S. firms. The greatest growth took place in Singapore and Malaysia. See UNCTAD, *International Subcontracting Arrangements,* Supplement 1, pp. 17–18.

This description of the timing of the move abroad, which is in rough accord with the output index constructed earlier, conflicts with other published estimates. See in particular the series given in U.S. Department of Commerce, *The U.S. Semiconductor Industry,* p. 84, which is based on information given in Finan, "The International Transfer."

U.S. employment abroad in electronics during the early years was also estimated in 1970 by Roger Stobaugh on the basis of information furnished him by the U.S. Electronics Industries Association. See Stobaugh, "The Economic Effects of the United States Electronic Industries' Use of Item 807.00 Tariff Schedules of the United States," submitted to the House Committee on Ways and Means, Trade and Tariff Proposals Hearings, 91 Cong. 2 sess., June 4, 1970, pp. 2849–57.

138. The geographical distribution of employment by U.S. affiliates producing electrical equipment, including components, in 1977, in thousands of employees, was

| | |
|---|---|
| Hong Kong | 18.8 |
| Indonesia | 5.3 |
| Malaysia | 23.6 |
| Philippines | 8.9 |
| Singapore | 25.2 |
| South Korea | 8.5 |
| Taiwan | 47.7 |
| Total, developing Asia and the Pacific | 158.4 |

U.S. Department of Commerce, *U.S. Direct Investment Abroad, 1977,* p. 38. A comparison of these figures with those given in table 3-25 yields the inferences offered in the text.

139. Hillebrand and others, "Industrial Restructuring in Singapore," pp. 15–16, 52.

*The Balance of Payments*

The little empirical evidence that exists suggests that foreign-owned semiconductor-assembly operations use significant amounts of nonlabor national inputs. This can be seen in table 3-27, in which the income and costs of U.S. electronic components affiliates in Asia are disaggregated into imported and national components. As remarked earlier, an overwhelming share of the output of these affiliates consists of semiconductors. The table shows that imports from the United States account for more than 40 percent of sales, and net profits, fees, and royalties another 5 percent.[140] The remaining 54 percent of sales is paid out in employee compensation, taxes, utilities and overhead, and purchase of inputs, some of which are imported from other countries.

To calculate the domestic resource costs of this foreign exchange, the various components of the 54 percent of sales composed of national inputs would have to be identified and priced appropriately.[141] Unfortunately,

140. In this instance total income and total sales are virtually synonymous, as can be seen by examining the data for majority-owned foreign affiliates (MOFAs). Total sales of affiliates other than MOFAs are not available.

141. To evaluate the effect of foreign assembly on the host country's foreign-exchange position and balance of payments, a conceptually precise approach would be to calculate the domestic resource costs of the nationally produced inputs used in assembly per dollar of foreign exchange produced and to compare the calculations with the domestic resource costs of earning a dollar of foreign exchange in alternative activities. If the only national input used were labor, the net inflow of foreign exchange would equal employee compensation plus whatever taxes on the profits of foreign operations were collected by the host country. The domestic resource costs of a dollar of foreign exchange would be the wage bill divided by the latter sum and multiplied by the appropriate exchange rate. If the price charged for labor supplied to foreign producers differed from the opportunity cost of labor used in the national economy, the wage bill in the numerator would have to be corrected for the divergence of market price from marginal social cost. In effect the wages of workers and income taxes are paid in foreign exchange, at a social cost to the domestic economy of the value of the workers' services forgone in the domestic economy. If workers are paid more by foreign producers than in the national economy, costs per dollar of exchange will decline.

On the other hand, if national inputs other than labor are used, the calculation will have to take into account the social costs of directing those resources from the national economy into the export enclave. A calculation of the domestic resource costs of assembly for export, then, will be greatly affected by the amount and type of national resources used. In particular, an export-oriented assembly operation using capital drawn from local capital markets—a factory established by a national entrepreneur, for example, that subcontracts assembly operations with foreign principals—may incur much higher domestic resource costs, especially if capital is very dear, as it usually is in a developing economy. Also, if the assembly operation, even if financed entirely by foreign capital, requires investments in infrastructure by the host country, the cost of those investments must be added into the domestic resource costs of the foreign exchange.

Table 3-27. *Income and Costs of U.S. Affiliates among the Developing Countries of Asia and the Pacific in the Manufacture of Electronic Components, 1977*

| *Element of income or cost* | *Millions of dollars* | *Percent of total income* |
|---|---|---|
| Total income | 1,622 | 100.0 |
| *Less:* Inputs imported from the United States | 661 | 40.8 |
| *Less:* Direct investment income[a] | 54 | 3.3 |
| *Less:* Net remittances of fees and royalties to parent firms | 22 | 1.4 |
| Net inflow of foreign exchange | 885 | 54.5 |
| Employment compensation | 195 | 12.0 |
| Operating expenses, overhead, taxes, inputs | 690 | 42.5 |

Source: U.S. Department of Commerce, Bureau of Economic Analysis, *U.S. Direct Investment Abroad, 1977.* Figures are rounded.

a. Reinvested earnings have not been subtracted.

lack of information on the structure of these costs prevents calculation of the socially correct shadow prices.

It is possible, however, to gauge the importance of semiconductor exports in terms of gross flows of foreign exchange. Table 3-28 displays the value of semiconductor production and exports of a number of Asian countries in 1979, in comparison with exports of manufactured goods and merchandise. Semiconductors are a large and significant share of the manufactured exports of Singapore, Taiwan, and the Philippines.[142]

While the precise contribution of semiconductor exports to the economic welfare of the host economies cannot be calculated, since the absence of data makes it impossible to compare foreign exchange earned from these activities with the alternatives, it is clear that they are a substantial source of foreign exchange for those economies. They are also a significant factor in the industrialization of those economies, as can be seen by their importance in manufactured exports and industrial employment.

### *Transfer of Technology*

Discussions of the transfer of technology through the foreign operations of multinational firms tend to be focused on two distinct sets of issues. The

142. In the Philippines exports of semiconductors soared from negligible levels in the early 1970s to half a billion dollars in 1980. See "Energy Development Export Incentives, Joint Venture Opportunities—The Philippines," *Business Week,* June 16, 1980, p. 36. In 1980 Philippine exports of SCDs amounted to almost $516 million and manufactured exports to a little more than $2 billion. See "Philippines Offers Significant Business Opportunities, U.S. Embassy Study Says," *Asian Wall Street Journal Weekly,* April 13, 1981, p. 3, special advertising section.

Table 3-28. *Importance of Semiconductors in the Manufactured Exports of Selected Developing Countries in Asia and Latin America, 1979*

| | *Exports of active components to developed countries*[a] | | | *Manufactured exports* | |
|---|---|---|---|---|---|
| *Country* | *Millions of dollars* | *Percent to the United States* | *Percent to Japan* | *Millions of dollars* | *As percent of all exports of merchandise* |
| Hong Kong | 151.3 | 60 | 2 | 15,156 | 54 |
| Singapore | 590.6 | 72 | 1 | 14,233 | 46 |
| Philippines | 274.4 | 76 | 10 | 4,601 | 29 |
| Malaysia | 792.3 | 84 | 3 | 11,077 | 16 |
| Korea | 371.5 | 72 | 17 | 15,055 | 58 |
| Taiwan[b] | 401[c] | n.a. | n.a. | 6,922 | 85 |
| Indonesia | 35.1 | 95 | 0 | 15,590 | 2 |
| Thailand | 52.0 | 99 | 0 | 5,288 | 15 |
| Brazil | 24.8 | 61 | 0 | 15,244 | 34 |
| Mexico | 138.1 | 99 | 0 | 8,768 | 36 |
| El Salvador | 54.2 | 91 | 2 | 1,029 | 16 |
| Barbados | 12.0 | 99 | 0 | n.a. | n.a. |
| Haiti | 4.1 | 56 | 0 | 184 | 32 |

Sources: Exports of active components, SITC 729.3, United Nations Statistical Office, *World Trade Annual, 1979;* manufactured exports, World Bank, *World Development Report* (Washington, D.C.: World Bank, 1982, 1983).

n.a. Not available.

a. Includes tubes as well as SCDs, as reported in the import statistics of twenty-four developed countries.

b. Figures for Taiwan are for 1976 and are based on World Bank, *World Development Report,* 1979, and U.S. Department of Commerce, *Global Market Survey—Electronic Components* (GPO, 1978).

c. Production of semiconductors.

first is whether workers gain valuable skills and discipline through their work in these firms. This issue will be discussed elsewhere in this book. The only point to be added here is that a semiconductor assembler reaches peak efficiency after about two or three months of experience, which does not indicate that a particularly high level of skill is attained.[143]

The second issue, and by far the most intriguing from the point of view of the host, is whether valuable process and product technology is transferred as nationals from the host country observe the technology of production, distribution, and sales. Semiconductor assembly using manual techniques is not a particularly difficult industrial process, and nationals from various countries have set up contract assembly plants, relying upon subcontracting arrangements with firms in developed countries for their business. Firms in the Philippines are particularly well known as independent subcontractors in semiconductor assembly.[144]

143. " 'No Hands' Assembly Packages Chips," *Electronics,* June 2, 1981, p. 38.

144. Some have permanent offices in "Silicon Valley," in California, where the arrangements are made. A Philippine subcontractor has even set up a U.S. assembly line using Philippine immigrant labor. *Northern California Electronic News,* May 12, 1980.

Though it may be argued that the value of this sort of simple assembly technology is low, the increasing complexity of the operations performed and equipment used in foreign plants is raising the technological level. Discrete semiconductors were being manufactured by local producers in Hong Kong by the early 1970s and more complex integrated circuit chips were being produced in Korea and Taiwan by the late 1970s.[145] A growing number of American firms began to locate complex testing equipment in Asia during the 1970s and, more recently, automated assembly equipment.[146]

Foreign assembly operations may therefore have been indirectly related to the technology used by local producers in chip manufacture.[147] While local entrepreneurs have successfully started contract assembly plants for semiconductors, which may have been related to experience in and observation of the operations abroad of foreign firms, experience in assembly is of limited relevance to the manufacture of the heart of the device, the etched silicon chip.[148] It is questionable just how much technology can be

145. See U.S. Department of Commerce, Domestic and International Business Administration, *Global Market Survey—Electronic Components* (GPO, October 1974); "Semiconductor Ventures Could Signal Hong Kong Shift to High Technology," *Asian Wall Street Journal Weekly,* February 16, 1981, p. 6; and "Gold Star Semiconductor Raising Loan for Move into Advanced Electronics," ibid., April 13, 1981, p. 7. Two local manufacturers began producing ICs in Hong Kong in early 1982; see "Two Firms Begin Making Hong Kong's First Chips," ibid., April 5, 1982, p. 20.

146. See "U.S. Firm's Plan to Assemble Semiconductors on West Coast Could Threaten Asian Producers," *Asian Wall Street Journal Weekly,* June 28, 1980, p. 16; ITC, *Competitive Factors,* p. 6; *Trade and Technology,* testimony of Robert Noyce before the Subcommittee on International Finance of the Senate Committee on Banking, Housing, and Urban Affairs, 96 Cong. 2 sess., January 15, 1980, p. 113; "The Drive for Quality and Reliability," *Electronics,* May 19, 1981, pp. 132, 145; "Automation May Erase Offshore Edge," ibid., April 21, 1982, p. 95; and Hillebrand and others, "Industrial Restructuring in Singapore," p. 48.

147. Direct transfer of technology has been based on joint ventures, such as Gold Star Semiconductor of Korea, one of the few non-Japanese Asian firms to produce its own chips, a joint venture with AT&T's Western Electric manufacturing arm, and on sending engineers to the United States for training and importing foreign production engineers, as did the manufacturers who recently began production of ICs in Hong Kong (see note 145). One Hong Kong firm is "sending its local engineers to a California semiconductor company with which it has close connections." The Hong Kong firms are thought to expect China to be an important market for their output, emphasizing the difficulty of preventing the export of technology, even when strict controls are placed on the export of the products that embody it.

148. Firms generally prefer to set up their own operations abroad, because it is cheaper—perhaps because capital is cheaper for them—but smaller firms not yet ready to absorb the fixed setup cost often choose to subcontract assembly. See Finan, "The International Transfer," p. 63; and Dicken, "How to Determine Fair Market Prices," p. 83.

transferred without the educational and research infrastructure that is required for its successful application. In fact, the experience of Japan seems to indicate that technology can be acquired successfully without direct investment, as long as the resources of skill and manpower that are needed to transmit it exist and access to proprietary knowledge can be negotiated. All the investment in the world will not transmit technology if the educated manpower required as a medium of transmission is lacking.[149] Training in assembly operations can add to the local stock of managerial and technical skills.[150]

In both Malaysia and Singapore, semiconductor firms have developed linkages to local vendors, most of them plastics companies and machine shops.[151] In a less developed economy, however, the skills and technology developed through these linkages are not necessarily of immediate use. In Malaysia, for example, where supporting machine shops do 80 percent of their business with semiconductor companies, there is little demand in the local economy for high-tolerance machining.[152]

### *Stability and Dependence*

Other important effects of assembly plants on a host economy have to do with the degree of stability and the dependence on foreign markets. If it did not cost anything for a developing country to shift resources to assembly activities, this would not be an issue. But shifting unemployed or displaced workers and fixed infrastructural or industry-specific investments are costs to the economy when demand falls in the industry in which those resources are employed. Variation in the level of output imposes costs on an economy, and the stability of demand is a factor with economic value when the return on resources committed to an industry is calculated. Insta-

149. Korean authorities, for example, acknowledge frankly that skilled manpower is the primary bottleneck in the future development of technology-intensive industries, including the semiconductor industry. See Korea Development Institute, *Long-Term Prospects for Economic and Social Development, 1977–91* (Seoul: KDI, 1978), pp. 149–50. Lack of technical skills has also been a constraint on the effort to create a technologically advanced electronics industry in Singapore. See Hillebrand and others, "Industrial Restructuring in Singapore," pp. 50–70.

150. In Malaysia, roughly half of a group of former managers and technicians worked outside the semiconductor industry. See Mark Lester, "Export Processing Zones and Technology Transfer in Malaysia," *Journal of the Flagstaff Institute,* 1981, p. 30.

151. Ibid., pp. 23–29; and Hillebrand and others, "Industrial Restructuring in Singapore," pp. 56–58.

152. Lester, "Export Processing Zones," p. 29.

bility also causes a certain amount of economic and political dependence. If demand can be affected by the decisions of some group, that group has a measure of bargaining power in its relations with the economy. Rather than shoulder the costs of shuffling resources about, policymakers in the host country may find it wiser to make economic concessions of a lesser cost.

In that sense dependence does not seem an important feature of the international semiconductor industry because of the fiercely competitive nature of the industry—as opposed, say, to some of the natural-resources industries. There have been few suggestions that foreign assembly operations, acting in concert, have been able to influence host-country economic policy decisions by threatening to close or reduce their operations.[153]

Yet cyclical instability is an important feature of the demand for electronics. An economy that places a significant share of its labor force or its capital in an electronics industry producing products for export may face a severe cost when the trough of the world business cycle hits. Ironically, business-cycle swings have had much more drastic effects on the home industry than on operations abroad, since firms are inclined to shut down their higher-cost home operations when rationalizing operations. Electronics assembly operations, for example, continued to be initiated in Malaysia and Singapore during the recessions of the 1970s.[154]

### *The "Footloose Industry" Issue*

The low transport costs and high mobility that led to the original migration of the semiconductor industry overseas might make local production levels sensitive to changes in the costs and attractiveness of a particular host country and, therefore, somewhat unstable. Variations in costs and political conditions have been accompanied at times by drastic and rapid changes in the international distribution of assembled output. It is easily shifted; even in a less developed economy, electronics assembly is much less capital-intensive than most other industrial activities.[155]

153. Nonetheless, firms generally choose to invest in areas in which labor, tax, and tariff policies are to their liking, and this fact has certainly influenced host countries to change their policies in an effort to attract investment.

154. Lester, "Export Processing Zones," p. 19; and Hillebrand and others, "Industrial Restructuring in Singapore," pp. 7–9.

155. In Singapore in 1979, for example, the electronics industry used about 40 percent of the net fixed assets per worker found in all manufacturing. See Hillebrand and others, "Industrial Restructuring in Singapore," p. 25.

Offsetting this sensitivity to cost factors is the importance of diversification of country-specific risks in the decisions of firms about where to produce or purchase inputs. Various sorts of evidence, from the statements of the managers of multinational semiconductor firms to the observed changes in the patterns of 806/807 imports, suggest that the diversification of country-specific risk in production is an important objective of firms engaged in production abroad.

Taking account of the riskiness of production abroad adds considerable complexity to a realistic analysis of the production location decisions of firms. Clearly, finding the least-cost location is not the sine qua non of selecting a production site abroad. Rather, a risk-averse producer should logically diversify production among a portfolio of sites, with considerable variation among average costs in these locations a distinct possibility. A simple model of production sharing that captures in a reasonably realistic way the problem of diversifying production location to reduce the political risks of foreign investment has been applied to actual data on the offshore operations of the U.S. semiconductor industry.[156] The analysis indicated that producers in that industry react quickly to perceived changes in costs and risks in the optimum location of their facilities abroad and that the optimal investment in any country is itself fairly sensitive to wage changes. Nevertheless, the reasonably high elasticity of output with respect to the

156. The econometric estimates imply that producers adjust investment portfolios rapidly in response to changes in production costs. The estimated coefficients of the model also seem to indicate that U.S. duty-free component–output ratios are fixed. Since the preponderant ingredient in the value of a U.S. duty-free component is an unassembled semiconductor chip, this merely confirms that the chip content of an assembled semiconductor is unaffected by the wage rate charged to the producer.

It is also possible to estimate the partial equilibrium elasticity of optimal capital invested in a location with respect to the wage in that location. It is a partial equilibrium estimate of the wage elasticity of investment, because various portfolio constants, reflecting the risks and returns available in financial markets, will also be altered as the rate of return in a location changes. If investment in a location is very small in relation to the size of the entire market portfolio of risky assets, however, these effects can be ignored by those who are concerned with the first-order effects of a marginal wage change on investment in one of many production locations.

The analysis indicated that the share of a location in all assets invested in the production of semiconductors responded to changes in wage rates with an elasticity close to $-1$. This would imply that moderately large changes in investment and production might be expected from changes in tax or wage policies that alter the return on investment in a particular location. See Kenneth Flamm, "The Volatility of Offshore Investment," *Journal of Development Economics,* forthcoming.

wage may also mean that a substantial monopoly rent can be extracted by setting taxes or wages correctly.[157]

## Conclusions

Like more pedestrian products, semiconductors were first pushed out of the country by the pressures of competition and an obliging technology that permitted the separation of labor-intensive assembly processes.

### *International Competition*

The move to foreign locations by the U.S. semiconductor industry was born in the fires of Japanese competition, beginning as an essentially defensive response to imports of cheap foreign transistors. It was also international competition, but of a different sort, that prompted a belated Japanese entry into assembling semiconductors in other countries. Factories were established during the late 1970s with the primary aim of servicing exports of consumer electronics to markets in industrial countries from Southeast Asian export platforms. The motivation for establishing these facilities was to gain access to the markets, and labor cost was a secondary consideration.

The major Japanese push in semiconductors, though, was reserved for the only real mass market, that for computer memory chips. It is in this arena that U.S. firms have been most threatened by Japanese competition. High levels of quality and reliability, important in components used in expensive equipment, such as computers, assisted in penetration of the market, and together with the large market tipped the economic balance in favor of assembly in highly automated facilities in Japan. Even here, however, growing protectionist sentiment within the United States and Europe has prompted Japanese producers to head off future conflict by setting up assembly lines within these markets.[158]

157. Since in many countries—Mexico and Haiti, for example—assembly wages are higher than wage levels within the domestic economy, there is some evidence that the benefits of such policies are already evident to national planners. Singapore, in particular, has used its wage policy both as a tool for switching its industrial base to less labor-intensive industries and as a way of charging a rent for what is widely perceived as a highly stable investment environment.

158. See footnote 108. The Japanese have also invested heavily in European production facilities within the tariff walls of the Common Market. See "Going for a Bigger Bite of the EC Chip Market," *Business Week,* October 6, 1980, p. 47.

In Japan, technology policy has been carefully coordinated with trade policy. Market access by foreign firms was limited and was used to force the licensing of key technologies to Japanese producers. Important projects were directed and financed under government auspices. Relatively cheap capital was channeled into the industry and probably hastened the adoption of automated lines.[159] Specialization in and cartelization of specific product lines reduced duplication.

While European firms were quick to follow U.S. producers of semiconductor devices onto the Asian export platforms, government policies within the EC quickly stanched the flows to these locations. In Europe, the intimate link between industrial policies and the structure of production is clearest. There, high levels of tariff protection make it uneconomical to import, except for the simplest devices, most of whose costs are attributable to labor-intensive assembly and packaging operations. For such highly labor-intensive devices, the huge difference in labor cost between the Far East and Europe can even offset the very high tariff charges. For more complex devices, where the chip and other materials represent a significantly larger part of the cost of the finished device, even the use of the outward-processing tariff provisions, when it is permitted, offers little relief, since the net effect of these provisions is still to impose a significant tax on the material content of the chip upon reimportation. Most production for the European market—whether by European, Japanese, or U.S. firms—is, as a consequence, assembled within the tariff walls of the EC.

European trade policy during this period is probably best interpreted as an effort to obtain technology cheaply: an attempt to force foreign manufacturers to set up operations in Europe as a means of encouraging joint ventures with European partners, the transfer of technology, and the creation of a strong indigenous European industry. The high tariff walls have been most effective in getting foreign-based manufacturers to set up affiliates in Europe. They have not proved effective in making European firms internationally competitive. More recently, European governments have been turning to subsidy policies as a means of increasing the competitiveness and technological competence of national producers.

159. For noneconomic, as well as purely economic, reasons. Because Japanese semiconductor firms have benefited from implicit or explicit government subsidies to investment, it seems unlikely that they could make use of these funds without paying attention to national priorities. It can be argued that part of the implicit social contract in Japanese industry, to which firms, workers, and the government are parties, is that in exchange for peace and cooperation from labor and assistance from the government, producers are committed to maintaining Japanese employment wherever it is possible to do so.

The policies that shaped the industry in the United States were much more uncoordinated and fragmented than were those in Europe and Japan, but they were equally effective in forming the industrial structure. Trade was considerably freer in the U.S. market; tariff levels have generally been lower than in all other markets, and the 806/807 tariff provisions were devised just as the move to foreign assembly began. Ironically, the 807 item was of little importance in the initial movement abroad, since labor content, then the principal cost in production, coupled with the vastly lower wage rates in Southeast Asia, swamped any savings in cost attributable to 806/807.[160] In recent years, increasing chip complexity has reduced the relative importance of labor cost and has probably made the 806/807 provisions a significant factor in some location decisions.[161] If current proposals to drop tariffs on high-technology products are implemented, tariff items 806/807 will no longer be used in the semiconductor industry.

While no explicit industrial policy shaped the U.S. industry, military demand for semiconductors was central to its development in the 1950s and early 1960s and is once again increasing in importance. Military users have special requirements for quality and reliability; every device must work properly every time. Commercial users, on the other hand, face a trade-off between cost and quality and can select the profit-maximizing combination. Every part supplied to military specifications was required to be inspected, tested, and "burned in" during prolonged operation by equipment manufacturers; these brute-force methods of quality control, required by the military, became standard in the American electronics industry. Japanese producers, on the other hand, who were completely dependent on the commercial electronics market, were free to adopt entirely statistical approaches to quality control, concentrating on improving processes of manufacture to the point where the defect rate was low enough to eliminate the need for costly and time-consuming testing and burn-in procedures.

Even more important, military demand has probably pulled American resources away from mass-market applications to custom military systems

160. See U.S. Tariff Commission, *Economic Factors Affecting the Use*, pp. 216–17.

161. See "U.S. Firm's Plan to Assemble Semiconductors on West Coast Could Threaten Asian Producers," *Asian Wall Street Journal Weekly*, June 28, 1980, p. 16. When cost comparisons are made, a critical difference between U.S. and Japanese producers is that Japanese-made chips are charged duty upon entry into the United States, while U.S.-made chips entering under the 806/807 tariff provisions are not.

with much smaller production runs and smaller commercial potential. While of great value in developing certain types of basic research, these systems have offered fewer opportunities for developing automated production technologies. Also, the long lead times on military systems often mean that they embody outdated technologies.[162] Both the military quality requirements and the scale of military systems have worked against the automation of assembly and testing by U.S. military contractors.

While assembly abroad has become important in other sectors faced with stiff competition, low transport costs, and significant labor content—apparel and television, for example—the semiconductor industry, marked by its obvious strategic importance, exemplifies the importance of state actions in determining the patterns of international trade and investment. It is thus clear that trade and industrial policies are crucial to an understanding of the fact that such vastly different production arrangements characterize the operations of U.S., Japanese, and European producers. Still, such policies have channeled underlying forces that are technological and economic in nature. In the face of a rapidly changing technology and a recent move toward significantly more protectionist and nationalist government policies, it is not clear that the current organization of production will persist.

*The Future of Assembly Abroad*

Advances in automation and the decreasing costs of automating assembly lines have recently triggered further discussion within the U.S. industry of the comparative costs of automating and having products assembled abroad.[163] Such discussion touches upon only one of many factors that make assembly abroad attractive, however, and it may be worth while to sketch out the principal points that will determine the way the present international structure of the semiconductor industry will change.

A number of powerful forces are at work that will maintain the cost advantages of a foreign production base. First and foremost, rapid technological advance in electronics seems certain to continue and will shorten

162. See "Cadence Slow for Military Sales," *Electronics,* August 25, 1982, pp. 76–77. The U.S. military, under the aegis of the VHSIC and other programs, is now directly funding the development of automated production technologies. See "Air Force to Recruit Robots for PC Boards," ibid., August 25, 1981, pp. 49–50; and "VHSIC Proposals Take Six Fast Tracks," ibid., September 22, 1981, pp. 89–96.

163. See "Automation May Erase Offshore Edge," *Electronics,* April 21, 1982, p. 95; and "Full Automation of IC Assembly Will Push Productivity to New Highs," ibid., August 11, 1982, p. 131.

even further the life of any new electronic product. Speeding up the rate of technical advance has even been advocated by U.S. firms as an effective counterattack against Japanese competition, with the objective of rendering obsolete the large fixed investments in capital-intensive factories and production technology that the Japanese have favored.[164] Technological advance will therefore continue to work against automated assembly at home.

The nature of the technological advance that continues will also tend to favor production abroad. As chip producers achieve greater levels of integration, cramming more devices onto a chip, manufacturers of electrical equipment will put more of their circuitry onto a single chip. This will lead to a proliferation of customized chips—and therefore to production on a smaller scale—favoring assembly technologies that do not require large fixed investments and are therefore more likely to be found abroad. Continued advances in the more general technologies of transport and communication will also favor continued movement abroad.

There are also factors working against foreign operations. Technology leads this list as well, since the continued cheapening of intelligence and control functions in production equipment makes automated bonding and assembly more attractive financially. Continual increases in the density of components on an integrated circuit discourage assembly abroad by making labor costs less and less important as a component of manufacturing costs. Other costs created by foreign operations—such as the need to hold inventories of increasingly expensive parts—will increase as chips become more complex and expensive, making assembly abroad less rewarding. Increasing emphasis on chip quality will also work in favor of automation and against labor-intensive assembly techniques.

Any rise in political and economic instability in the developing world will increase the perceived risks to capital and discourage foreign operations. As automation becomes cheaper, manufacturers may hesitate before installing newer and more expensive capacity abroad. The vulnerability of sophisticated equipment for the production of semiconductors to any sort of disruption is extreme.[165]

164. To quote an industry executive, "Innovation is the key. I think what we need to do is to have ways of obsoleting their capacity by the time they move on line." See "Semiconductors Face Worldwide Challenge," *Electronics,* May 19, 1982, p. 139.

165. Black soot producd by a fire in 1982 at the modern plant of a Japanese producer, which was turning out a million 64K memory chips a month, was expected to shut down production entirely for more than two months, and output was not expected to reach even 80 percent of the old level for perhaps six months. See "Oki Fire Halts 64-K RAM Production," *Electronics,* October 20, 1982, p. 75.

Rising protectionist sentiment in the industrial countries will also limit expansion abroad. While this will probably have little effect on production for the U.S. market, where U.S. producers have a substantial stake in easy access to the market for assembly imports, it has choked off European growth abroad and seems now to be checking further expansion by Japanese semiconductor assemblers in developing areas.

On balance, then, the forces producing the present international structure of production in the semiconductor industry seem likely to remain fundamentally unaltered. Europe will probably remain a protected market, largely untouched by foreign assembly arrangements. The Japanese will continue to produce their high-volume exports at home, and—as long as access to the market remains a delicate issue—will not expand their base on export platforms in the developing countries much beyond present levels. There will be some tendency for the more complex products of U.S. firms to be shifted back to automated facilities in the United States, but this will be a marginal readjustment rather than a reorganization of the industry. The U.S. market will therefore remain dependent on foreign assembly and testing. Continued rapid growth in semiconductor output will mean continued growth in foreign assembly. The existence of differentiated markets, of vastly different sizes, for different types and qualities of semiconductor devices, suggests that foreign assembly will remain an important feature of production flows in the international semiconductor industry.

## Appendix A: Estimating Growth in Foreign Assembly

Underlying the calculations of assembly abroad as a fraction of all U.S. shipments is the assumption that, since the U.S. price for a semiconductor is the same no matter where it is assembled and the cost of the U.S. materials used is also roughly the same, the total value added per unit shipped will be the same no matter where the unit is manufactured. Thus, the ratio of the index of value added abroad to the index of value added in the United States *and* abroad will be a function of the fraction of U.S. shipments assembled abroad.

Algebraically, let total value added in U.S. shipments be $TVA$, value added overseas in U.S. shipments $OVA$, U.S. value added in U.S. shipments $UVA$, value added abroad per unit assembled abroad $V_{off}$, total value added per unit (a constant) $V_{tot}$, units assembled offshore $X_{off}$, and all units assembled $X_{tot}$. Then $TVA = OVA + UVA = V_{tot} \cdot X_{tot}$; $OVA = V_{off} \cdot X_{off}$; and $OVA/TVA = (X_{off}/X_{tot}) \cdot (V_{off}/V_{tot})$.

If $OVA$ is not directly observable but is proportional to some index $I_{off}$, with constant of proportionality $k$, we have:

$$X_{off}/X_{tot} = (V_{tot}/V_{off}) \cdot (OVA/TVA)$$

$$X_{off}/X_{tot} = (V_{tot}/V_{off}) \cdot (kI_{off}/TVA)$$

$$= (V_{tot}/V_{off}) \cdot (kI_{off}/\ (UVA + kI_{off})$$

$$= \left[(V_{tot}/V_{off}) \cdot (k/\left(1 + \frac{(k-1)\ I_{off}}{UVA + I_{off}}\right)\right] \cdot [I_{off}/\ (UVA + I_{off})].$$

For $k$ close to 1 (our measured index of $OVA$ close to its true value), or $I_{off}/\ (UVA + I_{off})$ small (a small proportion of value is added offshore), we have, approximately,

$$\frac{X_{off}}{X_{tot}} = (V_{tot}/V_{off}) \cdot k\ [I_{off}/\ (UVA + I_{off})],$$

where $I_{off}/UVA + I_{off}$ is the index in table 3-10.

In reality, both $V_{tot}/V_{off}$ and $k$ have probably changed with the passage of time, while $V_{tot}/V_{off}$ has probably increased as more complex devices, a greater proportion of the value of which is reflected in the costs of designing and producing a functioning chip, have been introduced and assembly costs as a proportion of total cost have been reduced. On the other hand, increased testing abroad may have counteracted this trend to some extent, since this would increase $V_{off}$ in relation to $V_{tot}$, other things being equal. Since our measure of $I_{off}$ is dutiable 806/807 value, which includes some dutiable U.S. materials, $k$ must be less than 1. As the unfinished chip has come to be a greater and greater proportion of the value of U.S. materials used—and has been the main item admitted duty-free—with increasing chip complexity, $k$ must have moved closer to 1 with the passing years. Since, therefore, both $k$ and $V_{tot}/V_{off}$ have probably increased in the course of time, the index we are calculating—$I_{off}/UVA + I_{off}$—of value added abroad probably *understates* the true increase in $X_{off}/X_{tot}$, the fraction of output assembled abroad. Also, customs court decisions have substantially liberalized the definition of the sorts of operation on U.S. materials that are permissible if they are subsequently to reenter the United States duty-free. See Alan Lebowitz, *Item 807.00,* Mandel and Grunfeld Seminar

(New York: Mandel and Grunfeld, November 1979). This would lead to a decline in dutiable value and an understatement by the index of the increase in foreign operations.

## Appendix B: Estimating the Price Elasticity of Semiconductor Demand and the Cost Advantage of Assembly Abroad

To arrive at a crude estimate of the price elasticity of demand for semiconductor devices, it is possible to use the information on semiconductor input per unit of output given in footnote 9. To see this, first note that the price elasticity, $\eta_{Qp}$, is given by $\eta_{Qp} = \eta_{qp} + \varepsilon \cdot s$, with $\eta_{qp}$ the price elasticity of semiconductor demand per *unit* of consumer good; $\varepsilon$ the price elasticity of demand for the consumer good; and $s$ the cost share of semiconductor inputs in consumer good production.[166]

Since $s$ is quite small (see table 3-2; it never exceeded 0.06 in the industries of the 1972 input-output table), the second term can be ignored as long as $\eta_{qp}$ is reasonably large.

To estimate $\eta_{qp}$, note that cost reductions in semiconductors, which have been extremely large, have almost certainly swamped all other relative price movements affecting the use of semiconductors. If all input prices other than the prices of semiconductors have moved roughly proportionately to output price, then

$$\eta_{qp} = d \ln q / d \ln (P/P_x),$$

with ln the natural log and $P/P_x$ the price of semiconductor input in relation to the price of output.[167] Data on $q$ are referenced in footnote 9. Using time series data on the relative price of semiconductors and approximating the differentials by the first difference in time of the natural logs of

166. Let $Q = q(P)X[h(P)]$, with $Q$ total demand for semiconductors; $q$ demand per unit of output of consumer goods ($= Q/X$), a function of the price of semiconductors; $X$ demand for the final consumer good, a function of $h$, the unit cost of producing $X$—assumed equal to price—in turn a function of the price of semiconductors. Then differentiating with respect to $P$, $Q' = q'X + qX'h'$. By Shephard's lemma, $h' = q$, so

$$\eta_{Qp} = Q'\frac{P}{Q} = q'\frac{P}{q} + X'\frac{h}{X}h'\frac{P}{h} = \eta_{qp} + \varepsilon \cdot s,$$

which is the expression used here.

167. This follows from the fact that input demands are homogeneous of degree zero in

$q$ and $P/P_x$, their ratio will be an estimate of $\eta_{qp}$. This is done in table 3-29.

The estimated elasticities of demand per unit for semiconductor devices show a rather elastic demand, with estimates of about $-5.4$ for computers and estimates in the neighborhood of $-2.5$ for various other types of electrical equipment. Since aggregate elasticity of demand is a value-weighted average of the elasticity of demand by sector, aggregate elasticity of demand for semiconductors used in electronic output is about $-3.5$.

---

prices; that is, letting $P'$ stand for the price of another input (assume only one for expositional simplicity) and $P_x$ the price of output, $q(P,P') = q(P/P_x, P'/P_x)$.
Then, taking derivatives with respect to time,

$$\frac{dq}{dt} = \frac{\partial q}{\partial\left(\frac{P}{P_x}\right)} \frac{d\left(\frac{P}{P_x}\right)}{dt} + \frac{\partial q}{\partial\left(\frac{P'}{P_x}\right)} \frac{d\left(\frac{P'}{P_x}\right)}{dt}.$$

Assuming roughly constant relative prices for inputs other than semiconductors,

$$\frac{d\left(\frac{P'}{P_x}\right)}{dt} \cong 0.$$

Now, since

$$\frac{\partial q\,(P, P')}{\partial P} = \frac{\partial q\left(\frac{P}{P_x}, \frac{P'}{P_x}\right)}{\partial\left(\frac{P}{P_x}\right)} \frac{1}{P_x},$$

we have

$$\frac{dq}{dt} = \frac{\partial q\,(P, P')}{\partial P} P_x \frac{d\left(\frac{P}{P_x}\right)}{dt}$$

and

$$\frac{\partial q\,(P, P')}{\partial P} = \frac{\frac{dq}{dt}}{\frac{d\left(\frac{P}{P_x}\right)}{dt}} \frac{1}{P_x}.$$

Multiplying both sides by $P/q$,

$$\eta_{qp} = \frac{dq}{d\left(\frac{P}{P_x}\right)} \cdot \frac{\frac{P}{P_x}}{q},$$

the expression found in the text.

Table 3-29. *Estimated Elasticity of Demand for Semiconductor Input per Unit of Electronic Output, 1967–72*

| *Sector* | *Price index for sectoral output, 1967 (1972 = 100)* | *Estimated elasticity of demand for SCDs, 1967–72* ($\eta_{qp}$) |
|---|---|---|
| Computers and calculators | 98.6 | −5.4 |
| Radio and television receivers | 103.6 | −2.6 |
| Telephone and telegraph equipment | 83.8 | −2.6 |
| Radio and television communication equipment | 83.1 | −2.5 |
| Semiconductors | 115.1 | . . . |
| 1972 sales-value–weighted average, four electronics sectors | . . . | −3.5 |

Sources: See footnote 9; for calculations of elasticities of demand, see text. No correction for a technological advance in density levels of the components of integrated circuits has been made.

Not done were the calculations of elasticity for sectors other than electrical equipment, because their use of semiconductors is generally in electronic equipment used for internal consumption, and the elasticities so calculated would therefore also reflect the elasticity of demand for electronic equipment that contained the semiconductor.

These estimates of elasticity are crude, to be sure, but they are probably the best available.[168] They may be affected, however, by a serious negative bias. The price data used to construct table 3-29 are based on the wholesale price series of the U.S. Bureau of Labor Statistics for various types of semiconductor and probably reflect price declines in existing

168. The only other serious attempt found is that of Webbink, in *The Semiconductor Industry,* who regressed the log of aggregate demand for different types of semiconductor devices on log semiconductor price and the log of value of electronics sales. If the electronic output price index, which is unobserved, is negatively correlated with semiconductor prices throughout the period of his sample—roughly 1960–72—which is to be expected, and positively correlated with output—also to be expected, as demand for electronic products increased in spite of price increases—his estimate of the price elasticity will probably be biased toward zero. This is because the bias in his estimate of the price elasticity will equal $-by$, with $y$ the coefficient of the log of electronic sales and $b$ the coefficient of semiconductor price, in an auxiliary regression, of the—unobserved and omitted—log of electronics output price against the logs of semiconductor price and value of electronics output—the independent variables included. See Henri Theil, *Principles of Econometrics* (John Wiley & Sons, 1971), pp. 548–50, for a description of the principles determining the specification bias when an independent variable that might be included—that is, the log of electronic output price—is omitted.

types of semiconductor between 1967 and 1972 accurately. Around 1970, however, a significant advance was made in the production technology of integrated circuits. The number of circuit elements on a single chip was increased about four times for most computer chips;[169] this technological leap in levels of circuit integration is not reflected in the price series for existing chips. A 1972 integrated-circuit computer memory chip was equivalent to four 1967-generation computer memory integrated circuits. Other types of integrated circuit were also produced subsequently at much greater levels of complexity using the same technology.

Thus, on the average, a 1972 integrated circuit performed the functions of several 1967 integrated circuits. Since integrated circuits rose from 21 percent of the value of U.S. shipments of semiconductor devices in 1967 to 54 percent in 1972,[170] the census semiconductor output measure must significantly understate the amount of 1967-equivalent output produced in 1972, and the price index must overstate the cost of performing 1967-equivalent functions. The net effect will be to overstate the magnitude of the true price elasticity of demand.[171]

---

Webbink's own estimates of price elasticity (p. 88) were

| | |
|---|---|
| Linear ICs | −1.40 |
| Digital ICs | −1.62 |
| Silicon transistors | −0.65 |
| Germanium transistors | −1.73 |
| Silicon diodes | −0.77 |
| Germanium diodes | 0.28 |
| Lead-mounted rectifiers | −0.93 |
| Chassis-mounted rectifiers | −1.41 |
| Zener diodes | −0.69 |

He made no attempt to correct for changes in the complexity of ICs between 1960 and 1972.

The only other related estimate found is that of Robert W. Wilson, Peter K. Ashton, and Thomas P. Egan, *Innovation, Competition, and Government Policy in the Semiconductor Industry* (Lexington Books, 1980), who, on the basis of the observed price-quantity relations for memory bits sold between 1971 and 1979, guess the total price elasticity of computer memory bit demand, in MOS RAM ICs—not the elasticity per computer manufactured—to be about −2. They did not take into account changes in computer demand, and no actual price data for memory bits sold were used; instead, guesswork and the costs of memory bits in the most advanced design chips manufactured were used. Their estimate is therefore less useful.

169. Robert N. Noyce, "Microelectronics," *Scientific American,* vol. 237 (September 1977), p. 67.

170. U.S. Department of Commerce, Bureau of the Census, *1972 Census of Manufactures,* Industry Series (GPO, 1976), table 6A-1.

171. Call $x$ the measured percentage rate of increase in output between 1967 and 1972

The elasticity estimates given in table 3-29 support this conjecture. The sector that made use of the integrated circuits most affected by the great increase in density of components, computers and calculators, has an estimated elasticity roughly twice that of the other electronic equipment sectors, whose use of more discrete semiconductor devices and simple integrated circuits was affected less by the technological leap forward. Since table 3-29 in effect places an upper limit on the magnitude of the price elasticity of demand, it would also be convenient to place a lower limit on that elasticity.

This is done in table 3-30 by assuming that all 1972-generation integrated circuits performed the functions of the four 1967-generation integrated circuits. Implicitly, the demand for integrated circuits is treated as a demand for the electronic functions performed by the integrated circuits, so one 1972 integrated circuit and four 1967 integrated circuits would be perfect substitutes in the manufacture of an item of electronic equipment.[172]

---

and $y$ the measured percentage rate of decrease in price between 1967 and 1972. The calculated price elasticity (times $-1$) is just $x/y$. If, however, 1 unit of semiconductor sales in 1972 is equivalent to $N$ units sold in 1967 ($N > 1$), then the "true" price elasticity for 1967-equivalent devices is $(x + \ln N) / (y + \ln N)$, which will fall short of measured elasticity.

To see this, note that

$$\frac{d}{da}\frac{x + a}{y + a} = \frac{y - x}{(y + a)^2} < 0 \text{ for } x, y > 0, y < x \text{ (demand elastic).}$$

172. For a reasonable approximation this is probably not a bad assumption. An executive at Nippon Electric Company, for example, one of the biggest Japanese makers of ICs, explained in 1981 why Japanese producers were delaying mass production of the new generation of 64K computer memory chips, stating that "if 64Ks are introduced in the market, there will be no demand, since four 16Ks are less costly than one 64K." See "Japanese Electronic Firms Delay Plans to Mass-Produce 64-K Chips," *Asian Wall Street Journal Weekly,* April 6, 1981, p. 14.

The U.S. census index of 1972 IC output at 1967 prices was first multiplied by four, then multiplied by the 1967-dollar price index for ICs to arrive at a new estimate of the value of 1972 IC output at 1967 prices in terms of ICs of the type made in 1967 and used in the numerator of the calculated elasticity. The revised figure for the 1972 output of ICs at 1967 prices was then added to existing estimates of the value of the 1972 production of other types of semiconductors in 1967 prices and used as the divisor for 1972 production of all classes of SCDs at current prices to reach an implicit price deflator for a unit of 1972 output in terms of 1967 output. The original cross-weighted 1972 census price deflator for SCD output (1967 = 100) was 86.9. The implicit SCD price deflator, after revaluation of 1972 production of ICs at four times the original quantity index, in 1967 prices, was 30.9. This new price for 1972 semiconductors in terms of 1967 prices was then used in table 3-30 to recalculate the change in the relative price of semiconductors throughout the period 1967–72.

Table 3-30. *Estimates of the Lower Bounds of the Elasticity of Demand for Semiconductors*

| *Sector* | *Estimate of elasticity of demand* |
|---|---|
| Computers and calculators | −1.6 |
| Radio and television receivers | −1.2 |
| Telephone and telegraph equipment | −1.4 |
| Radio and television communication equipment | −1.4 |
| 1972 sales-value–weighted average, four electronics sectors | −1.5 |

Sources: Same as for table 3-29; calculations as described in the text.

This rather radical upward revaluation of the quantity of 1967-equivalent integrated circuits produced in 1972 almost certainly causes the elasticity estimates of table 3-30 to lie significantly below their true magnitudes, since most integrated circuits used outside the computer sector were probably affected much less by the higher chip-density levels, and even within the computer industry not all chips quadrupled in density. Thus, the true price elasticity per unit of demand for semiconductor input probably lies somewhere in the −1.5 to −3.0 range, with the clustering of values in table 3-29 for noncomputer uses suggesting the midpoint of that range, or around −2.3, as a decent point estimate.

### *The Cost Advantage of Foreign Assembly*

An estimate is needed of the relative price increase to users of semiconductors if assembly were to be relocated ($P_u/P_o - 1$). This cost increase depends, in turn, on two key parameters: the increase in assembly costs in the United States as a percent of total manufacturing cost with assembly abroad (call it $a$); and total manufacturing cost with assembly abroad as a fraction of the output price of semiconductor devices (call this ratio $b$). Then the cost difference will just equal $ab$, if the absolute difference between price and manufacturing cost remains roughly constant.[173]

173. That is, let price less manufacturing cost, with assembly abroad, equal a constant $\pi$. Let manufacturing cost abroad be $M_o$, manufacturing cost with domestic assembly $M_u$. Then

$$\frac{P_u}{P_o} - 1 = \frac{M_u + \pi}{M_o + \pi} - 1 = \frac{M_u - M_o}{M_o + \pi} = \frac{M_u - M_o}{M_o} \frac{M_o}{M_o + \pi} = ab,$$

as defined in the text. Since this difference between price and the cost of manufacture covers the costs of research and development, corporate overhead, and capital, it will remain approximately constant in a competitive industry as long as the technology of assembly does

To estimate how much more costly assembly in the United States would be is difficult, since only fragmentary information is available. The only real datum is a table in Finan, which can be reworked to estimate the cost differential, as in table 3-31. It indicates that in spite of the fact that increases in labor costs in the United States raised total manufacturing cost by 60 percent of its Singapore value, substantial savings in the costs of materials and in manufacturing overhead leave the net U.S. cost increase at about a third of the Singapore cost. The evidence on manufacturing costs suggests that, since assembly costs have shrunk in relative importance with the more advanced complex chips, this difference in cost may actually have declined somewhat in the aggregate by the late 1970s as demand for these types of chip soared.

The other critical parameter, manufacturing cost as a fraction of sales price, was also estimated by Finan to be about 0.65 in the early 1970s. In the late 1970s Dicken put the ratio at about 0.3 and 0.4 for a simple and a complex integrated circuit, respectively.[174] To some extent, the smaller ratios for 1979 may reflect demand pressures on prices in that year; they may also reflect the greater importance of the costs of research and development in the production of newer and more advanced chips.

If Finan's estimate of 0.33 is taken for $a$ and 0.65 for $b$, as appropriate to the early 1970s, the cost difference as a percent of sales price with assembly abroad, $P_u/P_o - 1$, was about 21 percent. If both ratios had dropped by the late 1970s, say to 0.25 for $a$ and 0.40 for $b$, as lower bounds, the increase in sales price would not have been less than 10 percent. It is therefore possible to hypothesize that in the early 1970s $P_u/P_o - 1$ was about 0.2, and in the late 1970s somewhere between 0.1 and 0.2.

The foregoing estimates refer to cost increases per unit when foreign

---

not change a great deal when it is brought back to domestic plants. If the transfer of assembly back to the United States, for example, led to the use of automated assembly techniques that required much more capital, $\pi$, which contains the return on that capital investment, might increase somewhat. Since assembly has become a relatively small part of the cost, however, $\pi$ would probably not increase a great deal, even with a switch to automation.

174. Estimates of manufacturing cost as a percentage of sales price were found as follows:

| *Percent* | *Description* | *Source* |
|---|---|---|
| 65 | For SCD industry in the early 1970s, with assembly in Singapore | Finan, "The International Transfer," p. 26 |
| 40 | 16K RAM, computer memory IC, 1979, with assembly abroad | Dicken, "How to Determine Fair Market Prices," p. 82 |
| 30 | Simple linear IC, 1979, with assembly abroad | Ibid., p. 83 |

Table 3-31. *Comparison of the Manufacturing Costs of Semiconductor Devices Assembled in Singapore with the Costs of Those Assembled in the United States, Early 1970s*

Percent of manufacturing cost with assembly in Singapore

| *Element of cost* | *Assembly in the United States* | *Assembly in Singapore* | *Increase or decrease with assembly in the United States* |
|---|---|---|---|
| Direct labor cost | 80 | 20 | 60 |
| Wafer fabrication | 12 | 12 | 0 |
| Assembly | 68 | 8 | 60 |
| Materials | 13 | 30 | −17 |
| Manufacturing overhead | 40 | 50 | −10 |
| Total cost | 133 | 100 | 33 |

Source: Finan, "The International Transfer," p. 66. To rework Finan's figures into this form, use the fact that the absolute direct labor cost of wafer fabrication, which was done in the United States, is constant, whether assembly takes place in the United States or abroad.

production is transferred back to the United States. Equation 3-1, however, measures the aggregate welfare effect of transferring assembly back to the United States. Since not all assembly took place abroad, however, the effect on the aggregate price level for semiconductors will be a weighted average of the effect on foreign output and on output already assembled in the United States. To put it more precisely, $P_o$, the price of a unit assembled abroad, must be replaced with $P_\alpha$, the average price of a unit with fraction $\alpha$ of output assembled offshore, so that $P_u/P_\alpha - 1$ is substituted for $P_u/P_o - 1$ whenever it appears in the text.

The average price of a semiconductor if there is no production abroad is just $P_u$. The average price with fraction $\alpha$ assembled abroad, $P_\alpha$, is $P_\alpha = \alpha P_o + (1 - \alpha)P_u$, with $P_u$ and $P_o$ the costs of domestic production and production abroad, respectively. Therefore,

$$\frac{P_u - P_\alpha}{P_\alpha} = \frac{\alpha(P_u - P_o)}{\alpha P_o + (1-\alpha)P_u} = \frac{\alpha\left(\dfrac{P_u - P_o}{P_o}\right)}{1 + (1-\alpha)\left(\dfrac{P_u - P_o}{P_o}\right)},$$

which is used in the calculations cited in the text. Using a range of 0.1 to 0.2 for $(P_u/P_o) - 1$ and an estimate of the fraction of output assembled abroad of 70 percent, the implied range for the average price increase as a fraction of the average price before relocating foreign assembly ($m$ in the text) is from 0.07 to 0.13.

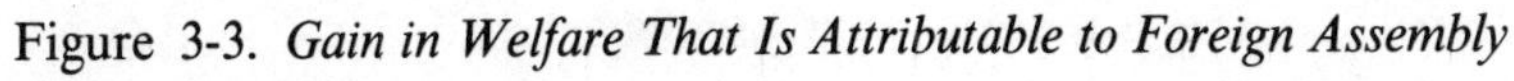

Figure 3-3. *Gain in Welfare That Is Attributable to Foreign Assembly*

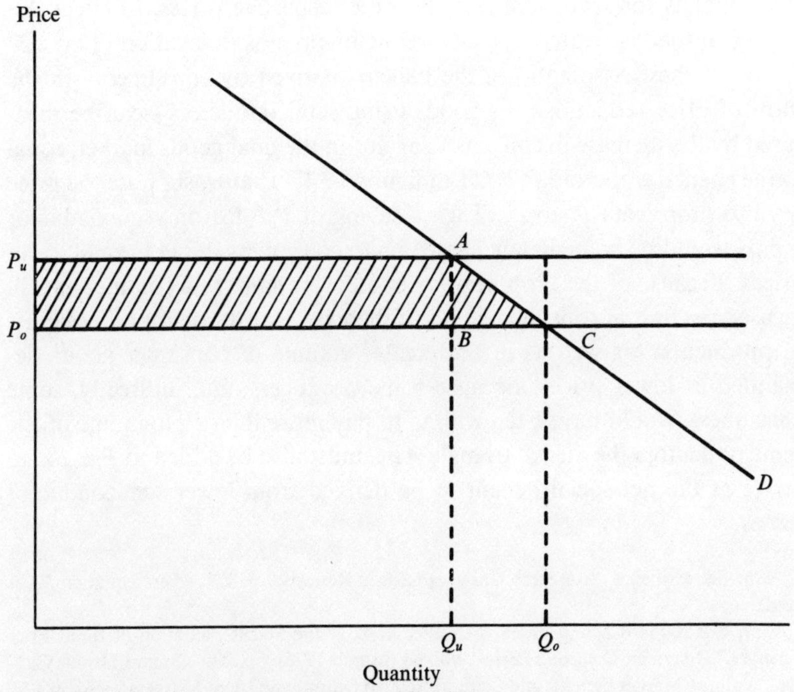


$D$ = demand for semiconductors as input to consumer goods industry
$P_u$ = price of a finished semiconductor manufactured in the United States
$P_o$ = price of a semiconductor assembled abroad
$Q_u$ = demand for semiconductors at price $P_u$
$Q_o$ = demand for semiconductors at price $P_o$

## *Cost-Benefit Considerations*

Figure 3-3 displays the theoretical framework used to construct social cost-benefit calculations, mainly for the purpose of illustration. Assume that all resources used in assembly, both domestically and abroad, are available in perfectly elastic supply to a competitive semiconductor industry and that there are constant returns to scale in assembly; $D$ is the demand curve for semiconductors as an input to the consumer goods industry;[175] $P_u$ is the price of a finished semiconductor when manufactured in

175. Technically $D$ is a compensated demand; that is, the demand for semiconductors that would prevail if, as the price of semiconductors and, therefore, the cost—the price, in a competitive consumer good industry—of finished consumer goods was changed, lump-sum transfers were made to consumers to maintain their satisfaction constant. As an approximation, however, the market demand will be used instead of the compensated demand curve. Robert Willig, "Consumer's Surplus without Apology," *American Economic Review*, vol. 66 (September 1976), pp. 589–97, shows that this is a reasonable approximation—that is, that the errors are generally minor.

the United States; $P_o$ is the price with assembly abroad; and $Q_u$ and $Q_o$ are the demands for semiconductors at these respective prices. In effect, assembly abroad is treated as a cost-reducing process innovation.[176]

Under these assumptions, the benefit received by consumers—in the form of price reductions for goods using semiconductors—can be measured by the increase in consumer surplus in the final goods market, equal to the shaded trapezoid $P_uP_oCA$ in figure 3-3.[177] That is, suppose the price were to drop from $P_u$ to $P_o$. Then a saving of $P_uP_oBA$ on semiconductor inputs would be immediately passed on to consumers in the form of lower prices. Because of the drop in price, moreover, more semiconductors will be used per unit of consumer goods, if there is substitution for other inputs in production, as well as in the greater volume of consumer goods demanded at lower prices. Because some producers and, indirectly, some consumers, would have been willing to pay more than $P_o$ for some of the semiconductors they used, triangle $ABC$ must also be added to $P_uP_oBA$ to arrive at the net social benefit to be derived from lower semiconductor prices.

176. See Griliches, "Research Costs and Social Returns," p. 422, where equation 3-1 is used.

177. See Richard Schmalensee, "Another Look at the Social Valuation of Input Price Changes," *American Economic Review,* vol. 66 (March 1976), pp. 239–43; and Dennis Carlton, "Valuing Market Benefits and Costs in Related Output and Input Markets," ibid., vol. 69 (September 1979), pp. 688–96.

CHAPTER FOUR

# The Assembly Industry in Mexico

JOSEPH GRUNWALD

IT is not surprising that Mexico has become the most important partner of the United States in assembly activities abroad. As a developing country it shares a nearly 2,000-mile border with a country in which wages are among the highest in the world and which is by far the largest producer in the world. The border is accessible, and transportation from almost any point in the United States to the border is cheaper than transportation to any overseas trading partner. Neither the geographic nor the cultural distance between the two countries is very great. Many U.S. entrepreneurs and business executives have been to Mexico, and for historical reasons as well as because of migration, its culture is diffused throughout many parts of the United States.

During the mid 1960s, when data on 806/807 trade first became available, Hong Kong was more than five times as important and Taiwan nearly as important as Mexico in the processing and assembling of U.S. components for reexport to the United States. By the end of that decade, Mexican operations were nearly twice as large as those of Hong Kong and about four times as large as those of Taiwan (see table 2-1). This shift took place despite the fact that wages were higher in Mexico. Mexican assembly operations now produce a significantly different product mix from that produced by Asian assemblers: the share of goods with low transport

This chapter benefited from the collaboration of El Colegio de México. A draft paper entitled "Evolución y perspectivas de la industria maquiladora de exportación en Mexico," by Federico Ballí Gonzalez, with the collaboration of Javier Villaseñor B. and José Meneses, of the Centro de Estudios Económicos y Demográficos of the Colegio served as background for the research for this chapter. The paper was submitted to the Second Seminar on North-South Complementary Intra-Industry Trade, sponsored by the United Nations Conference on Trade and Development and the Brookings Institution and held under the auspices of El Colegio de México in Mexico City, August 18–22, 1980. Specific points drawn from the paper are cited in footnotes to the chapter. The analysis and views expressed here are those of the author and should not be ascribed to Federico Ballí, his collaborators, or other staff members or officers of El Colegio de México.

costs, such as electronics and apparel items is smaller, the share of goods with high transport costs is larger. For this reason, Mexican output seems less sensitive to wage changes than Asian output; proximity to the U.S. transport network more than compensates for higher wages in the assembly of these products.

Proximity as a principal factor in that country's attractiveness was reinforced by Mexico's border industrialization program, put into effect during the mid 1960s. Aiming to absorb the border unemployment left by the termination of the bracero program between the United States and Mexico in 1964,[1] it allowed duty-free import of machinery, equipment, and components for processing or assembly within a twenty-kilometer strip along the border, provided that all the imported products were reexported.[2] Thus none of the output of the assembly operations, called *maquila* by Mexicans, could be sold within the country; the assembly plants are called *maquiladoras.*

Subsequent Mexican legislation, decrees, and administrative regulations expanded the scope of the maquila, first, by exempting the maquiladoras from the "Mexicanization" requirement of Mexican majority ownership,[3] and second, by permitting the establishment of maquiladoras anywhere in the country, subject to approval by the authorities. Mexico City and two other cities were intended to be off limits because of pollution problems, but special permission was granted for the establishment of several plants there; special incentives have also been offered for the establishment of plants in other locations. Foreign technicians and managerial personnel are allowed to reside in Mexico if their presence is considered necessary for the efficient functioning of the maquiladora. Customs procedures and other government formalities have been eased. As a further attraction to maquila operations industrial parks have been promoted, first along the border and then in the interior.[4]

1. Oscar J. Martínez, *Border Boom Town: Ciudad Juárez since 1848* (University of Texas Press, 1978), pp. 131–32.

2. Free zones have existed at the border since the 1930s; the first decree regulating temporary imports and exports was published in the Mexican federal register, *Diario oficial,* September 3, 1958.

3. The exception is the textile industry, whose exports are subject to the imposition of quotas by the United States. In that industry, Mexican ownership of assembly plants must be at least 51 percent, the usual minimum ownership requirement for economic activities in Mexico.

4. Until recently the only significant concentration of maquiladoras almost entirely outside industrial parks has been the one in Tijuana. Apparently commercial interests there have

The U.S. promoters' original conception of an idealized coproduction system with Mexico is the "twin plant" idea.[5] U.S. firms would establish two plants under a single management, one on each side of the border. The U.S. plant would perform the capital-intensive operations and the factory on the Mexican side, the labor-intensive processes. The U.S. plant would supply its Mexican counterpart with the component parts and the Mexican plant would return the assembled products to the U.S. side, possibly for further processing and for shipment to the various markets. The two plants would be close enough to one another for transportation costs to be minimal and a single management to be optimal. The costs of holding inventories, repair and maintenance, and other problems could be held to a minimum in the Mexican plant because supplies and technical support would be just a short distance away on the U.S. side.

The idea has won sufficient acceptance that the term "twin plant" has often been used incorrectly to describe all U.S. assembly operations in Mexico. In effect, the great majority of U.S.-owned maquiladoras are supplied from plants quite distant from the border, primarily in the Midwest but also in the East and the far West. Apparently many U.S. corporations have not thought that the savings in transportation costs and the advantage of a single management warranted the investment in an additional plant on the U.S. side of the border when plants that could supply the components already existed elsewhere. Although quite a few twin plants have been established along the border, particularly in the El Paso–Juárez region, there are not enough of them for the concept to be representative of coproduction activities between the United States and Mexico.

## The Importance of Assembly Plants to Mexico

Since 1965, when the border industrialization program got under way, a significant number of assembly plants have been established almost every

resisted industrial parks for fear of losing their free-port status. By 1980 a few new plants had been established in recently formed industrial parks in Tijuana. Industrial parks existed in Mexico before the establishment of the maquila program.

5. The concept was first proposed by Richard Bolin in a report by Arthur D. Little de Mexico, the Mexican subsidiary of the U.S. consulting firm, entitled "Industrial Opportunities for Ciudad Juárez," August 1, 1964.

Table 4-1. *Employment in Mexican Assembly Plants, Number of Plants, and Hours Worked, 1969–83*[a]

| Year | Number of plants | | Interior plants as percent of total plants | Total employment, all workers | | Interior employment, all workers | | Employment of production workers | | Average hours per month worked by production workers (millions of hours) |
|---|---|---|---|---|---|---|---|---|---|---|
| | Total | Interior | | Number | Percent change from preceding year | Number | Percent change from preceding year | Number | Percent change from preceding year | |
| 1969[b] | 108 | n.a. | n.a. | 15,858 | n.a. | n.a. | n.a. | n.a. | n.a. | n.a. |
| 1970 | 120 | n.a. | n.a. | 20,327 | 28.2 | n.a. | n.a. | n.a. | n.a. | n.a. |
| 1971[c] | 251 | n.a. | n.a. | 29,214 | 43.7 | n.a. | n.a. | n.a. | n.a. | n.a. |
| 1972[c] | 339 | n.a. | n.a. | 48,060 | 64.5 | n.a. | n.a. | n.a. | n.a. | n.a. |
| 1973 | 257 | 10[d] | 3.9 | 64,330 | 33.9 | 4,200[e] | n.a. | n.a. | n.a. | n.a. |
| 1974 | 455 | 26 | 5.7 | 75,977 | 18.1 | 4,852 | 15.5 | n.a. | n.a. | n.a. |
| 1975 | 454 | 36 | 7.9 | 67,213 | −11.5 | 5,069 | 4.5 | 57,850 | n.a. | 10.8 |
| 1976 | 448 | 42 | 9.4 | 74,496 | 10.8 | 6,964 | 37.4 | 64,670 | 11.8 | 12.3 |
| 1977 | 443 | 45 | 10.1 | 78,433 | 5.3 | 7.752 | 11.3 | 68,187 | 5.4 | 13.1 |
| 1978 | 457 | 37 | 8.1 | 90,704 | 15.6 | 8,317 | 7.3 | 78,570 | 15.2 | 15.1 |
| 1979 | 540 | 60 | 11.1 | 111,365 | 22.8 | 10,828 | 30.2 | 95,818 | 22.0 | 18.4 |
| 1980 | 620 | 69 | 11.3 | 119,546 | 7.3 | 12,970 | 9.8 | 102,020 | 6.5 | 19.2 |
| 1981 | 605 | 72 | 11.9 | 130,973 | 9.6 | 14,523 | 12.0 | 110,684 | 8.5 | 21.1 |
| 1982 | 585 | 71 | 12.1 | 127,048 | −3.0 | 13,821 | −4.8 | 105,383 | −4.8 | 20.0 |
| 1983 | 600 | 67 | 11.2 | 150,867 | 18.7 | 15,952 | 15.4 | 125,278 | 18.9 | 23.0 |

Sources: Departamento de Estadísticas Industriales, Secretaría de Programación y Presupuesto (SPP), and Secretaría de Patrimonio y Fomento Industrial (SEPAFIN).

n.a. Not available.

a. Except for 1970, figures for years earlier than 1974 may not be comparable to others in the series. Figures are rounded.

b. From El Paso Chamber of Commerce, as reported in *Trade and Tariff Proposals,* Hearings before the House Committee on Ways and Means, 91 Cong., 2 sess. (Government Printing Office, 1970), pt. 9, p. 3284; figures, as of July 31, 1969, may not be comparable to those for other years.

c. Figures as of July 1971 and August 1972, from Leopoldo Solís, "Industrial Priorities in Mexico," in United Nations Industrial Development Organization (UNIDO), *Industrial Priorities in Developing Countries* (United Nations, 1979), p. 109. Figures may not be comparable to those for other years.

d. Computed by subtraction.

e. Estimate, Banco de México, *Encuestas,* Cuaderno semestral no. 1 (December 1978), table 1.

year. In 1983, 600 maquiladoras were in operation, employing more than 150,000 persons (see table 4-1).[6]

The importance of employment generation is difficult to judge because "there are no reliable unemployment and underemployment statistics in Mexico."[7] Although employment in assembly production for U.S. firms is significant, the maquila labor force is a quite small part—less than 1 percent of the total—of Mexican employment. In the border region, however, maquiladoras are among the most important employers.[8]

Estimates of underemployment range from 27.4 percent to 52 percent of the labor force in 1978.[9] The unemployment rate at the border seems to be higher than in the rest of the country and, according to fragmentary information, appears to be rising.[10]

6. More than 1,000 maquiladoras were officially registered between 1965 and 1983. Many of these never began operations; some went out of business during the downturn of 1974–77. More about this later.

The maquiladora statistics are taken from tables, both published and unpublished, of the Mexican Secretariat of Programming and Budget—Oficina de Maquiladoras, Departamento de Estadísticas Industriales, Secretaría de Programación y Presupuesto (SPP). Many of these tables were supplied by the U.S. embassy in Mexico through the U.S. Department of State. Other statistics are from published and unpublished reports of the Ministry of Finance and Public Credit—Secretaría de Hacienda y Credito Publico (SHCP)—formerly the Ministry of Industry and Commerce—Secretaría de Industria y Comercio (SIC).

7. Victor Urquidi and Sofia Méndez Villarreal, "Economic Importance of Mexico's Northern Border Region," in Stanley R. Ross, ed., *Views across the Border* (University of New Mexico Press, 1978), p. 153.

8. The border region is made up of thirty-five municipalities located in the six states bordering the United States. Almost a third of the border population is concentrated in Tijuana and Mexicali, two cities on the California border, and almost a fifth in the largest border city, Juárez, the twin city of El Paso, Texas. These three municipalities accounted for half the border population according to the 1970 census, as reported by Urquidi and Méndez Villarreal, "Economic Importance," table 2, p. 142.

9. Michael Van Waas, "The Multinationals' Strategy for Labor: Foreign Assembly Plants in Mexico's Border Industrialization Program" (Ph.D. dissertation, Stanford University, 1981), note 253, pp. 195–96.

10. According to official Mexican census data, open unemployment in the border regions was slightly higher than the country average in 1970: 4.2 percent at the border, but only 3.8 percent for the country. See Joaquín Xirau Icaza and Miguel Díaz, *Nuestra dependencia fronteriza,* Archivo del Fondo 48 (México, D.F.: Fondo de Cultura Económica, 1976), table 11. Since these figures do not include those seeking work for the first time, they are underestimates. Urquidi and Méndez Villarreal, in "Economic Importance," p. 154, estimate the 1970 open unemployment at the border at about 7 percent. The estimates for 1970 made by two different Mexican commissions, however, indicate a significantly lower level of underemployment at the border than the national average. The low estimate is 9.2 percent at the border and 16.6 percent for the country; the high estimate is 16.1 percent at the border and 25.3 percent for all Mexico. See Urquidi and Méndez Villarreal, "Economic Importance,"

The value added generated by the maquiladoras in Mexico has been increasing sharply since the beginning of the border industrialization program.[11] At the end of 1981 it was running at an annual rate of more than a billion dollars according to peso figures from the Mexican Secretariat of Programming and Budget converted at the current rate of exchange (see table 4-2).

The maquila operations make a substantial contribution to Mexican foreign-exchange earnings. The precise magnitude is difficult to determine, primarily because of the leakage of Mexican maquila wages across the border to the United States. Various estimates have been made. *Comercio exterior,* the monthly review of the Mexican National Bank of Foreign Trade, cites other sources for the estimate that 60–75 percent of wages earned on the Mexican side of the border were spent in the United States during the 1970s.[12] Survey data elaborated by the Real Estate Research Corporation of El Paso, Texas, show that in August 1966, 20 percent of retail sales of durable goods in the El Paso metropolitan area were made to patrons living across the river in Juárez, Mexico, and the surrounding area. The corresponding proportion of retail sales in downtown El Paso was 30 percent.[13]

In the absence of specific survey studies, therefore, it is difficult to estimate the *net* leakage of the Mexican assembly payroll. There is no doubt that a good part of Mexican maquila wages are spent in the United States, perhaps between 40 percent and 60 percent, to take the latest assertion.[14] There is no estimate, however, of the expenditures made by U.S. residents in Mexico because of the existence of Mexican assembly operations for

---

table 11, p. 155. By including those who work only part of the year and those who receive less than the minimum wage, Bustamante arrives at an underemployment rate of 34.3 percent at the border. See Jorge A. Bustamante, "El programa fronterizo de maquiladoras: observaciones para una evaluación," *Foro internacional,* vol. 16 (October–December 1975), p. 187.

11. See table 4-2, note a, for the definition of value added in assembly operations.

12. Bustamante, "El programa fronterizo," pp. 186–87. See also *Comercio exterior de México,* vol. 24 (May 1978), p. 208. Donald Baerresen, *The Border Industrialization Program of Mexico* (Lexington Books, 1971) gives similar estimates for Mexican maquila wages spent on the Texas side of the border (p. 35).

13. *Trade and Tariff Proposals,* Hearings before the House Committee on Ways and Means, 91 Cong. 2 sess. (Government Printing Office, 1970), pt. 9, p. 3286.

14. *Actualidad,* a Mexican monthly review, vol. 2 (May 1, 1981), p. 14. After the massive devaluations of the Mexican peso in 1982, Mexican expenditures in the United States collapsed and U.S. purchases across the border in Mexico rose dramatically.

Table 4-2. *Total Value Added and Total Payroll in Mexican Assembly Plants, by Location, 1973–83*[a]

| *Location* | *1973* | *1974* | *1975* | *1976* | *1977* | *1978* | *1979* | *1980* | *1981* | *1982* | *1983* |
|---|---|---|---|---|---|---|---|---|---|---|---|
| | *Millions of current U.S. dollars* | | | | | | | | | | |
| *Value added* | | | | | | | | | | | |
| All plants | 197.0 | 315.6 | 321.2 | 352.2 | 314.9 | 438.6 | 637.9 | 770.8 | 977.8 | 847.0 | 828.7 |
| Border plants | 177.5 | 289.2 | 290.0 | 314.4 | 276.3 | 386.5 | 539.7 | 661.2 | 846.3 | 734.2 | 721.7 |
| Interior plants | 19.5 | 26.5 | 31.1 | 37.7 | 38.6 | 52.0 | 98.2 | 109.6 | 131.5 | 112.9 | 106.9 |
| *Total payroll*[b] | | | | | | | | | | | |
| All plants | 115.5 | 194.7 | 194.4 | 215.6 | 200.3 | 262.5 | 371.4 | 456.4 | 597.7 | 445.8 | 390.7 |
| Border plants | 107.7 | 181.4 | 180.1 | 199.9 | 183.8 | 241.8 | 339.6 | 413.7 | 537.2 | 402.4 | 354.0 |
| Interior plants | 7.8 | 13.3 | 14.2 | 15.7 | 16.5 | 20.7 | 31.8 | 42.7 | 60.5 | 43.4 | 36.7 |
| | *Index numbers of constant Mexican pesos (1975=100)*[c] | | | | | | | | | | |
| *Value added* | | | | | | | | | | | |
| All plants | 87.2 | 113.2 | 100.0 | 116.7 | 118.6 | 142.0 | 174.7 | 168.5 | 178.0 | 217.9 | 222.1 |
| Border plants | 87.1 | 114.9 | 100.0 | 115.3 | 115.2 | 138.6 | 163.7 | 160.1 | 170.6 | 209.2 | 214.4 |
| Interior plants | 89.2 | 98.2 | 100.0 | 126.6 | 150.1 | 173.9 | 277.7 | 247.4 | 247.2 | 299.3 | 295.5 |
| *Total payroll*[b] | | | | | | | | | | | |
| All plants | 84.5 | 115.4 | 100.0 | 118.0 | 124.6 | 140.4 | 168.0 | 164.8 | 179.8 | 189.4 | 173.0 |
| Border plants | 85.1 | 116.0 | 100.0 | 118.1 | 123.4 | 139.6 | 165.8 | 161.2 | 174.4 | 184.4 | 169.1 |
| Interior plants | 78.1 | 107.9 | 100.0 | 117.6 | 140.5 | 151.6 | 196.9 | 211.1 | 247.2 | 251.9 | 222.0 |

Sources: SPP and SEPAFIN tables, both published and unpublished; figures are rounded.

a. The economic concept of value added includes only payments to the factors of production, such as wages, rents, interest, and profits. In this and other tables, however, the term stands for the value added in Mexican assembly operations to the imported components and therefore includes local materials and utilities used.

b. Total payroll includes wages and benefits.

c. Deflated by the Mexican consumer price index. The CPI was chosen because the wholesale price index covers Mexico City only, and value added in Mexico consists primarily of wages, services, and profits, Mexican materials constituting only a small proportion.

U.S. firms. The facts are, according to data from the Banco de México, that both the border transactions and tourism have consistently earned Mexico substantial net foreign exchange, which since the mid 1970s has exceeded $1 billion a year.[15] Whether, and by how much, the surpluses on these accounts would have been larger in the absence of assembly operations for U.S. firms is still an open question.

In any event, as a net earner of foreign exchange maquila exports are

15. The Banco de México records separately estimates of expenditures of residents of the Mexican border region across the frontier in the United States and expenditures of U.S. residents in the Mexican border region. The two flows have shown a consistent surplus in favor of Mexico. In 1978 the surplus of $732 million represented 45 percent of Mexico's total border income, not including earnings from maquila exports; see Banco de México, *Indicadores económicos,* April 1979. This "retention coefficient"—the proportion of Mexico's border income that is not spent in the United States—fluctuates with the degree of overvaluation or undervaluation of the Mexican peso in relation to the U.S. dollar. In the Mexican balance-of-payments statistics "tourist income and expenditures" are measured as flows outside the border region.

important, since all the value added is exported (see table 4-3).[16] Thus since 1973 the exports of maquila services have earned for Mexico between 30 percent and 45 percent as much as total Mexican manufactured exports.[17]

## Characteristics of the Assembly Industry

Assembly operations tend to have special characteristics everywhere. They are generally more easily identifiable than other manufacturing processes and can usually be separated and done elsewhere, away from the earlier stages of production; most often they are less capital-intensive and do not require highly skilled labor.

In Mexico, in addition to these factors, the nature of the industry is heavily influenced by its proximity to the U.S. market. Not only are the costs of transport to that market less than from any other developing country, they can be reduced practically to insignificance through choice

16. Maquila exports are included in the service category rather than the merchandise export category in Mexican balance-of-payments statistics. They therefore do not correspond to U.S. import statistics under tariff items 806 and 807. The former include U.S. and other non-Mexican components as well as the Mexican value added. The dutiable value of 806/807 imports should reflect Mexican value added plus the value of non-Mexican and non-U.S. components. Data concerning Mexican maquila exports include Mexican assembly exports to all destinations, not only to the United States.

For these reasons, statistical discrepancies inevitably emerge between U.S. and Mexican data. In addition there are the usual discrepancies between values f.o.b. and c.i.f., there are lags in the recording of transactions, and some U.S. 806/807 imports come from Mexican assembly plants not under the maquila regime—plants that are in free zones and prefer to export under the free-zone regimes—and are therefore not listed in Mexican maquila statistics. On the other hand, there are maquila exports that contain no U.S. components or otherwise do not qualify for U.S. 806 or 807 tariff exemptions and are therefore not listed in U.S. data. Nevertheless, these factors may account for only part of the huge discrepancies, which have become wider each year. In 1983 the U.S. figure was more than twice as large as the Mexican. Until 1977 U.S. 806/807 dutiable import figures were used for the foreign-exchange earnings of the maquiladoras in the Mexican balance-of-payments statistics. Since 1978 the Banco de México has used the statistics of the Secretariat of Programming and Budget (SPP), which have been much lower than the U.S. import numbers. Because the SPP data are based on reports from the maquiladoras, it is possible, if not probable, that they represent significant underestimates. See table 4-3 for the discrepancies.

17. They earn more than twice as much if only those manufactures are considered that are similar to the maquila product lines. Earnings from maquila operation and from manufactured exports are not quite comparable. Maquila services are net of U.S. components and components of other countries for which assembly is done. They are thus net of most imports. Regular manufactured exports, however, include imported components and therefore tend to overstate net foreign-exchange earnings when they are compared with maquila earnings.

Table 4-3. *Comparison of Mexican and U.S. Data concerning Value Added in Mexican Assembly Plants, Exports of Mexican Assembly Services, and U.S. Dutiable Imports of Products Assembled in Mexico, 1973–83*

Millions of U.S. dollars

| *Year* | *Value added in assembly plants (1)* | *Net exports of Mexican assembly plants (2)* | *Dutiable value of U.S. 807.00 and 806.30 imports from Mexico (3)* |
|---|---|---|---|
| 1973 | 197 | 278 | 286 |
| 1974 | 316 | 444 | 464 |
| 1975 | 321 | 454 | 467 |
| 1976 | 352 | 536 | 536 |
| 1977 | 315 | 525 | 524 |
| 1978 | 439 | 452[a] | 714 |
| 1979 | 638 | 638 | 1,016 |
| 1980 | 771 | 773 | 1,155 |
| 1981 | 978 | 976 | 1,272 |
| 1982 | 847 | 832 | 1,383 |
| 1983 | 829 | n.a. | 1,808 |

Sources: Column 1, SPP tables, converted to U.S. dollars at prevailing rates of exchange (see table 4-16); column 2, Banco de México, annual reports, 1973–83; column 3, U.S. International Trade Commission (ITC), *Tariff Items 807.00 and 806.30: U.S. Imports for Consumption,* various years; figures are rounded.

n.a. Not available.

a. The 1978 figure was originally $714.3 million (Banco de México, 1978 annual report) but was revised downward 37 percent in the annual reports for 1979 and 1980.

of location within Mexico. Low transport costs in turn help determine the kinds of product that will be assembled. The long border between the two countries affects wages, ownership, and management by virtue of the ease of communication and therefore also of troubleshooting between the principals and the subsidiaries or subcontractors.

### *Products, Location, and Size*

The variety of Mexican assembly activities is wide and has been increasing. It ranges from toys and dolls and the sorting of U.S. retail-store coupons to sophisticated electronic equipment (see table 4-4). Imports in the ten most important product groups averaged about 80 percent of total value of assembly output imported by the United States from Mexico during 1969–71 but only about 70 percent during 1979–81. If television receivers and parts are excluded, the percentages drop from 60 to 45, indicating a diversification during the decade (see table 4-5).

Table 4-4. *Rank of Mexico among Countries from Which the United States Imports Assembled Manufactured Products under Tariff Items 807.00 and 806.30, by Selected ITC Category, 1970–71 and 1980*

| *Product category* | *1970–71* | *1980* |
|---|---|---|
| Television receivers and parts | 2 | 1 |
| Semiconductors and parts | 1 | 7 |
| Textile products | 1 | 1 |
| Office machines | 3 | 3 |
| Motor vehicle parts | 3 | 2 |
| Equipment for electric circuits | 1 | 1 |
| Electric motors and generators | a | 1 |
| Electrical conductors | a | 1 |
| Capacitors | a | 1 |
| Miscellaneous other electrical products | a | 1 |
| Radio apparatus and parts | a | 3 |
| Recording media | a | 1 |
| Luggage and handbags | a | 1 |
| Toys and dolls | a | 1 |
| Lumber and paper products | a | 1 |
| Scientific instruments | a | 1 |

Sources: 1970–71, magnetic tapes specially prepared by the ITC; 1980, ITC, *Tariff Items 807.00 and 806.30: U.S. Imports for Consumption, Specified Years, 1966–80* (ITC, June 1981).
a. Less than third place.

As the variety has increased, the composition of the product mix has changed. Textile products (including apparel), toys and dolls, and similar simple light industry constituted a fourth of all maquila output in 1969, but in 1981 they accounted for only a twelfth. Television receivers and parts, by far the most important single product group in Mexican assembly operations, now make up about a quarter of the total. Semiconductors and parts, which, with more than 16 percent of the total, were almost as important as the television group in 1969, accounted for less than 6 percent in 1980. Motor vehicle parts were not a significant assembly product in 1969, but in recent years they have occupied between the third and seventh place in order of importance in Mexico's maquila operations.[18]

The 600 maquiladoras operating in 1983 assembled at least $3.7 billion worth of products—the amount that was imported by the United States under tariff items 807 and 806 that year (see table 4-6). If products assembled in Mexico for other countries, principally Japan, are added, the value

18. See table 4-4 for the importance of Mexican assembly products in total U.S. 806/807 imports.

Table 4-5. *Ten Most Important Products Imported from Mexico by the United States under Tariff Items 807.00 and 806.30, 1969, 1973, 1978, and 1981*

| | *1969* | | *1973* | | *1978* | | *1981*[a] | |
|---|---|---|---|---|---|---|---|---|
| *ITC product category* | *Percent of total value* | *Rank* | *Percent of total value* | *Rank* | *Percent of total value* | *Rank* | *Percent of total value* | *Rank* |
| Television receivers and parts | 17.1 | 1 | 22.3 | 1 | 25.0 | 1 | 23.2 | 1 |
| Semiconductors and parts | 16.3 | 2 | 12.0 | 3 | 5.0 | 5 | 5.6 | 6 |
| Toys, dolls, and models | 11.9 | 3 | 2.8 | 9 | ... | ... | ... | ... |
| Textile products | 11.5 | 4 | 12.2 | 2 | 10.2 | 2 | 7.5 | 3 |
| Office machines | 9.0 | 5 | 7.5 | 4 | 2.8 | 10 | 3.5 | 8 |
| Electronic memories | 4.0 | 6 | ... | ... | ... | ... | ... | ... |
| Scientific instruments | 3.8 | 7 | ... | ... | ... | ... | 3.3 | 9 |
| Piston engines and parts | 2.9 | 8 | 2.6 | 10 | ... | ... | ... | ... |
| Hand tools and cutlery | 2.4 | 9 | ... | ... | ... | ... | ... | ... |
| Resistors and parts | 2.2 | 10 | ... | ... | ... | ... | ... | ... |
| Electric motors and generators | ... | ... | 2.8 | 8 | 3.8 | 6 | 5.8 | 5 |
| Equipment for electric circuits | ... | ... | 4.2 | 5 | 5.7 | 4 | 6.8 | 4 |
| Motor vehicle parts | ... | ... | 2.9 | 6 | 6.2 | 3 | 3.8[b] | 7 |
| Capacitors | ... | ... | 2.9 | 7 | 3.7 | 7 | ... | ... |
| Electrical conductors | ... | ... | ... | ... | 3.4 | 8 | 8.6 | 2 |
| Miscellaneous other electrical products and parts | ... | ... | ... | ... | 3.4 | 9 | 3.0 | 10 |
| Percent of value of ten most important products | 81.1 | ... | 71.2 | ... | 69.1 | ... | 71.1 | ... |
| *Addendum* | | | | | | | | |
| Total 806/807 value (millions of dollars) | 145.2 | | 651.2 | | 1,539.8 | | 2,655.6 | |

Sources: 1969, 1973, and 1978, magnetic tapes specially prepared by the ITC; 1981, special tabulations by the ITC.
a. Includes only 807.00 imports.
b. If 806.30 imports were included, this percentage would be 4.3.

Table 4-6. *Total Value of U.S. Imports from Mexico under Tariff Items 807.00 and 806.30, Dutiable and Duty-free Value, and Dutiable Value as Percent of Total Value, 1969–83*

Millions of U.S. dollars unless otherwise specified

| *Year* | *Total value (1)* | *Duty-free value (2)* | *Dutiable value (3)* | *Dutiable value as percent of total value (3 ÷ 1) (4)* |
|---|---|---|---|---|
| 1969 | 150.0 | 97.9 | 52.1 | 34.7 |
| 1970 | 218.8 | 138.3 | 80.5 | 36.8 |
| 1971 | 270.4 | 166.0 | 104.4 | 38.6 |
| 1972 | 426.4 | 256.3 | 170.1 | 39.9 |
| 1973 | 651.2 | 364.8 | 286.4 | 44.0 |
| 1974 | 1,032.6 | 568.7 | 463.9 | 44.9 |
| 1975 | 1,019.8 | 552.4 | 467.4 | 45.8 |
| 1976 | 1,135.4 | 599.9 | 535.5 | 47.2 |
| 1977 | 1,155.5 | 631.1 | 524.4 | 45.4 |
| 1978 | 1,539.8 | 826.0 | 713.8 | 46.4 |
| 1979 | 2,065.1 | 1,049.4 | 1,015.7 | 49.2 |
| 1980 | 2,341.4 | 1,186.3 | 1,155.1 | 49.3 |
| 1981 | 2,709.7 | 1,437.7 | 1,272.0 | 46.9 |
| 1982 | 2,837.5 | 1,454.1 | 1,383.4 | 48.8 |
| 1983 | 3,716.9 | 1,968.7 | 1,808.2 | 48.6 |

Sources: ITC, *Tariff Items 807.00 and 806.30: U.S. Imports for Consumption*, various issues; and special computer printouts from the ITC for 1983. Figures are rounded.

of the maquila output may well have reached $4 billion in 1983. About half the output consisted of U.S. components.

Most of the plants are concentrated in six towns along the border, from Tijuana, just south of San Diego, California, on the Pacific Ocean, to Matamoros, opposite Brownsville, Texas, near the Gulf of Mexico.[19] In 1983 about 11 percent of the total, 67 plants, were in the interior of the country (see table 4-1). The proportion, while still small, has been increasing. (In 1973 there were only 10 plants—less than 4 percent of the total at that time—located away from the border.) The plants in the interior are now situated in nearly every part of the country, including the three largest cities, Mexico City, Guadalajara, and Monterrey.

Not only the number of plants in Mexico's maquila industry but also

19. In 1980 the distribution of the plants among the six towns was as follows: 123 in Tijuana, 79 in Mexicali, 59 in Nogales, 22 in Agua Prieta, 121 in Cuidad Juárez, and 50 in Matamoros. In addition to the 454 plants in these towns, there were 97 factories located elsewhere along the border, with fewer than 20 plants in each location.

their size increased. Estimates indicate that there was an average of about 120 workers per plant during the early 1970s.[20] The number rose to about 160 during the mid 1970s, an average of about 200 workers per plant at the end of the decade and about 250 by 1983.[21]

The largest plants tend to be located in modern industrial parks; in Ciudad Juárez, where the largest industrial park for maquiladoras is located, the average reached 400 workers per establishment in 1983. Small plants prevail in the Far West: plants in Tijuana and Mexicali averaged about 130 workers each. Maquiladoras in the interior are slightly smaller than at the border.[22] Plant size also varies with type of product; furniture assembly is generally done in small plants, assembly of electrical machinery and equipment in large plants.

### *Ownership*

The majority of the maquila output in Mexico is produced by foreign subsidiaries operating in that country. And since 90 percent or more of the assembly is for the U.S. market, most of these subsidiaries are U.S.-owned or controlled.

Mexican capital, however, has also been important in maquila operations. While data are incomplete and contradictory, some patterns can be discerned. One Mexican source indicates that in 1979, the majority of the capital of only 259 of the 540 firms operating as maquiladoras—48 percent—was foreign; 95 percent of that came from the United States.[23] Another Mexican study says that 55 percent of the maquiladoras are wholly foreign-owned.[24] The U.S. embassy in Mexico cites a report that 35 percent of the firms had Mexican capital and managers in 1979.[25] A recent publication of the Third World Center in Mexico asserts that U.S. companies

20. Airgrams from the U.S. embassy in Mexico: A-265, dated June 4, 1971; A-388, dated June 30, 1972; and A-61, dated February 14, 1973.

21. Unpublished tables of the SPP.

22. The three plants in greater Mexico City were quite small, in 1983 averaging about 15 workers each, while in Guadalajara the 13 plants employed an average of more than 360 workers each.

23. Table submitted by the Secretaría de Hacienda y Credito Publico to the Second Seminar on North-South Complementary Intra-Industry Trade, sponsored by UNCTAD and the Brookings Institution, Mexico City, August 18–22, 1980. See also *Actualidad,* May 1981, p. 16.

24. Ballí and others, "Evolución y perspectivas," p. 33.

25. Unclassified section of cable 1071, dated January 21, 1980, from the U.S. embassy in Mexico City.

control 90 percent of all maquila operations in Mexico.[26] But in the same article there is a table in which it is shown that in 1978 only 11, or less than 30 percent, of the 38 plants established in the interior of Mexico were wholly U.S.-owned, while another 11 were wholly Mexican-owned; majority ownership of an additional 3 was Mexican, and between 16 and 40 percent of the capital of 4 more was Mexican. In other words, there was substantial Mexican capital in half the maquiladoras located in the interior of Mexico in 1978. Mexican capital is also involved in industrial parks designed for maquiladoras. The largest park of maquiladoras in the country, located in Ciudad Juárez, is Mexican-owned and operated.

In the past, most of the U.S.-controlled maquiladoras were subsidiaries of medium-sized multinational enterprises. More recently, however, some of the giants in U.S. industry have established assembly operations in Mexico. At least forty-eight of the Fortune 500 had maquiladoras in 1978. In addition, three of the largest Japanese firms and four of the top European industrial concerns operated assembly plants in Mexico that year.[27] The interest of Japanese and European companies in Mexican assembly production appears to be increasing.[28] While it is understandable that foreign participation would be greater in the maquila industry than in other economic activities, it should be noted that the share of all Mexican manufactured output produced by foreign transnational companies has increased since World War II.[29]

Foreign companies, instead of establishing their own subsidiaries, also subcontract with Mexican firms to undertake the assembly operation for them. Many of these are "captive" plants—that is, each produces for only one foreign company; the majority, however, each provide assembly services for two or more foreign enterprises. They can be found all along the

26. Ernesto Calderón, "Las maquiladoras de los paises centrales que operan en el Tercer Mundo," in *Maquiladoras,* Lecturas de CEESTEM (México: Centro de Estudios Económicos Sociales del Tercer Mundo [CEESTEM], 1981), p. 92.

27. Van Waas, "The Multinationals' Strategy," p. 34.

28. Federico Barrio, "El contexto historico de los programas federales para el desarrollo económico de la zona fronteriza," paper presented at Symposium on the Economic Development and Administration in the North Border Region of Mexico, Juárez, November 22, 1979, pp. 8–9; U.S. embassy cable 1071, January 21, 1980; and Lecturas de CEESTEM, pp. 92–93.

29. See, for example, Rhys Jenkins, "Foreign Firms, Manufactured Exports and Development Strategy: The Case of Mexico," *Boletin de Estudios Latinoamericanos y del Caribe,* no. 23 (Amsterdam, December 1977); R. S. Newfarmer and W. F. Mueller, "Multinational Corporations in Brazil and Mexico: Structural Sources of Economic and Noneconomic Power," prepared for the Subcommittee on Multinational Corporations of the Senate Committee on Foreign Relations, 94 Cong. 1 sess. (GPO, 1975), pp. 45–94.

border, but many are concentrated in the area along the California border, near their U.S. contracting companies. Most of the captive plants, principally those in the apparel industry, and some of the others receive much of the machinery and equipment for assembly operations on loan or on a rental basis from the subcontracting company in the United States. These are usually secondhand items, seldom up-to-date hardware. The fact that the equipment belongs to the foreign contractor—usually a U.S. firm—means that it can be withdrawn after completion of an assembly job. The usual agreement, however, calls for a continuing contractual relationship.

A variant of subcontracting used in Mexico is a temporary arrangement, generally called a "shelter plan," under which local and special firms in Mexico who "know the ropes" provide assembly services for a foreign concern until the foreign company is ready to establish its own subsidiary, enters into a long-term relationship with a Mexican firm, or decides not to assemble in Mexico. The firms that offer shelter plans range from consulting firms that only advise foreign companies wishing to set up shop in Mexico to well-equipped plants that can engage in a variety of assembly operations with machinery and equipment provided by the client.

The shelter plan thus permits a foreign company to try out assembly operations abroad without immediately having to make long-term commitments. The local firm "shelters" the foreigner from the red tape involved in initiating foreign production. This covers legalities in dealing with government offices, hiring and administration of workers and technicians, and compliance with rules, regulations, and customs. Since the foreign company's management personnel will be on the site, local procedures can be learned on the job.[30]

### *Capital Requirements*

Almost by definition, assembly operations, even in foreign plants that generally make up the largest maquiladoras, tend to have very low capital-to-labor ratios compared to those of other manufacturing activities. Ac-

30. For a discussion of the shelter-plan system see M. Richard Campbell, "Production Sharing, Implications for Industrial Promotion in Developing Countries," *Journal of the Flagstaff Institute,* vol. 3 (January 1979), p. 37. There is nothing that prevents the foreign company from continuing with the shelter-plan firm except that it is expensive and probably defeats the purpose of assembly abroad in the long run. In 1980, the fees charged by a shelter-plan concern varied between $2.00 and $2.50 an hour per direct labor employee. (From a brochure on the Nogales Shelter Plan, Nogales Industrial Park, Nogales, Mexico.) If there were fifty operators this could amount to about $250,000 for a single year.

cording to one Mexican economist, capital investment per worker was less than 10,000 pesos in the maquila industries of Mexico in 1974, while the capital investment per worker in all Mexican manufacturing industry was 62,000 pesos in 1970.[31] The difference may be exaggerated, because on the one hand, capital in the maquila industry may be underestimated, and on the other, compared to that in other developing countries the capital-to-labor ratio in manufacturing is very high in Mexico.[32] Nevertheless the gap between the capital requirements of maquila operations and the average for all manufacturing as reported in the Mexican industrial census is striking. It is likely that the difference has narrowed since the 1974 estimate, because larger and more capital-intensive assembly plants have begun operations in the country during the past decade. The available data are brought together in table 4-7, but comparisons between one period and another should only be made with great caution—particularly with the 1977 data, which are derived from a U.S. source and are not consistent with the Mexican statistics (see table 4-7, note a).

### *Value Added*

The difference in capital investment per worker in assembly operations and that in the rest of manufacturing also means that value added by the worker in the maquiladoras is lower than in other manufacturing plants. In 1975, until now the only year for which Mexican industrial census data and maquila information from the Secretariat of Programming and Budget coincide, the statistics indicate that the maquila value added per worker—approximately $4,800—is somewhat less than two-thirds of the total manufacturing value added per worker, $7,500.[33] If it is considered that

31. Leopoldo Solís, "Industrial Priorities in Mexico," in United Nations Industrial Development Organization (UNIDO), *Industrial Priorities in Developing Countries* (United Nations, 1979), pp. 108–09.

32. Machinery and equipment on loan (by the principal) to independent subcontractors, particularly in textile assembly, may not be reported to census takers. See Xirau and Díaz, *Nuestra dependencia fronteriza,* table 34.

33. Converted to U.S. dollars at official exchange rates. The source of maquila value added and employee data is the Oficina de Maquiladoras, Departamento de Estadisticas Industriales, Secretaría de Programación y Presupuesto (SPP), Mexico City; for all manufacturing, World Bank, *Mexico, Manufacturing Sector: Situation, Prospects and Policies* (World Bank, March 1979), table 3.4.

The difference in value added in assembly and value added in all manufacturing may be overstated because there is at least one sector in the maquila industry that cannot be classified as manufacturing, namely, the sorting of discount coupons clipped from newspapers and mailings and used in retail stores. The value added per worker in this maquila sector may be as much as 20 percent below the average.

Table 4-7. *Capital per Worker in Mexican Industry, 1970 and Selected Dates, 1972–77*[a]

| Area and date | *Gross fixed assets per worker in all manufacturing* | | | | *Machinery and equipment per worker in assembly industries* | | | |
|---|---|---|---|---|---|---|---|---|
| | *All sectors* | | *Electric and electronic sector* | | *All sectors* | | *Electric and electronic sector* | |
| | *Pesos* | *U.S. dollars* | *Pesos* | *U.S. dollars* | *Pesos* | *U.S. dollars* | *Pesos* | *U.S. dollars* |
| 1970 | | | | | | | | |
| Border towns | 35,174 | 2,814 | n.a. | n.a. | 7,314 | 585 | 8,308 | 665 |
| Mexicali | 38,179 | 3,054 | n.a. | n.a. | 3,553 | 284 | n.a. | n.a. |
| Tijuana | 19,476 | 1,558 | n.a. | n.a. | 5,586 | 447 | n.a. | n.a. |
| Nogales | 9,235 | 739 | n.a. | n.a. | 2,595 | 208 | n.a. | n.a. |
| Matamoros | 21,692 | 1,735 | n.a. | n.a. | 10,773 | 862 | n.a. | n.a. |
| Juárez | n.a. | n.a. | n.a. | n.a. | 11,685 | 935 | n.a. | n.a. |
| All Mexico | 62,880 | 5,030 | 34,420 | 2,754 | 7,314 | 585 | 8,308 | 665 |
| August 1972 | n.a. | n.a. | n.a. | n.a. | 5,200 | 416 | n.a. | n.a. |
| April 30, 1973 | n.a. | n.a. | n.a. | n.a. | 15,422 | 1,234 | n.a. | n.a. |
| June 1973 | n.a. | n.a. | n.a. | n.a. | 14,700 | 1,176 | n.a. | n.a. |
| January 31, 1974 | n.a. | n.a. | n.a. | n.a. | 14,536 | 1,163 | 12,439 | 995 |
| October 1974 | n.a. | n.a. | n.a. | n.a. | 9,300 | 744 | n.a. | n.a. |
| 1977 | n.a. | 9,043 | n.a. | 3,093 | n.a. | 5,433 | n.a. | 2,368 |

Sources: All Mexico, 1970, IX Industrial Census, as reported in *Centro nacional de información e estadisticas del trabajo* (Mexico, D.F., 1977), table 3.4.1.3, pp. 110–19; border towns, 1970, Joaquín Xirau Icaza and Miguel Díaz, *Nuestra dependencia fronteriza,* Archivo del Fondo 48 (Mexico, D.F.: Fondo de Cultura Económica, 1976), table 37 (based on IX Industrial Census); assembly industries, border towns, electric and electronic sector, 1970, Secretaria de Industria y Comercio (SIC), Dirección General de Industrias, *Posibilidades industriales del programa de maquiladoras* (Mexico, D.F.: SIC, 1974), pp. 85, 89; August 1972, June 1973, and October 1974, Leopoldo Solís, "Industrial Priorities in Mexico," in UNIDO, *Industrial Priorities in Developing Countries* (United Nations, 1979), table 15, p. 109; April 30, 1973, Xirau and Diaz, *Nuestra dependencia,* table 33; January 31, 1974, Victor Urquidi and Sofia Méndez Villareal, "Economic Importance of Mexico's Northern Border Region," in Stanley R. Ross, ed., *Views across the Border* (University of New Mexico Press, 1978), table 8, p. 150; 1977, U.S. Department of Commerce, Bureau of Economic Analysis, *U.S. Direct Investment Abroad 1977* (GPO, April 1981).

n.a. Not available.

a. To arrive at the figures for all manufacturing, the figures given for the net property of plant and equipment of Mexican affiliates of U.S. companies were divided by the numbers of employees in Mexico of these affiliates. A similar calculation was made for the assembly industries, using the corresponding data for the majority-owned foreign affiliates of U.S. companies (MOFA) in Mexico, under the assumption that MOFA are permitted to operate in Mexico only under the maquiladora program, since otherwise Mexican majority ownership is required. For obvious reasons, 1977 data are not comparable with data for earlier years.

average fixed capital per worker in all manufacturing may be at least three times that in the assembly industries, the output that can be obtained from a unit of capital in the latter is obviously about twice that in manufacturing as a whole.[34]

Value added per worker in assembly industries increased sharply be-

34. The comparison of capital requirements has been adjusted for underestimation of capital requirements in maquiladoras; unadjusted the ratio is 6:1 for 1974 as reported by Solís in "Industrial Priorities in Mexico" and almost 9:1 as reported in the 1970 census (see table 4-7). Using the relations of 3:1 for the capital–labor ratios and 1.5:1 for the value added–labor ratios, the value added–capital ratio in the assembly industry is twice as high as that in the total manufacturing sector in Mexico.

tween the early 1970s and the early 1980s. The severe recession, however, accompanied by massive devaluations of the peso in 1982 and the subsequent upsurge in Mexican inflation, reduced both the dollar value and the real value added per worker, in constant pesos, in 1983 (see table 4-9). It should be noted, however, that if value added is measured by the dutiable U.S. 806/807 imports from Mexico—the value added in Mexico to U.S. components—the recent picture looks quite different. Dollar value added per worker continued to rise rapidly, even after 1981, increasing by nearly a quarter to about $12,000 in 1983 (calculated from tables 4-1 and 4-6; see note 16 for a partial explanation of the discrepancies between U.S. and Mexican data).

In recent years, wages have accounted for more than half of total value added at the border but have averaged about 40 percent in the interior plants. Materials have made up about 2 percent of value added at the border and five times as much in the interior. Rents and utilities have also represented a higher proportion of value added in the interior, averaging well over a fourth, than at the border, where they have been less than 20 percent. Since 1978, the same has been true of profits and taxes, which have been more than 20 percent in the interior, less at the border (see table 4-8).[35]

35. An examination of U.S. import data may give an erroneous picture of the changing importance of foreign assembly operations for the host countries. As discussed in chapter 1, U.S. imports under tariff items 806 and 807 are divided into duty-free and dutiable imports. The latter represent the U.S. components that are reimported exempt from tariff, while the former represent the gross value added abroad, which is subject to tariffs. U.S. International Trade Commission data show that the proportion of dutiable imports in total 806/807 imports from Mexico rose steadily between 1969 and 1980, with a minor and temporary setback during 1977–78 as an aftereffect of the Mexican devaluation in the fall of 1976. In 1980 almost half these imports were dutiable, up from slightly more than a third in 1969 (see table 4-6).

The interpretation that, because the share of gross value added in Mexico increased, the linkages of U.S. assembly activities abroad to the Mexican economy increased must be regarded with skepticism. First, not only non-U.S., but also non-Mexican components are included in dutiable imports under 806/807 and, therefore, in this definition of value added in Mexico. As noted earlier the number of these components, primarily Mexican imports from the Far East for use in U.S. assembly plants, seems to have increased during recent years. Second, the product mix appears to have changed in favor of assembly sectors in which Mexican value added is more important, particularly television receivers and parts and motor vehicle parts, moving away from textiles (including apparel) and toys and dolls, where the relative value added is below the average. Third, Mexican wages and prices of gross value added components such as rents and utilities have risen faster than the value of U.S. components, thus contributing to a rise in the share of Mexican value added in U.S. 806/807 imports

Table 4-8. *Average Percentage Composition of Value Added in Mexican Assembly Plants, by Location, 1980–81*[a]

| *Component of value added* | *All plants* | *Interior plants* | *Border plants* |
|---|---|---|---|
| Wages and salaries | 63 | 43 | 60 |
| Materials and supplies | 2 | 12 | 3 |
| Rents and utilities (including transportation and maintenance) | 19 | 25 | 20 |
| Profits (including taxes) | 16 | 20 | 17 |
| Total | 100 | 100 | 100 |

Sources: SPP tables.
a. See table 4-2, note a.

The operations of the maquiladoras in the interior appear to have been successful. Value added per worker there averaged well over a third more than the value added per worker in the border maquiladoras during the decade 1974–83 (see table 4-9). In 1983 the profit shares of the maquiladoras in the interior were almost 50 percent higher than those at the border.[36]

### *Wages*

Maquila wages appear to have risen steeply during the mid 1970s, outpacing the consumer price index. The payroll per employee—both blue-collar and white-collar workers—increased about 16 percent in real terms in 1974 above that of the preceding year and about 7 percent from 1975 to 1976. Since 1977, remunerations per worker in maquiladoras have declined in constant prices so that by 1983 they were—in real purchasing power in Mexico—13 percent below the 1973 level (see table 4-10).[37] This does not mean that real maquila wages have fared much worse than wages in other manufacturing sectors. The average national index of official mini-

from that country. It is this effect, the rapid rise of the wage and utility bills, that does signify an important expansion of the linkages between the maquiladoras and the Mexican economy. U.S. import data, however, do not indicate whether or not the share of Mexican materials used in assembly plants has increased.

36. From unpublished tables of the SPP.

37. Data for the hourly compensation of production workers (which is calculated by dividing the payroll of production workers in assembly plants, excluding fringe benefits, by the hours worked by production workers, a series that is available only beginning with 1975) also show the 1976 rise and the subsequent decline in real terms; see table 4-11.

Table 4-9. *Value Added per Employee in Mexican Assembly Plants, 1973–83*[a]

| *Location* | *1973* | *1974* | *1975* | *1976* | *1977* | *1978* | *1979* | *1980* | *1981* | *1982* | *1983* |
|---|---|---|---|---|---|---|---|---|---|---|---|
| | | | | | *Thousands of U.S. dollars* | | | | | | |
| All plants | 3.1 | 4.2 | 4.8 | 4.7 | 4.0 | 4.8 | 5.7 | 6.4 | 7.5 | 6.7 | 5.5 |
| Border plants | 3.1 | 4.1 | 4.7 | 4.7 | 3.9 | 4.7 | 5.4 | 6.2 | 7.3 | 6.5 | 5.3 |
| Interior plants | 2.6[b] | 5.5 | 6.1 | 5.4 | 5.0 | 6.3 | 9.1 | 8.5 | 9.1 | 8.2 | 6.7 |
| | | | | | *Index numbers of constant Mexican pesos (1975 = 100)*[c] | | | | | | |
| All plants | 91.1 | 100.1 | 100.0 | 105.3 | 101.6 | 105.2 | 104.9 | 94.3 | 90.9 | 115.3 | 99.0 |
| Border plants | 95.4 | 100.4 | 100.0 | 106.2 | 101.3 | 104.6 | 100.5 | 92.7 | 90.4 | 114.8 | 98.8 |
| Interior plants | 59.4[b] | 102.2 | 100.0 | 93.8 | 98.2 | 105.9 | 130.7 | 97.3 | 86.8 | 109.8 | 93.9 |

Sources: Table 4-16 and SPP tables.
a. See table 4-2, note a.
b. Figure may not be comparable with figures for subsequent years.
c. Deflated by the Mexican consumer price index (see table 4-2, note c).

mum wages, put into constant prices, showed much sharper declines, as do the fragmentary data on average wages (see tables 4-10 and 4-11).[38]

For some purposes, however, it is advisable to express assembly wages in dollars. Converted into dollars, maquiladora wages increased enormously until 1981, the upward trend interrupted only by a temporary decline as a result of the 1976 devaluation of the peso.[39] Thus dollar wages increased more than 50 percent between 1973 and 1975—while Mexican purchasing power of assembly wages increased only 13 percent—and about 80 percent between 1977 and 1981. The massive 1982 devaluation

38. Theoretically there can be as many as 9,546 individual minimum wages, set by national and local commissions according to type of job and geographic area (86 occupational classifications for 111 geographic zones). By combining the zones into large geographic groups, the government has reduced the number, so that in January 1984 "only" 344 different minimum wages were set. They are set at the beginning of each year—and, during periods of high inflation, at other times during the year as well; see the issues of *Diario oficial* as of December 30 each year and *Salarios mínimos,* published annually by the Comision Nacional de los Salarios Mínimos. Minimum wages have been calculated here on the basis of unweighted arithmetic averages for each period. For the border figure the unweighted average of minimum wages in the border zones was used. The *national* unweighted average was used as a proxy for minimum wages in the interior. When a minimum wage was changed during a year, a day-weighted average was calculated for the year. Subsequent to the completion of this study a national arithmetic average weighted by the economically active population in each zone was published for each period since 1964 by the Mexican Minimum Wage Commission. The resultant weighted averages are somewhat higher than the unweighted averages because of the high proportion of the labor force that is entitled to above-average minimum wages, including those at the border; see Comisión Nacional de los Salarios Mínimos, *Salarios mínimos 1984* (Mexico, D.F.: CNSM, 1984).

39. The dramatic devaluation of 1982 again diminished Mexican incomes in dollar terms despite significant peso increases in wages.

Table 4-10. *Wage Indexes of Mexican Assembly Plants, in Constant 1975 Pesos and in Current U.S. Dollar Equivalents, by Location, 1973–83*[a]

1975 = 100

| | *Index of payroll per employee in assembly plants, in 1975 pesos* | | | *Index of payroll per employee in assembly plants, in current U.S. dollar equivalents* | | |
|---|---|---|---|---|---|---|
| *Year* | *All plants* | *Border plants* | *Interior plants* | *All plants* | *Border plants* | *Interior plants* |
| 1973 | 88.3 | 93.2 | 51.8 | 62.0 | 65.5 | 36.4 |
| 1974 | 102.1 | 101.4 | 112.0 | 88.6 | 88.0 | 97.2 |
| 1975 | 100.0 | 100.0 | 100.0 | 100.0 | 100.0 | 100.0 |
| 1976 | 106.5 | 108.7 | 85.3 | 100.3 | 102.2 | 80.2 |
| 1977 | 106.8 | 108.5 | 91.5 | 88.2 | 89.7 | 75.7 |
| 1978 | 104.1 | 105.3 | 92.2 | 100.0 | 101.3 | 88.6 |
| 1979 | 101.4 | 102.5 | 91.9 | 115.4 | 116.5 | 104.5 |
| 1980 | 92.7 | 94.0 | 82.3 | 132.1 | 133.9 | 117.2 |
| 1981 | 92.3 | 93.1 | 86.8 | 157.7 | 159.0 | 148.2 |
| 1982 | 100.3 | 101.3 | 92.5 | 121.3 | 122.5 | 111.7 |
| 1983 | 77.1 | 78.0 | 70.6 | 89.5 | 90.4 | 81.9 |

Sources: Table 4-16 and SPP tables.
a. Assembly plant payrolls include fringe benefits.

Table 4-11. *Index of Hourly Wages Paid to Production Workers in Mexican Assembly Plants, of Minimum Wages at the Border, and of National Average Minimum Wages, in Current and Constant Prices, 1975–83*[a]

1975 = 100

| | *Index of hourly wages paid to production workers in assembly plants* | | | | | | *Index of minimum wages, in constant 1975 prices (unweighted averages)* | |
|---|---|---|---|---|---|---|---|---|
| | *Current prices* | | | *Constant 1975 prices* | | | | |
| *Year* | *All plants* | *Border plants* | *Interior plants* | *All plants* | *Border plants* | *Interior plants* | *Border plants* | *National average* |
| 1975 | 100.0 | 100.0 | 100.0 | 100.0 | 100.0 | 100.0 | 100.0 | 100.0 |
| 1976 | 122.9 | 124.3 | 116.3 | 106.1 | 107.3 | 100.4 | 108.8 | 111.5 |
| 1977 | 155.0 | 155.9 | 165.0 | 103.7 | 104.3 | 110.4 | 107.5 | 110.5 |
| 1978 | 178.9 | 178.4 | 198.8 | 102.0 | 101.7 | 113.3 | 102.4 | 107.5 |
| 1979 | 200.9 | 200.9 | 228.8 | 96.9 | 96.9 | 110.3 | 98.1 | 106.2 |
| 1980 | 234.9 | 236.9 | 255.0 | 89.6 | 90.4 | 97.3 | 87.9 | 98.9 |
| 1981 | 295.5 | 296.4 | 333.7 | 88.2 | 88.4 | 99.6 | 57.2 | 49.8 |
| 1982 | 492.6 | 478.7 | 568.8 | 92.5 | 89.9 | 106.8 | 48.8 | 42.1 |
| 1983 | 773.4 | 753.9 | 862.0 | 75.0 | 75.1 | 72.4 | 38.1 | 32.7 |

Sources: Table 4-16; SPP tables; and Comisión Nacional de los Salarios Mínimos, *Salarios mínimos* (Mexico, D.F.: CNSM, various years).
a. See table 4-2, note a; wages here do not include fringe benefits.

caused a precipitous drop in wages converted into dollars, so the 1983 cost of wages was about 57 percent of the 1981 level (see table 4-9).

Wage changes in dollar terms have two implications. One has to do with the production costs of U.S. firms whose assembly operations are done through U.S. subsidiaries in Mexico. Although they pay their Mexican workers in pesos, it is the dollar cost of the wages that has meaning for U.S. firms. It is obvious that their Mexican wage costs increased much more rapidly than U.S. wages until 1981.

The other effect is on the behavior of assembly workers as consumers. Given the fact that the Mexican peso was freely convertible throughout the period under discussion, the sharp increases in border wages in dollar terms in relation to their stagnant or declining peso purchasing power in Mexico was a strong inducement for maquiladora employees to spend as much as possible of their wages across the border in the United States. Assembly workers on the Mexican side of the border found that the easily obtainable dollar equivalent of their peso wages rose much faster than prices in the United States. Another way of saying this is that the prevailing rates of exchange caused an ever greater overvaluation of the peso in relation to the dollar. With the 1982 devaluation, not only did the dollar become much more expensive, but convertibility became more difficult; in the interior of Mexico, free convertibility became practically nonexistent. Since then, it can be assumed, a much smaller proportion of Mexican border wages has been spent in the United States. This situation will continue to prevail unless considerable disparities in the movement of purchasing power between peso wages and their dollar equivalents emerge once more.

Minimum wages in the border areas tended to be considerably higher than the national average, exceeding the latter by more than half at the beginning of the Mexican border industrialization program. The influence of the high wages and prices on the U.S. side helped create this difference. Since then the border average has fallen behind so that by the early 1980s the difference between border wages and those in the rest of the country was reduced to less than 20 percent (see table 4-12). This may be a result of the announced government policy to equalize wage rates across the country or of a policy, stimulated by the downturn in assembly activities during the mid 1970s, to put the brakes on border wages in order to increase the attractiveness of maquiladoras there to potential investors. The weakness of the labor unions at the border, compared with those in the interior, may also have been a factor in the relative decline of wages there.

Table 4-12. *Unweighted Average Minimum Wages Converted to U.S. Dollars, All Mexico and at the Border, and the Relation between Them, 1970–83*

| | *Unweighted average daily minimum wage (U.S. dollars)*[a] | | |
|---|---|---|---|
| *Year* | *National* | *At the border* | *Border minimum wage as percent of national average minimum wage* |
| 1970 | 1.99 | 2.86 | 143 |
| 1971 | 1.99 | 2.86 | 143 |
| 1972 | 2.34 | 3.37 | 144 |
| 1973 | 2.45[b] | 3.52[b] | 144 |
| 1974 | 3.32[b] | 4.78[b] | 144 |
| 1975 | 3.84 | 5.52 | 144 |
| 1976 | 4.03[b] | 5.65[b] | 140 |
| 1977 | 3.51 | 4.91 | 140 |
| 1978 | 3.97 | 5.44 | 137 |
| 1979 | 4.64 | 6.16 | 133 |
| 1980 | 5.41 | 6.91 | 128 |
| 1981 | 6.82 | 7.82 | 115 |
| 1982 | 4.28[b] | 4.97[b] | 116 |
| 1983 | 3.26[b] | 3.81[b] | 117 |

Sources: *Diario oficial,* December, various years; and *Salarios mínimos,* various years.
a. Converted from pesos to dollars at the average annual rate of exchange.
b. The minimum wage was changed during the year; the rate for the year was averaged proportionately.

Despite some problems with comparability, the data show that average remunerations in the assembly industries have been significantly higher than official minimum wages. In the border plants they were running almost 10 percent higher than the border minimum level until 1973, and they were subsequently much higher. In the interior, assembly wages averaged more than 20 percent higher than the national average minimum wages during the period 1975–83 (see table 4-13).[40]

40. It should be noted that in order to be on the conservative side hourly minimum wages were calculated on the assumption that Mexican workers receive nonworking Sunday pay. To the extent that they do not, the calculated hourly minimum wages would be about 15 percent lower than indicated in the tables, thus enlarging the gap between minimum wages and maquila wages.

In a sample of 224 maquiladora workers in Tijuana, Monica-Claire Gambrill found in 1977–78 that 18 percent of all the workers received a wage lower than the minimum. Among the unskilled it was 21 percent lower; the percentages for women were higher, for men lower. About 36 percent of all workers and 20 percent of the unskilled received more than the minimum. See "La fuerza de trabajo en las maquiladoras," *Maquiladoras,* Lecturas de CEESTEM, pp. 15–16.

Wolfgang Konig found, on the basis of a sample of 622 workers in several selected cities at the border and in the interior, that maquila wages at the border were 101 percent and in the

Table 4-13. *Hourly Wages of Production Workers in Mexican Assembly Industries Compared with Official Mexican Minimum Hourly Wage, by Location of Assembly Plants, 1975–83*

| | *Hourly wages paid to production workers in assembly plants (pesos)*[a] | | *Assembly wages in border plants as percent of assembly wages in interior plants (1 ÷ 2)* | *Minimum hourly wage (pesos)*[b] | | *Assembly wages as percent of minimum wages* | |
|---|---|---|---|---|---|---|---|
| *Year* | *Border plants (1)* | *Interior plants (2)* | *(3)* | *Border region (4)* | *National average (5)* | *Border plants (1 ÷ 4) (6)* | *Interior plants (2 ÷ 5) (7)* |
| 1975 | 11.1 | 8.0 | 138.8 | 10.1 | 7.0 | 109.9 | 114.3 |
| 1976 | 13.8 | 9.3 | 148.4 | 12.7 | 9.0 | 108.7 | 103.3 |
| 1977 | 17.3 | 13.2 | 131.1 | 16.2 | 11.6 | 106.8 | 113.8 |
| 1978 | 19.8 | 15.9 | 124.5 | 18.1 | 13.2 | 109.4 | 120.5 |
| 1979 | 22.3 | 18.3 | 121.9 | 20.5 | 15.4 | 108.8 | 118.8 |
| 1980 | 26.3 | 20.4 | 128.9 | 23.2 | 18.2 | 113.4 | 112.1 |
| 1981 | 32.9 | 26.7 | 123.2 | 28.0 | 24.4 | 117.5 | 109.4 |
| 1982 | 65.5 | 54.6 | 120.0 | 38.0 | 32.8 | 172.4 | 166.5 |
| 1983 | 86.0 | 69.0 | 124.6 | 62.1 | 53.3 | 138.5 | 129.5 |

Sources: Columns 1 and 2, calculated from SPP tables, both published and unpublished; columns 4 and 5, *Diario oficial,* December 30 of each year and September 30, 1976, October 31, 1982, and June 13, 1983; see also *Salarios mínimos,* various years.

a. Does not include fringe benefits.

b. The official minimum wage is given as a daily wage under the assumption that workers are to be paid for nonworking Sundays. The hourly wage was calculated by multiplying the daily minimum wage by seven-sixths, then dividing by eight. Because the minimum wage was changed during 1976, 1982, and 1983, a day-weighted average was calculated for those years.

Assembly wages paid in plants in the border region have been consistently higher than in maquiladoras in the interior of Mexico. While the gap appears to have declined in recent years, it still averaged about 25 percent from 1980 to 1983.

To summarize: Average Mexican wages in the border regions adjoining the United States are considerably higher than in the interior of the country. The difference has been declining, apparently as a result of deliberate government policy and weak labor unions at the border. Wages in the assembly industries have followed this pattern. Nevertheless both at the border and in the interior the wages paid in assembly industries have been higher than respective minimum wages. Insofar as wage differentials are important for foreign assembly operations, the lower wages in the interior of Mexico provide a stronger attraction.

### *Use of Mexican Materials*

The share of materials and supplies provided by the domestic economy is an important indicator of the linkages that foreign assembly activities have for the Mexican economy. That percentage has been exceedingly small. With the exception of 1976, when it rose to 3 percent, it hovered around 1.5 percent of the total use of components and supplies, both imported and domestic, during the period 1975–83. In the plants in the interior, however, the use of domestic materials has been considerably greater, the domestic content ranging from 4 to 15 percent of total materials used (see table 4-14). Given the differences in inflation rates between Mexico and the United States, it is difficult to interpret a change in proportion with the passage of time. If prices of Mexican materials rise more than the prices of materials imported from the United States and the rate of exchange remains fixed, then the proportion of local material used may go up in value without increasing in physical volume. The converse is true

interior of the country 124 percent of the respective minimum levels; see "Efectos de la actividad maquiladora fronteriza en la sociedad mexicana," paper presented to the National Symposium on Frontier Studies, El Colegio de México, University of Nueva Leon, Monterrey, January 24–27, 1979, p. 8. *Actualidad,* May 1981, asserts that the maquiladoras constitute 5 percent of "the national manufacturing activity, but [receive] only 4.17 percent of employee remunerations, which makes them not very remunerative for labor," p. 16 (author's translation).

Table 4-14. *Mexican Materials and Supplies Used in Mexican Assembly Plants as Percent of All Materials and Supplies Used, by Location, 1975–83*

| *Year* | *All plants* | *Border plants* | *Interior plants* |
|---|---|---|---|
| 1975 | 1.4 | 0.8 | 9.9 |
| 1976 | 3.0 | 2.1 | 15.4 |
| 1977 | 1.5 | 1.6 | 6.1 |
| 1978 | 1.5 | 1.0 | 6.9 |
| 1979 | 1.4 | 0.9 | 7.9 |
| 1980 | 1.7 | 0.8 | 10.0 |
| 1981 | 1.3 | 0.8 | 7.1 |
| 1982 | 1.3 | 0.8 | 6.9 |
| 1983 | 1.3 | 1.0 | 4.4 |

Source: SPP tables.

when a sharp devaluation takes place. This is illustrated in table 4-14, which shows the declines in the proportions for the interior in the years following the devaluations of 1976 and 1982.

## The Main Issues of Assembly Operations in Mexico

Because of the magnitude of Mexican involvement in assembly activities for foreign firms, its merits for the country have been debated extensively. Benefits have been questioned, and serious negative effects on the Mexican economy and on society as a whole have been attributed to the assembly arrangements. The critique centers on three principal issues: the absence of significant linkages of assembly activities to the Mexican economy, the effects on the labor force and on society in the areas in which maquiladoras are concentrated, and the vulnerability of maquiladoras to swings in the U.S. business cycle and their general dependency on decisions made in the United States and elsewhere outside Mexico.

### *Linkages*

A persuasive argument can be made that by their very nature assembly services for foreign companies constitute an enclave in the Mexican economy. First, it was noted that only a trivial percentage of the materials used in these operations is of Mexican origin. Second, according to several recent studies discussed below, the employment generated by the maquiladoras tends not to absorb "traditional" unemployment and underemployment. Third, the bulk of the maquiladoras are concentrated in towns along the U.S. border. Many of the towns are virtually isolated from the economic heartland of Mexico geographically and by the lack of adequate infrastructure. Fourth, most of the jobs created are unskilled and, almost by definition, it is argued, will remain so. The labor force therefore receives little training. Fifth, although many of the assembly plants use sophisticated equipment and technologies, there is little transfer of technology to the rest of the Mexican economy. Sixth, it is said that wages are destined to remain low, not only because of the low skill requirements of assembly production but also because of the effort to keep these activities attractive to foreign manufacturers. In addition, only part of the wages paid to assembly workers are spent to buy Mexican goods and services, because the population near the border is accustomed to shop across the frontier for a significant portion of its requirements. Thus, it is argued, the income generated by assembly production for foreign manufacturers will provide only a limited stimulus to the Mexican economy.

The institutional framework for maquila operations reinforces their economic isolation. In general, maquiladoras are not permitted to sell on the national market but must export their entire production. This is understandable, since these are in-bond industries, whose imports of components are exempt from Mexican import duties provided that they are reexported after assembly—although in the interim, the maquiladora must post a bond in the amount of import duties plus potential penalties.

Most of the commercial relations of the maquiladoras are therefore with foreign companies, especially with U.S. multinationals, rather than with Mexican producers and consumers. Add to that the fact that even when maquiladoras are not subsidiaries of U.S. companies, many plants, particularly in the apparel industry, operate with machinery and equipment provided and owned by the U.S. contractors; the resultant picture is of an enclave of Mexican assembly activities that is tied much more strongly to the United States than to the rest of Mexico.

There is little doubt that this picture is close to reality as it has existed until now. It is open to question, however, whether the coproduction relationship between industrial and developing countries is such that it creates a permanent straitjacket that does not permit the eventual integration of assembly production into the national economy. The experience of Korea and Taiwan, not to mention that of the city-states of Hong Kong and Singapore, seems to point in the opposite direction.[41]

Interviews with both U.S. and Mexican managers of maquiladoras indicate that attempts were made to increase the use of Mexican components and materials in assembly operations.[42] According to the managers, most of the attempts failed because of one deficiency or another of potential Mexican suppliers: rigorous specifications could not be met because of deficiencies in quality control (important particularly in the electrical and electronics industries); delivery schedules could not be met; production capacity was insufficient; and, most often mentioned, prices were too high. All these are typical symptoms of industries of newly industrializing countries. They are also characteristic of the import-substitution type of industrialization, in which protected firms have not yet attained international competitiveness. In principle, these weaknesses can be overcome as the incipient industries mature and become more efficient.

The other side of the coin is that there are no strong incentives for Mexican manufacturers to do business with maquiladoras or for the establishment of assembly operations with Mexican capital. Given the protection of Mexican industry and the uncertainties of foreign markets, producing for secure domestic markets may not only yield greater returns but may also be easier than meeting the demanding requirements of foreign firms and consumers. The image of the maquiladora as the footloose foreigner ready to move on whenever greater profits beckon elsewhere, moreover, does not encourage Mexican firms to make long-term commitments in the assembly business.

The low participation of Mexican capital and entrepreneurship in maquiladora activities will limit the transfer of technology from assembly operations to the Mexican economy. This limitation is itself a barrier to greater Mexican involvement in coproduction with foreign companies. Unless the circle is broken linkages will remain weak; Mexican enterprises

41. For data on domestic materials used in assembly operations in Korea and Taiwan, see chapter 7, note 23. In the city-states of Hong Kong and Singapore, national integration cannot be considered a problem. But even in Singapore there has been a deliberate government policy to squeeze out the maximum from assembly activities for foreign manufacturers by increasing wages, although it may mean losing those operations that require low-skilled labor (see chapter 3).

42. Border visits, March 1980.

will continue primarily to furnish packing materials and janitorial supplies for the maquiladoras rather than the manufactured components for assembly in substitution of foreign materials.

The enclave image is also fostered by the near absence of any "forward" linkages, because the sale of maquiladora output on the domestic market is all but forbidden. Among other things, maquiladoras could provide Mexican producers with sophisticated subassemblies at lower prices than they pay for them now. This might enable Mexican firms to use high-technology inputs that they now cannot afford. If so, the maquila could contribute to the technical upgrading of Mexican industrialization. The official government decree for maquiladoras seems to permit Mexican assembly plants, under some circumstances, to supply the internal market as long as certain domestic content requirements are met. In practice, however, by the end of 1979 only four such plants had been approved and "all operate under rigidly imposed conditions." The government "has been under pressure from domestic producers to repeal this enabling legislation because of claims of unfair advantage."[43] Protected Mexican firms fear the competition of the low-priced products of the maquiladoras. The perception of an "unfair advantage" is particularly great if the assembly plants are subsidiaries of U.S. firms.

Incentives for establishing assembly plants in the interior of the country could be of particular benefit to the national integration of assembly operations. Plant location in the interior could increase the content of domestic materials, increase the participation of national firms, and diminish, if not eliminate, the leakage of purchasing power—and foreign exchange—into the United States that occurs at the border. The benefits would be magnified if plants could be located in the depressed regions of the interior of the country.

*Employment*

The striking aspect of the labor force in Mexican assembly industries is the high proportion—more than three quarters of the total—of women (see table 4-15). Some observers attribute this to the hiring practices of maquiladora managers, who want to obtain a docile crew of production

43. Quotations from unclassified telegram #3126 from the U.S. embassy in Mexico, January 21, 1980.

Table 4-15. *Distribution of Production Workers in Mexican Assembly Industries, by Sex, Location, and Industry, 1980*

| | *Number of persons employed* | | | *Sex distribution (percent)* | |
|---|---|---|---|---|---|
| *Location or industry* | *Total* | *Men* | *Women* | *Men* | *Women* |
| All locations | 102,020 | 23,140 | 78,880 | 22.7 | 77.3 |
| Border | 91,308 | 21,455 | 69,853 | 23.5 | 76.5 |
| Interior | 10,712 | 1,685 | 9,027 | 15.7 | 84.3 |
| Industry | | | | | |
| Food | 1,260 | 334 | 926 | 26.5[a] | 73.5[a] |
| Shoes and apparel | 14,126 | 2,888 | 11,238 | 20.4 | 79.6 |
| Furniture and parts | 2,779 | 2,425 | 354 | 87.3 | 12.7 |
| Machinery and transport equipment (non-electric) | 7,522 | 3,052 | 4,470 | 40.6 | 59.4 |
| Machinery and accessories (electric and electronic) | 52,393 | 9,369 | 43,024 | 17.9 | 82.1 |
| Other | 8,767 | 2,787 | 5,980 | 31.8 | 68.2 |
| Services | 4,395 | 554 | 3,841 | 12.6 | 87.4 |

Source: SPP tables.
a. Border plants.

workers.[44] Most of these women are quite young and have not previously been in the labor force.[45]

Relatively few of the female maquiladora workers are heads of households, and most of them provide only supplementary income for their

44. See, among others, María Patricia Fernández-Kelly, *For We Are Sold, I and My People: Women and Industry in Mexico's Frontier* (Albany: State University of New York Press, 1983); Mitchell A. Seligson and Edward J. Williams, *Maquiladoras and Migration Workers in the Mexico–United States Border Industrialization Program* (University of Texas Press, 1981); Wolfgang Konig, *Towards an Evaluation of International Subcontracting Activities in Developing Countries* (United Nations, Economic Commission for Latin America, 1975), p. 106; Konig, "Efectos de la actividad," p. 13; Baerresen, *The Border Industrialization,* p. 35; Gambrill, "La fuerza de trabajo," pp. 23–26; Van Waas, "The Multinationals' Strategy," chaps. 7, 8, and 9; and Bustamante, "El programa fronterizo," pp. 201–04.

45. See, among others, the sample surveys undertaken by the authors mentioned in the previous footnote. Probably the best of the wider surveys, but only tangentially related to the present discussion, is by Seligson and Williams, *Maquiladoras and Migration.* The Fernández study covered only Ciudad Juárez and the Gambrill survey only Tijuana.

About two-thirds of the women workers are younger than 25 years of age. In electronics the proportion is 85 percent, with a median age of less than 20 years. The average age is considerably higher in the apparel industry, about 26 years; see Fernández, *For We Are Sold,* pp. 50–51. Konig found that 45 percent of maquila workers had not previously been in the labor force, although they were over 16 years of age. See "Efectos de la actividad," p. 8.

families. The lesser dependence of these workers on their jobs would make them vulnerable to easier dismissal or forced resignation (in order to avoid severance pay) if their productivity in these exacting jobs should decline after a few years.[46]

What seems to be clear is that maquila workers in Mexico are not drawn from the traditionally unemployed or underemployed but from a sector of the population that never worked or looked for work. Therefore, one of the original main objectives of the Mexican border industrialization program, which was to absorb the rural male migrant workers left stranded by the termination of the bracero arrangement with the United States, has not been met by the establishment of assembly operations for foreign manufacturers in the country.

On the other hand, women who enter the labor force through maquila employment do not tend to leave the labor force when they become separated from their jobs. Once they have gained a certain measure of independence through working, they will probably look for work after they have lost their first jobs, particularly if they are under pressure to continue making the financial contributions that have helped them and their families to achieve higher standards of living. It is therefore argued that the maquiladoras create their own labor pool. It is easy to conclude from this that, rather than helping to reduce unemployment, the introduction into Mexico of assembly production for foreign manufacturers has worked to increase the "reserve army of the unemployed."

Questioning of maquiladora executives about the high proportion of female workers in their plants almost invariably brings the same responses: women are more dexterous at assembly tasks than men—having smaller hands as well, which is an asset particularly in the assembly of electronic microcomponents—they are more used to and, therefore, more patient with routine assignments, and, according to the managers, comparatively few men apply for such jobs in any event.

There is little support for the assertion that women workers have greater manual dexterity than men, even for delicate assembly operations. Further questioning of plant managers in Mexico and Haiti reveals that men on the assembly lines, whether in sewing or electronics, are at least as efficient as women.[47]

46. Compare the discussion of the same subject in chapter 5.

47. Fernández, *For We Are Sold*, pp. 81–82; Van Waas, "The Multinationals' Strategy," pp. 200–01; and interviews by the authors at the Mexican border, March 19–26, 1980.

The fact is that the preponderance of female workers in assembly production seems to be universal and is not confined to developing countries. The proportion in the United States appears to be higher than in Mexico, averaging 90 percent in most assembly activities.[48]

The employment of women in occupations such as sewing appears to be culturally determined in most parts of the industrial and industrializing world. It seems to be a small step from experience with the needle to the learning of electronics assembly, which requires detailed attention to small components. It may also be culturally determined that men are less patient with delicate, repetitive routines. It is not clear, therefore, whether the employment of women is based on a design for exploitation in order to maintain lower wage scales through easier control and manipulation of a more docile work force. What seems to be clear is that Mexican assembly plants are not unique in employing a high proportion of women.

Consideration of other aspects attributed to the preponderance of female employment in maquiladoras, such as working conditions, health effects and, particularly, the effects on the family and society are beyond the scope of this study.[49] It seems safe to say, however, that the employment of a greater proportion of women not already in the labor force is a phenomenon of the path of economic development in modern times. There will be confusion of social roles—not only between male and female, but also between parent and daughter—and other disintegrative effects on the traditional family. Social adjustments of this type are painful and sometimes costly, but they are a part of the contemporary process of economic development. Perhaps the introduction of assembly activities into particular regions of Mexico has accelerated the coming of the adjustment problems there.

48. In the U.S. semiconductor industry, for example, 92 percent of the assembly operators in September 1977 were women. Contrary to expectations, there was no significant difference in the female proportion among skill levels and, curiously enough, in the South, an even larger proportion of women—97 percent—were employed at the highest skill level than in the lowest level of assembly operations, where women were 91 percent of the total. Bureau of Labor Statistics, *Industry Wage Survey: Semiconductors, September 1977,* Bulletin 2021 (GPO, 1979), p. 7. In the U.S. apparel and accessories industry, 81.4 percent of the total labor force was female. Bureau of Labor Statistics, *Employment and Unemployment during 1979: An Analysis,* Special Labor Force Report 234 (U.S. Department of Labor, 1980), table 30, p. A-29.

49. For a discussion of these factors see Fernández, *For We Are Sold;* Gambrill, "La fuerza de trabajo"; Van Waas, "The Multinationals' Strategy"; and the references given therein.

A further argument about the maquila labor force, which goes beyond the employment problem, has to do with the linkage effects of maquila labor. Far from contributing to the upgrading of the labor force, it is said, assembly production causes the "deskilling" of the workers. Some of the discussion is reminiscent of the debates surrounding the industrial revolution. Before being employed in the maquila sewing operations, for example, many of the women workers had acquired high-level skills—in needlework, for example—perhaps applied only in the home. In their present work place, however, they must perform the most elementary, although precise, operations again and again. Those maquila workers who had had previous experience had often used their judgment and skills earlier to a higher degree than they do in their current assembly tasks.[50]

A general observation, made frequently in leftist literature, points to the tendency in manufacturing, no matter how high the level of technology and sophistication of the product, to break down complex production into ever simpler component processes.[51] At each successive stage of decomposition, less and less skill is required to perform the tasks. Assembly operations, more than other kinds of production, may be especially subject to continuing simplification, the aim of which is to make workers (and machines) ever more efficient.

Whether or not maquiladoras are unique in this tendency is open to question. Although the deskilling claim in the previously cited study was made in comparison of maquila work and previous jobs, the same study also contains information that indicates an upgrading of the labor force in assembly production.[52] Assembly-line supervisors are almost invariably drawn from among the line workers, and upward mobility does not appear to differ from that in assembly plants in the United States. The average skill level in certain assembly industries can also rise, when wage increases

50. Gambrill, for example, found that among those in her sample of maquiladora workers in Tijuana who had had previous jobs, about 25 percent of the previously skilled and semiskilled descended into the unskilled category in assembly work; see "La fuerza de trabajo," table 13. There is also an interesting intergenerational comparison, which shows that about three times more fathers of assembly workers than their offspring were classified as skilled or semiskilled.

51. See, for example, Harry Braverman, *Labor and Monopoly Capital* (New York: Monthly Review Press, 1974). It was applied to foreign assembly production by Van Waas, "The Multinationals' Strategy," pp. 70–77 and passim.

52. Gambrill, "La fuerza de trabajo," tables 14–17. The sample data show that a significant portion of workers changed jobs within the plant and that, among those, more than twice as many went to higher-skilled positions than to lower-skilled ones.

make the lowest-skilled operations unprofitable so that they have to be transferred to other locations where wages are lower.[53]

In surveying the negative aspects of foreign assembly production regarding labor, it is important to see them in the context of the whole Mexican economy. It was found that average maquiladora wages have been higher than minimum wages everywhere, and minimum wages at the border are still well above those in the rest of the country. It is quite certain, therefore, that average maquila wages are higher than Mexican wages for equivalent work. Labor unions seem to be as active in maquiladoras as elsewhere, although they are unevenly distributed along the border.[54] The picture painted in the literature is that, with some notable exceptions, labor unions in assembly plants, as well as in some other Mexican economic sectors, tend not to represent the interests of their members very well.[55] This, however, seems to have little to do with the proportion of women in the maquila work force. It would also be useful to compare labor conditions, upward occupational mobility, and other aspects of employment in maquiladoras with those existing in nonassembly plants. At present, reliable data that are the result of such comparisons are not available, but impressionistic information indicates a not unfavorable position of maquiladoras in relation to other factories in Mexico.

One important point regarding the supply of labor in Mexico remains to be made. The usual discussion centers on the large pool of persons available to do low-skilled jobs. The scarcity of skilled and highly trained persons urgently required by the growing Mexican economy has not often

53. See Van Waas, "The Multinationals' Strategy," pp. 77–78, for a brief report of upgrading of skills in a Mexican electronics assembly plant at the border, while the less skilled jobs were being transferred to a new plant in the interior, where wages are lower. The same point is made in a cable from the U.S. embassy in Mexico dated January 21, 1980, which refers to maquiladoras of two large U.S. companies at the border spinning off plants to the low-wage interior, to which the most labor-intensive operations are channeled, keeping the more highly skilled operations in the border plants.

54. Nearly all assembly plants along the eastern part of the U.S. border are unionized. This is so particularly in the state of Tamaulipas, which includes the maquiladora centers of Matamoros and Nuevo Laredo. In the latter city, as will be seen, interunion rivalry destroyed a large part of the assembly activities. The rate of unionization diminishes as one moves west, and in Ciudad Juárez, the largest assembly concentration, it is only about 50 percent. Farther west, as in Tijuana, there is relatively little union activity.

55. For a detailed discussion of the activities of unions in Mexico, and in assembly plants in particular, see Van Waas, "The Multinationals' Strategy," pp. 107–35 and passim, and the sources cited there as well. A majority of managers interviewed in plants without unions indicated that they would welcome unionization in order to regularize labor relations. See also Ballí, "Evolución y perspectivas," appendix B, p. A-39.

been an important concern. Yet this scarcity has become a significant obstacle to efficient economic development. The assembly plants also are in constant need of trained manpower (engineers, technicians, managers, plant supervisors, accountants, and so on). Between 1975 and 1979 technical and administrative personnel constituted about 13–14 percent of the total maquiladora work force.[56]

Sometimes maquiladoras import their skilled labor, in some instances they train high-level manpower, and they also hire trained Mexicans. For these, the assembly plants compete with other Mexican enterprises. This competition will be to the detriment of the economic development of the country if the maquiladoras have "unfair" market power because of their foreign connections and resources.

### *The Dependency Issue*

The U.S. recession of 1974–75 was traumatic for the promoters of Mexican assembly industries. Some maquiladoras closed down; many workers were laid off. The Federal Reserve Bank of Dallas reported the closing of thirty maquiladoras by April 1975 and the loss of about 35,000 jobs, or more than 40 percent of the 1974 labor force.[57] The decline for all 1975 turned out to be less dramatic; the net loss was only one plant. Another eleven closed during the following two years. But almost one hundred additional plants opened between 1977 and 1979. The net job loss was less than 9,000, or less than 12 percent from 1974 to 1975, and by 1977 employment was about 2,500 persons above the 1974 level (see table 4-1). Value added increased about 2 percent in dollar terms and fell 12 percent in real terms in 1975. Production volume declined only in the border plants; in the interior real value added increased 2 percent in 1975 (see table 4-2).[58] Thus, while the effect of the U.S. recession on maquiladora operations seemed for a few months to have been swift and severe, assembly activities bounced back relatively quickly.

56. Since then there has been an increase. In 1983 technical personnel averaged 10.8 percent and administrative workers 6.1 percent of the total assembly work force (SPP tables). Part of this increase can be attributed to the economic recession and part to the greater use of technicians in maquiladoras.

57. "Border Industries," *Business Review,* July 1975, p. 1. See also Solis, who gave the same job-loss figure in "Industrial Priorities in Mexico," p. 108.

58. In dollar terms there was a sharp decline in 1977 owing to the massive devaluation of the Mexican peso toward the end of 1976.

A closer examination of data from the Mexican SPP and the U.S. ITC reveals that the shock wave of the U.S. recession was concentrated in the electrical and electronic assembly industries. Apparel and textiles were not affected. Employment in these industries increased slightly from 1974 to 1975. Geographically, only the border maquiladoras appear to have been affected. Average annual employment in the interior continued to increase. On the border, the effect was uneven. The principal maquiladora towns in the west, Nogales and Tijuana, suffered the most. Ciudad Juárez, in the center of the border region, and the maquiladora city in which value added is greatest, suffered no net declines in employment and production. Although many plants closed there, new maquiladoras opened, and employment increased 45 percent between 1974 and 1977.

The most striking relative decline in both employment and output, beginning in 1974 and continuing through 1976, seems to have had nothing to do with the U.S. recession and took place in Nuevo Laredo, on the far eastern Texas border. Employment fell almost 70 percent during that period and value added in real terms more than that. What happened there was what one observer calls a "worker rebellion," provoked in part by conflict among labor unions.[59] Nuevo Laredo accounts for more than a third of the temporary total net loss in assembly employment in Mexico that was attributed to the 1974–75 economic downturn in the United States and a similar proportion of the temporary decline in Mexican assembly production. If what happened there, which is unrelated to the U.S. recession, is deducted from the national totals, recovery in Mexican assembly activities appears to be even faster, with employment reaching 1974 levels by the end of 1975.

The bulk of the remainder of the temporary losses in jobs and production of 1975 in the maquiladoras can be accounted for by Tijuana and Nogales. Most of the affected maquiladoras in the two towns were plants of fly-by-night firms with small, easily portable investments.[60] Such firms are particularly sensitive both to the business cycle and to increases in wage rates.

A sharp rise in Mexican wages aggravated the effects of the U.S. reces-

59. For an interesting description and analysis, see Van Waas, "The Multinationals' Strategy," especially pp. 296–310. The turnaround of the catastrophic decline in assembly activities in Nuevo Laredo began in a rather gingerly way in 1976, but the upturn has been slow. By 1983 employment and value added in real terms were still only about half what they had been in 1973–74 (Mexican SPP data).

60. A whole plant is reported to have disappeared during one three-day weekend. See, for example, "Border Industries," *Business Review,* July 1975, p. 6.

sion. There was an average 36 percent jump in minimum wages in 1974, when the consumer price index increased only 23 percent. Wage increases continued to outpace Mexican inflation until 1976, reaching a level 24 percent above the 1970 level in real terms (see table 4-16). Since all the output was exported, however, primarily to the United States, and the peso rate of exchange remained fixed, wage costs in assembly firms rose with the nominal wage increases, especially in the U.S. subsidiaries that use dollars for working capital. Minimum wages in U.S. dollars doubled between 1971 and 1976, and even if this increase were to be deflated by some U.S. price index relevant to the import of assembly products from Mexico, real wage costs in the assembly plants would appear to have risen well over 50 percent during that period.

The jump in minimum wages was reflected in the payroll cost per employee, which rose more than 60 percent in dollar terms between 1973 and 1975 (see table 4-10). If the sharp price rises in the other components of Mexican value added, such as rent and utilities, which follow the much higher inflation in Mexico than in the United States, are also considered, then it can be seen that the weaker assembly companies could not withstand the cost squeeze in the face of declining U.S. demand. The devaluation of the Mexican peso during the final months of 1976 reduced the wage bill and other local costs of Mexican export industries—including especially assembly production—whose accounting must be in terms of their dollar earnings.[61]

Despite the devaluation relief, many of the small firms that closed their Mexican plants during the mid 1970s did not return. Although there has not been an explicit government policy to keep out the fly-by-night firms—those firms that want to take a quick profit and run—a certain self-policing by the assembly industry has taken place since that time. All the principal industrial parks screen the applications for the establishment of plants with an eye toward keeping out those that do not promise reasonable stability and continuity.[62] The composition of assembly plants in Mexico changed, and by the end of the decade there was a considerably larger proportion of well-established and reputable companies operating in the

61. In the case of imports from U.S. subsidiaries and some other related-party trade, the U.S. Customs Service requires a dollar estimate of the Mexican cost of production, to which customs adds an imputed profit figure to arrive at value added in Mexico, which is dutiable under tariff items 806/807 (see the appendix to chapter 2).

62. Interviews with the director of the Nogales Industrial Park, July 13, 1978, and March 20, 1980; with the manager of the Bermudez Industrial Park, Juárez, March 24, 1980; and with several consultants who specialize in setting up industrial parks.

Table 4-16. *Various Economic Indicators for Mexico, 1969–83*

1975 = 100

| *Year* | *Consumer price index* *(1)* | *Index of monthly earnings* *(2)* | *National minimum wage (average for year)* *(3)* | *Rate of exchange, pesos to U.S. dollar (average for year)* *(4)* |
|---|---|---|---|---|
| 1969 | 54.0 | 49 | 43.8 | 12.5 |
| 1970 | 56.6 | 51 | 51.0 | 12.5 |
| 1971 | 59.7 | 54 | 51.0 | 12.5 |
| 1972 | 62.7 | 59 | 60.3 | 12.5 |
| 1973 | 70.3 | 65 | 71.1 | 12.5 |
| 1974 | 86.8 | 84 | 81.2 | 12.5 |
| 1975 | 100.0 | 100 | 100.0 | 12.5 |
| 1976 | 115.8 | 127 | 129.3 | 15.4 |
| 1977 | 149.5 | 168 | 165.3 | 22.6 |
| 1978 | 175.4 | 192 | 187.6 | 22.8 |
| 1979 | 207.4 | 224 | 219.0 | 22.8 |
| 1980 | 262.1 | 270 | 257.9 | 23.0 |
| 1981 | 335.2 | 359 | 337.7 | 24.5 |
| 1982 | 532.6 | 489[a] | 475.0 | 55.0 |
| 1983 | 1,115.8 | n.a. | 772.1 | 120.1 |

Sources: Columns 1, 2, 4, International Monetary Fund, *International Financial Statistics,* various issues; column 3, calculated on the basis of weighted average minimum wages 1964–84, published in table "Salarios mínimos generales" (Mexico, D.F.: Comisión Nacional de los Salarios Mínimos, 1984).

n.a. Not available.

a. Average of first three quarters.

country than during the early 1970s. The size of assembly plants increased, the average number of workers per plant rising from 116 in 1971 to 251 in 1983.[63]

Thus, given a mix of more responsible companies and a larger investment in assembly operations, it is safe to assume that maquiladoras will be less prone to "pack up and go" whenever negative, but temporary, forces are encountered. Of course, a severe and prolonged deterioration of economic conditions can lead to serious losses of income and employment for the maquiladoras. The most recent data, however, indicate that the prolonged and severe U.S. economic recessions of 1980–82 had only an insignificant and short-lived negative effect on assembly activities in Mexico for U.S. firms. ITC data show that U.S. 806/807 imports from Mexico rose about 16 percent above those of the preceding year in 1981, 5 percent in 1982, and 31 percent in 1983, in which year they were thus 80 percent higher than the prerecession 1979 level (see table 4-6). Official Mexican

63. Solís, "Industrial Priorities in Mexico," p. 109; and SPP tables.

figures reveal a drop of less than 3 percent in the number of plants from 1980 to 1981, while employment continued to rise. Only in 1982 was there a decline, which proved to be temporary, in the number of production workers, but white-collar employment rose. By 1983 there was a considerable expansion in the number of production workers; average employment in maquiladoras was 35 percent greater than in 1979 and the average number of hours worked was 25 percent higher (see table 4-1). In 1980 there was a slight temporary decline, in constant dollars, in value added in Mexico, but a strong recovery followed, so by 1983 it was 27 percent higher than it had been in 1979 (see table 4-2). U.S. import figures for dutiable 806/807 imports show an uninterrupted increase in the value added to U.S. components in Mexico, reaching in 1983 a level 78 percent higher than that of 1979.

Although the growth of the assembly industry in Mexico after 1982 can be related in part to the devaluations of that year, the effects of the recent recession in the United States confirm the conclusions drawn from the experience of the mid 1970s: the downturns of the U.S. business cycle are reflected to a much smaller degree, if at all, in Mexican assembly activities for U.S. firms. A shakeout of unstable firms takes place, but output and employment expand with a smaller number of plants, as U.S. companies transfer more of their labor-intensive operations to low-cost locations abroad.

In summary, the dependency issue merits concern. Assembly production may be more sensitive to external economic conditions and decision-making than some other economic activities within Mexico. After all, foreign assembly has been directed exclusively toward exports, and it is natural that sales will depend on foreign markets. These activities also are tied to foreign decisions, either through the operation of foreign subsidiaries or through international subcontracting. Yet it was shown that downturns in assembly operations that were attributable to U.S. recessions were relatively mild and short-lived. Their effects were particularly small compared to the declines in Mexican manufactured exports during these periods, not including assembly, which dropped 14 percent in 1975.[64]

64. World Bank, *Mexico, Manufacturing Sector,* table 1.2. It should be noted that the growth of the Mexican economy as a whole declined significantly between 1974 and 1976 and between 1981 and 1983. See World Bank, *Special Study of the Mexican Economy: Major Policy Issues and Prospects,* vol. 2, Statistical Appendix (World Bank, May 30, 1979), p. 25; and *Mexico: Recent Economic Development and Prospects,* Statistical Appendix (World Bank, April 3, 1984), table 3.3.3, p. 31; see also UN Economic Commission for Latin America, *Economic Survey of Latin America 1980* (Santiago: ECLA, 1982), table 18, p. 16.

*Maquiladoras and Migration*

Three assertions have been made about the influence of maquiladoras on migration. The first is that the establishment of assembly plants at the border has stimulated massive internal migration from the interior of Mexico to the border; the second is that the maquiladora serves as a jumping-off place for migration to the United States by those it has brought to the border from the interior; the third, inconsistent with the preceding assertion, is that the creation of assembly jobs in Mexico causes migration to the United States to diminish.

Regarding the first point, the fact is that the border population has grown faster than that of any other region in the country except greater Mexico City. A few of the border municipalities, notably Tijuana, have grown more rapidly than Mexico City. About 5 percent of the Mexican population live there now. A significant part of the growth, however, took place before the beginning of the maquiladora program. The average annual growth rate in the border region between 1950 and 1960 was 6.3 percent, while it was only 3.1 percent for the whole country. Between 1960 and 1970, the period during which the maquiladora program began, the growth rate slowed to 4.1 percent, still higher than the national rate of 3.4 percent. Some attribute the slowdown to the ending of the bracero program in 1964.[65]

Another fact is that a large proportion of the border population, about 29 percent in 1970, or almost a third of the population of the three largest border cities, Juárez, Tijuana, and Mexicali, were not born there; the national average of persons not born where they live was only 15 percent.[66] Census data for 1980 are not yet available, but all indications point to a continuation of migration to the border at a rate that exceeds the internal migration rate for the country as a whole.

The importance of the maquiladoras in attracting the migrants is debatable. They had nothing to do with the highest recorded rate of migration to the border, during the intercensal years of 1950–60. Subsequently they must have been responsible for some migration, as would any focal point of employment. In the studies of maquiladora workers cited earlier, it was found that about 80 percent of the workers interviewed in Tijuana were not born there and that more than two-thirds came from states away from

65. See Bustamante, "El programa fronterizo," pp. 190–91.

66. Ibid., p. 191; and Urquidi and Méndez Villarreal, "Economic Importance," table 2, p. 142.

the border;[67] in Juárez somewhat less than two-thirds of the respondents were not born there and about a quarter came from states not on the border.[68] In both studies a minority of the migrants were found to have come to the towns in order to work in maquiladoras—about 10 percent of the migrant workers in the Tijuana assembly plants, or about 20 percent if the motive to emigrate to the United States is also included.

In the more comprehensive study by Seligson and Williams it was found that "at most approximately 4 percent of *all* [maquiladora] *workers* . . . were interstate migrants motivated to move to the border in search of BIP [that is, maquiladora] employment."[69] Part of the apparent discrepancy between this figure and those given in the other studies cited is explained by the fact that the vast majority of the assembly worker migrants arrived as children "accompanied by members of their families, generally parents and siblings."[70] The median age of migrants arriving at the border was 10.5 years.[71] Also, plant managers tend to prefer hiring persons who have had a few years of residence in the hope that they will be more stable employees.[72] About 80 percent of the interstate migrant maquiladora workers had lived for more than three years in the cities in which they were interviewed, and only 5 percent had lived there less than a year.[73] In conclusion, the answer to the question of how important the assembly plants have been in giving impetus to internal migration to the northern border is "not very," at least until the late 1970s.

The second assertion mentioned at the beginning of this section merits a similar response: In none of the studies cited has any evidence been found that maquiladoras at the border have served significantly as jumping-off points for migration to the United States. "Interstate migrants working in the *maquiladora* industry . . . possess no peculiar ambitions concerning migration to the United States. . . . Indeed, the migrants are more prone to choose a location in the interior of Mexico than those

67. Gambrill, "La fuerza de trabajo," pp. 28–29.

68. Fernández, *For We Are Sold,* tables 7 and 8, p. 58.

69. Seligson and Williams, *Maquiladoras and Migration,* p. 162; see also p. 73.

70. Fernández, *For We Are Sold,* p. 59. The same conclusion can be reached from Seligson and Williams, *Maquiladoras and Migration,* chapter 3.

71. Seligson and Williams, *Maquiladoras and Migration,* appendix 2, pp. 78–79; the appendixes are available only in the original version of the work, which was submitted as a report to the Department of Labor; see U.S. Department of Labor, National Technical Information Services, Report DLMA 21-04-78-29-1.

72. Border interviews, March 1980.

73. Seligson and Williams, *Maquiladoras and Migration,* pp. 67–68. The migrant maquiladora workers had lived an average of 10.3 years at the border in mid 1978.

workers born on the border."[74] About 15 percent of maquiladora workers had been in the United States, legally or illegally. Among the male workers, the percentage was higher, about 29 percent, but even this is much lower than a recent survey showed for Jalisco, a Mexican state more than 1,000 miles south of the border, where 50 percent of male workers had had experience as migrants to the United States.[75] Only 13 percent of interstate Mexican migrant assembly workers said that they planned to work in the United States.[76]

These findings are not surprising, given the nature of the maquiladora work force. Most of it consists of women, primarily of urban background, a quite different population group from the male rural workers and peasants who usually constitute the aliens who have entered the United States illegally.[77]

The same reasoning invalidates the third assertion often made, that "for each job that is created by the maquiladora industry there is possibly one less alien that would go to the United States."[78] The people who cross the border into the United States without documents are generally not potential maquiladora workers. Just as the establishment of the border industrialization program through the creation of the maquiladora system could not absorb, as intended, the unemployed and underemployed men who were left stranded when the bracero program ended, this system also cannot stem the migration to the United States. Two different populations are involved: the erstwhile braceros and present undocumented aliens, who are generally rural males, and the assembly workers, who are generally urban females.

Of course, this point should not be exaggerated. No kind of job creation at the border in Mexico can be entirely neutral in respect to migration across the border. It will have some holding effect on people, keeping some from migrating. Even if a female assembly worker never thought of emi-

74. Ibid., p. 146.

75. Ibid. The Jalisco study was made by Wayne A. Cornelius, *Mexican Migration to the United States* (MIT Press, 1978), and is discussed in Seligson and Williams, *Maquiladoras and Migration.*

76. Ibid., table IV.8, p. 104.

77. Ibid., pp. 122–23; see also Richard Mines and Alain de Janvry, "Migration to the United States and Mexican Rural Development," *American Journal of Agricultural Economics,* vol. 64 (August 1982), pp. 444–54.

78. Ramiro Zuñiga, of the trade association that represents the maquiladora plants, speaking on National Public Television on "Border Business," *MacNeil/Lehrer Report,* March 12, 1979.

grating, her earnings might keep a man who did intend to cross the border from doing so.

In this respect the establishment of maquiladoras in the interior of Mexico may be much more effective. They may help keep potential interstate and intercountry migrants in place. Here it is interesting to note that Seligson and Williams found almost half the migrants working in assembly plants at the border saying that they would go back home (to the interior of Mexico) if similar employment were available there.[79]

Much of this discussion of the migration issue is based on the conditions that prevailed during the late 1970s. The flow of people across international borders, like the flow of goods and services and financial resources, is greatly affected by the rate of exchange. The sharp devaluations of the Mexican peso in 1982 made Mexican wages much lower in dollar terms, thereby greatly widening the gap between Mexican and U.S. wages. Aggravated by the severity of the economic recession in Mexico, the debt crisis, and the ensuing austerity program, by 1984 the wage gap had become so large and real wages so low that the maquiladoras for the first time encountered difficulties in holding onto their workers. Tardiness and absenteeism rose, and the high wages across the border in the United States proved to be an irresistible lure for many maquila workers.[80]

79. Seligson and Williams, *Maquiladoras and Migration,* p. 166.

80. See, for example, Matt Moffett, "U.S. Companies with Factories in Mexico Are Having Difficulty Retaining Workers," *Wall Street Journal,* July 17, 1984, p. 33; see also U.S. embassy in Mexico, airgram A-63, October 2, 1984.

CHAPTER FIVE

# Foreign Assembly in Haiti

JOSEPH GRUNWALD, LESLIE DELATOUR,
KARL VOLTAIRE

HAITI is among the poorest countries of the world. The country with the next lowest income level in the Americas, Honduras, has more than twice the GNP per capita of Haiti, which was estimated by the Inter-American Development Bank in 1982 at $311. The Dominican Republic, with which Haiti shares the island of Hispaniola and which had a population just a few percent higher than Haiti's 5.3 million in 1983, has earnings per person nearly four times as great.

Manufacturing in Haiti is of recent origin. It is confined primarily to the processing of food, beverages, agricultural materials, and basic items such as shoes, clothing, soap, and cement. National income figures—as well as most other statistics—are still rudimentary, but the World Bank estimates the contribution of manufacturing to gross domestic product (GDP) to have reached about 18 percent by 1981.[1] Most of the increase took place during the 1970s, after a decade of near stagnation.

## The Importance of Assembly Production in Haiti

The growth of assembly industries has been an important element in the recent dynamism of the Haitian economy. Between 1970 and 1980 the value added in Haitian assembly plants increased more then twenty-three

1. World Bank, *Economic Memorandum on Haiti,* Report 3931-HA (Washington, D.C.: World Bank, May 25, 1982), p. 106. The United Nations preliminary estimate is 13.2 percent for 1981. See Economic Commission for Latin America (ECLA), *Economic Survey of Latin America, 1981* (Santiago: United Nations, 1983), p. 471. The Inter-American Development Bank (IDB) estimates the 1981 and 1982 manufacturing shares in GDP to be 16.2 percent. See IDB, *Economic and Social Program in Latin America,* 1983 report, pp. 345, 349. Figures of 16–17 percent for the manufacturing contribution to GDP are mentioned in Association des Industries d'Haiti, "The Industrial Sector in Haiti: Situation, Prospects and Policies" (Port-au-Prince: ADIH, 1981), p. 3.

times, or at an average annual rate of 37 percent (see table 5-1). Even in real terms, the growth was 22 percent a year, deflated by the implicit import price deflator of the United States. In part the dramatic upsurge was aided by government incentives and by changes in the political environment.

Assembly activities have benefited from two types of incentives: new production firms are exempt from income taxes for five years, following which they are subject to partial payments in increasing yearly proportions, so that after ten years they must pay the full tax; and a franchise is granted to assembly firms that exempts them from any tariff duties on imports. The franchise is given indefinitely for production all of which is exported. This covers assembly production. For production that is sold on the domestic market, the franchise is given on a temporary basis, because the firm is expected to use local materials as inputs after the first few years.

There are no free-trade zones in Haiti that cater to export industries. While in Port-au-Prince there is a successful industrial park which is run by a government agency, it emerged as a result of the growth of assembly plants rather than contributing to their emergence.

Thus, unlike that in other countries, assembly production in Haiti is not an in-bond activity in the strict sense. Although assembly production cannot be sold domestically, any firm can obtain a duty-free import franchise whether it exports or not. More than half of all manufacturing output, including assembly, is exported, and there are many firms that produce for both the home market and the export market.

With the advent of a new government in the early 1970s, investors' perceptions of political stability improved. The new environment permitted the huge wage gap between Haiti and the United States to become an enormous attraction for assembly production. Many Haitian professionals and entrepreneurs who were abroad during the preceding regime returned and established businesses for the purpose of assembling U.S. components.

While there are no exact figures, estimates by the U.S. embassy in Haiti and by the World Bank put the number of assembly plants in 1980 at about 200, employing approximately 60,000 persons. All the assembly plants are in Port-au-Prince, the capital and by far the largest city. Assuming a dependency ratio of 4 to 1, this means that assembly operations supported about a quarter of the population of Port-au-Prince in 1980.

Assembly activities in Haiti have been concentrated in sporting goods,

Table 5-1. *Total Value, Dutiable Value, and Duty-free Value of U.S. Imports from Haiti under Tariff Items 806.30 and 807.00, 1969–83*[a]

Millions of U.S. dollars unless otherwise specified

| *Year* | *Total value of 806/807 imports (1)* | *Duty-free value of U.S. components (2)* | *Dutiable value added in Haiti (3)* | *Dutiable value as percent of total value (3÷1) (4)* |
|---|---|---|---|---|
| 1969 | 4.0 | 2.4 | 1.6 | 39.8 |
| 1970 | 6.1 | 4.0 | 2.1 | 34.4 |
| 1971 | 9.1 | 5.9 | 3.2 | 35.2 |
| 1972 | 16.1 | 11.0 | 5.1 | 31.7 |
| 1973 | 28.5 | 20.3 | 8.2 | 28.8 |
| 1974 | 56.5 | 43.0 | 13.5 | 23.9 |
| 1975 | 54.7 | 40.2 | 14.5 | 26.4 |
| 1976 | 78.1 | 56.6 | 21.5 | 27.5 |
| 1977 | 84.3 | 61.3 | 23.0 | 27.3 |
| 1978 | 104.9 | 76.1 | 28.7 | 27.4 |
| 1979 | 133.7 | 94.5 | 39.2 | 29.3 |
| 1980 | 153.8 | 105.3 | 48.5 | 31.5 |
| 1981 | 171.3 | 117.1 | 54.2 | 31.6 |
| 1982 | 181.0 | 126.2 | 54.8 | 30.3 |
| 1983 | 197.4 | 139.4 | 58.0 | 29.4 |

Sources: Special magnetic tapes from the U.S. International Trade Commission (ITC); and ITC, *U.S. Tariff Items 807.00 and 806.30: Imports for Consumption,* various issues.

a. U.S. imports from Haiti under tariff item 806.30 amount to less than $50,000 a year.

particularly baseballs, and textiles, including apparel (see table 5-2). Haiti is the world's principal exporter of baseballs and ranks among the top three in overseas assembly of textile products and stuffed toys. During the period 1969–72, more than half of Haiti's assembly exports that entered the United States under U.S. tariff item 807.00 consisted of baseballs. While still growing in absolute amounts, their importance in the total declined to less than a quarter during the mid 1970s and less than a sixth in 1983. Clothing and textile products have grown much faster, from less than a quarter during 1969–72 to well over a third of exports to the United States under tariff item 807.00 since 1973. More than 90 percent of Haiti's textile exports go to the United States under tariff item 807.00; in 1983 Haiti accounted for 12 percent of such imports by the United States.[2] It should be noted, however, that the volume of Haitian shipments of textiles

2. There have been occasional U.S. imports from Haiti under U.S. tariff item 806.30, which permits the duty-free entry of U.S. components processed abroad. The amounts, however, were very small, usually less than $50,000, so these imports constituted a trivial proportion of U.S. imports from Haiti.

has not grown significantly in recent years, so Haiti's share of the total U.S. import market declined from 1.2 percent in 1979 to 0.8 percent in 1983.[3] There is little doubt that the textile quotas imposed on Haiti by the United States in 1973 under the International Multi-Fiber Agreements have limited the expansion of Haitian textile exports, particularly during recent years.[4]

The facts that about 60 percent of the exports from Haiti are not subject to any restraints and that on the average less than half the aggregate quotas are used do not mean that the bilateral agreements have no negative effects on Haitian output.[5] First, categories not specifically under restraint are still subject to large uncertainties. At any moment the U.S. government may request consultation for items that are perceived as threatening disruption of the market. Unless shipments fall off significantly, the results of these consultations are either mutually agreed-upon limits or unilaterally imposed restraints. Second, the output of potential investors may be too large to be accommodated by the unused portion of the quota, which means that the quota will remain underused. Third, the quota limitation becomes a binding constraint whenever there is a clear comparative advantage, such as the highly labor-intensive sewing of brassieres in Haiti. Finally, textile exports grew rapidly until 1973, then slowed after the signing of the first bilateral restraint during that year.[6]

During the mid 1970s, stuffed toys and dolls became number three in Haiti's assembly production but then declined in rank, as did other "traditional" products that were significant initially. Electrical (and electronic) machinery, equipment, and parts have rapidly grown in importance and

3. The increasing value of Haitian exports to the United States in the face of near stagnant quantities is accounted for primarily by shifts in the composition of such exports. There were changes, not only from low-priced to high-priced products, but also from low quality to high quality within given product lines.

4. During the two years that preceded the 1973 textile agreement the volume of Haitian textile exports virtually doubled each year, from 8.4 million square-yard equivalents (SYE) in 1971 to 15.7 million SYE in 1972 and 30.3 million in 1973. After that a decade passed before exports doubled again; they reached 62 million SYE in 1983 (unpublished data from U.S. Department of Commerce, International Agreements and Monitoring Division, Office of Textiles and Apparel).

5. The data underlying these statements are contained in Performance Report, Textile and Apparel Bilateral Agreements and Unilateral Import Restraints, U.S. Department of Commerce, International Agreements and Monitoring Division, Office of Textiles and Apparel (Government Printing Office, 1984).

6. There was a dramatic upsurge in assembly production, particularly of brassieres, in the Dominican Republic, which was the effect of postponing the signing of a quota agreement until 1979.

Table 5-2. *The Ten Most Important U.S. Imports from Haiti under Tariff Item 807.00, by ITC Product Group, as Percent of Total U.S. 807.00 Imports from Haiti, Ranked among U.S. 807 Imports from Haiti and among U.S. 807 Imports from All Countries, 1970, 1978, and 1981*[a]

| | *1970* | | | *1978* | | | *1981* | |
|---|---|---|---|---|---|---|---|---|
| *Product group* | *Percent of total value of U.S. 807 imports from Haiti* | *Rank among U.S. 807 imports from Haiti* | *Rank among U.S. 807 imports from all countries* | *Percent of total value of U.S. 807 imports from Haiti* | *Rank among U.S. 807 imports from Haiti* | *Rank among U.S. imports from all countries* | *Percent of total value of U.S. 807 imports from Haiti* | *Rank among U.S. 807 imports from Haiti* |
| Baseballs and softballs | 52.2 | 1 | 1 | 23.3 | 2 | 1 | 18.2 | 2 |
| Textile products | 24.6 | 2 | 6 | 37.8 | 1 | 3 | 35.6 | 1 |
| Equipment for electric circuits | 1.9 | 6 | 9 | 2.9 | 7 | 4 | 10.3 | 3 |
| Television receivers and parts | 2.9 | 4 | 8 | ... | ... | ... | ... | ... |
| Fur and leather products | 2.4 | 5 | ... | ... | ... | ... | ... | ... |
| Office machines | ... | ... | ... | 5.3 | 4 | 11 | ... | ... |
| Toys, dolls, and models | 3.6 | 3 | 5 | 7.2 | 3 | 2 | 4.3 | 5 |

| | | | | | | | | |
|---|---|---|---|---|---|---|---|---|
| Resistors and parts | 1.3 | 10 | ... | ... | ... | ... | ... | ... |
| Electric motors, generators, and so on | 1.6 | 8 | ... | 1.9 | 9 | 3 | 3.1 | 8 |
| Tape recorders and players | 1.6 | 9 | ... | ... | ... | ... | ... | ... |
| Valves and parts | 1.8 | 7 | ... | ... | ... | ... | ... | ... |
| Miscellaneous other machinery | ... | ... | ... | ... | ... | ... | 1.8 | 9 |
| Capacitors | ... | ... | ... | 3.4 | 6 | 3 | 3.9 | 6 |
| Miscellaneous electrical products and parts | ... | ... | ... | 4.1 | 5 | ... | 3.8 | 7 |
| Luggage, handbags, and the like | ... | ... | ... | ... | ... | ... | 4.8 | 4 |
| Gloves | ... | ... | ... | 1.7 | 10 | 3 | 1.7 | 10 |
| Miscellaneous other articles | ... | ... | ... | 2.4 | 8 | ... | ... | ... |
| *Addendum* | | | | | | | | |
| Total 807.00 value (millions of dollars) | 6.1 | ... | ... | 104.9 | ... | ... | 171.1 | ... |

Source: Special magnetic tapes from the ITC.

a. U.S. imports from Haiti under tariff item 806.30 were negligible.

now constitute more than 30 percent of Haitian assembly exports to the United States; its share was a little more than 10 percent in 1970. Equipment for electric circuits alone accounted for more than 10 percent of Haitian assembly exports, making it the third most important assembly product group in 1981 (see table 5-2). The establishment of luggage assembly at the end of the 1970s has put this product group in fourth place among Haitian assembly industries.

The available data indicate that value added in assembly plants now constitutes about a quarter of all industrial value added in Haiti, whereas it constituted less than 6 percent in 1970.[7] Contributing about two-thirds of the country's industrial exports, assembly production now earns almost a third of Haiti's yearly foreign exchange receipts from exports.[8]

It is clear that in the case of Haiti, the effect of assembly operations on employment, income, and the balance of payments is of considerable importance. These effects and some more subtle ones will be discussed later in the chapter. At this point, let it be noted that Haiti's weight in the world coproduction system is far greater than its size—in both population and income—in the world community. Of about fifty countries that imported substantial quantities of U.S. components for assembly in 1980, Haiti ranked ninth, with imports of more than $105 million (see table 2-1). It held a similar position among developing countries in respect to value added in the assembled articles that were exported to the United States. While its share in third world assembly operations is still small—about one twenty-fifth of Mexico's value added and one-eighth of that of Singapore—after Mexico it is the most important assembly country in Latin America.[9]

7. Calculated from World Bank, *Economic Memorandum on Haiti,* tables 2.1 and 2.4, on the basis of import price deflators given in the *Economic Report of the President, January 1981,* table B-3.

8. Estimates of the authors, confirmed by an unpublished "Economic Note for the Haitian Subgroup" of the World Bank, Latin American and the Caribbean Regional Office, November 23, 1983, p. 32. According to the World Bank the industrial sector was still a net user of foreign exchange as late as 1977. See World Bank, *Current Economic Position and Prospects of Haiti,* Report 2165-HA (December 22, 1978), vol. 1, p. 25.

9. Although in 1982 total 807 shipments to the United States from Haiti—$180 million—were about 50 percent higher than 807/806 shipments of $123 million from Brazil, Haitian value added of $54 million was about half as great as value added in Brazil, which was $105 million. As indicated in chapter 2, Brazil is more like a developed country in respect to 807 shipments, incorporating relatively small quantities of U.S. components into Brazilian automobiles.

## Characteristics of Assembly Operations in Haiti

The nature of the assembly industry is not the same in all countries. Haitian assembly operations differ from the Mexican maquiladoras in most respects. The differences are explained not only by the small size or the level of development of the country but also by political and social factors. Data in this section were obtained from two sample surveys undertaken as part of the research for this chapter—one a survey of enterprises, the other, of workers. See the appendix to this chapter for further details.

### *Ownership and Structure*

Unlike Mexican assembly production, which is done largely through subsidiaries of U.S. companies, Haitian assembly activities rest to a great extent on Haitian entrepreneurship. Almost 40 percent of the firms in the sample are Haitian-owned, a third are foreign-owned, and 30 percent are joint ventures.[10] Most of the Haitian-owned firms are concentrated in textile assembly, where almost two-thirds of the firms are locally owned. In electronics and the miscellaneous category, joint ventures predominate; in baseballs, foreign companies. Even in foreign firms, most of the managers are Haitian. Of forty-nine firms that responded to the question, about three quarters had local managers.[11]

It should be noted that several firms, especially in the baseball category, that had been wholly owned by Haitians were sold to foreign interests before the sample was taken. The oldest assembly enterprises are Haitian, and their average age is ten years. The youngest are foreign-owned, with an average age of seven years, and the ages of the joint ventures are in between. No change in the pattern of ownership can be discerned during recent years. Less than a third of the firms were established during the five years that immediately preceded the survey, and more of these were wholly Haitian-owned than were wholly foreign-owned; almost a third of the total were owned jointly.

10. In a third of the joint ventures, majority ownership is Haitian. Not all the foreign-owned firms are U.S. subsidiaries; there are several that are owned by foreign citizens who reside in Haiti. These could have been classified as local firms. In the classification used here, however, local firms are those 100 percent of which is owned by Haitian citizens.

11. In separate random visits of the authors to Haitian assembly plants in February 1980, all the managers interviewed were Haitian.

Most of the companies interviewed do assembly work for U.S. principals.[12] Those that are not wholly owned by U.S. manufacturers usually work with machinery and equipment supplied by U.S. principals. About three quarters of the forty-seven respondents to the survey said that the principals usually furnish the machinery and two-thirds said that the principals always do so. This arrangement, which is a special form of an arm's-length relationship, reduces the risks faced by both the subcontractor and the principal. The former does not have to venture his own capital, and having his customer's machinery is some assurance that the principal will not run out on the contract. The principal, on the other hand, can have his production abroad without having to establish a subsidiary company and without having to make a large capital investment. The machinery that he lends to his subcontractor is usually secondhand, often fully depreciated, and in any event he can take it back when a contract has been completed. That there is Haitian entrepreneurship is demonstrated by the fact that about three quarters of the local firms reported that they initiated the relationship with the principal. In many instances the Haitian enterprise has a relationship with more than one principal. The overall average is three U.S. principals per Haitian firm, and there may be as many as an average of nine for local firms in the electronics sector.

It should be noted that, aside from Haitian entrepreneurship, a strong reason for local ownership of assembly plants may be that government bureaucracy and red tape keep foreign firms from establishing their own subsidiaries in the country. This means that, as foreign enterprises become used to doing business with Haiti and learn the ropes—not to speak of any improvement coming about in the bureaucracy—more of them will invest directly in Haitian assembly production rather than subcontract with independent Haitian firms.

### *Size of Firms*

As might be expected, foreign firms are larger than locally owned assembly companies. While the labor force is about equally distributed

12. This does not mean that all the output is shipped to the United States. Some of it may go to U.S. customers in Europe or Canada at the direction of the U.S. parent company. The amounts so shipped, however, usually represent only a small proportion of the production that is shipped to the United States.

among Haitian, U.S., and jointly owned enterprises, the average number of workers per foreign enterprise is about 480, the average per Haitian firm about a third less.[13] Since some firms have more than one plant, employment per plant is significantly lower than the average of about 400 workers per firm in the sample. The best available estimate is about 300 workers per plant, which is many more than in other manufacturing enterprises in Haiti. About two-thirds of the employment in assembly plants is concentrated in the one-third of the enterprises that employ more than 400 workers each. Assembly firms that produce for export are therefore the largest employers in the country.

By far the largest plants, both in employment and in square feet, can be found in baseball assembly, followed by electronics, in which they are only slightly larger than the average, and by textiles, in which they are somewhat smaller than the average. The smallest plants are to be found in the miscellaneous category.

Capital investment in assembly is extremely low. An average figure is difficult to arrive at because, as indicated earlier, many of the local firms receive from their principals machinery and equipment, the value of which could not be included in the survey. Taking only those firms which responded that the principals never provided the machinery, the average capital invested was about $740,000 in 1979. The average investment was nearly three times as large in electronics, but only about a third as large in textiles. The capital requirements of most local assembly companies are, of course, much less because the principals furnish most of the machinery and equipment. Capital is therefore not a great restraint upon a Haitian who wants to enter the assembly business. The difficulty of finding a principal in the United States is probably a greater barrier.

Similarly the ratio of capital to labor is very low. The approximate average of $1,500 per worker for assembly operations is far less than the $25,000 found in Haitian import-substituting enterprises. On the other hand, average utilization of capacity of about 75 percent in assembly plants is twice that in industries that produce for the domestic market. Part of the reason is that assembly plants—whether Haitian-owned or subsidiaries of foreign companies—have a regular relationship with their princi-

13. The differences in size between foreign and domestic firms and among assembly sectors is confirmed by the ranking according to square feet of factory space.

pals abroad and therefore work closer to capacity than Haitian firms that produce primarily for the slow-growing local markets.

### *Wages*

Haiti, like most countries, has minimum-wage laws. No matter how low the minimum wage may be in a developing country, the temptation is for economists to claim that it is too high, even in very poor countries, as long as there is a vast pool of underemployed persons, as there is in Haiti. That the minimum wage is higher than the opportunity cost of labor in Haiti can be demonstrated by the fact that the daily earnings of persons who work at home under contract to more formal enterprises—the "put out" system—are usually between half and a tenth of the official minimum wage.[14]

It might therefore be claimed that more capital-intensive methods are employed in Haiti than would be warranted by the true opportunity cost of labor—the shadow price—particularly in industries that work for the domestic market, where, as indicated earlier, the average capital per worker is more than $25,000. On the other side of the coin, however, capital is not heavily subsidized in Haiti, as it is in many developing countries. Long-term financing is generally not available, and there are neither special interest rates nor special exchange rates or licenses for the import of capital. It was indicated that in the assembly-for-export sector, moreover, the capital–labor ratio is less than a tenth of the average in the industries that produce for the home market.

Average wages reported by the enterprises in the survey were more than a quarter higher than the official minimum wage of $51 a month, if a five-day week, the usual work week in assembly operations, is taken as the norm (see table 5-3). Although the implications of the law are not clear, strict interpretation of it might mean a legal monthly minimum of $69 a month, including nonworking Sunday pay, rather than the average wage in the enterprise sample of $65 a month. According to the World Bank, "the law stipulates a normal working week of 48 hours, 8 hours per day."[15]

14. Simon M. Fass, *Families in Port-au-Prince: A Study of the Economics of Survival* (Washington, D.C.: Office of Urban Development, U.S. Agency for International Development, September 30, 1977), pp. 109–10. The most significant aspect of this problem is that, according to Fass, even the public sector practices this kind of dual system, not by subcontracting but simply by hiring people on a temporary basis and paying them lower daily wages than "regular" permanent employees, even if they do the same job.

15. World Bank, *Economic Memorandum on Haiti,* p. 145.

Table 5-3. *Comparison between Wages Reported in Surveys of Firms and Workers in Haiti and Official Minimum Wages, December 1979*[a]

U.S. dollars

| | | | *Minimum monthly wages* | | | | |
|---|---|---|---|---|---|---|---|
| *Sector* | *Monthly wages reported by firm* | *Monthly wages reported by workers* | *Twenty-two days per month*[b] | *Twenty-four days per month*[c] | *Twenty-six days per month*[d] | *Thirty days per month*[e] | *Official minimum daily wage* |
| Textiles | 64 | 54 | 48 | 53 | 57 | 66 | 2.20 |
| Electronics | 72 | 59 | 57 | 62 | 68 | 78 | 2.60 |
| Baseballs | 60 | 51 | 53 | 58 | 62 | 72 | 2.40 |
| Miscellaneous | 63 | 59 | 51 | 55 | 60 | 69 | 2.30 |
| Average | 65 | 55 | 51 | 55 | 60 | 69 | 2.30 |

Sources: Leslie Delatour and Karl Voltaire, "International Subcontracting Activities in Haiti," paper prepared especially for the present study, tables IV-11 and V-4; World Bank, *Economic Memorandum on Haiti,* Report 3931-HA (Washington, D.C.: IBRD, May 25, 1982), table 2.5, corrected by the authors.

a. Detailed information on the Haitian minimum-wage law could not be obtained. One provision of the law is for non-working Sunday pay under certain circumstances, principally after a worker has worked forty-eight hours in a six-day week. Workers in most assembly plants, however, work only a five-day week. Monthly minimum wages, therefore, were calculated on the basis of four different assumptions, as noted in the four columns under that heading.

b. Five-day week.

c. Five-and-a-half-day week.

d. Six-day week.

e. Seven-day week.

Foreign firms pay a little more, local firms somewhat less than the average of $65 a month found in the survey, and, as expected, wages are higher in electronics than in textiles (for details and explanations, see table 5-3).[16]

In the survey of workers the respondents reported receiving about $10 a month less in the various categories than the figures given by the managers in the enterprise survey. It should be noted that the wages reported by the worker are the take-home pay and are therefore less than the wages reported by the firms. Nevertheless, the average monthly wage of $55 reported by the workers was almost 8 percent higher than the official minimum, assuming a five-day week. The average monthly wage paid in Port-au-Prince in 1975–76, on the other hand, was $45 in clothing manu-

16. The labor cost to the employer is 32 percent higher than the wage in order to cover legal fringe benefits and social security. For details see ADIH, "The Industrial Sector in Haiti," appendix II, p. 94. The figures given were adjusted by the authors. If workers work more than forty-eight hours or at night, they are legally entitled to time-and-a-half pay. They are also entitled to a paid rest day (ADIH, "The Industrial Sector in Haiti," p. 33). Often, however, the wage laws are not enforced in Haiti, and workers receive the regular rate of pay for overtime and do not receive Sunday pay. It should be recalled that most production workers in Haiti (all those in the underlying sample) are paid on a piece-rate basis. The piece rate is determined by dividing the minimum wage by a productivity norm set on the basis of time-and-motion studies.

facture and $49 in industries similar to other assembly operations.[17] The workers in the sample who had had previous experience reported an average monthly wage of $38 in their previous jobs, about 70 percent of the wages they reported in their present jobs.

There is no question that their wages put assembly workers in the upper income groups in Haiti. According to a 1976 survey, 70 percent of the households living in Port-au-Prince had incomes of less than $40 a month.[18] Even allowing for inflation this would still be less than the average take-home pay reported by the assembly workers in the survey.

Given that fact and the existence of the put-out system in the subcontracting industry in Haiti, it might be expected that a majority of the firms would consider the minimum wage too high. The survey did not show this. In reference to the productivity of the workers, only 10 percent of the managers considered the minimum wage too high, while 73 percent considered it adequate and 17 percent considered it too low. In reply to another question in the enterprise survey, more than 80 percent of the respondents said that they would not hire additional workers if the minimum wage were abolished. This included even a majority of those who considered the minimum wage too high.

This does not mean that the minimum wage is irrelevant. It only suggests that the existence of the minimum wage in 1979–80 did not noticeably affect the level of employment. It should be noted that almost 60 percent of the assembly subcontractors in the sample charge their principals piece rates that are the piece rates paid to the workers plus overhead and a profit markup. The number of jobs created, therefore, is determined to a great extent by the demand for Haitian labor by the principals in the United States. That demand, in turn, largely depends on the difference between U.S. and Haitian wages, differences in productivity, tariffs, taxes, transportation costs, and so on. According to the responses in the survey, about half the firms reported that their productivity was about equal to

17. Calculated with data from World Bank, *Haiti: Urban Sector Survey,* Report 2152-HA (April 19, 1979), table 2.1. The table reports total salaries (in gourdes) and number of employees according to registration in the national insurance system (OFATHA). The fixed rate of exchange of five gourdes to the U.S. dollar has been in effect for many years.

18. Simon M. Fass, "Port-au-Prince: Awakening to the Urban Crisis," in Wayne A. Cornelius and Robert V. Kemper, eds., *Latin American Urban Research,* vol. 6, *Metropolitan Latin America: The Challenge and the Response* (Sage Publications, 1978), pp. 155–80.

that of U.S. firms with comparable product lines and activities, while about a fifth said that it was superior. The available evidence seems to support these findings.[19]

As long as the difference between labor costs in the United States and those in Haiti greatly exceeds the sum of transportation costs and the U.S. tariffs on Haitian value added, there will be an economic incentive for U.S. companies to subcontract the labor-intensive parts of their production processes in Haiti. This does not imply that minimum wages, if enforced, can be pushed higher and higher as long as the difference is large enough to cover the other costs mentioned. First of all, to push minimum wages continually upward might cause distortions in the Haitian economy, such as large-scale substitution of capital for labor, which would have serious implications for a labor-abundant, poverty-stricken economy. Second, if the difference were not large enough, it might still cover transportation, tariff, and other direct costs yet not be sufficient to offset the bureaucratic and political risks in Haiti, which are perceived as formidable. Assembly business might thus be lost if wages rose to much higher levels, even if they remained lower than those of international competitors.

### *The Labor Force*

Haiti is not different from other countries in having a high proportion of women in assembly plants. The 75 percent found in the survey is slightly smaller than the proportion in Mexico. In Haiti, however, women seem to constitute a much larger share of the total labor force than in Mexico and in many other countries.[20] Abject poverty forces most adult women to go

19. C.R. Droesch estimates Haitian productivity in subcontracting as equal to 75–80 percent of that in the United States. See United Nations Industrial Development Organization (UNIDO), *La Sous-traitance internationale en Haiti,* Project HA1-77-801 (UNIDO, March 1979), p. 16. Richard Bolin, director of the Flagstaff Institute, supplied the authors with hourly labor costs in Haiti and put productivity of the better-trained Haitian workers virtually at par with U.S. levels in textiles and electronics.

20. See Fass, *Families in Port-au-Prince,* pp. 80–81; International Labour Office, *Haiti: Problemes de main d'oeuvre et d'emploi* (Geneva: ILO, 1976), p. 46; and World Bank, *Haiti: Urban Sector Survey,* p. 19. The World Bank showed a labor-force participation rate of 52 percent in 1971. Fass found a rate of 76 percent in St. Martin, a slum section of Port-au-Prince. Except for Lesotho, Haiti, with a labor force 55 percent of whom are women, has the highest labor-force participation rate among fifty-five of the developing countries listed by Mats Lundahl in his *Peasants and Poverty: A Study of Haiti* (St. Martins Press, 1979), table 2.14.

to work. It is also reported that in Port-au-Prince women outnumber men by 30 percent.[21]

Before working in the assembly plants in which they were interviewed, more than half the women held other jobs or were looking for work. Well over 90 percent said that they would remain in the labor force if they were to lose their present jobs. Their responses were not substantially different from those given by men. The principal difference was that almost a quarter of the women workers—but half the men—were attending school before taking assembly jobs.

In Haiti as in other countries, two main reasons are offered for the predominance of women in assembly plants: women, unlike men, possess the manual dexterity needed in assembly operations, and they are more docile and less militant than men. Yet in the survey men were found to be more productive than women. Since workers are paid piece rates, their wages should reflect their output. Average wages of men were nearly 10 percent higher than those of women.[22] Regarding docility, labor militancy is still unknown in Haiti. Indeed, more than three-fourths of the workers did not know what a labor union is, and in none of the fifty-one firms in the sample was labor organized. The high proportion of women in the assembly work force in Port-au-Prince is probably due in part to the more abundant supply of female labor there and in part to cultural factors already referred to in the study of Mexico.

Almost three quarters of the assembly workers were born outside Port-au-Prince, yet the assembly industries have not been a particularly strong stimulus to migration.[23] At the time of the survey, the migrant worker had been in Port-au-Prince an average of fourteen years, long before the assembly industries emerged as a significant force in the economic development of Haiti.

The existence of a large labor pool for assembly work is demonstrated by the selectivity exercised in hiring practices. Since the minimum wage is higher than what needs to be paid for unskilled labor in the informal sector, assembly managers give preference to persons with some skills, such as literacy and previous experience. In the face of a literacy rate of

21. Fass, *Families in Port-au-Prince,* pp. 50–51.

22. It is, of course, possible that the tasks performed by men and women in the sample were not identical.

23. Only 6 percent of the migrant workers listed assembly work as a reason for migration. About a third came to look for work in general, another third for family reasons, and more than a fifth to go to school.

only a quarter of the adult population in Haiti, more than half the enterprises—in electronics more than three quarters—always require literacy and generally pay higher wages than those that never require it as a condition of employment.[24] Vocational training, surprisingly, was not required by many firms; the highest level required is in textiles, where only a quarter of the companies insist on it. Although about half the firms—more in textiles, fewer in electronics—require prior experience, they do not pay higher wages than firms that do not require it.

Whereas few assembly enterprises say that they require vocational training, about half the workers in the sample reported that they had had such training. About a third of the workers interviewed had had previous assembly experience and another 5 percent had worked in nonassembly jobs. While neither vocational training nor previous experience seemed to make much difference in workers' earnings, education is positively correlated with assembly wages. More than 90 percent of the assembly workers reported that they had had at least one year of schooling. A third had had some high school, and 44 percent had completed elementary school. These levels are far higher than those for the country as a whole and also significantly higher than those for Port-au-Prince, where the educational level is much higher than in the rest of the country.[25] Reflecting the difference in wages, the highest educational level was found in electronics and the lowest in baseball assembly.

Compared with Mexico and other countries in which assembly activities take place, the average age of assembly workers in Haiti is high—about 29 years. It is somewhat lower in electronics and a little higher in the other assembly categories. Age, unexpectedly, is not correlated with wages. This finding is consistent with another that indicates that seniority of workers in the factories is unrelated to their earnings. Surprisingly, female workers in electronics are younger than their male colleagues yet earn more, while in textiles they are older and earn less. These findings appear to say that learning on the job is not rewarded, that there is no learning, or that productivity declines with time spent on the job. The last may be a consequence of boredom with routine tasks or a decline in efficiency with age. In

24. The adult literacy rate was 23 percent in 1976, the last year for which such data are available. See World Bank, *Haiti: Country Data* (January 30, 1981).

25. Uli Locker found that 54 percent of the slum dwellers he interviewed had had some schooling; see *Rural Urban Migration and the Alleged Demise of the Extended Family: The Haitian Case in Comparative Perspective,* Working Paper 20 (Montreal: Center for Developing Area Studies, McGill University, August 1977), p. 9.

either case, since piece rates prevail the result would be lower wages. It may be too early, however, for any pattern to emerge, since the average seniority is just under four years, and about half of the workers have been in their present jobs less than three years.

*Linkages*

Much is made of the apparently weak linkages in developing countries between assembly activities and the rest of the economy. In Haiti, however, the rudimentary status of overall industrial development combined with the predominance of imported inputs would lead to the assumption that intersectoral linkages are weak in general.

Although assembly plants in Haiti are not isolated from the rest of the economy as they are in other places through in-bond and free-zone restrictions, the output of sophisticated assembled intermediate goods, such as computer harnesses and integrated circuits, could hardly serve as inputs for Haitian industries in a forward linkage, nor, for that matter, could the output of assembled finished goods, such as baseballs, wigs, stuffed toys, and relatively expensive clothing, find a ready market in the country.

In respect to backward linkages, however, significant progress has been made. In the assembly production of cassettes, for example, the plastic shells are purchased from a local producer; in baseballs and softballs, the core is now fabricated in Haiti and the glue is supplied locally; some threads are also purchased on the domestic market even though the relation of quality to price may not be up to international standards. All these items were formerly imported.[26]

Despite the increased use of local materials in baseballs, there was no increase in the share of dutiable value—that is, value added in Haiti—as a percent of total value of U.S. baseball imports from Haiti under U.S. tariff item 807.00. Value added in Haiti averaged about a third of total value of assembled products exported to the United States, according to data obtained from the U.S. International Trade Commission. In some product groups there was a noticeable expansion of the Haitian share of assembly export value after the mid 1970s, perhaps indicating both a greater use of Haitian materials and an increase in local wages and profits (see table 5-4).

If the overall proportion of Haitian value added in total U.S. imports from Haiti is examined through a number of years, a decline can be ob-

26. This does not mean that all imports in these assembly activities have been replaced by domestic production. Most of the components are still foreign; in the assembly of baseballs for use in professional games, the core materials and the glue are still being imported.

served until 1974, then a gradual increase until 1981 (see table 5-1). Part of the swing is a result of changes in the composition of output. The early decline appeared to be attributable to the use of more expensive U.S. components, as U.S. producers became more confident of Haitian assembly capabilities. The subsequent rise in Haitian value added might be attributed to higher relative wages and to the greater attention being paid to quality control in Haitian assembly plants, which increased the payroll component of value added through the employment of more highly paid testing personnel, inspectors, and supervisors.[27] This seems to be true of the assembly of office machines, the dutiable value of which rose from 6 percent of total U.S. 807 imports from Haiti in 1973, the first year of production, to about 30 percent in 1982 and 1983, and of assembly of miscellaneous electrical products and parts, of which the dutiable value rose from less than 10 percent in the mid 1970s to 31 percent in 1981. In almost all categories more than a quarter of total export value is added in Haiti; in gloves it has been about half since 1977, probably because of the increased use of local leather (see table 5-4).[28]

The most important indirect linkage of assembly operations to the Haitian economy is through the consumption expenditures of assembly workers. If the U.S. embassy figure of 60,000 workers and the $55 average monthly wage reported by the workers in the survey are used, the result is a total annual wage bill of almost $40 million.[29] If most of this amount were spent on food, shelter, simple clothing, and transportation, items that would have a very low import content, the effect on Haitian economic development would be substantial. Profits and the incomes of managers

27. For example, in electronics the salaries of foremen and supervisors represent 32 percent of the wages of production workers, while the average for the sample survey is 15 percent.

28. Both in textiles and in baseballs, in the course of time, Haitian firms assembled more expensive U.S. components, which in baseballs offset the effects of the increasing use of Haitian materials in an erratic manner. In textiles, changes in the composition of products may have contributed to the decline of the value-added share until 1976. (Brassieres, however, have remained the largest single component.) Since then there has been a steady increase in that share.

29. This is a higher level than the figure that can be derived from the 1980 dutiable value of $49 million reported by the ITC. Assuming that about $2 million of value added in assembly output was exported to countries other than the United States and that wages constitute about two-thirds of value added, the assembly payroll in Haiti would amount to $34 million in 1980. For the sake of comparison let it be noted that the total payroll of Haiti's 19,000 civil servants was about $23 million in 1977 (see World Bank, *Current Economic Position,* vol. 2, table 5.6, p. 149). Assembly employment thus appears to be more important than the civil service in creating an urban middle class in Haiti.

Table 5-4. *Total U.S. Imports of Selected Products from Haiti under Tariff Item 807 and Dutiable Value as Percent of Total Value, 1969–81*

Total values in millions of dollars; dutiable values in percent

| | *Textiles* | | *Baseballs* | | *Toys and dolls* | | *Office machines* | | *Equipment for circuits* | |
|---|---|---|---|---|---|---|---|---|---|---|
| *Year* | *Total 807 value* | *Dutiable value* | *Total 807 value* | *Dutiable value* | *Total 807 value* | *Dutiable value* | *Total 807 value* | *Dutiable value* | *Total 807 value* | *Dutiable value* |
| 1969 | 1.0 | 46.4 | 2.0 | 38.6 | 0.1 | 44.2 | a | a | 0.1 | 25.2 |
| 1970 | 1.5 | 38.3 | 3.2 | 34.7 | 0.2 | 37.7 | a | a | 0.1 | 21.4 |
| 1971 | 1.8 | 36.2 | 5.0 | 36.7 | 0.3 | 38.4 | a | a | 0.4 | 18.2 |
| 1972 | 4.1 | 35.0 | 8.0 | 31.8 | 0.4 | 40.0 | a | a | 0.8 | 17.1 |
| 1973 | 10.1 | 29.9 | 9.2 | 29.7 | 1.2 | 33.0 | 1.7 | 5.9 | 1.0 | 27.0 |
| 1974 | 19.7 | 25.3 | 12.4 | 29.8 | 2.2 | 28.9 | 4.6 | 4.4 | 1.9 | 21.2 |
| 1975 | 19.4 | 25.2 | 13.6 | 31.8 | 3.0 | 28.3 | 3.1 | 6.9 | 1.1 | 25.5 |
| 1976 | 27.1 | 23.8 | 16.8 | 37.6 | 6.1 | 31.4 | 6.3 | 10.4 | 2.2 | 23.6 |
| 1977 | 30.7 | 24.7 | 17.4 | 29.2 | 7.2 | 30.3 | 5.5 | 13.7 | 2.3 | 30.6 |
| 1978 | 39.7 | 27.6 | 24.4 | 25.6 | 7.6 | 29.6 | 5.5 | 17.6 | 3.1 | 25.8 |
| 1979 | 46.2 | 29.9 | 28.4 | 24.9 | 10.0 | 28.5 | 6.3 | 26.8 | 8.1 | 25.8 |
| 1980 | 53.0 | 30.8 | 29.5 | 26.8 | 8.5 | 28.8 | 3.9 | 56.1 | 11.4 | 21.1 |
| 1981 | 61.0 | 31.9 | 31.5 | 29.9 | 7.4 | 33.3 | 1.5 | 37.9 | 17.6 | 23.1 |

Source: Special magnetic tapes from the ITC.
n.a. Not available.
a. Zero or less than $50,000.

might have a lesser effect, since substantial portions would be spent either abroad or on imported luxury items.

In respect to transfer of technology, there is a flow of technical assistance between the foreign principals and the Haitian assembly plants. Well over half the firms in the survey reported that foreign principals always provide technical assistance and an additional few indicated that they sometimes do. Much of the assistance comes in the form of foreign technicians sent by the principal on a temporary basis. About 60 percent of the assembly firms that responded said that foreign technicians visit regularly, and well over a third reported that they regularly send their own technicians abroad for training. Since the majority of assembly factories are in Haitian hands, new working methods and production techniques can easily be transferred to other sectors of the Haitian economy, particularly because some Haitians simultaneously operate other businesses as well as assembly plants.

Table 5-4 (*continued*)

Total values in millions of dollars; dutiable values in percent

| *Capacitors* | | *Electric motors* | | *Gloves* | | *Miscellaneous electrical products* | | *Luggage and handbags* | | *Miscellaneous other machinery* | |
|---|---|---|---|---|---|---|---|---|---|---|---|
| *Total 807 value* | *Dutiable value* | *Total 807 value* | *Dutiable value* | *Total 807 value* | *Dutiable value* | *Total 807 value* | *Dutiable value* | *Total 807 value* | *Dutiable value* | *Total 807 value* | *Dutiable value* |
| a | a | a | a | a | a | a | a | n.a. | n.a. | n.a. | n.a. |
| a | a | 0.1 | 10.1 | a | a | a | a | n.a. | n.a. | n.a. | n.a. |
| a | a | 0.1 | 13.8 | 0.1 | 38.6 | a | a | n.a. | n.a. | n.a. | n.a. |
| a | a | 0.1 | 13.3 | 0.1 | 40.8 | 0.1 | 28.6 | n.a. | n.a. | n.a. | n.a. |
| a | a | 0.2 | 16.4 | 0.3 | 38.3 | 0.3 | 14.9 | n.a. | n.a. | n.a. | n.a. |
| 0.3 | 24.0 | 0.2 | 24.8 | 1.1 | 40.9 | 1.1 | 10.4 | n.a. | n.a. | n.a. | n.a. |
| 2.8 | 21.1 | 0.5 | 39.0 | 1.2 | 35.7 | 1.3 | 7.5 | n.a. | n.a. | n.a. | n.a. |
| 6.0 | 23.9 | 1.3 | 31.4 | 1.4 | 44.3 | 2.0 | 9.8 | n.a. | n.a. | n.a. | n.a. |
| 4.5 | 27.2 | 1.8 | 33.1 | 1.5 | 50.0 | 2.6 | 11.8 | n.a. | n.a. | n.a. | n.a. |
| 3.5 | 20.7 | 2.0 | 35.6 | 1.7 | 53.2 | 4.3 | 13.4 | 0.9 | 29.1 | 1.7 | 26.8 |
| 1.9 | 35.3 | 2.0 | 45.5 | 2.1 | 50.7 | 6.1 | 15.8 | 3.3 | 30.6 | 2.1 | 29.1 |
| 5.7 | 48.1 | 2.7 | 35.7 | 2.1 | 47.1 | 7.2 | 22.7 | 4.7 | 31.8 | 2.5 | 29.4 |
| 6.7 | 28.3 | 5.3 | 28.1 | 2.9 | 48.6 | 6.6 | 31.0 | 8.2 | 37.8 | 3.0 | 34.6 |

### *Stability*

Subcontracting is generally perceived to be a volatile business, so assembly operations are expected to be unstable. Two possible reasons for instability in these activities are sensitivity to the external business cycle, particularly in the United States, and the involvement of footloose U.S. industries and fly-by-night enterprises out to make a fast profit and run.

Regarding the first, a look at table 5-1 shows that Haitian assembly exports to the United States increased by leaps between 1969 and 1983. The only interruption of the monotonic expansion occurred in 1975, when there was a 3 percent decline in total export value after it had doubled in 1974 its value in the preceding year. This slight break can probably be attributed to the U.S. recession of 1974–75 and was caused entirely by a drop of 7 percent in the value of U.S. components used for assembly. Haiti, however, was not adversely affected; to the contrary, assembly activities generated a rise of more than 7 percent in Haitian value added in 1975. In textiles in 1975 there was a barely noticeable hesitation in the steady increase, and the only product group in which a significant decline can be found is equipment for electric circuits, the total decline in value added of which hardly amounted to $250,000. The U.S. recession of 1980–82 did not have a negative effect on Haitian assembly operations for the U.S. market. Growth in value added in Haiti slowed from 1981 to 1982, though the decline was less than 3 percent in real terms when deflated by the U.S. consumer price index excluding food. But in 1983 it was almost 50 percent greater than in prerecession 1979.

The assembly firms in Haiti seem to have a sanguine outlook regarding the fragility of their operations. Nearly half of them believe that a U.S. recession will not affect them, according to the survey taken at the beginning of 1980, when a business downturn abroad threatened. Textile companies are the least optimistic of the assembly firms; the most optimistic are those that assemble stuffed toys. Depending on the industry, either a supply-side or a demand-side explanation is given. The supply-side assumption is that in a business downturn the U.S. principals will have an additional incentive to reduce production costs and therefore will move more operations abroad; the demand-side assumption is that consumers will shift from expensive products to cheaper ones—that is, that instead of buying fancy electronic gadgets for children, adults will give them stuffed toys.

In this respect, it is interesting to note that in Haiti light manufactured exports that use local materials appear to have been deeply affected by the U.S. recession of 1974–75. There was a decline of about a quarter in these exports from 1974 to 1975 and a further decline in the following year, so the value of 1976 exports was almost a third lower than that of 1974. Only in 1978 were 1974 export levels reached again in nominal terms.[30] Exports of light manufacture also suffered on account of the U.S. recession of 1980–82.[31]

In respect to the argument that footloose industries impart instability, the record shows that only a few products assembled abroad have emerged

30. World Bank, *Haiti: Economic Memorandum,* p. 100; and World Bank, *Economic Memorandum on Haiti,* p. 119. The decline was dominated by the collapse of exports of "coated and impregnated textiles," which dropped more than 80 percent from 1974 to 1975 and never recovered. It is not clear whether this was caused by the imposition of import quotas by the United States.

31. World Bank, "Economic Note for the Haitian Subgroup," p. 32.

and disappeared, while most product lines have increased steadily.[32] Because most of Haiti's assembly plants require small capital investments, it is surprising that so few industries have disappeared. This does not mean that there have been no fly-by-night operators and that no subcontractors in Haiti were hurt, but this kind of instability appears to have had only small effects on the Haitian economy.

Furthermore, Haitian assembly operators have learned to protect themselves against the ups and downs of subcontracting. Almost all the firms in the sample work with more than one U.S. enterprise and the majority subcontract with more than two principals each. This often tends to smooth fluctuations in the total orders, thereby reducing the risk. It will be especially true if the local enterprise assembles several different product lines, each of which may be subject to diverse seasonal and cyclical variations.

The low capital requirements in this business permit the local entrepreneur to diversify his assembly operations so that he can work for U.S. firms in different industrial sectors, either simultaneously or by shifting his work force from one assembly production to another according to the external demand. It was observed in the survey that the low capital–output ratio enables some firms, with only minor modifications in their factories and equipment, to move from baseballs to cassettes or from electronics to textiles, as they lose contracts for one product but find them for another. Thus, it is not the foreign principal that is footloose but rather the Haitian firm, which displays high mobility between foreign principals or production sectors. It is this flexibility, a manifestation of perceptive Haitian entrepreneurship, that has given stability to the growth of assembly activities in Haiti.

## Conclusions

Assembly production has become an integral part of economic activities in Haiti. It is not a marginal appendage, as in some countries that are

32. The only significant rises and falls were in the following categories (complete products, parts, or both), listed in descending order of magnitude: office machines, electric tubes, jewelry, recording media, valves, internal combustion engines, and watches. But except office machines, output of these never exceeded $1.5 million, with only about $300,000 of value added. In the last two product groups value added in the peak year was $10,000 or less. Information about disappearances at the plant level is not available. (Data from special magnetic tapes supplied by the ITC.)

engaged in these operations, but a principal contributor to the economic development of Haiti and the leading edge of its industrialization. It has been the most buoyant sector of the Haitian economy for the past decade. The best estimate is that value added in assembly activities now constitutes more than a quarter of all income generated in the manufacturing sector and provides almost a third of the country's export earnings.[33] While the employment it creates, estimated by the authors at 60,000 persons in 1980, may seem small in relation to the total labor force of more than 2.5 million, it is probably as large as employment in all the rest of the modern manufacturing sector in the country.[34]

The strong linkages of assembly plants to foreign companies do not seem to have introduced extraordinary instability into the Haitian economy. While there is a dependence on foreign orders or contracts, Haitian entrepreneurs have learned to protect themselves against the extremes of this dependency, often by spreading the risk among several foreign firms and assembly products.

The foreign principal, in turn, apparently wants to keep the dependency relationship to a minimum: while prepared to provide machinery and equipment to the Haitian assembly plant, the principal does not provide much financing. Only 7 percent of the firms interviewed in the survey reported that they were in debt to the principal. Nearly all the rest borrowed from private banks in Haiti.[35]

It would be difficult to support the assertion that, as in Mexico, assembly activities form an economic enclave in Haiti. First of all, Haiti is at the bottom of the development ladder, so linkages among its economic sectors are weak and it is still far from having an integrated economy. Second, assembly production is concentrated in the economic and population center of the country, metropolitan Port-au-Prince, and not in a remote region far removed from the capital, as in Mexico.[36] There are no laws that explicitly restrict assembly plants to a free-trade zone or to in-bond operations. There is, however, a formal legal barrier to selling assembled items with

33. Table 5-1; and World Bank, "Economic Note for the Haitian Subgroup," pp. 26, 32.

34. Based on data in World Bank, *Economic Memorandum on Haiti,* p. 144.

35. Apart from wholly owned subsidiaries, where the financial link is obvious, only when the foreign principal has equity participation does he frequently provide financing: about half the joint ventures reported borrowing from the U.S. contractor.

36. Nevertheless, a decentralization of assembly activities would be desirable in Haiti as well. In areas of the country where extreme poverty exists living costs are lower than in Port-au-Prince, and it would make sense to have lower minimum wages there than in the capital in order to absorb part of the vast pool of underemployed.

imported components on the local market. At present, assembly firms have no strong economic incentives to sell at home, where the demand for their products is weak in relation to export demand.

The lack of tight integration of assembly operations into the rest of the economy is not too different from the relatively weak linkages among other industries that use imported materials. This is particularly true of many of the new import-substituting industries that depend on imported inputs.

The basic problem of national economic integration is the low level of economic development. As income levels rise and better public policy helps ease supply constraints, the various economic sectors, including assembly industries, are tied together more closely, thereby increasing their contribution to the economic development of the country. In the meantime, the linkages in assembly production have not been trivial; they compare favorably with linkages in other economic activities in the country. Not only do the incomes generated by assembly production create a significant demand for local goods and services, but assembly production has also provided a substantial stimulus to the banking, transport, and communications sectors, as well as to food services in or near the factories for the assembly workers.[37] While some local components, such as materials for baseball cores, leather for shoes and handbags, plastic cases for cassettes, and corrugated cartons and other packing materials are used in assembly production, any substantial increase in the use of local inputs must await the elimination of supply problems in other sectors, particularly in agriculture.

In the context of an underdeveloped economy such as that of Haiti, assembly operations help significantly in the transfer of technology. The mere existence of these activities, which constitute perhaps half the country's modern sector, introduces workers to factory discipline and to new equipment and working methods. Even if, as the World Bank reports, the average training period for assembly work is only two months, it provides skill levels far higher than the mean of the Haitian labor force.[38] As shown earlier, there is a considerable interchange of technicians between the Haitian plants and the U.S. principals. And the mere fact that assembly operations and other production activities are often carried on within the same

37. Bank credit to the private sector increased from $13 million in 1970 to $184 million in 1979. According to one source, foreign banks came into Haiti mainly in response to the demand by the assembly industry. See ADIH, "The Industrial Sector in Haiti," p. 12.

38. Figure from World Bank, *Current Economic Position,* vol. 1, p. 23.

firm makes an unusual economic and technological isolation of the former highly unlikely.

Barring a deterioration of the political situation in Haiti, indications are that the dynamism of assembly production will remain alive. The vast majority of the firms interviewed—84 percent of them—expected a further growth of subcontracting activities and said that they planned to expand their own operations.[39] At least until 1983, the optimism of the managers has been borne out by the facts: value added generated in assembly production in Haiti in 1980 was nearly a quarter greater than in the preceding year, and growth continued in 1981, 1982, and 1983, despite a dramatic decline in GNP and in other exports.

## Appendix: A Note on the Sample Surveys Used

Much of the analysis in this chapter is based on two detailed sample surveys conducted during December 1979 and January 1980 in Port-au-Prince, Haiti, by Leslie Delatour and Karl Voltaire. They reported the results in a paper entitled "International Subcontracting Activities in Haiti," prepared especially for the present study. It was submitted to the Second Seminar on North-South Complementary Intra-Industry Trade, sponsored by the United Nations Conference on Trade and Development and the Brookings Institution and held under the auspices of El Colegio de México in Mexico City, August 18–22, 1980. One of the two sample surveys deals with the enterprises, the other with the workers in assembly industries. They were administered by two Haitian contractors chosen for their intimate knowledge of the assembly sector in Haiti and their privileged access to industrialists. The detailed results of the surveys are available from the authors.

In Haiti the designation *assembly* is also given to firms using local materials in producing goods for export. Thus assembly firms are divided into those that use local materials and those that use imported materials. The former do not concentrate on assembly operations but produce a complete product, usually for export, although some of their output may be sold on the home market. Those "assembly" firms that use local inputs are not as significant as the true assembly industries that use imported components; the former exported only about $16 million worth of light manufactures in

39. This despite the fact that some of them were operating below capacity at the time of the survey (probably because of seasonal factors).

1978, the latter $29 million worth.[40] The former are not considered assembly firms here. The survey was confined to those enterprises that assemble, at least in part, imported components. Some of the firms included in the sample, however, do both export and sell on the domestic market.

The enterprise sample, consisting of fifty-one firms, some of which had more than one plant, was selected from a list of assembly companies supplied by the Haitian government and the U.S. embassy in Port-au-Prince. The selection was made at random within four broad categories: electronics, textiles (including clothing), sporting goods (primarily baseballs and softballs), and miscellaneous.[41] Both the absence of formal accounting and managerial information techniques and the aura of secrecy regarding sales and profit figures limited the amount of hard data that could be extracted. Nevertheless, enough information was obtained to make possible an examination of the basic features of the industry.

The sample of 500 workers was spread among the fifty-one firms; about ten were selected at random from each. Only piece-rate workers—no foremen or supervisors—were included. The questions, although printed in a formal questionnaire, were asked orally, in Creole rather than in French, in order to facilitate communication.

Given the absence of precise information about the universe, it is impossible to determine the representativeness of the samples. There are disagreements between the various reports consulted as to how many firms there are in the assembly sector and as to how many workers they employ. The sample used here of fifty-one firms employing a total of 20,000 workers gave results that seem consistent with figures of the World Bank and the American embassy.

Since these are the first intensive surveys of enterprises and workers in Haiti, little of the information obtained can be compared with data previously available.

40. The comparison was made with value added in assembly exports (see table 5-1) so as not to count the value of U.S. components (total assembly exports were $105 million). The difference between assembly exports from local materials and those from imported materials has widened in recent years. In 1981 and 1982, value added in Haiti of 807 exports to the United States was about twice as much as the value of exports made from domestic materials ($54 million and $27 million, respectively, in 1981 and $55 million and $28 million, respectively, in 1982); see table 5-1 and World Bank, "Economic Note for the Haitian Subgroup," p. 32.

41. Half the firms in the "miscellaneous" category are firms that assemble stuffed toys; the others are a firm that sorts coupons for U.S. manufacturers who have issued them to the public for discounts in supermarkets and retail stores, a shoe-assembly firm, and a wig-assembly firm.

CHAPTER SIX

# Assembly Activities in Colombia

JOSEPH GRUNWALD
WITH JUAN JOSÉ ECHAVARRÍA

THE striking aspect of Colombian assembly activities for the U.S. market is an explosive growth—a sixtyfold increase in only four years, 1970–74—followed by a sudden evaporation of that momentum. Between the mid 1970s and 1980 total assembly exports to the United States fluctuated roughly around the 1975 level, then began to increase, reaching $30 million in 1983, a third of which was value added in Colombia (see table 6-1). Before reflecting on the reasons for this unusual growth pattern and the small size of the sector, a few words on its background and characteristics are in order.

## Characteristics

As a middle-income Latin American country, although far above average in population and area, Colombia is now the fifth largest industrial producer in the region. As in most of the import-substituting economies of Latin America, export of manufactures came late. It is concentrated in textiles, particularly clothing, which accounts for about a quarter of total industrial exports, excluding fuel oil (see table 6-2). Yet because of the preponderance of coffee, manufacturing exports have contributed less than a fifth of the country's total export earnings.

This chapter had the benefit of a lengthy paper entitled "Colombia: A Typical Non-Assembly Country," prepared by Juan José Echavarría for this project. It provided background material and some research findings for this chapter. Echavarría applied an extensive questionnaire to a sample of eighteen enterprises out of a total of approximately sixty Colombian firms that were doing assembly work for foreign firms. The Echavarría survey, as it will be referred to hereafter, was presented at the Second Seminar on North-South Complementary Intra-Industry Trade, sponsored by the United Nations Conference on Trade and Development and the Brookings Institution and held under the auspices of El Colegio de México in Mexico City, August 18–22, 1980.

Table 6-1. *U.S. Imports from Colombia under Tariff Item 807.00, Dutiable and Duty-free, and Imports of Principal Products as Percent of Total, 1969–83*[a]

| | Value of imports (millions of dollars) | | | As percent of total | | |
|---|---|---|---|---|---|---|
| Year | Total | Dutiable | Duty-free | Dutiable | Textiles | Toys and dolls |
| 1969 | 0.4 | 0.1 | 0.2 | 34 | 99.7 | * |
| 1970 | 0.3 | 0.2 | 0.1 | 69 | 94.5 | * |
| 1971 | 0.7 | 0.5 | 0.2 | 68 | 94.7 | * |
| 1972 | 1.5 | 0.8 | 0.7 | 52 | 99.2 | * |
| 1973 | 6.7 | 2.2 | 4.5 | 33 | 99.2 | * |
| 1974 | 18.7 | 5.6 | 13.1 | 30 | 98.9 | 0.1 |
| 1975 | 20.4 | 6.0 | 14.4 | 30 | 99.8 | * |
| 1976 | 14.3 | 5.1 | 9.2 | 36 | 98.4 | 0.8 |
| 1977 | 14.6 | 5.5 | 9.0 | 38 | 96.0 | 3.7 |
| 1978 | 21.5 | 8.2 | 13.3 | 38 | 95.7 | 4.2 |
| 1979 | 25.2 | 9.6 | 15.5 | 38 | 94.8 | 4.7 |
| 1980 | 19.9 | 7.8 | 12.1 | 39 | 93.8 | 5.6 |
| 1981 | 25.8 | 10.3 | 15.5 | 40 | 94.1 | 5.8 |
| 1982 | 28.0 | 9.4 | 18.6 | 34 | 98.9 | 1.0 |
| 1983 | 29.8 | 9.7 | 20.0 | 33 | 99.9 | * |

Sources: U.S. International Trade Commission (ITC), *Tariff Items 807.00 and 806.30: U.S. Imports for Consumption*, various years, and printouts of special magnetic tapes prepared by the ITC.

* Zero or less than 0.05 percent.

a. U.S. imports from Colombia under item 806.30 never amount to more than $50,000.

Export assembly operations are small, not only in comparison with those of Mexico and Haiti, but also in relation to the size of the Colombian economy. Value added in these activities, consisting mostly of the assembly of apparel, has not averaged more than about 4 percent of the incomes generated in the whole textile industry. Only in the exports of specific product groups to the United States is assembly output of real importance. Thus more than 97 percent of U.S. imports of women's blouses and men's shirts from Colombia came in under item 807.00 in 1978 (see table 6-3).[1]

The assembly of toys and dolls was of some importance during recent years. Much of it, however, cannot be detected under U.S. 807 statistics. "Pop-up" toy books for children, for example, assembled in Colombia from paper and cardboard from the United States, do not qualify under tariff item 807 because, besides being assembled manually, the U.S. com-

1. Unlike the Philippines, Mexico, Haiti, and other countries, Colombia assembles almost no brassieres or other body-supporting garments, which carry relatively high tariffs and are usually the principal textile products assembled elsewhere.

Table 6-2. *Importance of Value Added in Textile Assembly Exports to the United States Compared with Total Exports of Textiles and of Manufactured Goods from Colombia to the World, 1970–81*

| | | *Exports of textiles*[a] | | *Dutiable 807.00 exports of textiles to the United States* | | *Total 807.00 exports of textiles to the United States* | |
|---|---|---|---|---|---|---|---|
| *Year* | *Manufactured exports (millions of dollars)* | *Millions of dollars* | *As percent of total* | *Millions of dollars* | *As percent of total textile exports* | *Millions of dollars* | *As percent of total textile exports* |
| 1970 | 71.2 | 18.7 | 26.3 | 0.2 | 1.1 | 0.3 | 1.5 |
| 1971 | 97.9 | 26.7 | 27.3 | 0.5 | 1.7 | 0.7 | 2.5 |
| 1972 | 146.8 | 42.6 | 29.0 | 0.8 | 1.9 | 1.5 | 3.5 |
| 1973 | 233.9 | 81.9 | 35.0 | 2.2 | 2.7 | 6.7 | 8.2 |
| 1974 | 376.7 | 154.0 | 40.9 | 5.6 | 3.6 | 18.7 | 12.1 |
| 1975 | 294.2 | 102.4 | 34.8 | 6.0 | 5.9 | 20.4 | 19.2 |
| 1976 | 364.0 | 139.0 | 38.2 | 5.1 | 3.7 | 14.3 | 10.1 |
| 1977 | 365.2 | 88.0 | 24.1 | 5.5 | 6.1 | 14.6 | 16.0 |
| 1978 | 496.3 | 194.7 | 39.2 | 8.2 | 4.0 | 21.5 | 10.5 |
| 1979 | 549.1 | 150.4 | 27.4 | 9.6 | 6.1 | 25.2 | 15.9 |
| 1980 | 596.9[b] | 146.7[b] | 24.6 | 7.8 | 5.0 | 19.9 | 12.8 |
| 1981 | 632.4[b] | 157.6[b] | 24.9 | 10.3 | 6.1 | 25.8 | 15.5 |

Sources: Table 6-1 and Colombian data as reported in World Bank, "Colombia: Economic Development and Policy under Changing Conditions," vol. 2, Statistical Appendix, Report 4444-CO (World Bank, August 1983), table 3.2, p. 28.

a. "Textiles" includes clothing and footwear but not cotton fiber.

b. Preliminary estimate.

Table 6-3. *Total Exports and the Principal Assembly Exports of Colombia to the United States and the Importance of Value Added, by Product Group, on the Basis of U.S. Import Data, 1978*

| | *Millions of dollars* | | | |
|---|---|---|---|---|
| *Product group*[a] | *Total exports*[b] | *Assembly exports*[c] | *Assembly exports as percent of total exports* | *Value added in Colombia as percent of total assembly exports*[d] |
| Women's, girls, and infants' blouses | 7.1 | 6.9 | 97.9 | 40.2 |
| Men's and boys' miscellaneous wearing apparel | 7.1 | 6.0 | 84.7 | 36.8 |
| Women's, girls', and infants' suits, coats, jackets, and skirts | 5.1 | 4.5 | 87.3 | 41.1 |
| Women's, girls', and infants' miscellaneous wearing apparel | 1.9 | 1.6 | 84.0 | 20.7 |
| Men's and boys' shirts | 0.9 | 0.9 | 97.3 | 38.1 |
| Total wearing apparel | 31.8 | 20.6 | 64.7 | 38.5 |
| Toys and dolls | 1.3 | 0.9 | 69.7 | 28.8 |
| Total manufactured exports | 120.5 | 21.5 | 17.9 | 38.1 |

Source: Printouts of special magnetic tapes prepared by the ITC.
a. ITC classifications; see ITC publications on tariff items 807.00 and 806.30.
b. Total U.S. imports from Colombia.
c. U.S. 807 imports from Colombia.
d. Dutiable value as percent of value of 807 imports.

ponents are cut and printed in Colombia.[2] Under the 807 category, therefore, the import of assembled toys and dolls became insignificant during the early 1980s (see table 6-1).

### *The Incentive Systems*

For many years, Colombia has tried to promote manufactured exports. An incentive system called Plan Vallejo, initiated in 1959 and subsequently strengthened, provides for duty-free import of inputs and also for subsidies in the form of tax credits for production to be exported. One aspect of the plan is geared to assembly operations and thus constitutes the counterpart to the U.S. 807 tariff item. That part of the plan applies only to assembly done in bond, which means that the product must be exported and cannot be sold on the domestic market.

There seem to be serious problems in the application of Plan Vallejo. They range from bureaucratic delays to the requirement that before a fabric that is also produced in Colombia can be imported duty-free, a

2. It will be recalled that the U.S. components must be identifiable—uncut and unprocessed—in the assembled product in order for it to qualify for import under item 807.

letter of approval has to be obtained from the relevant textile firm. These administrative complications have greatly reduced the value of the export incentive system for both regular and assembly exports of textiles. Given the short season in clothing, a delay of only a few weeks in obtaining Plan Vallejo approval can be disastrous. Morawetz shows how Colombia's advantage in distance over the Far East can thereby be nullified.[3] It should be noted, however, that compared to those of other Latin American exporters of textiles to the United States under item 807, Colombia's transport costs are high (see table 6-4).

Another part of the export incentive system is the establishment of free-trade zones in the country. In an effort to help decentralize industry, Colombia's six free-trade and industrial zones were established outside Bogotá and Medellín, where much of Colombian industry is concentrated. With the possible exception of the zone in Barranquilla, the oldest one, and the one in Cali, a city that already had a relatively high concentration of industry, the free-trade zones did not stimulate much industrial activity. A large part of what they have done has been focused on warehousing rather than on manufacturing. Thus neither the free-trade zones nor the Vallejo Plan has provided significant incentives to do assembly work for export.

### *Subcontracting*

Subsidiaries of U.S. firms engaged in assembly of U.S. manufactured goods in Colombia are relatively rare—although such enterprises do assemble a large share of the knockdown parts for the local market. The firms in this sector, majority ownership of more than 90 percent of which is by Colombians, have an arm's-length relationship with U.S. companies from whom they subcontract. Yet about a fourth of U.S. textile imports are considered in U.S. statistics as transactions by related parties, which means that one party owns at least a 5 percent interest in the other. Nevertheless, this proportion is much smaller than it is in Mexico, the Dominican Republic, Costa Rica, and El Salvador, other textile producers in Latin America that assemble for the United States (see table 6-4).

Almost all enterprises do assembly to U.S. specifications. The clothes, for example, are nearly always designed and the fabric manufactured and

3. David Morawetz, *Why the Emperor's New Clothes Are Not Made in Colombia* (Oxford University Press for the World Bank, 1981), pp. 78–82 and 120–21.

Table 6-4. *U.S. Imports of Textiles and the Importance of Related-Party Imports, 807.00 Imports, and Transport and Insurance, from Sixteen Countries, 1978*[a]

| Country | Total textile imports (millions of dollars) | Percent of total imports: Imports under item 807.00 | Related-party imports[b] | Transport and insurance |
|---|---|---|---|---|
| Mexico | 181.7 | 86.5 | 62.6 | 0.4 |
| El Salvador | 30.8 | 83.9 | 54.0 | 2.9 |
| Brazil | 29.7 | 0.03 | 12.8 | 6.6 |
| Haiti | 43.5 | 91.1 | 19.1 | 3.5 |
| Dominican Republic | 47.3 | 97.9 | 70.8 | 2.9 |
| Colombia | 31.8 | 64.7 | 25.5 | 4.8 |
| Costa Rica | 28.0 | 99.8 | 61.3 | 2.9 |
| Korea | 632.5 | 0.9 | 7.6 | 10.2 |
| Hong Kong | 1,153.5 | 0.1 | 2.7 | 8.8 |
| Taiwan | 807.6 | 0.1 | 1.3 | 9.5 |
| Singapore | 113.7 | 0.03 | 0.3 | 8.0 |
| Philippines | 139.6 | 13.3 | 37.4 | 10.1 |
| Malaysia | 23.0 | 0.0 | 0.0 | 8.5 |
| Canada | 38.9 | 4.5 | 46.5 | 0.2 |
| West Germany | 57.8 | 0.1 | 24.2 | 5.6 |
| Japan | 336.3 | 0.1 | 18.7 | 6.9 |
| Sixteen countries | 3,696.0 | 8.7 | 11.5 | 8.2 |
| All countries | 4,641.0 | 8.8 | 11.9 | 8.2 |

Source: Printouts of special magnetic tapes prepared by the ITC.
a. "Textiles" includes all of Schedule 3, Tariff Schedules of the United States of America, in which there were 807 imports.
b. "Related-party" trade refers to trade between firms one of which owns at least 5 percent of the other (see chapter 2).

cut in the United States and shipped to Colombia, together with buttons and zippers, to be sewn and assembled for reshipment to the United States. Although the U.S. principals rarely supply machinery and equipment to the Colombian firms, as they often do for Haitian and Mexican firms, they usually do provide their Colombian subcontractors with technical assistance. Also contrary to the Haitian case, it is generally the U.S. firm that initiated the assembly contract. It is not unusual for a Colombian firm operating close to capacity that has assembly contracts with the U.S. principal to subcontract part of a contract to other Colombian enterprises. In this way many firms have entered into direct arrangements with U.S. companies.

On both sides of the assembly relationship there is a spreading of risks. The U.S. company will often contract with more than one Colombian firm, usually one large long-term contract with the principal partner and one or more smaller short-term contracts with other Colombian firms. (This is in addition to the subcontracting of assembly work by Colombian companies.) On the other side, Colombian enterprises engaged in assembly operations average two foreign principals per firm, according to the Echavarría sample.

## What Happened?

After a dramatic upsurge during the first half of the 1970s, the comparatively wide fluctuations of Colombian assembly for export are puzzling (see table 6-1). Is subcontracting inherently unstable? Are fluctuations therefore introduced from outside Colombia? Is this particularly true of assembly of clothing, a highly volatile sector because of the changes in fashion?

In the Echavarría survey, it was found that the assembly contracts of two-thirds of the Colombian firms had been canceled at one time or another. Almost half the cancellations originated with the Colombian firms. When the U.S. principal canceled, it was always because the Colombian firm (according to the Colombian firms' own testimony) could not meet the contract specifications. Usually the U.S. company then transferred the contract to another Colombian enterprise. It is obvious, therefore, that cancellations are not the whole reason for the slowdown and fluctuation in Colombian assembly production since 1975.

Although there was a sharp drop in total exports of clothing from Colombia to the world during the U.S. recession of 1974–75, Colombian assembly exports to the United States rose dramatically. The increase was pronounced in the value of U.S. components assembled in Colombia, which jumped from $4.5 million in 1973 to $13.1 million in 1975 (see table 6-1). After the strong U.S. economic recovery in 1975, assembly operations in Colombia declined. Notable increases were to be observed again during the world recession of the early 1980s. U.S. components imported for assembly in Colombia rose more than half between 1980 and 1982 (see table 6-1).

Two forces, one coming from the United States, the other from Colombia, may have been behind this phenomenon. First, as indicated earlier, U.S. firms seeking to cut costs have an especially strong motivation to shift labor-intensive operations abroad during a recession to areas in which wages are low. On the other hand, Colombian firms, as will be seen, wish to take up the slack in their production, both for export and for the domestic market, during the recession by assembling foreign components for export.

The general decline in total textile exports from Colombia has been attributed to a drop in the profitability of exporting in relation to the profitability of selling at home.[4] Various factors account for this change: a rise in the protection of domestic production; an increase in bureaucratic obstacles to exporting; overvalued rates of exchange; a decline in the productivity of labor; and other elements that restrain international competition. Because of these features, prices of domestic fabrics have increased to a level 75 percent above world prices and, despite low wages, labor costs in Colombia have surpassed those in Hong Kong, Korea, and Taiwan. Thus, exporting garments has become difficult for Colombian producers even if they are able to do so with lower-priced imported fabrics. If the requirements that export products must meet high standards of quality, specifications, and delivery schedules are added, it becomes clear that selling on the domestic market is not only easier but much more profitable.

Assembly exports are sheltered from some of these problems, however. By definition, assembly production is done with imported materials; it will therefore be more profitable than conventional exports based on high-priced domestic fabrics. Also, the productivity of labor can be improved through technical assistance provided by the principal. Nevertheless, as long as domestic production is protected through import licenses, tariffs, and administrative restraints on imports and competition, selling at home will generally be preferred over assembly activities for the U.S. market.[5]

Why, then, do Colombian firms engage in assembly production for the U.S. market? According to the Echavarría survey, transfer of technology is a principal motivation for Colombian firms to subcontract with U.S. companies. Technicians and managers from the U.S. company regularly visit the subcontracting Colombian firm, and often key persons from the Colombian enterprise will spend some time in training at the U.S. plant. The

4. This phenomenon is examined in detail in Morawetz, *Why the Emperor's New Clothes.*

5. In the Echavarría survey none of the firms interviewed claimed that their assembly activities were more profitable than producing for the domestic market. In fact, a 20–30 percent difference in profit was claimed in favor of the home market. It should be noted that from the mid 1970s until 1981 there was a steady increase in the proportion of 807 import value added in Colombia, rising from 30 percent to 40 percent in 1981 (see table 6-1). This may be attributable to rising wages and profit shares in assembly activities. Since 1981 both the share and the absolute amount of value added have declined again as the sharp devaluations of the Colombian peso have caused a drop in the cost of assembling the increasing value of U.S. components.

Table 6-5. *U.S. Imports of Textiles under Item 807.00 from Seven Countries, 1970 and 1974–83*[a]

| | Total textile imports under item 807.00 (millions of dollars) | | | | | | | |
|---|---|---|---|---|---|---|---|---|
| *Country* | *1970* | *1974* | *1975* | *1976* | *1977* | *1978* | *1982* | *1983* |
| Mexico | 21.0 | 117.3 | 124.5 | 131.4 | 131.2 | 157.2 | 207.4 | 161.1 |
| El Salvador | 0.3 | 9.0 | 12.6 | 17.9 | 18.9 | 25.9 | 8.1 | 5.6 |
| Haiti | 1.5 | 19.7 | 19.4 | 27.1 | 30.7 | 39.7 | 62.6 | 73.7 |
| Dominican Republic | 0.1 | 5.5 | 10.9 | 20.1 | 31.1 | 46.4 | 116.9 | 137.0 |
| Colombia | 0.3 | 18.5 | 20.4 | 14.1 | 14.0 | 20.6 | 27.7 | 29.7 |
| Philippines | 0.8 | 13.1 | 13.8 | 13.2 | 16.0 | 18.6 | 29.9 | 23.0 |
| Costa Rica | 2.1 | 10.1 | 10.8 | 19.0 | 22.7 | 27.9 | 45.3 | 62.5 |
| All countries | 43.0 | 220.8 | 237.8 | 277.4 | 311.6 | 409.6 | 649.7 | 627.5 |

Source: Printouts of special magnetic tapes prepared by the ITC.

technology thus acquired can be applied to the domestic and other export production activities of the firm. The assembly relationship, moreover, gives the Colombian clothing manufacturer early access to information about changes in styles and new trends in fashions.

Probably the more important incentive to engage in assembly production for export is that it gives the Colombian firm the opportunity to fill gaps in production whenever other export business or domestic demand or supply declines, so that plant capacity will always be used as fully as possible. When there is a downturn in domestic production, workers need not be fired—a very expensive action in Colombia, where high severance pay is mandatory—and machinery and equipment need not become idle.

Colombian firms that have any ambition to improve their export capabilities might therefore be willing to sacrifice part of their profits by substituting assembly work for some domestic production in order to learn from their U.S. customers how to cut costs, improve quality and styling, and upgrade the skills of their labor force. If the degree of competition at home were higher, all companies would be interested in producing more efficiently and with greater quality and might therefore benefit from engaging in some export assembly work.

### *Effects on U.S. Firms*

That which makes for stability in Colombian firms, however, creates instability for the U.S. principals. The lack of reliability of Colombian assembly output has been responsible for a shift of U.S. 807 imports away

Table 6-5 (*continued*)

| *Dutiable value as percent of total value of textile imports under item 807.00* | | | | | | | | |
|---|---|---|---|---|---|---|---|---|
| *1970* | *1974* | *1975* | *1976* | *1977* | *1978* | *1982* | *1983* | *Country* |
| 26.8 | 30.0 | 31.7 | 30.9 | 28.5 | 29.5 | 28.7 | 22.2 | Mexico |
| 26.8 | 21.0 | 26.0 | 29.2 | 32.4 | 34.1 | 29.0 | 27.9 | El Salvador |
| 38.3 | 25.3 | 25.2 | 23.8 | 24.7 | 27.6 | 31.6 | 27.8 | Haiti |
| 20.8 | 27.2 | 26.2 | 28.2 | 30.7 | 31.9 | 34.1 | 32.6 | Dominican Republic |
| 71.0 | 29.3 | 29.6 | 35.6 | 38.2 | 38.6 | 33.7 | 32.7 | Colombia |
| 55.7 | 90.0 | 89.8 | 90.0 | 88.8 | 88.9 | 77.7 | 83.5 | Philippines |
| 31.7 | 26.0 | 29.1 | 30.2 | 32.7 | 36.2 | 20.3 | 22.9 | Costa Rica |
| 35.3 | 34.0 | 34.7 | 34.8 | 35.4 | 38.3 | 38.7 | 34.3 | All countries |

a. "Textiles" includes all of Schedule 3, Tariff Schedules of the United States, in which there were 807 imports.

from Colombia to other Latin American countries after 1975 (see table 6-5). Haiti, for example, exported about the same amount of textiles to the United States under 807 as Colombia did during 1974–75, yet by 1983 Haiti's 807 textile exports amounted to $74 million, while Colombia's were only $30 million. Nevertheless, a modest, albeit fluctuating, assembly business has continued between the United States and Colombia, as both sides have accommodated themselves to the relationship. Just as Colombian firms tend to use export assembly operations as a cushion in order to keep their labor force, plant, and equipment in full use, so too U.S. manufacturers use short-term subcontracts with Colombian enterprises as a way of taking care of the short-term fluctuations in their assembly needs.

## Conclusions

Export assembly operations began in Colombia during a period when conditions for export appeared favorable compared to production for the home market. Later, export conditions deteriorated and selling at home became far more lucrative and convenient. As fill-in work, assembly production began to fluctuate according to the requirements of Colombian firms, for as long as assembly and domestic production are considered substitutes in a zero-sum situation, employment in one can expand only at the expense of the other.

It is in the last sense that assembly activities can be regarded as making their primary contribution: they provide the needed flexibility for Colombian clothing manufacturers to maintain their production on an even keel. When there is a downturn in domestic production, workers need not be fired, expensive severance pay can be saved, and machinery and equipment need not become idle. Ironically, therefore, assembly operations for export, far from introducing instability, a charge frequently made in other countries, is a stabilizing element for the Colombian economy.

On the other side, this situation has brought instability to U.S. clothing manufacturers who have found it difficult to make long-term plans for their assembly needs in Colombia. Most of the expansion in the assembly business has therefore gone to other Latin American countries in the Caribbean basin.

CHAPTER SEVEN

# Overview

THE international reorganization of production examined in this book is an essentially reactive strategy of firms in industrial countries that face competition from low-cost imports. In an attempt to defend domestic markets against international competition, rather than as an aggressive move against competitors at home, producers have transferred abroad production processes in which they have lost their international competitive advantage. The value of such a strategy depends on the relative costs of labor, transport, and communications, the importance of quality, the risks to investment, and the economic costs of the principal alternative to labor-intensive assembly—automation. It has been on the whole a successful way for threatened firms in industrial countries to retain competitiveness and for developing countries to exploit their own comparative advantage.

Assembly production abroad, therefore, is a sharp manifestation of the North-South dichotomy: capital-intensive, high-technology production in industrial countries; low-skilled, labor-intensive production in developing countries. The system produces global benefits as well as serious misgivings. In the North, the movement abroad creates adjustment problems for large pockets of the unskilled that remain in manufacturing industry; in the South, the growth of assembly production for export raises the specter of a trap that will perpetuate a low-grade labor force and rudimentary production activities. The southern perception is nurtured by the absence of strong linkages of assembly activities to the rest of the economy, particularly in the larger developing countries.

Assembly activities are concentrated in two types of manufacture: electronics and apparel. In both, the value-to-weight ratios are high and transport costs are therefore low. Both can be manufactured in sequential operations that can be separated in time and space without affecting the quality of the product. They are goods with relatively short life cycles, as fashions and technologies change. Both types of product require extensive routine assembly operations, which can be performed either by unskilled labor or by sophisticated machines. An ample supply of low-wage labor can keep production costs internationally competitive. Automation as an alternative to manual assembly generally requires a large fixed-capital investment. Its attractiveness will therefore depend on the relative cost of capital and the size of the production flow that can repay the capital charges.

In all countries, subcontracting between independent firms appears to be the principal mode of having assembly done abroad in the apparel industry. In electronics, however, such operations are usually carried out by subsidiaries of multinational enterprises. In complex, high-technology industries it can be risky for a U.S. company not to control all manufacturing processes: valuable technology may leak to competitors, and independent subcontractors may not have the skills and techniques to undertake precision operations to the exacting standards for which the U.S. firm must bear responsibility to its customers.

Assembly of the same type of product can be found in many countries and a single firm often maintains similar production facilities in several locations abroad. Because wage levels in these locations are widely divergent and the costs of transport and communications are different, the return on investment abroad varies substantially from one place to another. Country risks, such as potential political and economic disturbances, also have a significant influence on decisions on the location of assembly operations for the home market. Diversifying production among countries is therefore an explicit strategy for reducing these risks, which loom large in the generally poor low-wage countries.

The trade-off between risk and economic return available in a particular assembly location will depend on both the technological characteristics of the product and the wage rates of the country in question. To weigh these factors, a simple framework for investment decisions has been constructed and estimated, using data from the semiconductor industry.[1] In the model, firms evaluate the political and economic risks to investment specific to every country and select a portfolio of production locations that reflects the optimal combination of risk and return available to investors. The calculations reveal that in semiconductor production, the only

1. For details see Kenneth Flamm, "The Volatility of Offshore Investment," *Journal of Development Economics,* forthcoming.

industry to which the model was applied, firms react rather quickly to changes in relative wages, though the long-run effect of a wage increase is a moderate decline in employment. These findings support some elements of the anecdotal portrait of a "footloose" industry painted by critics in the third world.

Yet the Mexico study shows that assembly output in that country does not appear to be highly wage-sensitive. The mix of products assembled there tends toward heavy items with relatively high transport costs. It will take large differences between wages in Mexico and those in other developing countries to offset its advantages of geographic and cultural proximity and a perception of relatively little risk.

## Production Abroad and the Industrial Countries

The transfer of labor-intensive operations to locations abroad affects the industrial countries by lowering the costs of assembled goods to their consumers. It alters the relative availability of labor and capital, the wages, and the profit rates in the domestic economy and fosters the equalization of factor prices internationally.

The traditional trade-theory view of these matters is often that struggles over import competition pit the incomes of specific workers against the general level of economic welfare. If workers whose incomes are reduced as a consequence of imports were offered a suitable system of transfers, the economy as a whole would benefit. The extra income created by trade will more than pay for the transfers required by the workers affected, so liberalization of trade leaves everyone better off. Underlying these arguments is the assumption that a system of perfectly competitive markets guarantees the employment of all resources, including labor, in the economy. When this assumption does not hold, policies other than free trade may also be required to ensure improvements in social welfare.[2]

2. For one thing, the system of welfare and minimum wages in most industrial countries creates a floor for wages, so if the wage for unskilled labor that would ensure full employment falls below that socially set level, unemployment is created. For another thing, in the presence of insufficient effective demand, free trade alone may not be optimal. For examples of this in the literature, see Michael Bruno, "Import Competition and Macroeconomic Adjustment under Wage-Price Rigidity," in Jagdish Bhagwati, ed., *Import Competition and Response* (University of Chicago Press for the National Bureau of Economic Research, 1982); and Richard Brecher, "Money, Employment, and Trade Balance Adjustment with Rigid Wages," *Oxford Economic Papers,* vol. 30 (March 1978), pp. 1–15.

From a practical point of view, even if markets do guarantee full employment in the long run, there may be significant transitional costs associated with the relocation of an industry, as displaced workers are forced to move, search for new employment, and, possibly, be retrained. These frictional "adjustment" costs are likely to have an effect on any calculation of the net benefits from cheaper imports.[3] While in theory a system of transfers can be worked out to guarantee labor that its standard of living will not decline as a result of socially desirable changes in trade arrangements, these transfers have, in practice, not generally been made.[4]

### *Consumers*

The obvious objective of U.S. firms in transferring assembly work abroad is to reduce the costs of production, which means lower prices to consumers. In 1978, cost savings from Mexican operations have been estimated to have been between $8,000 and $14,000 per employee a year.[5] On this basis, rough calculations yield a total direct saving from Mexican assembly production of between $1 billion and $2 billion in 1980. The reduction in cost to U.S. firms from assembly operations in all countries might be more than twice that amount, since wages are higher in Mexico than elsewhere in U.S. assembly operations abroad, and less than half the

3. See J. Peter Neary, "Intersectoral Mobility, Wage Stickiness, and the Case for Adjustment Assistance"; Michael Mussa, "Government Policy and the Adjustment Process"; and Peter Diamond, "Protection, Trade Adjustment Assistance, and Income Distribution"; all in Bhagwati, ed., *Import Competition and Response.*

4. See Graham Glenday, Glenn P. Jenkins, and John C. Evans, *Worker Adjustment to Liberalized Trade: Costs and Assistance Policies,* Staff Working Paper 426 (World Bank, October 1980); George R. Neumann, "The Direct Labor Market Effects of the Trade Adjustment Assistance Program: The Evidence from the TAA Survey," and Louis S. Jacobson, "Earnings Losses of Workers Displaced from Manufacturing Industries," both in U.S. Department of Labor, *The Impact of International Trade and Investment on Employment* (Government Printing Office, 1978); and Malcolm Bale, "Estimates of Trade-Displacement Costs for U.S. Workers," *Journal of International Economics,* vol. 6 (August 1976), pp. 245–50.

5. M. Richard Campbell, "Production Sharing, Implications for Industrial Promotion in Developing Countries," *Journal of the Flagstaff Institute,* vol. 3 (January 1979), p. 36. Taking the approximate differences in U.S. and Mexican wages yields similar results. In 1978 the differences between Mexican minimum wages per hour at the border and hourly earnings in the United States, as reported by the U.S. Department of Labor, were $5.38 in all of manufacturing, $5.04 in the electrical industry, and $3.15 in the apparel industry. (Because of the 1982 devaluation of the peso, the wage gap more than doubled in 1983.) The assumption in using these differences for an approximation of savings in cost is that there is little substitution of capital for labor; the estimates of savings should therefore be interpreted as an upper bound.

total employment in these activities was in Mexico. Although this represented less than 1 percent of U.S. value added in manufacturing in that year, the savings in cost on individual products are substantial. The gain in welfare to purchasers of semiconductors was estimated to be about 10 percent of the value of consumption. In the aggregate, then, savings to consumers as a result of production abroad are likely to be significant, although concentrated in only a few products.

### *Producers*

Rather small differences in cost can spell life or death for a firm. There is evidence that production arrangements in other countries have allowed certain businesses to remain internationally competitive in the face of serious threats from imports. Large-scale production abroad originated as a response to low-wage competition in the semiconductor industry and became an entrenched feature of the U.S. industry; it has also permitted some U.S. producers of television sets to stay afloat as low-wage Asian producers entered the U.S. market.

It can be expected that U.S. producers operating abroad are more likely to use U.S. intermediate inputs in their products than foreign manufactures. Production abroad thus tends to boost the U.S. content of a given volume of assembled imports. If the assembled article is to enter the U.S. market free of duty under tariff items 806/807, a component manufactured abroad must be cheaper than a U.S.-made component (net of the cost of transport abroad) to compete. This fact works to increase the demand for exports of U.S. components.

In industries less subject to foreign competition, however, production abroad may merely create extra profit—economic rent—that is pocketed by producers. In certain lines of apparel subject to U.S. import quotas, for example, production abroad with savings in U.S. tariffs through item 807 probably enables some U.S. firms to claim some of the implicit rents received by those who are allotted part of the U.S. quota.

### *Labor*

It is clear that the displacement of workers in an industry going abroad is, for an industrial country, the principal negative effect of such movement. Measuring the effects, however, is difficult, since to make precise calculations would require information or assumptions about the price elasticity of demand for the product, the technology that determines the demand for labor, the price elasticity of supply for assembly services abroad, the vulnerability of the domestic industry to competitive imports in the absence of a move abroad, and the indirect employment content of U.S. components, materials, and supplies going into foreign facilities.[6] Such "job counting" studies of the employment effects of foreign investment generally conclude that the net change can be either positive or negative, depending on the precise magnitudes and assumptions used in the calculations.[7]

The study of the semiconductor industry indicates that the "direct" employment effect of production abroad—that is, excluding indirect effects on employment in other industries that supply components or use the finished product—compared with the hypothetical situation that might have been created by simply banning all imports of semiconductors, is negative: forcing assembly back onto U.S. soil might increase employment in the industry by 30,000–60,000 jobs, but at the cost of significant losses in employment in the more highly skilled occupations.[8]

Other data confirm that there have been significant job losses in industries affected by foreign assembly. Between April 1975 and July 1982, more than 170,000 workers in the apparel and textile industries and 75,000 workers in the electrical and electronics industries successfully sought certification by the U.S. Department of Labor of eligibility for trade-adjustment assistance. Of the workers in electronics, about 27,000 were in radio and television receiver plants, 8,600 in the manufacture of semiconductors, and about 19,000 in other electronic-component plants.[9]

6. Ideally, more subtle, indirect effects, such as the effect on substitutes, need also to be measured, which requires a knowledge of their price and cross-price elasticities.

7. For a review of these studies, see Daniel J. B. Mitchell, *Labor Issues of American International Trade and Investment* (Johns Hopkins University Press, 1976); and chapter 4 of C. Fred Bergsten, Thomas Horst, and Theodore H. Moran, *American Multinationals and American Interests* (Brookings Institution, 1978). With one set of assumptions, J. M. Finger arrives at a positive effect on U.S. employment in an evaluation of the special tariff provisions for assembly abroad. See his "Trade and Domestic Effects of the Offshore Assembly Provision in the U.S. Tariff," *American Economic Review,* vol. 66 (September 1976), pp. 598–611; also "Offshore Assembly Provisions in the West German and Netherlands Tariffs: Trade and Domestic Effects," *Weltwirtschaftliches Archiv,* vol. 113 (1977), pp. 237–49.

8. It is not clear, however, what the effect of the trade restrictions assumed in these calculations would be on the foreign sales of U.S. producers.

9. These figures reflect only workers applying for trade-adjustment assistance who were partially or fully eligible for assistance. The numbers were:

After each U.S. recession the ratio of U.S. production workers to total employment in U.S. industries assembling abroad has declined. This confirms the conclusion, drawn from the experience of certain developing countries, that during a business downturn producers seem to reduce their high-cost operations in the United States in favor of production abroad, and the trend is not reversed during the subsequent economic recovery. Recessions are therefore more harmful to U.S. employment than to assembly employment abroad.

The workers who suffer most in the two industries most strongly affected by foreign production, apparel and electronics, especially in the least-skilled assembly jobs, are women. Empirical studies tend to show that adjustment costs for displaced female workers are greater than for male workers of the same ages and skill levels.[10] Periods of unemployment of displaced women workers, for example, seem to be much longer than those of male workers, at all ages. Assembly abroad is thus likely to cause acute problems of employment displacement. It seems inequitable for unskilled working women to bear costs that are more than compensated for by lower costs to consumers.

Because certain vulnerable segments of the U.S. labor force have borne the brunt of retrenchment, the importance in total employment of the more highly skilled segment remaining in the United States has increased. Since skilled workers are less likely to be laid off in response to a downturn, fluctuations in total employment in an industry may have decreased. This seems to have been the case in the semiconductor industry.

Production abroad, then, has wrought permanent change in the composition of the demand for labor in that part of the industry left behind. The least skilled and the marginally employed—those for whom displacement is most costly—are those most strongly affected. Ironically, though, the demand for assembly workers seems to increase with the technological

| | *Eligible workers (thousands)* | |
|---|---|---|
| *Industry (SIC no.)* | *Fully eligible* | *Partially eligible* |
| Textile products (22) | 23.3 | 2.0 |
| Apparel (23) | 138.7 | 7.1 |
| Electrical and electronic equipment (36) | 71.7 | 3.2 |

Figures are from unpublished U.S. Department of Labor computer printouts and are totals for the period June 1975–July 1982.

10. For evidence on these points, see Glenday, Jenkins, and Evans, *Worker Adjustment to Liberalized Trade;* Neumann, "Direct Labor Market Effects"; Jacobson, "Earnings Losses"; and Bale, "Estimates of Trade Displacement Costs."

changes in design that increase the use of electronic components. Savings in cost realized through movement abroad, in turn, may have helped stimulate those design changes.

### *Long-Run Prospects for the Unskilled*

Concern for the effects of changes in patterns of production and trade on the demand for unskilled labor in the industrial countries is not unique to the industries that engage in coproduction abroad. Nonetheless, an analysis of the mix of skills in U.S. industrial employment reveals that those industries which use much more than the average amount of unskilled labor coincide closely with the assembly industries examined here (see table 7-1). More than half the unskilled workers in U.S. manufacturing in 1978 were in these labor-intensive industries, and more than a third were in electrical and electronic equipment, apparel and textile products, and motor vehicles. If only assemblers are considered, 97 percent were in manufacturing, 68 percent in the labor-intensive industries, and 53 percent in electronics and motor vehicles. Thus, in the United States, unskilled manual labor in general and assembly labor in particular is largely concentrated in manufacturing, and within manufacturing it is found in precisely those industries that have tended to shift assembly operations to other countries.

In the aggregate, this may not seem to be a critical issue. Unskilled operators, excluding those in transport, made up about 8 percent of U.S. employment in 1978. But these occupations are highly concentrated in assembly industries: a quarter of employment in all U.S. manufacturing, nearly a third of employment in electronics, and roughly two-thirds of employment in apparel. And even if services remain sheltered from low wages in the third world, it is difficult to imagine the 60 percent expansion of service employment that would be required to absorb the continued and steady displacement of all the unskilled in manufacturing. (There were about 8 million unskilled nontransport operators in the U.S. economy in 1978 and about 13 million service workers.) Since these service jobs generally pay substantially less than jobs in manufacturing, the continued displacement of the unskilled will mean the end of their relatively high incomes in Western industrial societies.

Traditional trade theory predicts that wages, as well as other factor prices, will be equalized across countries. Because the underlying assump-

Table 7-1. *Importance of Unskilled Labor in Labor-intensive U.S. Industries, 1978*[a]

| Industry | *Unskilled operators as percent of total employees in industry listed* | | *Unskilled operators as percent of total unskilled employment in all industries* | |
|---|---|---|---|---|
| | *All unskilled operators*[b] | *Assemblers only* | *All unskilled operators*[b] | *Assemblers only* |
| Furniture and fixtures | 37 | 9 | 2.5 | 3.9 |
| Pottery | 46 | 2 | 0.3 | 0.1 |
| Cutlery and other hardware | 22 | 9 | 0.5 | 1.4 |
| Engines and turbines | 19 | 10 | 0.3 | 1.1 |
| Farm machinery | 20 | 12 | 0.4 | 1.5 |
| Office and accounting machines | 18 | 12 | 0.2 | 0.7 |
| Electronic computing equipment | 13 | 9 | 0.5 | 2.1 |
| Other nonelectrical machinery | 18 | 8 | 2.3 | 7.0 |
| Household appliances | 35 | 22 | 0.9 | 3.5 |
| Radios, television sets, and communication equipment | 24 | 12 | 1.9 | 6.3 |
| Other electrical equipment | 32 | 16 | 5.4 | 17.3 |
| Motor vehicles and equipment | 29 | 18 | 3.8 | 15.3 |
| Mobile dwellings | 28 | 9 | 0.4 | 0.9 |
| Miscellaneous transportation | 29 | 15 | 0.2 | 0.6 |
| Scientific instruments | 24 | 14 | 0.6 | 2.4 |
| Optical and health-service supplies | 25 | 8 | 0.7 | 1.5 |
| Watches and clocks | 36 | 20 | 0.1 | 0.5 |
| Meat processing | 43 | 1 | 2.0 | 0.2 |
| Apparel and accessories[c] | 64 | 0 | 9.8 | 0.0 |
| Miscellaneous fabricated textile products | 51 | 2 | 1.3 | 0.3 |
| Rubber products | 40 | 2 | 1.6 | 0.5 |
| Leather tanning and finishing | 53 | 1 | 0.2 | [d] |
| Nonrubber footwear | 62 | 2 | 1.4 | 0.3 |
| Other leather | 51 | 7 | 0.4 | 0.4 |
| All labor-intensive industries | n.a. | n.a. | 37.7 | 68.1 |
| All manufacturing | 25 | 5 | 69.3 | 96.7 |
| All industries | 8 | 1 | 100.0 | 100.0 |

Source: Calculated from data in U.S. Department of Labor, Bureau of Labor Statistics, *The National Industry-Occupation Employment Matrix, 1970, 1978, and Projected 1990,* Bulletin 2086 (Government Printing Office, 1981).

n.a. Not available.

a. "Labor-intensive industry" is defined as a sector in which the proportion of unskilled labor is 160 percent or more of the fraction of unskilled employed in all industries.

b. Excluding transportation employment.

c. Sewing is not considered to be assembly.

d. Negligible.

tions are often violated, one does not always expect to observe this equalization. But the assembly industries in many ways do approximate those assumptions, and a process leading to equalization of wages seems to be under way. Continued downward pressure on real wages of the unskilled manufacturing worker seems likely.

## Assembly Production and Developing Countries

The benefits of assembly production to host countries are significant. In economies with large unemployed or underemployed resources, assembly activities offer opportunities for low-cost employment and the creation of income. In most countries with important assembly operations, net foreign exchange earned from assembly contributes significantly to the external balance. Experience in Mexico and Haiti seems to indicate that capacity utilization and hours worked are higher in assembly than in the rest of the economy. In addition to the smaller capital requirements per job than in other sectors, most of the workers in these activities were previously not in the labor force, were not employed, or were engaged in occupations in which their productivity was substantially lower.

### *Employment*

A feature that seems to characterize all assembly activities is a predominantly female work force. A great many ills, ranging from the disruption of the family to exploitation of the workers, have been attributed to this fact. The wages of women have been generally lower than those of male workers in assembly plants, as in other economic activities, but the comparison cannot be controlled for occupation and other factors. In apparent contrast to those in the developed countries, an overwhelming proportion of the female workers are young and unmarried, with the upper age limit at roughly the mean age of marriage for factory women in their local societies.[11] Many of these young women participate formally for the first time in the labor force as export assembly-plant workers, and critics charge that rather than eradicating unemployment, this may actually induce it by en-

11. In the industrial zones of Taiwan, where detailed data on workers by age and sex is available, 85 percent of the labor force are female, 41 percent are women under the age of twenty, 75 percent women under thirty. See Export Processing Zone Administration, *Essential Statistics* (Taiwan, December 1979), p. 20. (In Haiti, female workers seem to be older than elsewhere, perhaps in part because of the rather informal nature of the marriage bond in the local population.) On the other hand, affiliates of German apparel firms in the industrial countries, for example, employed some 22 percent of the labor force more than forty years old in 1974, while affiliates in the developing countries employed only 5 percent. See Fölker Fröbel, Jürgen Heinrichs, and Otto Kreye, *The New International Division of Labor,* tr. Pete Burgess (London: Cambridge University Press, 1980), table I-14, p. 114.

couraging groups that might otherwise not do so to join the labor force.[12]

The fact is that women predominate in certain assembly operations everywhere in the world; developing countries are not unique in that respect. What is new, however, is that the introduction of assembly production into developing countries has accelerated the entrance of women into the labor force. This may also have accelerated the disruptions and the adjustment problems that usually appear as the proportion of women gainfully employed increases in the course of economic development.

In large countries, assembly activities have not been extensive enough to employ a significant share of the labor force. Of all developing countries, Mexico has the largest employment in assembly production for the U.S. market, yet assembly jobs constitute less than 1 percent of the total Mexican labor force. Their effect is concentrated in the towns along the northern border, where they make up about half of manufacturing employment.

Around the world, assembly for foreign manufacturers probably did not employ more than about 1 million workers in the mid 1970s, while total open unemployment in the third world was estimated to be 33 million.[13] Yet it is a critical source of employment in certain small countries, particularly in the Caribbean basin, such as Barbados and Haiti, and it is fairly important in some countries in Asia, including Singapore and Hong Kong and, to a lesser extent, South Korea and Taiwan.

With respect to migration, the effect on Mexico is limited by the fact that assembly for export has created much of its own labor force there by bringing in primarily young women from urban areas who were formerly not active economically. Most of the undocumented workers in the United States have tended to be males from rural areas. If this trend continues, an increase in assembly employment will have little effect on Mexican migra-

12. Although the criticism is expressed primarily in relation to Mexico, the phenomenon of assembly industries being responsible for large increases in female labor force participation is documented elsewhere as well. See Boum Jong Choe, "An Economic Study of the Masan Free Trade Zone," in Wontack Hong and Anne O. Krueger, eds., *Trade and Development in Korea* (Seoul: Korea Development Institute, 1975), for data on Korea. For data on Singapore, see Cheng Siok-Hwa, "Singapore Women: Legal Status, Educational Attainment, and Employment Patterns," *Asian Survey,* vol. 17 (April 1977), pp. 358–74; and Chang Chen-Tung, "Female Employment and Fertility Behavior," in Peter S. J. Chen and James T. Fawcett, eds., *Public Policy and Population Change in Singapore* (New York: The Population Council, 1979).

13. See Fröbel, Heinrichs, and Kreye, *The New International Division of Labor,* tables 3-7 and 3-8, pp. 308–10, and table 3-13, p. 340.

tion to the United States. In the small countries of the Caribbean basin, however, where assembly operations constitute a significant part of employment and where in the poorest countries, such as Haiti, female participation in the labor force has traditionally been high, the pressures to emigrate would probably be greater without such activities.

As noted in the case studies on Mexico and Haiti, wages in assembly plants in those countries tend to be at or above the legal minimum. Since evasion of minimum wage requirements seems widespread in both countries, the wages paid there to assembly workers are probably significantly higher than a market wage.[14]

Because they tend to be more visible and their environment more closely regulated than those of other firms, working conditions in assembly plants are generally thought to be somewhat better than in firms of similar size in the rest of the country, though undoubtedly they are unsatisfactory by developed-country standards.[15] On the other hand, special concessions to limit the rights of workers have been granted to assembly firms in some countries.[16]

### *Balance of Payments*

The single most important benefit of assembly production to developing countries appears to have been its contribution to the balance of payments. Net export earnings have been running between 30 percent and 50 percent of the total value of assembly output. For many developing countries this constitutes a significant proportion of the foreign exchange earned from the export of manufactured products (see table 7-2). Particularly in the Caribbean basin, and in many of the least-developed countries

14. In many developing countries minimum wages are ceilings rather than floors. For Mexico, see U.S. Department of Labor, Bureau of International Labor Affairs, *Country Labor Profile: Mexico* (GPO, 1979). For Haiti, see Association des Industries d'Haiti, "The Industrial Sector in Haiti: Situation, Prospects, and Policies" (Port-au-Prince: ADIH, 1981), p. 54.

15. United Nations International Development Organization (UNIDO), *Export Processing Zones in Developing Countries* (Vienna: UNIDO, August 1980), pp. 22, 33. In a survey undertaken by the Swedish Ministries of Foreign Affairs and Trade it was found that labor legislation is generally enforced in most export-processing zones. Ibid., p. 18.

16. Fröbel, Heinrichs, and Kreye, *New International Division of Labor,* pp. 320, 361–64; and Deepak Nayyar, "Transnational Corporations and Manufactured Exports from Poor Countries," *Economic Journal,* vol. 88 (March 1978), p. 77. Even in socialist China, export-processing zones have been given special privileges not available in other parts of the economy. In some instances, export-oriented assembly industries have been legally exempted from local labor laws. For a discussion of the situation in Malaysia, see "Unions Have U.S. Electronics Makers Scared," *Business Week,* June 13, 1983, p. 53.

of Asia as well, assembly exports are a crucially important source of foreign exchange.

In some countries, foreign-exchange earnings from assembly exports to the United States under 806/807 exceed earnings from exports entering the United States under the Generalized System of Preferences (GSP). This is true for Mexico, the fourth largest beneficiary of the GSP in 1980 (among 140 countries), and other important beneficiaries, such as Singapore, Malaysia, Haiti, and El Salvador.[17]

The lure of foreign exchange has been the primary motive for socialist countries to promote export assembly operations within their borders.[18] In the last few years China has moved vigorously toward setting up export-processing zones, compensation trade agreements, and other institutional arrangements aimed at encouraging the setting up of assembly plants for foreign manufacturers.[19] It now permits joint ventures. A significant share of manufactured exports from Hong Kong is probably made up of reexports of production assembled in Chinese plants. Much of the output of electronic watches from Hong Kong, for example, is assembled in China.[20] Other socialist countries have been hosts to assembly plants for some time. Yugoslavia, East Germany, Hungary, and Romania have had much to do with the West German trade in apparel assembly.[21]

### *Linkages*

Since assembly production is often clustered in compact and politically discrete free manufacturing zones, it is criticized as an enclave of foreign interests, not subject to the same political and economic forces that regulate the business environment in other parts of the country. The lack of integration of these production activities into the rest of the host economy

17. For comprehensive data on the first years of the GSP, see House Committee on Ways and Means, *Report to the Congress on the First Five Years' Operation of the U.S. Generalized System of Preferences (GSP),* 96 Cong. 2 sess. (GPO, 1980).

18. Fröbel, Heinrichs, and Kreye, *New International Division of Labor,* pp. 97–98; and Fox Butterfield, "China's Trade Plan Has Capitalist Tinge," *New York Times,* December 27, 1979.

19. Butterfield, "China's Trade Plan"; Butterfield, "Chinese Region Imitates Taiwan in Search for International Trade," *New York Times,* April 21, 1980; Jerome Alan Cohen, "A Year of High Adventure in Coming Joint Ventures," *Far Eastern Economic Review,* March 7, 1980, pp. 44–45; and Brenton R. Schlender and Vigor Fung, "Shenzhen Economic Zone Thrives amid Inadequate Services, Dearth of Managers," *Asian Wall Street Journal Weekly,* May 21, 1984, p. 3.

20. "Hong Kong Moves In," *Business Week,* May 5, 1980, p. 106.

21. Fröbel, Heinrichs, and Kreye, *The New International Division of Labor,* pp. 71–75, 108–10.

is a particularly sensitive issue in Mexico, where assembly plants are concentrated in the distant border region. It is not surprising that this has produced an image of a foreign enclave. U.S. subsidiaries predominate, U.S. managers and technicians commute from their homes on the U.S. side of the line, and evidence of U.S. influence can be seen everywhere in the border region. The assembly operation itself appears to be hermetically sealed off from the rest of the country. U.S. components cross the border in bond to a plant often only a few blocks away and go back again in assembled form with almost no leakage into Mexico. As seen from the distant capital, Mexico City, the border region appears more nearly integrated with the United States than with Mexico.

The weakness of assembly linkages derives in part from laws and regulations governing that activity. Because the use of tax and tariff incentives, for example, generally prohibits the shipment of large volumes of assembly output to the national markets, there is little opportunity for national producers to use assembly products as inputs to production for the national market.

In the development of backward linkages, some countries have made greater progress. Contrary to the situation in Mexico, where Mexican inputs into assembly plants tend to be confined primarily to janitorial supplies and packing materials, the substitution of nationally produced inputs for materials formerly imported has been observed in other countries.[22] In the export-processing zones in Taiwan and Korea, the content of national materials has increased considerably—to about a fifth and a fourth, respectively, of the value of exports.[23]

The low domestic content in Mexico is due in part to the fact that, in the absence of significant transport costs (as along the Mexican border), Mexican suppliers of components for U.S.-bound exports must actually produce at a lower price than the price at which the component is available in the United States. This is so because Mexican inputs are subject to duties upon entering the United States, while components produced in the United States are exempt under tariff items 806/807. Thus the competi-

22. For the Haitian example see chapter 5; see also UNIDO, *Export Processing Zones,* pp. 25–29.

23. Before 1976, domestic material content of exports was 9 percent in Taiwan and 17 percent in Korea. See Export Processing Zone Administration, *Essential Statistics,* various years; and Republic of Korea, Ministry of Commerce and Industry, *Masan Free Export Zone in Facts and Figures* (Seoul, circa 1979).

tiveness of foreign inputs is restricted to the most labor-intensive items, on which the difference in labor cost will offset the surcharge when a duty is added to the price of the item in U.S. customs. Perhaps for the same reason, even in more distant Taiwan, linkages of Japanese firms to domestic subcontractors seem more common than those of U.S. firms.[24]

In many countries, of course, protection of domestic industries has contributed to making the cost of national materials higher than that of imported U.S. components in assembly production. Apart from price considerations, the lack of international competition in domestic markets has also made it more difficult for firms to meet either production and delivery schedules or specifications and high standards of quality. The same factors have sometimes restrained the investment of national capital in assembly operations.

Nevertheless, the near absence of transportation costs does put potential Mexican suppliers of components at a greater disadvantage than firms in the Far East. There high transportation costs afford some protection to domestically produced assembly inputs. Even in Mexico assembly plants in the interior of the country, from which transportation costs to the United States are much higher than those from the border, use a considerably larger percentage of national materials.

One of the most important concerns of developing countries is the transfer of technology. The extent to which assembly operations transmit productive knowledge and skills to nationals of the host country is difficult to document. A significant number of assembly operations require some training and experience. In the semiconductor industry, for example, it takes about three months to reach peak efficiency as an assembler. Since many in the assembly work force are involved in their first industrial work experience, there may also be some inculcation of industrial labor discipline. Specific assembly tasks, however, such as those taught in electronics, often use proprietary high-technology components unavailable in the national economy, and the skills that they require are of lesser value outside the export enclave.[25]

Foreign firms involved in assembly operations do train significant numbers of host-country nationals as lower- and middle-level managers and

24. Gustav Ranis, "Industrial Development," in Walter Galenson, ed., *Economic Growth and Structural Change in Taiwan* (Cornell University Press, 1979), p. 248.

25. See UNIDO, *Export Processing Zones,* p. 31.

often offer independent subcontractors technical assistance that can be of considerable value as they learn to organize production flows and processes. As mentioned earlier, there are examples in Colombia of national apparel firms whose productivity has doubled because of technical assistance supplied by foreign contractors.

The transfer of product and process technology seems to be much rarer. Most assembly plants perform a limited number of the production steps required in production of industrial output, and most of the design, research, and production of high-technology intermediate components remains in the industrial countries. There are, however, a few recent examples of more technologically advanced steps being transferred to locations abroad.[26]

Indeed, Singapore has been experimenting with a policy of deliberate and substantial wage hikes in an attempt to move its industrial output away from low-wage, low-productivity products and toward high-wage, high-productivity, high-technology products.[27] The objective is to force producers to automate, mechanize, and, wherever possible, substitute skills and capital for unskilled labor. Another aim is to discourage the migration of foreign workers into Singapore.[28]

An examination of assembly production across countries reveals that its acute economic isolation in Mexico is an extreme case. Linkages have been stronger nearly everywhere else, particularly in some Asian countries and even in poverty-stricken Haiti. In Colombia, assembly activities seem to be completely integrated into the economy. Nonetheless, value added in Mexico has constituted a larger share of its total assembly output than the

26. Simple semiconductors are now being produced by local firms in Far Eastern countries, though it is not clear that this is necessarily related to the assembly operations that existed in those countries earlier. In Singapore, Philips, the Dutch producer of electrical and electronic products, now designs all locally manufactured audio products with a 150-person research-and-development team, the largest in the country; Hewlett Packard and Nestlé also do some research and development locally. See "Singapore: 2000" (advertising supplement), *Scientific American,* August 1981, p. S5.

27. Andy McCue, "Singapore Businesses Brace for Expected Wage Raises," *Asian Wall Street Journal Weekly,* June 9, 1980, p. 16; Ian Gill, "Investment Sag Prompts Singapore Policy Change," ibid., January 5, 1981, pp. 1, 20; S. Karene Witcher and Ian Gill, "Singapore Faces Sharp Rise in Wages as Guidelines End," ibid., May 25, 1981, p. 16; and Wolfgang Hillebrand and others, "Industrial Restructuring in Singapore: Technological Decision-Making and International Cooperation in the Electronics Industry" (Berlin: German Development Institute, 1981, mimeographed).

28. The export-processing operations were so successful in increasing employment that 100,000 foreign workers, most of them from Malaysia, Indonesia, and Sri Lanka, were recruited. See *Far Eastern Economic Review,* October 19, 1979, pp. 81–83.

corresponding proportions in Haiti, Colombia, and many other developing countries (see table 2-1). This is so not only because of a different mix of products, but also because Mexican wages are higher and make up a larger share of total value added than they do elsewhere.

### *Dependence and Stability*

It is often argued that assembly production for foreign companies as a step toward industrialization creates an industrial structure that is dependent on demands and markets that are entirely foreign and over which the host country has no control. Hence the economy is subject to fluctuations in income and employment imported from abroad.[29] The declines in output and the layoffs that occurred in processing and free zones in many parts of the world during the 1974–75 recession are usually used to make this point.

External linkages do transmit disturbances in the international business cycle to national economies, and the vulnerability of an economy to external fluctuations is an important issue. The issue, however, arises with all types of exports, not just those produced in assembly plants by foreign firms or their local subcontractors. The question must be asked, therefore, how assembly exports vary in relation to all manufactured exports. Because assembly production in developing countries tends to be concentrated in apparel and electronics, products the demand for which is notorious for its volatility throughout the business cycle, it might be expected that increasing assembly activities would add to the vulnerability of exports during a world recession.

The data in table 7-2 give a rough answer. The ratio of exports to the United States under tariff items 806/807 to all manufactured exports is presented through a period that includes the world recession of 1974–75. If assembly exports were more sensitive to a recession than manufactured exports in general, this ratio might be expected to drop during 1974–75. The ratio did, in fact, drop somewhat during the recession in Hong Kong and Singapore, both of which are relatively high-cost locations for assembly production, and in Barbados. On the other hand, 806/807 exports to the United States grew much more, or declined much less, than all manufactured exports in at least six of the listed countries during the recession.

29. Fröbel, Heinrichs, and Kreye, *The New International Division of Labor,* pp. 368–69, 383–85.

Table 7-2. *Exports to the United States under U.S. Tariff Items 806.30 and 807.00 as Percent of Total Manufactured Exports, Selected Countries, 1970 and 1973–81*[a]

| *Country* | *1970* | *1973* | *1974* | *1975* | *1976* | *1977* | *1978* | *1979* | *1980* | *1981* |
|---|---|---|---|---|---|---|---|---|---|---|
| Barbados | 42.5 | 41.7 | n.a. | 40.4 | 39.4 | 42.7 | 47.1 | 51.0 | 62.0 | n.a. |
| Brazil | 1.2 | 2.0 | n.a. | n.a. | 3.7 | 4.3 | 3.8 | 2.8 | 1.7 | 1.8 |
| Colombia[b] | 0.5 | 2.2 | 4.8 | 6.8 | 3.8 | 3.2 | n.a. | 3.9 | 2.6 | 3.2 |
| Dominican Republic[b] | 2.6 | 30.3 | n.a. | 16.8 | n.a. | 128.3 | 120.8 | 125.2 | 152.0 | 160.0 |
| El Salvador[b] | 0.6 | 4.5 | 15.2 | n.a. | 32.9 | 38.4 | 45.7 | 49.0 | 35.0 | n.a. |
| Haiti[b] | 63.3 | 198.9 | 226.7 | 177.8 | 187.3 | 180.1 | 181.0 | n.a. | n.a. | n.a. |
| Hong Kong | 6.4 | 4.6 | n.a. | n.a. | 2.8 | 3.4 | 3.4 | 3.1 | 3.1 | 3.8 |
| Indonesia[b] | n.a. | n.a. | n.a. | n.a. | 4.3 | 10.1 | 8.9 | 8.0 | 10.0 | 6.9 |
| Korea | 4.4 | 3.5 | n.a. | 3.1 | 3.0 | 3.2 | 2.6 | 2.7 | 2.2 | 1.8 |
| Malaysia | 0.6 | 7.1 | 21.7 | 25.5 | 29.3 | 33.8 | n.a. | 33.0 | 34.0 | 40.0 |
| Mexico | 60.5 | 60.6 | 97.0 | 115.6 | 119.0 | 105.3 | 96.0 | 117.0 | 139.0 | n.a. |
| Philippines | 9.0 | 6.3 | n.a. | 17.7 | 19.6 | 18.1 | 25.9 | 28.0 | 35.0 | 40.0 |
| Singapore | 7.6 | 12.6 | n.a. | n.a. | 10.2 | 10.1 | 8.9 | 9.0 | 8.8 | 8.7 |
| Thailand[b] | n.a. | n.a. | n.a. | n.a. | 2.4 | 2.2 | 6.2 | 4.1 | 5.3 | 6.2 |

Sources: Total manufactured exports, United Nations Commission on Trade and Development (UNCTAD), *Handbook of International Trade and Development Statistics, 1980* and *1983* (UNCTAD, 1981, 1984); 806/807 exports, U.S. International Trade Commission (ITC), *Tariff Items 807.00 and 806.30,* various years.

n.a. Not available.

a. U.S. imports under 806/807 from certain countries exceed the total manufactured exports of those countries because some countries, such as Mexico, do not count these exports in their trade statistics and some, such as Haiti, count only the value added; also, small quantities of nonmanufactured exports come into the United States under 806/807.

b. Only 807; the values of 806 exports are negligible or zero.

All three of the country studies in this book indicate that recessions in the United States had only small negative effects, if not positive effects, on assembly production abroad. On balance, then, 806/807 exports seem to have fared much better during the recession than all manufactured exports in the low-wage locations and somewhat worse than all manufactures in the high-wage locations. Mexico belongs in a special category because of its low transport costs to the United States. In Colombia, a surge seems to have taken place as local garment makers switched capacity from the depressed local markets to U.S. exports.

This pattern is consistent with the rationalization of operations by assembly producers during times of recession. When demand plummets, it is most economical to shift output to low-cost locations in order to cut variable costs. The production sites that suffer are in the industrial countries and in the most expensive foreign locations for assembly, while assembly plants in lower-cost countries seem to do rather well in export sales compared to what all national producers of exported manufactures are able to do.

U.S. 807/806 imports from a few advanced East Asian countries have leveled off, not because of a U.S.-induced drop in demand, but because these countries have succeeded in substituting their own materials for U.S. components and have thus been able to export the entire product, which enters the United States as a regular import rather than under tariff items 806/807. U.S. 807 imports from Colombia have been unstable since the mid 1970s. Again, this cannot be attributed to fluctuations in U.S. demand, because assembly is used by Colombian firms to stabilize their *total* production levels.

In many countries in which there is arm's-length subcontracting for assembly work, both sides usually diversify their risks by contracting with more than one firm at a time. This also tends to smooth out large fluctuations. Thus, contrary to expectations, and as confirmed by the three country studies in this book, assembly activities have shown a remarkable stability in developing economies. In most of them value added in assembly has been continuously increasing.[30]

The general stability and growth of assembly production in many developing countries implies that such activities are not exceptionally sensitive to changes in relative wages among countries. There will be shifts of individual firms and products from one country to another. There is also some evidence of an upgrading of the skill level in assembly production as wages rise.

Sharp increases in relative wages, however, will provoke shifts in the location of manufacture of products with high ratios of value to weight, such as semiconductor devices, which will tend to be more footloose because of their low transport costs. Thus the steep wage increases in Mexico during the mid 1970s contributed to the shift of semiconductor assembly to Malaysia and other East Asian countries.[31] This was probably the single

30. The resilience of an assembly relationship, once established, can be great enough to withstand the most severe noneconomic upheavals. Witness the survival of assembly output in El Salvador during years of enormous political trouble: the 1982 value added in assembly for the U.S. market was still two-thirds as great as value added at the peak, in 1979, when the armed conflict began, greater than in preupheaval 1977, and still greater than in most countries of the Caribbean basin.

31. Although Mexico's world share of U.S. semiconductor assembly imports declined sharply from a high of 28 percent in 1971 to less than 5 percent in 1982, the volume of Mexican semiconductor output continued to increase and was significantly greater in 1982 than ever before. On the other hand, despite wages that are high compared to those in other host countries, Mexico has done rather well in electrical assembly other than of semiconductors. In television apparatus and parts, for example, Mexico is now far ahead of any other assembler, having doubled its world assembly share from about a third during the late 1960s and early 1970s to more than two-thirds during the early 1980s. (Compare table 4-4. Analysis based on ITC magnetic tapes.)

most important loss of a market share in a major assembly product attributable to shifts in relative wages that can be noted among countries.[32]

Within a certain range, geographic proximity and political stability can make the U.S. demand for assembly production in a neighbor country less wage-elastic. For these reasons, the variety of 807 products produced abroad is much wider in both U.S. neighbors, Mexico and Canada, than in any other country that processes U.S. components for return to the United States.

32. The wage hikes decreed by the government of Singapore in its attempt to switch production from less highly skilled assembly operations to more complex products in capital-intensive and skill-intensive industries also caused a decline of foreign investment. See Gill, "Investment Sag Prompts Singapore Policy Change"; and *Asian Wall Street Journal Weekly*, March 23, 1981, p. 20.

CHAPTER EIGHT

# Policy Implications and Conclusions

THE benefits of assembly operations abroad have been questioned by both sides. In the United States, the opposition comes from that segment of the labor force which is injured in competition with unskilled workers in the third world. In the developing countries, doubts have come from those concerned with the development of an indigenous industrial base. The major decisions revolve around the evaluation of immediate versus long-run effects. As is true of many questions of economic development, these dilemmas are difficult to resolve.

Assembly production offers immediate gains for both developed and developing countries. It would therefore be to the benefit of both sides to reconcile the interests of U.S. workers and third world industrial development in this process of restructuring industry. Measures to ease the adjustment of U.S. assembly workers to increased foreign competition are needed, as are measures designed to use assembly operations for the U.S. market to widen the industrial base of developing countries.

## U.S. Policies

While both types of policy are in the long-term interest of the United States, there is an intrinsic conflict in the short term. Strengthening the linkages of assembly operations in developing economies implies increasing the use of local materials. This will tend to reduce employment in U.S. industries that supply components for the assembly plants abroad.

Yet industrial development overseas is of benefit to the United States for simple but compelling reasons. Apart from the clear advantages of a prosperous and stable world system, U.S. consumers benefit from lower costs of a growing volume of traded goods, U.S. producers benefit from broader markets for their products, and U.S. workers benefit from reduced foreign immigration.

The moving of manufacturing operations abroad seems likely to continue at its present pace. Trade has steadily grown in importance to the U.S. economy, and assembly abroad has become an increasingly significant part of U.S. trade. Assembly production has been most important in products that are under pressure from foreign competition and is likely to accelerate during periods of slow economic growth. The 1980s seem to promise both greater international competition and slow growth. U.S. assembly labor will be affected to an increasing extent.

The effects of foreign assembly on the domestic labor force will be essentially the same as the effects of the other important structural force that will affect unskilled U.S. workers in the coming decade, automation. The most important task for the United States government is to assist the workers who will be displaced. Much of this labor force, mainly less highly skilled women, will benefit from retraining.

Programs aimed at helping those forced out of assembly industries should be part of a broader policy toward the U.S. labor force. As international competition intensifies during the coming decade, it is essential that U.S. workers be given the incentives and the assistance that they will need if they are to increase their competence.

*Facilitating the Reorganization of Industry*

The substantial growth of coproduction activities since the 1960s has been essentially the result of the workings of free world markets. The pressures of international competition have induced firms in industrial countries to seek the redeployment of production stages in which they were no longer competitive. Government policies may have facilitated the process, but they have not been its basic engine. Measures taken by industrial countries, among which U.S. tariff items 806.30 and 807.00 are the most prominent, have stimulated assembly operations abroad, as have actions by developing countries that wanted to share in such coproduction. Without the establishment of free-trade zones, special tariff and tax treatment, and in-bond arrangements, many developing countries, particularly those in which the barriers to trade and investment are high, would have had difficulty in attracting assembly production from the industrial countries.

*Quotas.* If an orderly process of industrial reorganization is seen as desirable, high priority should be given in developed countries to the removal of those barriers, such as quotas and "voluntary" restraints, that are particularly burdensome to the poorer countries. The current international multifiber arrangement is a prime example. Under it the United States imposes textile quotas on many of the poorest developing countries, including several with which coproduction relations in the manufacture of apparel exist. Not only do such protectionist measures stand in the way of efforts to facilitate industrial redeployment, but they also harm those low-income countries the economic development of which is of particular concern to the United States. Consideration should be given to the removal of quotas from the countries in which income is the lowest.

Take the case of Haiti, the country with the lowest income in the Caribbean basin, an area in which the U.S. government has taken a special interest.[1] Given the relatively insignificant share of U.S. imports that originates in Haiti—less than 1 percent during 1981–83—the justification of U.S. restraints on imports from Haiti is not obvious. Indeed, as a small supplier, Haiti should be protected by article 6 of the Multi-Fiber Agreement (MFA), which provides not only for more favorable terms for developing countries but also for avoidance of "restraints on exports from participating countries whose total volume of textile exports is small in comparison with the total volume of exports of other countries."[2]

Of special significance to the discussion in this book is the MFA mandate that "special and differential treatment" be given to the type of trade that is subject to U.S. tariff item 807.00, because such trade, which constitutes an extension of U.S. operations, cannot be considered as disrupting the U.S. market.[3] The United States has ignored these provisions in its bilateral agreements under the MFA. Small suppliers, such as Haiti, are not exempt from MFA restrictions, and imports from them under item 807

1. The following discussion of the effects of U.S. textile-import restraints on Haiti is based on a report submitted by Leslie Delatour, who in 1982 and 1984 acted as one of Haiti's principal negotiators in the U.S.-Haiti bilateral restraint agreements under the Multi-Fiber Arrangement (MFA) of the General Agreement on Tariffs and Trade (GATT).

2. GATT, *Arrangements Regarding International Trade in Textiles (MFA),* TEX. NG/1, December 20, 1973, p. 9. These provisions were reaffirmed in paragraph 12 of the *Protocol Extending the Arrangement Regarding International Trade in Textiles,* L/5256, December 23, 1981, of which the United States was also a signatory.

3. GATT, *Arrangements Regarding International Trade in Textiles,* article 6, paragraph 6, p. 9, reaffirmed in *Protocol Extending the Arrangement,* paragraph 13, p. 7.

are subject to MFA quotas. This may produce such a puzzling—if not absurd—outcome that the replacement of a full import from a large-quota country with an 807 import from a small-quota country might not be possible, even though such a replacement would mean the creation of U.S. production and employment.[4]

The quota itself becomes a factor of production in the international distribution of the production of certain items. A potential investor who is considering assembly abroad, perhaps in order to remain competitive in the face of rising imports, must take into account not only the cost of labor, the cost of transportation, and so forth, but also the question whether a given country has a quota large enough to accommodate his output. Since the size of the quota under the bilateral agreements depends on past performance, the earlier producers are granted larger quotas than more recent producers. Thus, the existence of individual bilateral agreements freezes the international division of labor by preventing the moving of production facilities from older producing areas to newer areas. The system thus penalizes smaller countries that are recent, low-cost producers as well as some U.S. firms and workers and all U.S. consumers.

*Tariff sparing.* While U.S. tariff items 806/807 could be regarded as a component of the liberalization of trade, a paradoxical aspect is that the higher the general tariff levels, the more effective the provisions of 806/807 will be in promoting foreign assembly with U.S. components. As tariffs decline the value of 806/807 diminishes. It is likely that in some instances firms do not use 806/807 for certain eligible assembly products, largely because the subjective costs of applying for the tariff exemption—the filing of the necessary forms, and so on—exceed the tariff savings. In any movement toward general liberalization of trade, 806/807 will be used less and less.

Some products that enter the United States under 806/807 could be assembled abroad and imported profitably without these tariff provisions. Foreign assembly of other products, particularly textiles, using U.S. components could not take place without the benefit of these tariff items.

4. According to background information presented by the Haitian negotiators to the U.S.-Haiti bilateral restraint agreement, there were several instances in which U.S. investors could not shift facilities from the Far East to Haiti because of insufficiently large quotas. In all these instances, Haitian production would have been assembly using U.S.-produced components, and the articles produced would have replaced full imports from the Far East that compete with U.S. products.

The Generalized System of Preferences (GSP), which represents complete tariff exemption, appears to be a superior incentive to 806/807.[5] As expected, since 1976, the year the GSP went into effect, some products assembled abroad have returned to the United States under the GSP rather than 806/807. But not all products are eligible for the GSP. Assembly items, moreover, do not qualify if the value added abroad is less than 35 percent of the total value of the assembled product.[6] This requirement is sometimes the deciding factor in determining whether to use the GSP or 807.[7]

A streamlining of 806/807 might make those tariff provisions more efficient and increase the linkages of assembly for foreign manufacturers to the domestic host economy without diminishing the incentive to use U.S. materials. First, given the small magnitude of imports under item 806.30 in relation to imports under item 807.00—about 2 percent during the period

5. It is important to remember that tariff items 806/807, unlike the GSP, were not designed originally as a preference measure favoring developing countries. During the 1960s well over 90 percent of the use of 806/807 was made by industrial countries. Only with the dramatic expansion of assembly activities abroad since then have duty-free imports from developing countries under those tariff items far exceeded those from the industrial countries, although the latter still constitute more than half of total 806/807 value.

6. There are other elements that disqualify the use of the GSP: some communist countries and certain other developing countries are excluded, and when imports of a given product from a given country exceed 50 percent of total U.S. imports or if they exceed a certain value—$25 million in 1975, rising each year with the increase in U.S. gross national product (GNP)—imports of that product from that country are not eligible. Under the Caribbean Basin Initiative (CBI) proposed by the U.S. Executive in February 1982, eligibility for the GSP would be lowered to require a minimum local content of 25 percent. The CBI includes the countries of the Caribbean and Central America. See U.S. Department of State, *Background on the Caribbean Basin Initiative,* Special Report No. 97 (GPO, March 1982).

7. Both 807 and the GSP apply to stuffed toys, for example. The GSP, with its complete exemption from tariffs, will be used if the sewing and stuffing of the toys, the cutting, or both are done abroad, because the sum of the value of those operations will generally exceed 35 percent of the total value; the value added abroad will probably fall short of 35 percent if only the sewing is done there, so 807 will be used. See ITC, *Supplement to Summary of Trade and Tariff Information, Dolls and Stuffed Toy Animals,* Publication 841 (ITC, December 1982), p. 5. Because the use of the GSP will always be preferred over 806/807, its requirement of 35 percent domestic content may actually penalize those who make massive use of U.S. components. Duties must be paid on value added to U.S. components of U.S. assembly imports when the value of the U.S. components exceeds 65 percent of the total value, which means that the GSP cannot be used. Other products from developing countries, however, may enter the United States entirely free of duty under the GSP, even though they do not contain any U.S. components. While the GSP may sometimes discourage the use of U.S. components, 806/807 always encourages it.

1980–82—it would be a good idea to combine the two tariff items. Second, the provision of 806 that permits the processing and transformation of U.S. components without affecting their tariff exemption upon reentry into the United States should be incorporated into 807 (or a combined 806/807 item).[8] As 807 stands now, a substantial change in the U.S. component made abroad during assembly disqualifies it from tariff exemption upon reimport in assembled form into the United States. This eliminates the cutting, mixing, and other processing of U.S. components abroad if they are to be brought back duty-free.[9] The broadening of 807 to include such operations in developing countries would increase national linkages by extending the opportunities for local participation in assembly production. At the same time it might also broaden the use of U.S. components.[10]

A more extreme step to create linkages would be the selective application of a blanket removal of duties from goods assembled in the poorest developing countries. The 806/807 provisions have the effect of making U.S.-produced inputs cheaper than foreign inputs in foreign assembly for the U.S. market, even if costs are identical. Replacing them with a complete tariff exemption for assembled goods, thus including the value added abroad, would encourage greater use of foreign inputs. While ultimately U.S. consumers would benefit from lower-priced goods, this measure could cause a decline in the use of certain U.S.-produced components. Therefore such an action should be reserved for the developing countries with the lowest incomes, or for those that in any event would be in need of substantial resources on concessional terms.[11]

8. It will be recalled that 806 applies only to metal articles and has other limitations that should not be applicable to a new, combined tariff item.

9. As noted earlier, the rigid interpretation of 807 that the U.S. component had to be separable from the assembled product in order to be eligible for tariff exemption has been eased by administrative and court decisions through the years. But any significant modification still disqualifies the U.S. component from duty-free entry.

10. If the value of a foreign component processed abroad plus the U.S. tariff is less than the value of a U.S. component processed abroad without the U.S. tariff (but including transport charges from the United States), the processed foreign component will be imported. If the value of the foreign component processed abroad plus the U.S. tariff is greater than the value of the U.S. component processed abroad without the U.S. tariff on the U.S. component (but including the cost of transport from the United States), the processed U.S. component will be imported—provided that processing abroad does not disqualify it from U.S. duty-free treatment.

11. This proposed measure is an essential ingredient in the Caribbean Basin Initiative as it was originally presented by the U.S. Executive in February 1982.

*Assisting Industrial Development Abroad*

The image of assembly production as an enclave in the host economy is nurtured by the strikingly small percentages of local material used in these operations in many locations. In the case of Mexico, not only is the supply of national materials tiny, but Mexican ownership and the use of Mexican capital in assembly activities are in the minority.

The main obstacles to increasing the local content of assembly production have to do with shortfalls of potential supplier factories that operate from a less sophisticated industrial base: production costs are too high, quality control is too low, capacity is insufficient, production and distribution planning is inadequate, so delivery schedules and other specifications cannot be met, and so forth. Some of these deficiencies can be attributed to trade barriers that insulate the markets in developing countries from foreign competition. As long as the domestic economy is growing, the local firm will find it easier to work only for the secure national market and not to worry about the uncertainties of foreign markets or world prices or the demanding requirements of foreign firms and consumers.

Protection aside, the fact is that many local producers who might be potential suppliers of assembly plants are in infant industries and are in need of technical assistance. The U.S. principals and their assembly subsidiaries are in an ideal position to provide it, because they know precisely what it takes to become a competitive supplier of materials for assembly production for the United States. Although their offering technical assistance to these producers might lead to substitution of indigenous materials for some U.S. ingredients, the steadily evolving high-technology components and materials would continue to be supplied by the United States. Still, in some instances it would be a significant step forward to move from local provision of nothing more than janitorial supplies to inputs of, say, locally made wiring in the assembly of electrical and electronic products or threads, buttons, and other accessories in the assembly of apparel. As long as assembly activities abroad keep growing at past rates, this shift would not signify an absolute decline in the use of U.S. components.

The question remains who would bear the cost of the technical assistance. Both sides in the coproduction relationship presumably have some interest in ensuring that technical assistance will be provided and that it will be effective. With some exceptions the record shows that until now that interest has not been strong enough to produce significant flows of technical assistance. Special government incentives by one or both sides seem to be necessary to stimulate the transfer of technology; in many instances technical assistance is costly and compensation for it is required if it is to be forthcoming. Apart from direct aid that would provide the resources to pay for it, additional incentives that the U.S. government might offer are limited.

Some incentives already exist; recent changes in customs valuation procedures have defined "assists"—the cost of technical assistance provided by U.S. firms for their subsidiaries and foreign subcontractors—as an element of the U.S. duty-free component.[12] As business expenses they would also presumably be exempt from U.S. income taxes. But it appears that an additional stimulus to the transfer of technology must be furnished by the government of the recipient country.

It is clear that subcontracting with local firms in developing countries is more conducive to the transfer of technology than operating assembly plants abroad through U.S. subsidiaries. The subcontractor in the developing country would not only benefit directly from working with the U.S. principal but could also transfer the knowledge acquired to production for the domestic market, thus spreading the effects.[13] Not only would a shift from subsidiary assembly production to subcontracting eliminate the intermediary in the transfer of technology, but the delinking of assembly plants from the United States would also remove the pejorative image of assembly abroad as an enclave.[14]

## Policy Implications for Developing Countries

Assembly production is of more than trivial significance for developing countries. While it is not the engine of economic development, the assembly sector has been an important generator of income, employment, and foreign exchange. In smaller countries such as Haiti this sector has provided the main thrust toward industrialization.

12. See Revision of Title V, Section 402 of the Tariff Act of 1974 in the *Trade Agreements Act of 1979,* Report of the House Committee on Ways and Means, to Accompany H. R. 4537, 96 Cong. 1 sess (GPO, 1979), pp. 255–56.

13. These benefits will be facilitated when domestic firms are permitted to produce for the domestic market and to export assembled products, as will be discussed in the next section.

14. As it would in Mexico, where some hold the view that assembly operations have "denationalized" the border region.

Despite their positive and important contributions, however, assembly activities have been regarded with some ambivalence by policymakers of developing countries. Few are proud of assembly operations. They are considered by some as a demeaning activity, a service performed for foreigners, like taking in their dirty laundry.[15]

In part the lack of enthusiasm is a result of the isolated nature of assembly activities. In the case of Mexico these activities are geographically concentrated. Add to that the perception that assembly production constitutes a stage of international capitalism that serves the interests of foreign owners, that it does little to train and upgrade the labor force, that domestic inputs are small, that there is hardly any transfer of technology, that it creates an industrial structure dependent on the whims of foreigners who, searching the world for opportunities for easy profit, are quick to transfer their business to whatever country it is in which wages are lowest, and the image emerges of an enclave activity that makes a small contribution indeed to economic development.

Furthermore, it is assumed—and not without some justification given the historical record in Mexico—first, that the key to assembly development is foreign investment; second, that the key to greater foreign investment in assembly plants is maintainence of as wide a gap as possible between wages in the developing country and those in the United States; and finally, that therefore all incentives to promote assembly activities must take the form of reducing the cost of labor in the developing country. This would inevitably lead to the making of concessions to the foreign companies by bending national labor laws, tax laws, and others. Various requests for concessions have been reported, including "the establishing of a special labor code to . . . employ workers on temporary contracts," easier dismissals, tax relief for workers who would receive less than minimum

15. The special treatment of these activities is reflected in the way a sale of assembly products abroad is accounted for in Mexico's balance of payments, not as an export but as a service, just like tourism, transportation, and insurance. In past efforts to attract foreign investors, the government of Mexico did not go out of its way to promote investment in assembly operations for foreign companies. In a sixteen-page special advertising supplement sponsored by Mexico, maquiladoras, or assembly activities, were not mentioned once, although investment in manufacturing was featured conspicuously. See "Mexico's Sunny Economic Climate," special advertising section, *Newsweek*, June 1, 1981. The U.S. businessman would not know by reading the supplement that assembly opportunities existed in Mexico, much less that such activities generated more than $2.3 billion of U.S. imports, including U.S. components, from Mexico in 1980.

wages, lower social security payments for a shorter work week, and so forth.[16]

These doubts prompt the question in a developing country whether resources put into assembly operations might not be better used in other sectors that would produce immediate and strong linkages for national industrialization. This question applies primarily to the use of domestic capital, because funds from foreign sources intended for assembly production would generally not be available to other sectors.

It is not clear whether from the social viewpoint scarce national capital resources are best invested in assembly production activities, in physical and social infrastructure, or in industries in which technological externalities and linkages seem more extensive and more dynamic. Making rigorous empirical calculations in the attempt to answer this question is not only statistically difficult, it requires conceptual frameworks that do not easily accommodate the dynamic elements essential to policies aimed at accelerating the process of economic development. While it is clear that national enterprise in Mexico has gained little from enclaves made up primarily of foreign firms that use foreign inputs, it is unlikely that Mexico would be better off without them. It is also clear that national enterprise in poverty-stricken Haiti has gained substantially. There, the alternatives to employment in assembly activities are generally much less desirable.

Thus, while one critique of assembly production is focused on the lack of integration of assembly activities into the national economy and polity, another criticizes assembly production as dead-end industrialization. Policies emerging from the first kind of critique will seek to increase the linkages of assembly activities to the rest of the economy. Policies based on the second will do just the opposite: they will aim to divert national capital to areas deemed more productive socially. The enclave nature of this production may therefore be a deliberately created outcome.

So either these activities are judged to be ill suited for national capital and a controlled foreign enclave is deliberately created or they are seen as potentially productive areas for national entrepreneurship and an effort is made to break down the enclavelike aspects of assembly operations. But it makes no sense to hold both views and pursue contradictory policies.

16. "In-Bond Industry: Recent Evolution and Perspectives," *Comercio exterior,* vol. 24 (May 1978), p. 210; see also Jorge A. Bustamante, "El programa fronterizo de maquiladoras: observaciones para una evaluación," *Foro internacional,* vol. 16 (October–December 1975), pp. 188–89.

The position taken here is that, given large underused resources, assembly production offers the host country short-run economic opportunities. We have concluded that the economic and social benefits of assembly production can be increased significantly through its greater integration into the national economy. This means that growth in assembly operations should not be surrendered to foreign firms and that greater involvement of national enterprise is necessary if economic linkages are to become important. Fiscal subsidies might broaden the benefits to be derived from assembly production by encouraging national firms to seek, and foreign companies to provide, training and technology.

Existing policies of free-trade zones, in-bond arrangements, tariff exemptions and duty drawbacks, special tax treatment, waiving of requirements of national ownership and content, and similar measures are designed to expand assembly operations, but not to integrate them into the economy. The economic limit to such policies will be reached when further growth in assembly can be undertaken only by bidding away scarce resources from other profitable sectors. Long before then, however, a political limit may be reached if such policies are seen as creating a privileged activity that is sealed off from the rest of the economy.

In general, support of assembly activities should be subordinated to broad policies, such as import substitution and export promotion, that will stimulate industrialization. Some of these will also affect assembly production favorably. Trade-liberalization policies, for example, would increase competition and force national firms to reduce costs. At present there is little incentive for protected oligopolistic industries, which are sometimes foreign-owned, to be efficiency-conscious. Standards of quality are often low, production and delivery schedules haphazard.

Heightened competitiveness would facilitate greater participation of national enterprises in assembly activities. Lower costs would enable firms to reduce prices of products that could serve as inputs for the assembly plants. Competition would also raise their standards of performance so that they might be able to meet the more stringent requirements of export production, both as potential suppliers to assembly plants and as operators of them. Thus trade-liberalization policy, while designed as part of an overall economic development strategy, might contribute to increases in the national content of assembly products and the participation of local capital in export activities.[17]

17. It would be possible to arrive at the opposite conclusion with respect to least-developed Haiti. That country has been unique among developing countries in the scant use of

As long as trade restrictions insulate the national producer from foreign competition, special incentives may be needed for national capital to venture into assembly activities as suppliers or operators. A strong inducement in some countries—in Mexico, for example—would be to eliminate the restrictions on simultaneously producing for the domestic market and assembling for export. This would permit the fuller utilization of capacity in existing plants and reduce the risk to national capital of investment in assembly plants. Fluctuations in both domestic and foreign business can be smoothed if they can shift between production for the domestic market and production for export, as has been permitted in Colombia. In order to avoid charges of unfair competition from powerful foreign subsidiaries, limiting the opportunity to sell on the domestic market, at least initially, to companies whose majority ownership is Mexican might be considered.[18]

The attractiveness of assembly to local enterprise could be enhanced in countries in which this activity is particularly isolated, as it is in Mexico, by lifting the restrictions on the sale of in-bond assembly products on the domestic market. Although these sales would not be exempt from customs duties on imported materials, they would make assembled items available to the domestic economy at lower cost than if they had to be reimported after their return to the United States—if through nothing else than saving the costs of two-way transportation.[19]

---

tariffs for industrial promotion. The real level of protection has declined, not because of deliberate government policy to liberalize trade, but because the country relies on specific tariffs rather than ad valorem tariffs. In an inflationary situation it means that import duties will represent a diminishing proportion of the total value of imports. If this erosion of protection is combined with a creeping overvaluation of the currency, as domestic inflation exceeds external price rises, incentives to domestic production will be weakened. The trend is to substitute imports for domestic materials. Add to this structural rigidities introduced by such factors as patterns of land use and tenure and the inelasticity of domestic supply becomes one of the most serious obstacles to economic development. The reversal of this trend does not call for all-out import substitution such as was practiced in many Latin American countries during the 1950s and 1960s. This indeed would be a disastrous policy for such a country as Haiti. But it is almost equally absurd for some existing import-substituting industries in Haiti to have increased the import content of their material inputs to nearly 100 percent. With rational policies Haiti could supply more domestic inputs to its industries.

18. In Mexico, under the present law, this would apply in any event to nonassembly investment.

19. Normal import duties should be paid in order to avoid unfair competition of in-bond assembled items with goods produced entirely locally.

Such a measure could strengthen the economic linkages of assembly production. It would be particularly important for Mexico, where the domestic economy has been all but shut off from the output of the maquiladoras. Lower prices would benefit not only consumers but also producers, who might use sophisticated subassemblies—too expensive before—as inputs in their industries.

While policies that would make it possible to combine assembly and nonassembly production and would open the domestic market to assembly plants would stimulate the entry of national firms into assembly operations, the immediate beneficiaries would be U.S. subsidiaries abroad. Because this poses a political problem, it might also be a sizable obstacle to the introduction of such policies. A policy that permitted local sales of assembly output in exchange for an increase in national content might overcome the problem. This would provide incentives for U.S. assemblers to furnish technology and financial aid to domestic suppliers of inputs and for indigenous industry to support greater access to local markets by U.S. assembly subsidiaries.

The quid pro quo between market access and technical and managerial assistance would reward U.S. firms with increased sales as they worked to enhance the competence of local enterprises to become efficient suppliers of components and other inputs to the U.S. plants. At the same time the local availability of assembly output would stimulate indigenous industry, while the relaxation of the export requirement of in-bond production would attract national capital into assembly production.

At present U.S. foreign economic policy is firmly opposed to national-content requirements abroad, such as obliging U.S. subsidiaries to use a minimum percentage of local materials in their production for the domestic market. But because the measure proposed here would benefit all sides, a more flexible U.S. attitude toward national-content policies in developing countries would be desirable.

Perversely, bureaucratic rigidities and stumbling blocks have fostered a large extensive participation of local firms in export assembly operations in some countries, such as Haiti. Domestic entrepreneurs have a comparative advantage over foreigners in knowing how to get things done in the bureaucratic maze—how to pass goods through customs in a day instead of a month, for example. But increasing the involvement of local capital should have a sounder basis than adeptness in running an obstacle course. The streamlining of administrative procedures deserves high priority among development policies. This is especially true for external transactions that are particularly sensitive to bureaucratic delays.

## Concluding Remarks

This study has shown that firms in industrially advanced countries collaborate with firms in developing countries in the manufacture of a variety of products. To a large degree the collaboration takes place within multinational enterprises, usually between a parent company based in an industrial country and its foreign subsidiaries. This is the prevailing mode of operation in the high-technology electronics field. In other product lines, particularly textiles, the tendency is for a company in the industrial country to contract with an independent firm in the developing country.

The primary motivation for this kind of coproduction is to reduce production costs by using the large low-wage labor pools in developing countries. This is the main reason that U.S. firms go abroad. For Japan, however, the principal motive appears to be to secure local and third-country markets.[20]

The implication of much of what has been said here is that policy should smooth the way to more sophisticated coproduction stages between industrial and developing countries. It also implies that subcontracting between independent firms in developing countries and U.S. firms should be encouraged. Subcontracting, rather than the intra–U.S. firm activities that now predominate abroad, facilitates the transfer of technology and provides the opportunity for national firms to improve their expertise

20. The general preference of Japanese managers is to keep interrelated production activities not only close to home but also close to the principal plant. This is derived from the principle of producing at each stage only the subcomponents that will be needed at the next stage of production. See, for example, Urban C. Lehner, "The Nuts and Bolts of Japan's Factories," *Wall Street Journal,* March 31, 1981.

Korea and Taiwan are the principal foreign locations for Japanese production. Besides U.S. firms, Japanese companies are the main foreign operators of assembly plants in Mexico. The output of those assembly plants, however, which are among the largest in the country and assemble electronic products primarily, does not return to Japan but is destined principally for the U.S. market. (Such products can enter the United States as Mexican-made, reducing the effect of direct Japanese exports to the United States.)

With respect to Japanese motivations in the semiconductor industry see chapter 3; with respect to the automotive industry, see Hak K. Pyo, *A Case Study on the International Subcontracting Arrangements by Japanese Automobile and Parts Manufacturers in Selected ESCAP Developing Countries* (Bangkok: Economic and Social Commission for Asia and the Pacific, 1981), p. 37.

through practical experience. From the U.S. side, however, the specter can be raised that moving from assembly operations abroad through U.S. subsidiaries to subcontracting might be the overture to the transfer out of the United States of all the production processes in an industry, with the consequent loss of jobs and profits. As long as the technological innovation and knowledge of the United States is substantially superior to that found in developing countries, however, the production design and high-tech processes of an industry will remain in the United States.

### *The Cycle of Reorganizing International Industry*

So the assembly system that now prevails between the United States and Mexico, some countries in the Caribbean basin, and the Far East can be regarded as a temporary phenomenon. The forces of economic development will push toward a greater participation of developing countries in many production processes in a continuing coproduction relationship. The internationalization of industry, in a broad sense, seems to have become a lasting feature of the world economic system.

The world economy has passed through successively more comprehensive stages of integration, markets for traded goods and, more recently, financial markets having meshed together across national boundaries into a truly international structure. Labor markets are also in the process of being integrated into an international system, not only through migration, but also through trade.

In a global scheme of a changing international division of labor, coproduction can be seen as a principal feature of the international reorganization of industry. As long as sharp differences between wages in economically advanced countries and those in less developed regions persist, the rationale for assembly production abroad will remain. As developing countries that are hosts to such operations become more technically advanced, however, their labor forces more highly skilled, and their industries more efficient, they will be able to produce more and more of the components that have hitherto been imported for assembly exports to the United States.

There is some evidence that more complex assembly operations are introduced gradually as the labor force becomes more highly skilled and relative wages rise in a developing country. Judging by the mix of industries in various countries from which the costs of transportation to the United States are similar, there seems to be a fairly significant relation between wage levels and average skills in assembly work associated with the industries that are prevalent in the countries in question. Thus in Haiti, where wage levels are the lowest in the Caribbean basin (including Mexico and Central America), the largest proportion of the assembly jobs are in sporting goods, toys and dolls, and apparel, product lines usually considered to require the lowest level of labor skills. In El Salvador, where wages are higher, a larger proportion of the assembly jobs are in electronics and other industries associated with a somewhat higher skill level than is the product mix in Haiti. And in Mexico, where wage levels are the highest, the mix is of the most sophisticated assembly industries, requiring the highest levels of skill to be found in the region. Furthermore, in time the skill level in assembly operations will tend to rise within a given country. It seems to have done so in Mexico, judging by the change in the composition of its assembly products.

As countries climb up the development ladder their ability to participate in more advanced assembly activities will increase as well. The international assembly system will therefore be in continuous but gradual flux, associating the least developed countries with tasks that require only basic labor services and moving to more advanced developing countries with more sophisticated assembly operations that demand more highly skilled labor and greater material inputs.

*Automation*

The big question is whether the cycle outlined here will be interrupted by a movement toward automation. Until now automation has been cost-effective when production runs are sufficiently long and quality requirements are high. As automated methods become more sophisticated, robots will be able to make the change from handling one product line to another in much less time. This will reduce costs of operation and will also make automation worth while in short production runs for articles that change rapidly in technology or style.

Will automation, then, bring foreign assembly production back home to industrial countries? It might still be economically rational to transfer automated assembly abroad. If automation becomes economically viable, automated assembly may take place abroad as long as differences in cost persist and are not outweighed by the perception of greater risk.

There are already many examples of the growing use of automated equipment in assembly plants abroad. While the operation itself is not labor-intensive, the ancillary operations can use a great deal of labor. Materials handling, preparation, cleaning, and inspection can be done by workers who are not highly skilled. Only the design, programming, and maintenance of the equipment require skilled technical personnel. Thus as long as differences in wage costs greatly outweigh transportation costs, even automated assembly for the U.S. market might be cost-effective in developing countries. As an example, it might make sense for Japanese and other foreign firms to automate assembly for the U.S. market in labor-abundant Mexico as long as there are significant savings in transporting components rather than finished products across the ocean; also, automation would avoid the hassle associated with having to manage a foreign and—for Japan—culturally very different labor force.

Nevertheless, it would take an enormous improvement in the economic efficiency of automation to offset the economies derived from the vast, inexpensive, and easily trainable labor pool of the developing world. The transfer of automated assembly abroad involves substantial capital investment. Risks in foreign lands will have to be weighed much more carefully and sensitivity to political and social factors needs to be much greater than is required by manual assembly technology. Automated assembly abroad might therefore be severely limited, extending only to developing countries in which the risks are perceived as being low. Part of the investment risk might have to be borne by the developing countries themselves. It is not unlikely that large firms in the more advanced developing countries will eventually invest in robots and do their own automated assembly.

It is likely, however, that when automation becomes profitable, the motive for having products assembled abroad will diminish and some portion of assembly operations will return to the United States. This will be particularly true if the cost advantage of assembly in developing countries is eroded by growing political instability, rising labor militancy, increasing bureaucratic obstacles, and other heightened risks. Such conditions would accelerate the movement toward automation and bring assembly production back to the industrial country. While the return of assembly operations to the United States through automation would cost many jobs in the developing countries, however, it would create few assembly jobs in the United States.

Most current trends thus appear to point to the end of relatively high wages and standards of living for the unskilled in manufacturing in the Western industrial societies. Growing efficiency in the newly industrializing countries may enable them to carry on ever larger portions of manufacturing processes that have been the province of advanced industrial countries. And growing automation will have similar effects on the work force in the industrial country.

The significance of the international reorganization of product flows within a single industry is that the present high wages for unskilled labor in the United States will no longer be insulated from international competition. Technological advances in the United States are unlikely to offset this trend. So what is left is a fundamental long-term policy choice for industrial societies. One choice is to face a reduction in the comparatively high standards of living of the least skilled and, with it, possibly a period of social and political turbulence. The other alternative is to eliminate those sectors of the labor force that are in direct competition with workers in developing countries through investment in education and training, in effect shifting the composition of the labor force to more highly skilled occupations.

In the long run, of course, the outcome may well be the same: the elimination of the unskilled from the industrial work force. The choice is, in effect, between laissez faire and state intervention in education, training, and other forms of investment in human capital. Given the social costs of an unplanned transition and the amount of skilled labor required by an increasingly important high technology, large-scale investment in upgrading the U.S. work force should be the preferred choice.

# Index